Sydney Morgan, William Hepworth Dixon

Lady Morgan's Memoirs

Sydney Morgan, William Hepworth Dixon

Lady Morgan's Memoirs

ISBN/EAN: 9783742809599

Manufactured in Europe, USA, Canada, Australia, Japa

Cover: Foto ©Thomas Meinert / pixelio.de

Manufactured and distributed by brebook publishing software (www.brebook.com)

Sydney Morgan, William Hepworth Dixon

Lady Morgan's Memoirs

LADY MORGAN'S MEMOIRS:

AUTOBIOGRAPHY,

DIARIES AND CORRESPONDENCE.

VOL. I.

Second Edition.

LONDON:
WM. H. ALLEN & CO., 13, WATERLOO PLACE, S.W.
MDCCCLXIII.
[*The Right of Translation and Reproduction is Reserved.*]

LEWIS AND SON, PRINTERS, SWAN BUILDINGS, MOORGATE STREET.

PREFACE.

LADY MORGAN bequeathed her papers and Journals to me, with a view to their publication. The collection was large, as she had preserved nearly every line written to her—from the letters of princes and statesmen, the compliments of poets, of exiles and heroes, down to the petitions of weavers, chimney sweeps and servant girls—even the invitations sent her to dinner, and the address cards left at her door. Many of these trifles of the day have no value now; a hundred years hence, if kept together, they may serve to illustrate, with singular brightness and detail, the domestic life of a woman of society in the reign of Victoria. My duty in the matter of this publication was clear enough. Lady Morgan had not only proposed to write her own Memoirs, but had made a considerable progress in her task. A good part of a volume had been prepared under her own eyes for the press; much of the correspondence to be used had been marked; and the copious diaries in which she had noted the events of her life and the course of her thoughts, supplied nearly all the additions which could be desired. Under these circumstances, it appeared to me that Lady Morgan could be judiciously left to tell her own story in her own way.

In this preparation of her papers, Lady Morgan had received a great deal of valuable assistance from Miss Jewsbury; more than once in her conversations with me she had referred with satisfaction to this assistance, and even expressed a desire, that after her death, Miss Jewsbury should complete the arrangement of her papers. My own choice would have led me, independently, to the quarter pointed out by Lady Morgan, and I have pleasure in bearing witness to the fact that Miss Jewsbury undertook the task with alacrity, glad of the opportunity of working out in some degree her ideas of Lady Morgan's character and work.

In this labour many eager hands have joined. The services of Lady Morgan's nieces, Mrs. Inwood Jones, and Mrs. Geale, have been constant and indispensable.

As Lady Morgan's literary executor, I have thought this explanation due to the reader. In the credit which may arise from this book, I have no part. Lady Morgan is here substantially her own biographer. Whatever escapes from the original author belongs of right to Miss Jewsbury. I claim no other merit in this affair than that of having faithfully obeyed the wishes of the dead.

W. HEPWORTH DIXON.

November 26, 1862.

NOTE.

In the new edition many errors of the press, especially in the names and quotations, have been corrected. Lady Morgan's writing, like Counsellor Bell's "*third* hand," was one that neither she nor anybody else could read. If errors have still escaped notice, it is hoped they may be found few in number and of little importance.

January 1, 1863.

CONTENTS.

	Page
PREFATORY ADDRESS	1
CHAPTER I.—A Birthday	5
CHAPTER II.—The Christening	11
CHAPTER III.—Impressions of Early Childhood	16
CHAPTER IV.—The National Theatre Music Hall	23
CHAPTER V.—My Education	28
CHAPTER VI.—My Instructors	80
CHAPTER VII.—My Father	40
CHAPTER VIII.—My Father's Story continued	59
CHAPTER IX.—My Mother	69
CHAPTER X.—Thomas Dermody—the Poor Scholar	85
CHAPTER XI.—My Mother's Death	93
CHAPTER XII.—After my Mother's Death	98
CHAPTER XIII.—Kilkenny	118
CHAPTER XIV.—Early Girlhood	123
CHAPTER XV.—At Drachlin	154
CHAPTER XVI.—Brachlin continued	168
CHAPTER XVII.—From Drachlin to Dublin	179

CONTENTS.

	Page
CHAPTER XVIII.—Illustrations of the Autobiography	191
CHAPTER XIX.—Period of 1801	205
CHAPTER XX.—Still a Governess	227
CHAPTER XXI.—After leaving Fort William	241
CHAPTER XXII.—A successful Authoress	257
CHAPTER XXIII.—The Wild Irish Girl	276
CHAPTER XXIV.—Old Irish Hospitality	295
CHAPTER XXV.—A New Friend and a Brother-in-law	311
CHAPTER XXVI.—Ida of Athens	321
CHAPTER XXVII.—First taste of Criticism	343
CHAPTER XXVIII.—The condemned Felon	353
CHAPTER XXIX.—1800—Friends and Countrymen	363
CHAPTER XXX.—Dr. Morgan and Dr. Jenner	372
CHAPTER XXXI.—Old Friends and New	383
CHAPTER XXXII.—Baron's Court	380
CHAPTER XXXIII.—The Missionary	407
CHAPTER XXXIV.—Visit to London	419
CHAPTER XXXV.—Lady Morgan painted by herself and Sir Thomas Lawrence	429
CHAPTER XXXVI.—Engaged to be Married	440
CHAPTER XXXVII.—Between Cup and Lip	459
CHAPTER XXXVIII.—Lady Morgan	520

PREFATORY ADDRESS.

To those who have lived all the days of their life in society, who know the elements of which it is composed—its proneness to that peculiar feature of morbid civilization called Ridicule, of which no savages except the New Zealanders have any notion,—it is no faint effort of moral courage to exhibit themselves even in Kit-cat, and with all appliances and means to boot, *de se peindre en pied!*

The author of the following pages has, however, lived so continually before the scene, even from her earliest childhood upwards; she has been so often drawn from the life—caricatured to the uttermost—abused, calumniated, misrepresented, flattered, eulogized, persecuted; supported as party dictated or prejudice permitted; the pet of the Liberals of one nation, the *bête-noire* of the ultra set of another; the poor butt that reviewers, editors and critics have set up,—that she may, perhaps, be pardoned for wishing to speak a few true and final words of herself.

The success of my first Irish national novel, *The Wild Irish Girl*, my attempts to advocate liberal opinions in my works on France and Italy, when I stood forth in the cause of civil and religious liberty, dipped many a pen in gall against me which would otherwise have more gently scanned my faults. However, here I am once more, and to you, dear, kind, fair-judging public, who are always for giving a fair field and no favour, and who are always willing to take the odds for those who "show pluck" and who "hit out," to you I dedicate these pages, in which I have entered the circumstances of my life, *sans peur et sans tache*. *Memoires pour servir* generally mean either "serving out" one's friends and enemies, or feeding a morbid appetite for secret slander. I can promise no scandal, neither can I open a biographical ledger, after the fashion of Miss Betsy Thoughtless and others, with an "I was born, &c., &c.," or "the villain who deceived me was quartered in the town where my father lived;" nor yet can I pretend to give a description of the "scene of rural innocence where first I saw the light."

The sum of my long experience in society leaves in its total a large balance in favour of what is good. I have no reason to complain of memory; I find in my efforts to track its records, guided by the fond feelings of my life, and warmed by the fancifulness of my Celtic temperament, bright hues come forward like the colours of the tesselated pavement of antiquity when the renovating water is flung upon them. I pause here for a moment to mention as a curious physiological fact, that this memory is much preserved to me through musical association. My father died singing an Irish cronan; and when in the confusion of illness I have spent weariful hours in the visions of the night, I have cheered gloom and lightened pain by humming a song of other times, which embodied dear remembrances and sustained memory by music. The songs taught me on my father's knee, have lost nothing of their power even to the present day. I have other links connecting me with the past; of the many kind and illustrious friends whom I have made through life, I have never lost one except by death; and I am now enjoying in the second and third generation of those who are gone, the distinction conferred upon me by the personal kindness of their grandsires. One of the chief temptations to present the principal facts of my life to the public, has been to prove the readiness with which society is willing to help those who are honestly and fervently ready to help themselves. I would wish to impress on young people who are beginning life as I did, dependent on their own exertions, the absolute need of concentrated industry; a definite purpose, and above all, conduct dictated by common sense, as absolutely essential to give genius its value and its success. No woman, from Sappho downwards, ever fell out of the ranks without finding that her "self-sacrifice" was only another name for indulged selfishness. "The light that leads astray" is *not*, and never will be, "light from Heaven."

11, William Street, Lowndes Square,
    March 2nd, 1857.

LADY MORGAN'S MEMOIR.

CHAPTER I.

A BIRTHDAY.

Mon ami le chèvre commences par le commencement.

"I was born under fortunate auspices; the sun was in the sign of the Virgin, at the utmost degree of elevation; the aspects of Jupiter and Venus were favourable to the day, Mercury testified no signs of hostility, Saturn and Mars were neutral. The moon, however, then near her full, was an important obstacle. She retarded my entrance into the world until the moment had elapsed." Thus writes Goëthe! Such is the opening of the autobiography of one of the most celebrated European writers of the eighteenth century, and yet it sounds very like a page out of the biography of Catherine de Medicis, dictated by the director of her religion of magic, and the reference to Venus and Mercury might favour the supposition. It is, however, the utterance of that mind which led the German intellects of the day; which assisted to found its dreamy philosophy, and gave to his country a literature unknown to it before.

This dependence on astrology opens a very nice volume of mysticism for the more *spirituelle* of the sexes, and pleads in favour of that miscalled "the weakest."

> "That when weak women go astray,
> Their stars are more in fault than they."

For myself, I reject the doctrine altogether, and stand on my own responsibility.

However, these astrological reveries are pleasant things to lie by upon, like the purchased intercession of "licensed" advocates with the higher powers; to attribute the actions of life to the revolutions and movements "of stars in their courses," spares an immensity of trouble and anxiety, and to have one's position determined by the signs of the zodiac is a comfortable look out. Had my little horoscope been cast at the moment of my birth it would have found its subject "mantling into life" under the influence of the "Star of the West," that charming, sentimental Hesperus, who is described as leading on the "silent hours," which are not the worst in the twenty-four, and who seems to hang over the Emerald Isle, with a brighter effulgence than elsewhere. In freeing myself from all dependence on the planets, I take the opportunity to enter my protest against DATES. What has a woman to do with dates? Cold, false, erroneous, chronological dates — new style, old style, — precession of the equinox, ill-timed calculation of comets, long since due at their stations, and never come! Her poetical idiosyncracy calculated by epochs, would make the most natural points of reference in woman's autobiography. Plutarch sets the example of dropping dates, in favour of incidents, and an authority more appropriate to the present pages—Madame de Genlis— one of the most eminent female writers of any period, who began her own memoirs at eighty, swept through nearly an age of incident and Revolution without any reference to vulgar eras "signifying nothing;" the times themselves though "out of joint," testifying to the pleasant incidents she recounts and the changes she witnessed. I mean to have none of them.

In the hour when I first drew breath, and felt life's first inaugural sensation—pain, the world took part in the hour and the day. It was the festival of humanity, of peace and good will to man, of love and liberty and high distinction to woman, of glory to the motherhood of nations — the accomplishment of the first desire of *her*, who was created, not born; the desire "to be as gods, knowing good from evil"—the head and front of human science. I was born on *Christmas Day*; in that land where all holy days are religiously celebrated, as testimonials to faith, and are excuses for festivity—in " Ancient ould Dublin."

Bells tolled, carols were intoned, the streets resounded with joyous sounds, chimneys smoked, and friends were preparing to feast the fasters of the previous week, in that most Catholic of countries. Holly and ivy draped every wall, and many happy returns of the season were offered on all sides; supper tables without distinction of religion, High Church and Low Church, Catholic and Protestant, alike took the benefit of "the good the gods provided." Guests were assembled, and all awaited the announcing hour as it struck from the belfry of St. Patrick's Cathedral, the echoes booming down all the close old streets of Dublin, and overpowered all the minor bells of the seven churches of its most saintly neighbourhood.

There was, however, on that joyous night, one round table distinguished above most others, by the wit and humour of the *convives*. The master of the feast was as fine a type of the Irish gentleman as Ireland ever sent forth. His name was Robert Owenson. Beside him sat one whose name in Ireland was long celebrated and is not yet forgotten, as belonging to one of the greatest wits of his country and time, Edward Lysaght, long the captain of the university boys, that formidable body of learned and privileged insubordinates, and who had lately been admitted to the Irish bar. Others there were also, though then unknown to fame, except for their social endowments.

The lady who had the best right to preside on the occasion of this most Christian festival, as she was herself truly the sincerest of Christians and best of women, had retired early in the evening to her chamber, on the plea of "indisposition;" but still not deeming it indicative of any immediate catastrophe. But before the great clock of St. Patrick had chimed out the second hour of the new born anniversary, another birth had taken place, and was announced by a joyous gossip to the happy father, who instantly disappeared. The guests, far from dispersing, waited for him (though not with empty glasses), and when he returned, nearly an hour after, and announced the birth " of a dear little Irish girl—the very thing I have always wished for"—the intelligence was responded to by a half suppressed cheer, mellow as a Low Mass, and hearty wishes of long life to her!

The news was "a reason fair to fill their glass again," the father with difficulty dispersed the jolly crew by accepting Lysaght's proposal that they should all meet that day month at the christening of the little heathen, and that he, Ned Lysaght, should be the sponsor, "and vow three things in her name," which he had never been able to observe in his own.

A faint and childish voice caught the ear of Counsellor Lysaght as he was trudging home to his remote lodgings. It preceded him for many paces, and he could just detect that the air, so plaintive and broken, was a Christmas carol. The snow was falling and the night was cold; he overtook the little singer, a female child, just as her song was expiring in the following words:—

"Christmas comes but once a year,
And when it comes it brings good cheer—"

and she sank on the steps of a splendid mansion in Stephen's Green, brilliantly lighted up and resounding with festive sounds.* He attempted to raise her, but she was lifeless; she still grasped her little ballad in her hand. He called to an old watchman who was

* It was Shelburne House, now an hotel.

growling forth the hour near the spot, and begged his assistance to convey the poor child. She was placed before a large fire, and Lysaght procured the assistance of an unfortunate woman who was passing by to attend to her till morning; but when he returned to her at an early hour, the child was lying where he had left her. She was dead. He picked up her ballad, and sent a person to convey her little remains to the Hospital fields, the great burial place of the poor who could claim no other. The incident took possession of his imagination, for he had a great deal of passionate sentimentality. As soon as my mother was able to receive any one, the future sponsor of her little girl was admitted at the particular desire of my father, and for her he recited the following little carol while she rocked the cradle of her own precious infant.

> "An orphan who not long before,
>   Had lost her parents, fond and tender,
> Dropped near a lord and lady's door,
>   Who had no child, and lived in splendour;
> She breathed a strain of genuine woe.
> Hoping to catch the ear of pity,
> She simply sung this simple ditty,—
> Oh, happy Christians, great and good,
> Afford a helpless infant food,
> For Christmas comes but once a year,
> And when it comes, it brings good cheer."

The first effort of memory exhibited by the baby who was rocking in the cradle when it was recited, was called forth by being taught by rote the above stanzas—it was long before she got it by heart—but her "pity gave ere charity begun," for she wept at the tale long before she understood its tragedy.

CHAPTER II.

THE CHRISTENING.

*The O'Rourke's noble feast shall ne'er be forgot
By those who were there, and those who were not.*

"THE *fête* that was to celebrate my entrance into the Church of England, as "by law established," and thus become an "inheritor of the kingdom of Heaven," was, according to the law and custom of Ireland from the days of St. Patrick—a dinner. The "christening dinner" admitted of no exclusion—the Catholic Bishop of Cashel (though at that time the existence of a Catholic in Ireland was not admitted), might take his place beside the Primate of all Ireland, "without let or molestation," to use the words of the Irish passports of that day.

I have the list before me of the choice guests who graced the table on that day, in whose favour penal laws were forgotten, and for that day at least all prejudices were relaxed.

At the head stands the name of Father Arthur O'Leary, a Dominican friar, the most eloquent preacher

of his day, a learned casuist, a popular gentleman in
society, and an excellent patriot. He was proud of
being the friend and correspondent of many illustrious
Englishmen, gentlemen and statesmen, and his Irish
vanity showed itself alone in being proud of this.

The Rev. Mr. Langley, a missionary of Lady Huntingdon's College, of Trevecca, comes next; he was my
mother's cousin, and at this time a guest at Moira
House.

Counsellor Macnally, who was the author of some
very popular dramas of the day.

The Rev. Charles Macklin, nephew to Macklin the
actor and dramatic writer; he was so great a favourite
with my father, that he chose him to perform the ceremony of inaugurating me into the church militant.
But his preaching, however eloquent, was not equal to
his skill in playing the Irish bagpipes, that most
ancient and perfect of instruments. The "piper that
played before Moses" is still an Irish adjuration, and
a personage who is at any rate sworn by.

Kane O'Hara, who first introduced high burlesque
into dramatic literature; he was the author of *Midas,
Poor Kelsan, The Golden Pippin, &c.*

Signior Giordani, the eminent composer, an early
friend of my father's.

Captain Jephson, author of two popular tragedies,
the *Count of Narbonne* and the *Carmelite*.

Richard Daly, of Castle Daly, patentee of the
Theatre Royal, Dublin.

Edward Tighe, of Woodstock, the finest dramatic
critic of the day, from whose judgment there was no

appeal. He was great uncle to the charming author of "Cupid and Psyche."

The dear, kind Joseph Atkinson, the treasurer of the Ordnance;

> ——— describe him who can,
> An abridgment of all that was pleasant in man;

he was the early friend of Moore, the dear and almost paternal friend of the wild Irish girl and her sister, at a time when such friends were the most necessary to both.

Counsellor Lysaght, the Irish improvisatore in his youth, the eloquent barrister and prime wit in his middle age.

Sir Thomas and Lady Bell—the lady was my godmother.

When I close the list with the names of Robert Hitchcock, the historian of the stage, and his beautiful daughter, Lady Green—

> "Il catologo eccolo là!"

I knew them all in my early girlhood, and some of them long after my happy marriage; him, in particular, whom Moore thus characterised:—

> "The sunny temper bright when all is strife,
> The simple heart above all worldly wiles,
> Light wit that plays along the calm of life,
> And stirs its languid surface into smiles."

If the company was national, the dinner was quite as national as the guests who partook of it; and a branch of shilealagh, from its own wood near Dublin, flourished as a Christmas tree in the centre of the table.

Of course that "precious baby" was brought in; her health was drunk with "three times three," by the style and title of "Foghau Foh!" in less classic phrase —"wait awhile."

My father sang first in Irish and then in English Carolan's famous song of "O'Rourke's Noble Feast," whilst the chorus was swelled by all the company:—

> "Oh, you are welcome heartily,
> Welcome gramachree,
> Welcome heartily,
> Welcome joy!"

I am sorry not to be able to tell all this as a "credible witness" of the scene narrated, for being but a month old I understood nothing about it; but I have so often heard of it from my father as I sat upon his knee, that my testimony, although but hearsay evidence, may be accredited.

Many years after this notable event, Counsellor Lysaght, an eminent barrister, going the Munster circuit, bivouacked for the night (as was then usual with great lawyers), at the house of a friend in Tipperary. He stole into the drawing-room, which was full of company — not to interrupt a song which a young girl was singing to the harp; it was the Irish cronan of "Emuck ac Nock — Ned of the Hill;" the air was scarce finished when he sprang forward and seized the harpist in his arms, exclaiming:—"This must be Sydney Owenson—it is her father's voice—

none but an Irish voice could have such a curve in it, and she is my godchild!"

In the vicissitudes of Irish friendships he had not seen his godchild since the christening dinner, and had nearly fought a duel with her father in the meantime. Now holding her at arm's length, but holding her fast, and throwing up his head and eyes, he burst forth in the following impromptu lines:—

> "The muses once found me not very sober,
>   But full of frolic at your merry christening,
> And now, this twenty-third day of October,
>   As they foretold, to your sweet lays I'm listening.
> Tho' when I'd vowed and promised for the best,
> The heathen hussies turned it to a jest;
> At pomps and vanities, and wicked world,
> They sneered, and up their saucy noses curled;
> Renounce the devil, too, in your new name
> They substituted wit, and grace, and fame;
> And then around thy baby brow they bound
> A wreath of laurel, with some shamrock crowned,
> Poor me they plied with draughts of rosy wine,
> Foretelling I would one day have some strains divine
> From the young Christian of the festal hour—
> 'Tis done! I bow to their prophetic power.*

* A fragment of this poem has appeared in the Life and Poems of Edward Lysaght, Esq., published after his death.

CHAPTER III.

IMPRESSIONS OF EARLY CHILDHOOD.

IN the latter half of the last century, and on the evening of a dreary winter's day, a lumbering post-coach, the Irish *retturino*, the "leathern convenience" of that time (like those of Italy of the present day), between the infrequency of stage-coaches and the perils of an Irish "po'-chay," crept up the ill-paved hill of an old street in the oldest part of old Dublin, called Fish Shamble Street, from its vicinity to the Liffey, a rather Irish nomenclature, as the Liffey had no fish and the street no shambles. Mr. Denis Reddy, was the celebrated proprietor, and he drove it himself, with his own horses thirty miles a day, providing the charge committed to his care with provisions and every accommodation on the road, when there were any, which was not always the case. He sat on his own coach-box, and, from time to time, let down the front glass to talk to his freight, which on the present occasion was an English lady, with two little girls and two maids. The journey had only been from the little town of Portarlington.

On the brow of the hill, the carriage drew up before a ponderous double gate of an apparently old dismantled fabric, which flanked a court and lane to the right, and presented in front a *corps de logis*, from whose portals streamed a flash of bright lights and many flickering shadowy figures. A gaunt man with flaring lanthorn stood at the gate, apparently waiting for the party, and ringing a bell he came forward with, "Och you're welcome, marram, to the great music hall! and ten thousand welcomes and to the childre! I am Pat Brennan, plaise yer honour, the man about the place, from the beginning of time and before! Shure here's the masther, long life to him!" With much love and great impatience in his countenance, the "masther" attempted to open the carriage-door with a vehemence that almost shook it from its propriety; the maids and the children screamed, whilst Mr. Reddy, coming to the rescue, cried out, "Don't be affeard, Mrs. Owenson, its only this divil of a door, that takes the staggers betimes!" The next moment the lady and children were in the arms of the happy husband and father, who, drawing the arm of the lady through his own, and taking the eldest child by the hand, whilst the other was carried by the maid, proceeded through the cavernous entrance before them, into a vast space, with an atmosphere of dust and smoke, whilst every species of noise and clatter and sounds uncouth, the fall of hammers, the grinding of saws and the screwing of wheels; "the crash of matter and the fall of worlds," reverberate on every side. The party having crossed a long plank that shivered over an open pit, where some remains of velvet-covered seats were still visible, landed over a spiky orchestra on a stage, representing some architectural ornaments of former grandeur, which were vainly pointed out to cheer the lady by the proprietor of this strange, wild, fantastic place. The mother thought most of her children and their maid, as they stumbled along through mounds of sawdust and mountains of chips; whilst the workmen in brown paper caps with lights fixed on them (an ingenious suggestion), cleared the way with much kindness and courtesy. They at last reached the extremity and entered a large well-proportioned room to the right, where a blazing fire of wood and turf under a capacious and beautiful marble chimney-piece, was a welcome sight; above it swung on a moveable scaffolding, an artist of no mean courage, painting what might have been a proscenium, above which the Irish motto of *Cead mille Falthae*, glittered in gold letters.

"This will be the green-room," said the gentleman, "there is no such green-room in either of the Royal theatres; and in this room, my dear Jenny, Handel gave his first concert of the MESSIAH, which the stupid English had not the taste to encourage him to produce in London!" The lady smiled for the first time, and the little girl, who was in the habit of asking about everything, said, "Papa, was Handel a carpenter?" but received no answer, the gentleman going on to do the honours of the green-room.

"Sydney," said her mother peevishly, "don't talk,

but mind where you tread; there! you have nearly fallen into a paint-pot, and spoiled your beautiful new cardinal!" This was the first sentence that had escaped the lady's lips since her entrance into her cheerless future domicile. Sydney stood checked—not convinced—her papa was vexed and mortified, and the party silently followed Pat Brennan, who, opening a door and holding up his lanthorn, exposed the fearful sight of a roof half fallen in, and the floor covered with indescribable rubbish. The gentleman dragged him back by the arm and clapped-to the door of the mysterious chamber, but not before Pat Brennan, with the garrulity of a cicerone, had observed to the lady, "That's the 'Death Chamber,' Marram! where the flure gave way while Napper Tandy was making his grand speech; and hundreds and thousands, aye more, of the citizens of Dublin, were murthered and killed!"

The lady shuddered, but the gentleman led on through a gloomy court-yard, touched off by a rising moon, which exhibited the ruder aspect of the place, and from whence they ascended a very wide but not steep flight of stairs, which evidently meant to represent steps cut out of a rock, whilst branches of trees, gushing waters, and pendant stalactites glittering with frost hung on every side.

"Thim is a part of the old Ridottos,"—at that moment an enormous cat sprang across, and Pat Brennan did not soothe the fears which its appearance created, by the cool observation—"and that is one of the wild cats the place is full of, with *stings in their tails!* Aye, indeed, Marrum, and it's thrue; but only for them we could not live with the *rots!*"

"Get on before us, Pat, and hold up your lanthorn," said the gentleman, angrily.

The stairs gradually narrowed till they terminated in a narrow gallery which led through clusters of rocks, by way of entrance into a large square space, apparently surrounded by beautiful pastoral scenery, and lighted by a *real* moon, which shone in from the skylights of the painted ceiling.

"And now, marram," said Pat Brennan, "ye're welcome to the Dargle, for it's the Dargle ye see all about you, and Mr. Grattan's house in the middle; and there's the waterfall, and ——" but the rest of his words "the gods dispersed in empty air," for the attention of the poor wearied and frightened guests was called to an object in the centre of the room, less picturesque, but infinitely more interesting at that moment—a table, plenteously and luxuriously covered, a lofty branch of lights in the centre which might have figured at the royal banquet of Macbeth; a blazing fire, sofas and chairs; a gentleman in a white jacket and cap was settling the dishes on the table, whom Pat Brennan introduced as Mr. Mulligan, the master's son of the "Strugglers," the greatest tavern in the world in regard of its beef steaks and punch royal, "and there's of it before the fire that 'll warm all your hearts."

From the garrulity of Pat Brennan, his master saw that he judged of the merits of the punch from experience, and he dismissed him with,—

"You may go, now, Brennan; see to the getting in of the luggage."

The table was immediately surrounded by the parents and the children, whilst "below the salt," *i. e.*, at a little table in the corner, the maids did ample justice to the feast before them.

Brennan, in spite of orders, remained *de service*, and Mr. Mulligan, with a bow that Brennan told the maids "cost his mother a dollar when he learned to dance," returned to the "Strugglers," whilst the party left behind proved that,—

L'homme en mangeant remonte ses ressorts."

Within an hour the whole party, except the gentleman, had retired to rest. The maids occupied a "shake down," the lady and the little girls adjourned to an apartment called by courtesy a bedroom, but which had served the purpose of a hermit's cave at the last ridotto. It had been made comfortable for present use.

The maids, however, did not fare so well, for Molly, the children's maid, a semi-French importation from Portarlington, told her mistress the next morning that "the life was frightened out of her by Betty calling out to her, 'are ye awake, Mrs. Molly? the rats are dragging the bed from under me!'"

These wild, incredible, and apparently fabulous scenes require an explanation, but they are indelibly photographed on a memory from which few things that ever impressed the imagination have been effaced.

* NOTE.—Lady Morgan was not superstitiously exact about supplying the "missing links" in her recollections and impressions of her early life; and no explanation was ever written of this whimsical introduction to the domestic Dublin life of her father; but the fact was simple enough—viz.: that the portion of the old music-hall, which was destined to serve as the family residence, had not been finished or put in order; hence the necessity of fitting up a lodging for a few nights in the midst of things in general. We can understand that Lady Morgan felt it more irksome to "explain" than to "describe."—ED.

CHAPTER IV.

THE NATIONAL THEATRE MUSIC HALL.

The opening of this theatre was the continuation of a history of many comic and tragic events, from its foundation as a chantry to the church of the Holy Trinity, to this last and most indiscreet undertaking to transform it to a theatre.

The opening of the theatre was, moreover, an event of considerable importance to Mr. Owenson and his family.

The first performance was to be altogether national, that is, Irish, and *very* Irish it was. The play chosen was *The Carmelite*, by Captain Jephson, with an interlude from Macklin's farce of *The Brave Irishman*, and a farce of O'Keefe's, *The Poor Soldier*. The overture consisted of Irish airs ending with the Volunteer's March, which was chorussed by the gallery to an accompaniment of drums and fifes. An Irish audience was always *en rapport* with the stage, and frequently commented aloud on an absurdity in the actor, public or private, in a manner to excite quite as much laughter as any farce that might be going on. One night, an anxious friend in the pit close to the orchestra, perceived that his cousin on the stage, by an unlucky rent in a critical part of his dress, was exciting laughter not set down in his part;—put his hand to his mouth in an aside, and said in a stage whisper, "Larry! Larry! there's the laste taste in life of yer linen to be seen!"

This, by way of parenthesis,—to proceed with our "opening day," or rather night:

My father wrote and spoke the prologue in his own character of an "Irish Volunteer."

The audience was as national as the performance; and the pit was filled with red coats of the corps to which my father belonged; and the boxes exhibited a show of beauty and fashion, such as Ireland above all other countries could produce. What added to the *éclat* of the evening was the first appearance on any stage of an Irish lady of rank—the Honourable Mrs. Mahon—then known by the pretty cognomen of the "Bird of Paradise." She was the daughter of Lord Perry, afterwards Lord Limerick. She imprudently eloped with her singing master, Mr. Mahon, the Irish Mario of his time, her family threw her off, and she was obliged to share the artistic exertions of her husband.

The National Theatre flourished. Everybody took boxes, but few paid for them. Orders were given in profusion, when, lo! in the midst of the apparent success of this rival to the great Royalties, Government granted an exclusive patent for the performance of the legitimate drama to—Mr. Daly! with the additional honour of creating him deputy Master of the

Revels, a distinction which had nearly fallen into abeyance. In a capital so dramatic as Dublin, the event made a great sensation, which, however, soon subsided, but not before my father's friends had devised legal grounds to sue for remuneration for his losses. Mr. Daly agreed to an arbitration. Lord Donoughmore and the Right Honourable Denis Bowes, M.P., were the arbitrators, and became guarantees to my father for an income of three hundred a year for ten years, on the promise that no paid actor or actress should appear on the boards of the National Theatre. My father also accepted, provisionally, the deputy managership of the Theatre Royal; and every one appeared contented, except the creditors for debts incurred in getting up this phantom theatre.

The cousinhood of Ireland extends itself beyond the Green Island to remote lands, and if the

"Blakes and O'Donnels whose fathers resigned
The green hills of their youth, amidst strangers to find,
That repose which at home they had sought for in vain,"

there were others of the "thirteen tribes of Galway," who sought a more tranquil and certain mode of existence, through the commercial genius which had probably lain hid amid the domestic warfares of Ireland, but which was now coming forth in various parts of the continent, wherever the vine flourished. Among the respectable and respected commercial houses in France, the Ffrenches of Bordeaux were and are one of the most flourishing concerns. The custom of Ireland alone would have sufficed to make their fortune in the sole article of claret.

My father boasted of his claims to relationship with this eminent family—a claim never denied; and his witty and clever letters had long kept up a correspondence with his cousin Ffrench of Bordeaux; the value of his Irish news and Irish fun being paid back in frequent presents of wine and liqueurs, with pretty *cadeaux* sent to my mother of scented pincushions and *sac d'ouvrage*, worked by the nuns, and smelling of pious incense. One of these I well remember; it was of yellow satin, embroidered in holy devices in white silk, of which my mother made a present on account of the *smell*, she said, but more probably on account of the Catholic devices which emblazoned it.

My father proposed himself as "commercial correspondent" of their house. He told them his story in his own pleasant yet pathetic way; and proved his fitness to become a Dublin wine-merchant, by his intimacy with all the great wine drinkers of the day, gentle and simple! He referred them to his connections in Connaught.

The Ffrenches acceded to his proposition, and consigned a cargo of wines to his account. Such was his interest, that before they were delivered, he obtained "the freedom of the six and ten per cents," which was considered a high commercial honour at that time in Dublin; but of its nature and advantages I am utterly ignorant, and I don't suppose that my father knew much more, except that Sir John Ferns, the great wine-merchant of the day, had found some difficulty in obtaining it.

Grand changements des décorations in the Music

Hall! The vast vaults of the Holy Trinity which had served the purposes of Juliet's burial, were now dried up, cleansed, heated, lighted by day and watched by night. The rubbish of old theatrical properties was shovelled out, and pipes, hogsheads and flasks of precious contents were rolled in. A Connaught clerk was seated at his desk, and accounts were opened with many O's and Macs, who had long rolled their own claret to their own cellars at little cost but much risk.

The pretty theatre and its adjoining rooms were leased out for public meetings. The family dwelling-house was enlarged by the addition of other apartments, and made comfortable. Before the ensuing winter my mother, whose confusion had been worse confounded by all the chances and changes her fortunes had undergone, was settled with her little family in Dublin, with her pretty retreat at Drumcondra in reserve, and whilst my father's life was "double, double, toil and trouble," she passed the quiet tenor of her days in avocations suited to her domestic habits.

Her greatest anxiety was for the education of her little girls, and her next for the salvation of mankind through the influence of the Countess of Huntingdon.

CHAPTER V.

MY EDUCATION.

My father now always spent his Sundays at home with us, and as much of his other days as his commercial, convivial, and dramatic avocations would allow.

My mother seldom went to church, but my father, from the time we could toddle, took us to church himself, where our endurance of hanging legs and cold feet was recompensed by the divine music for which the two cathedrals were and are still celebrated.

He shared all my mother's anxiety about the education of his two little girls, which was, however, only fitfully carried on.

My mother had in her mind the recollection of a model child who had lived fifty years before, a traditional piece of Shropshire perfection. She was the daughter of the good Sir Rowland Hill, of Hawkesley, near Shrewsbury, of whose family my mother was proud to be a humble branch. This child had read the Bible twice through before she was five years old, and knitted all the stockings worn by the coachmen!

My mother's ambition was that I should emulate this bright example of juvenile excellence, but all in vain. I could not even learn the few verses which open the genealogy of the Patriarchs.

My sister Olivia, who was given over to the tuition of Molly, was not much more apt. Neither my father nor my mother took into account, or seemed aware that our education was going on under an influence stronger than any book learning could exercise—the education of circumstances. Every incident as it arose developed a faculty; it excited an imitation. There was a great power of mimicry in both myself and my sister. For myself, I figured away in all the trades and occupations that came within my scope. I imitated Jemmy McCrackem, my father's hairdresser, to the life, and opened a shop which I furnished with my father's theatrical wigs, and opened it in the only window that looked into the street. I wrote over this window an advertisement that ran thus:—

SYDNEY OWENSON,
"SYSTEM, TETE AND PERUKE MAKER."

This was the invariable form of inscription over the doors of old Irish coiffeurs.

I could go through the whole process of hair dressing (which was then a most arduous one), from the first papillotes to the last puff of the powder machine.

I became a chimney-sweep from my observation of a den of little imps who inhabited a cellar on the opposite side of the way.

A propos to the chimney sweeps, my mother sent

me to a day-school, to "keep me quiet," a few doors from our own house.

It happened one day the chimney of our school-room took fire. Every one screamed, but no one offered a remedy. I had seen a fire in our own chimney put out by the cleverness of my little neighbours the sweeps. I flew across and called on them to follow me. I found them assembled at their dinner, sitting on a bag of soot. They seized their scrapes and brushes and all followed me to the rescue. The burning soot was soon dragged down; fumes, and flames, and soot, and smut filled the atmosphere of Mrs. Gaine's neat schoolroom.

The little boys had probably saved lives and property, but the schoolmistress angrily asked "who had sent them?" They pointed to me and said:

"Little Miss, there."

"Then let little Miss pay you!" said she, and seizing me by the shoulder, she hurled me down the door-steps, saying:

"Go home, you mischievous monkey!"

The injustice of this to myself, and the black hand I commanded, but above all the epithet, for a monkey has been ever my favourite aversion!

I ran up the court to our house, crying bitterly, and followed by my clients.

My father and mother, who were standing at the window, saw us pass, and rushed to the door, as did, of course, the servants.

I was scarcely to be recognised, and when appealed

to could only answer with passionate sobs; but one of the little sweeps took *la parole*, and said:

"Well, plaise your honour, Mr. Owenson, little Miss here called us to put out Mother Gaine's chimney, who said she would not give us nothing, but that Miss might pay us!"

My father endeavoured to command his gravity, though my mother could not command her anger, and he said:

"Well, Sydney, I suppose you have wherewithal to recompense these young gentlemen for their allegiance to your command?"

I could only sob out:

"Papa, you have *two and eightpence of mine*, give it to them all."

My father took out an English half-crown, and said:

"There, gentlemen, is sixpence a-piece for you."

The little sweeps then threw up their caps, with the "cry" of the street (which had its "aboo" as well as the Fitzgeralds and O'Donnels). "Long life to yer honour—success—all happiness and nothing but pure love!" and this sooty troupe galloped away, while I was handed over to Molly to be punished and purified, as justice or mercy might prevail, according to my merits. From that moment these wretched little victims of the cruel social economy of the day became the objects of my especial compassion and protection. I very early wrote in their behalf, and I was the first who applied the *ramoneur* to an Irish chimney in my own house.

Though my mother could never teach me to read, she taught me hymns and poetry by rote, which incited me to write rhymes on my own account. I had many favourites among cats, dogs and birds, my mother's reprobation and the servants' nuisance; but I turned them all to account and wove them into stories, to which I tried to give as much personal interest as old Mother Hubbard bestowed on her dog.

The head favourite of my menagerie was a magnificent and very intelligent cat, "Ginger," by name, from the colour of her coat, which though almost orange was very much admired. She was the last of a race of cats sacred in the traditions of the Music Hall. Pat Brennan,

"The mad historian of the ruined towers,"

held them in the greatest reverence mingled with superstitious awe. Brennan was a good Catholic, but rather given to exaggeration, which rendered his testimony to matters of fact proverbially questionable; and it became a bye word among unbelieving neighbours when any one told a wonderful story, to ask, "Do you know Brennan? Well, then, enough said!" After this, there was nothing left for the disconcerted narrator but to walk away. One of his stories was—that the monastic cats had *stings* in their tails, which after their death were preserved by the monks for purposes of flagellation, or by the nuns—Brennan was not sure which!

Ginger was as much the object of my idolatry as if she had had a temple and I had been a worshipper in ancient Egypt; but, like other deities, she was reprobated by those who were not of my faith.

I made her up a nice little cell, under the beaufet, as side-boards were then called in Ireland—a sort of alcove cut out of the wall of our parlour where the best glass and the family "bit of plate"—a silver tankard—with the crest of the Hills upon it (a dove with an olive branch in its mouth), which commanded great respect in our family.

Ginger's sly attempt to hide herself from my mother, to whom she had that antipathy which animals so often betray to particular individuals, were a source of great amusement to my little sister and myself; but when she chose the retreat of the beaufet as the scene of her *accouchement*, our fear lest it should come to my mother's knowledge, was as great as if we had been concealing a moral turpitude.

It was a good and pious custom of my mother's to hear us our prayers every night; when Molly tapped at the parlour door at nine o'clock, we knelt at my mother's feet, our four little hands clasped in hers, and our eyes turned to her with looks of love, as they repeated that simple and beautiful invocation, the Lord's Prayer; to this was always added the supplication, "Lighten our darkness we beseech Thee;" after which we were accustomed to recite a prayer of our affectionate suggestion, calling a blessing on the heads of all we knew and loved, which ran thus, "God bless papa, mamma, my dear sister, and Molly, and Betty, and Joe, and James, and all our good friends." One night, however, before my mother could pronounce her solemn "amen," a soft muttered "purr" issued from the cupboard, my heart echoed the appeal, and I added, "God bless Ginger the cat!" Wasn't my mother shocked! She shook both my shoulders and said, "What do you mean by that, you stupid child?"

"May I not say, 'Bless Ginger?' I asked humbly."

"Certainly *not*," said my mother emphatically.

"Why, mamma?"

"Because Ginger is not a Christian."

"*Why* is not Ginger a Christian?"

"Why? because Ginger is only an animal."

"Am I a Christian, mamma, or an animal?"

"I will not answer any more foolish questions to-night. Molly, take these children to bed, and do teach Sydney not to ask those silly questions."

So we were sent off in disgrace, but not before I had given Ginger a wink, whose bright eyes acknowledged the salute through the half-open door.

The result of this was that I tried my hand at a poem.

The jingle of rhyme was familiar to my ear through my mother's constant recitation of verses, from the sublime Universal Prayer of Pope to the nursery rhyme of Little Jack Horner; whilst my father's dramatic citations, which had descended even to the servants, had furnished me with the tags of plays from Shakespeare to O'Keefe; so that "I lisped in numbers" though the numbers never came.

Here is my first attempt:

"My dear pussy cat,
  Were I a mouse or rat,
    Sure I never would run off from you,
You're so funny and gay,
With your tail when you play,
  And no song is so sweet as your "mew;"
But pray keep in your press,
And don't make a mess,
  When you share with your kittens our possot;
For mamma can't abide you,
And I cannot hide you,
  Except you keep close in your closet!

I tagged these doggrels together while lying awake half the night, and as soon as I could get a hearing in the morning I recited them to the kitchen, and no elocution ever pronounced in *that* kitchen (although it was dedicated to Melpomene, whose image shone on an orchestra that had been converted into a dresser, the whole apartment being the remains of the fantastic Ridotto, though now being converted to culinary purposes in the same floor as our dining-room), no elocution had ever excited more applause. James undertook to write it down, and Molly corrected the press. It was served up at breakfast to my father, and it not only procured me his rapturous praise but my mother's forgiveness.

My father took me to Moira House; made me recite my poem, to which he had taught me to add appropriate emphasis and action, to which my own tendency to grimace added considerable comicality. The Countess of Moira laughed heartily at the "infant Muse" as my father called me, and ordered the housekeeper to send up a large plate of bread and jam, the earliest recompense of my literary labours.

CHAPTER VI.

MY INSTRUCTORS.

ALL this time the education of the children, a favourite theme of discussion and disputation, proceeded in a desultory manner.

The moment nature broke out into anywhat noticeable act, discipline was brought in, and a master was found for the time being, which always proved to be a very short time indeed.

Once, accompanying my father and mother in a very John Gilpin trip, to spend the day at Castle Bellingham, I was so struck with the pretty church on the roadside, that while dinner was preparing I made a sort of sketch of it with the pen and ink and paper generally found lying on inn tables.

My father and mother were astounded, and a future Angelica Kauffmann was predicted in me over our chickens and bacon.

My mother was delighted that my first attempt should have been a sacerdotal one, and immediately on our return to town a drawing-master was sought for, and one was found who rejoiced in the name of Martin. He encouraged my mother's hopes, and put me at once to indite a cherub's head.

My cherub was really wonderful; my mother said it was *miraculous;* and so it would have been if I had had any hand in it; but to tell the truth, it owed all its merit to the genius of my master. One day that the black chalk was committed to my unpractised hand, on my mother's sudden entrance, my cherub's head ran the risk of being converted into a negro's. Mr. Martin was mad; and putting a large lump of bread into my hand, saying, "There, Miss, take out the effect of the jaw with this piece of bread."

Caligraphy and mathematics succeeded to the finer "art."

One morning when we were at breakfast with my father and mother—that is, my sister and myself—at our own little table, with bread and milk, the servant announced a visitor by the style and title of "Mr. Mark Tully."

"Stay a moment, James," said my father to my affrighted mother, *qui dans ce mot là reconnaissait notre sang*—and anticipated a cousin; while my father, in a coaxing tone, said: "My dear Jenny, this is a poor fellow from Lough Rea; once a flourishing schoolmaster, a great mathematician and copper-plate writer. I think we might make use of him for the children, though he has now taken to another line of life."

At this moment James introduced a gaunt, ungainly looking man, with a pedlar's pack in one hand and a short stick in the other.

He looked extremely frightened. My good-natured father rose to meet him with:

"Marcus Tullius Aufidius, my brave fellow, how does the world use you?"

"Thank your honour for axing."

"Will you take a cup of tea before we drop into *shanahos*?" said my father.

"Thanks be to your honour, the thimble full, if ye plaze."

"Here, Sydney," said my mother, "take the gentleman this cup of tea."

Replacing the cup and saucer on the table, I took out my silver thimble out of the tidy little "house-wife" that hung to my side; I filled it with tea and presented it to the pedlar.

My mother tried to look angry and my father too.

"She is a silly child," said he, "but she means no harm."

"Oh, God bless her, Mr. Owenson, she is a fine lively little cratur, and will come to good yet!"

My father at once proposed us as his pupils in the noble art, in which at present I certainly do not excel.

Paper was got—lines were ruled, and Marcus Tullius Aufidius gave me a line of strokes and a line of A's and B's to copy.

"Now, Miss, broad strokes down—hair strokes up."

I not only copied these strokes but I copied his most ridiculous mouth, which he opened and shut to correspond with the ups and downs of his pen.

My little sister tittered, my father and mother, though angry, could not suppress their smiles; the susceptible Marcus Tullius took offence and rose in wrath, saying:

"Och, then, Miss is too cliver for me entirely."

"Well, then," said my father, "to ease your burden, we will for the present take your Connemara stockings, and bye-and-bye your instructions."

My mother now hastened to make a bargain. My father at once purchased a pound's worth of the "Connemara's," and Marcus Tullius shouldered his pack, made his scrape, and never after returned, while I, perhaps, lost the chance of becoming as good a mathematician as Voltaire's *Marquise de Châtelet*, or any other poor French philosopheress who assisted to make Newton known in Paris.

CHAPTER VII.

MY FATHER.

Who was my father? to whom in these few pages I have dedicated so much recollection.

My father was a Celtic Irishman, my mother was a Saxon; and "I had the good fortune," as Paddy O'Carrol says, "to come over to Ireland to be borned."

My father was—an actor! But he shall tell his own tale; or, rather, I will try to relate it as I heard it from his lips many a time and oft, sometimes spoken, sometimes sung.

My father devoted as much of his time to domestic enjoyment as his profession and public life would admit of. In the course of my early and after years, it was a source of infinite delight to me, to hear him narrate in broken episodes, traits and incidents of his own story and of the times in which he lived, mingled with relations of habits, customs and manners still existing in Ireland down to the close of the last century. They were so impressive in their character and musical in their narration, that they seized on my imagiration,—for I was a very impressionable child,—and were the cause of the first purely Irish story ever written; it has since been known as *The Wild Irish Girl*. But to go on with my father and his story, which he told us by fragments, it was a romance in itself. I repeat that it was not told in spoken narrative, but interspersed with delicious Irish melodies, and given out with an emphasis and gesticulation not less eloquent than his language, which was "music spoken."

MY FATHER'S STORY.

"St. Patrick was a gentleman and come of decent people."
Met. Hist. of St. Patrick.

"We were kin to the Braghlaglans, Callagans,
Connors and Brides also."—*Irish Song.*

At the beginning of the last century many of the manners and customs and national habits of Ireland in the middle ages still existed. The rustic amusements of the gentry as well as of the peasantry, were of a character that enlisted some of the most violent passions of Irish temperament; a dance begun in utmost jollity *on* the sod, often ended by laying one of the performers *under* it; and a duel was not rare that arose from some mere awkwardness in the canonical performance of the rite of hands across and back again in a country dance. The hurling matches in the provinces were the Olympic games of ould Ireland; the athletæ of Connaught would challenge the rival hurlers of Munster. County against county, but more frequently Bally against Bally came forth in mutual and picturesque defiance, not unaptly imaged forth in the wrestling contest of *As You Like It*. The first ladies of the neighbourhood frequently presided as umpires; whilst the combatants, whose chief claims were their personal prowess, enlisted in their ranks young men of the first families, as well as the prime youth and manhood of the "mere Irishry."

Early in the last century, a celebrated hurling match took place in Connaught, sustained by the gentry, farmers and squirearchy of the neighbouring counties of Sligo and Rosscommon. All the chief gentry of the neighbourhood were present, the flower of Irish youth of both sexes. It was the custom to award to the victor of the field a ribbon to wear at his breast, or some other simple mark of distinction, presented by the Queen of Beauty of the day.

On this occasion, the Queen of Beauty was Sydney, the orphan grand-daughter of Sir Malby Crofton; the victor of the day was Walter MacOwen, *Anglice* Owenson, a gentleman according to the genealogy of Connaught, but a farmer by actual position. He was very handsome in person and tall in stature, and of noted prowess in all contests like the present. The lady was a descendant of the house of Crofton, which settled in Ireland in the days of Elizabeth. The head of the family was made escheator-general of the province, by Sir Henry Sydney, who was the governor of Connaught. In the partition of the lands and estates of the Irish, the "Escheator-general" did not forget himself; he left at his death six brave sons to inherit six good estates; the second of these sons settled at

Longford House, in Sligo, where a Sir Malby Crofton still lives at the present day.

The fair Queen of Beauty who then graced Longford House was smitten with the grace and bravery of the young victor in the hurling match; she probably intimated, or at least allowed him to discover, that he had

> "Wrestled well—and overthrown
> More than his enemies."

The young man was not "afraid to take his fortune up." The result was, that shortly after the hurling match, there was what the people of the country called an "abduction," and the Crofton family a "*mésalliance* never to be forgiven;" in matter-of-fact speech, they ran away by mutual consent, and were married beyond all power of protest or disapprobation of friends to separate them.

The young bride, with great good sense, entirely accepted her new position, and made the best of it.

She was an extremely clever woman, who discharged her duties in all respects as a farmer's wife, and obtained in the condition of life to which she had descended, the respect and influence she was calculated to have won in her own sphere. But the marriage was none the less indiscreet, neither was it a happy one, for she had *not*, like Desdemona,

> "beheld Othello's visage in his mind."

Her husband seems to have been a jolly, racketting Irish boy; he was frequently absent on all manner of rustic frolics, hurling matches, fairs and other occasions, for the display of his vanity and those qualities which had bewitched her, but from which now, so far as she was concerned, all glamour had departed.

She was a woman of genius, a poetess and musician; she cultivated her natural gifts, and found in art a resource against unavailing regret for the position in life which she had left, and it was her best preservative against disgust at her present surroundings. She was appreciated by her Irish neighbours, who love music and song; they gave her the *sobriquet* of *Clasagh na Valla*, or the "Harp of the Valley;" she was eminent for her skill as a performer on the Irish harp, and for her poems in the Irish tongue; so her life did not pass entirely without sympathy and recognition. She had one son, named Robert, who seemed to unite the most remarkable peculiarities of both his parents.

He resembled his father in stature and personal beauty, and he had the artistic and poetical instincts of his mother; he had also a magnificent musical voice of extraordinary compass. His mother devoted herself to giving him the best education in her power; in this she had the good-natured assistance of the parish priest, who was an ex-member of the Jesuits' College of Liege, and occasionally, the Protestant incumbent of the parish gave his aid. The young pupil of this combined instruction showed his gratitude by impartially intoning Low Mass in the early Sabbath morning with Father Mahony, and later in the day singing the New Version of Sternhold and Hopkins in the parish church with his mother, who was a Protestant. In this way, with a little French taught by Father Mahony with the true Belgian accent, a little Latin and English, together with reading in a few volumes of Irish traditionary lore belonging to his mother, who also gave him his musical, poetical and historical teaching, from the first arrival of the Crofton down to the latest contemporary grievance, the education of the young Robert Owenson went on until he had reached his seventeenth year.

About that time a great sensation was caused in the neighbourhood by the arrival of a stranger bearing the name of Blake, who proceeded to take possession of the castle of the Blakes of Ardfry, after a long interregnum, as the lineal descendant of the original proprietors of the estate.* He had been brought up in foreign parts, and was the possessor of a large West Indian property in addition to his Irish estate. He was a man of great eccentricity, singular accomplishments, and an utter stranger to the habits and manners of the country in which he was called upon to succeed to an ancient property. Mr. Blake was struck with the originality of all he saw around him in Ireland. He was anxious also, as a landlord, to improve the condition of the peasantry on his estate, and to study their habits.

A Protestant himself, he, nevertheless, visited impartially both the Protestant and Catholic places of worship in the parish. One Sunday, when he attended High Mass, he was struck with the beauty of a young fresh voice which rose distinctly above all others. He

* The Blakes of Meulo were a branch of the ancient family of Ardfry.

was somewhat surprised, when an hour later he heard the same voice in the Protestant Church accompanied by a female soprano of great delicacy and some science, singing the magnificent hymn:

"O come, loud anthems let us sing."

Mr. Blake was an eminent musician, fresh from the schools of Italy and Paris.

He soon made himself acquainted with the name, quality, and residence of the owners of the two voices, and the next day paid a visit in form to the persons who had so charmed and surprised him.

The manners and style of Clasagh na Valla convinced him that he was in the presence of a gentlewoman. Her husband was absent on one of his many frolics. It was new to Clasagh na Valla to have the society of one of her own class, and the motives of kindness which had brought Mr. Blake, although expressed with some coldness and formality, nevertheless worked upon her and warmed her to a degree of communicativeness which possibly surprised him. She told him her history, and ascribed the ruin of her husband's family, and its present low estate, to the dishonesty of a member of Mr. Blake's family in former times.

A Catholic, Mac Owen, had once entrusted some landed property to a Protestant Blake. A Bill of Discovery was filed by him against the owner, the ruin of the confiding Catholic ensued, and the traditional memory of the wrong had become exaggerated in its progress until it had become the standing grievance of the family, and in Clasagh na Valla it had certainly found the most eloquent and spirited of its narrators. Right or wrong in her belief, her eloquence and beauty interested the Lord of Ardfry; and whether he believed or not the imputation upon the memory of his remote kinsman, it is certain that he conceived the notion of turning the peculiar talents of young Owenson to his own account; the *naïveté* and natural abilities of the boy promising amusement to one who was much in want of it. He offered to receive Robert Owenson into his family, if his parents would part with him, and to make him his own special *protégé*. He promised that he should receive such an education as would fit him for any liberal profession, and for the position of a gentleman in society.

The parents consented. Clasagh na Valla was proud of the effect her eloquence had produced. She beheld her son already restored to the position in life which she believed to be his lawful birthright, out of which he had been defrauded by the accident of her having married below her station. The father consented; probably he was not able to stand against his wife's eloquence; possibly he could not get leave to say a word against it, and possibly, too, he may have thought it a fine thing for his son "to get his own again" from a Blake; at all events, it is certain that with the consent of all parties Mr. Blake took young Owenson into his own house and made him his companion.

Mr. Blake was not a good person to whom to entrust the destinies of a young man. He was an intellectual epicurean, profoundly selfish, and prepared to make every accident of his life subservient to his use, convenience, or delectation; confirmed in celibacy, and living only for himself, he saw he could make of his *protégé* a submissive dependent, an accomplished companion and an efficient future secretary, likely to be useful to him in the management of his estate, from being versed in Irish affairs from early habits and associations; above all, he would make a *maestro de capella*, who, after the fashion of foreign houses, would superintend his music and infinitely contribute to his amusements.

Young Owenson resided with Mr. Blake so long as he continued on his Irish estates, but Mr. Blake soon grew weary of the monotony of this remote existence and of provincial pursuits — the improvement of his tenantry included.

After a few months he set out to go to London, where he had a house in Russell Street. He stopped a few days *en route* in Dublin. Amongst other reasons, he wished to furbish up and render presentable the young wild Irishman he was about to introduce to his London acquaintance and friends. The Connaught suit of genuine ratteen was exchanged for the fashionable costume of the day; his luxuriant black locks — shaggy and picturesque — were transformed into the *coiffure poudré* and *ailes de pigeon* which had succeeded the wigs of the preceding half-century. Thus dressed and disguised, he accompanied Mr. Blake to the Theatre Royal, Crow Street, to witness the performance of "Coriolanus," by Mossop, the great tragedian of the age, whose father, a Protestant clergyman in France, had christened my father nearly twenty years before. In the same font, Oliver Goldsmith (who was my father's second cousin once removed) had also been christened, and by the same clergyman.

This was the first theatre he had entered—the first dramatic performance he had ever witnessed—he was not ignorant of Shakespeare, for Shakespeare has at all times been more read and better understood, or rather felt, even in the remote provinces of Ireland, than in the country which has the glory of his birth. The drama was, at this epoch, in Ireland at the *acmé* of its popularity and its influence. Dublin supplied London with its best actors and its best dramatists, and the Irish stage was, for a time, almost a fourth power in the state. Young Owenson was "not touched but rapt, not wakened but inspired." From that moment the son of *Clasagh na Valla* had discovered his vocation, and, though in future years he worked it out under the influence of a far different temperament to that of his countryman Mossop, the impression and intention remained indestructible.

In a few days from this memorable night, Mr. Blake and his young *protégé* arrived in London, at the comfortable mansion of the former in Great Russell Street. He lost not a moment in seeking to render those abilities available, for which he had chosen his young charge on so short an experience. Mr. Blake was well acquainted with all that was most eminent in the musical society of London — professional and amateur, of which his own house was the resort. Among the most celebrated was Dr. Arne, the reviver, perhaps it might be said, the founder, of English opera, the composer of *Artaxerxes*, and of many operas now forgotten. Arne was particularly skilful in instructing vocal performers. The young Irish melodist gave him a proof of the quality of his voice, which he declared to be one of the finest baritones he ever heard, and particularly susceptible of that quality of intonation then so much admired and now so much out of fashion, the *falsetto*, then introduced from the Italian school. Arne had at that time completely merged his reputation as a teacher in his higher qualification of a *maestro*; and his grand opera of *Artaxerxes* placed him at the head of all English composers; he, therefore, declined taking his friend's musical *protégé* as his pupil, but strongly recommended him to Dr. Worgan, the celebrated blind organist of Westminster Abbey, rival of Dr. Burney, and the first singing master of the day. Dr. Worgan accepted the cultivation of a voice and ear so rare and perfect, and Mr. Blake paid a liberal entrance fee for the admission of his *protégé* into the evening classes, twice a week, of this singularly gifted blind instructor. The mornings of young Owenson were otherwise employed; he was placed for some hours daily under the tuition of the Rev. Mr. Eyle, who kept one of those academies then numerous in London, where elocution, mathematics, the English classics and the rudiments of Latin were taught; similar to that opened by Mr. Sheridan, the father of Brinsley Sheridan, on his retreat from his arduous reign over the insatiable vanities of an Irish theatre and the caprices of an Irish audience.

The rest of the young man's time was devoted to the domestic *régime* of his protector; a good arithmetician, as most Irish lads are, he audited the Irish accounts, which were forwarded by Mr. Blake's agent from the county of Galway; he took the foot of his dinner-table, having been systematically taught to carve by the old butler, a jealous and confidential servant, and, above all, he sung his delightful Irish melodies with their genuine Irish words, to the very bad accompaniment of Mr. Blake himself on the harpsichord, whose incompetent performance induced the young amateur to study *counterpoint*, and so accompany himself. Owenson had charge of the house in Russell Street in the absence of his protector on visits to the seats of his friends in the country, among whom was Lord Clare the protector of Goldsmith.

Mr. Blake only once visited his estates in Ireland during the residence in his family of young Owenson, whom he treated with a condescension too marked ever to be construed into familiarity; a circumstance which often roused "the blood of the Mirabels," and occasioned a petulance of manner better becoming a wild chief of the MacOwens in other times, than a dependent of the Anglo-Norman gentleman of the present. Of all the advantages which that dependant enjoyed from his position, the excellent male society occasionally assembled at Mr. Blake's table, was the most profitable and delightful; almost all the literary men of the day were among his guests, and the Gerard

Street Club were, with Garrick himself, his frequent guests; but there was one, above all others, among these high bidders for immortality, who had a peculiar interest in young Owenson's heart and the strongest claim on his admiration—this was his countryman and relative, Oliver Goldsmith. His parents had furnished him with a letter of introduction to Goldsmith; and those claims made upon him for their son on the plea of kith, kin and relationship;—ties always admitted in Ireland to the remotest generation, were accepted with all that genial cordiality peculiar to Goldsmith's happy temperament. A difference in age of nearly twenty years, still left Goldsmith nearly upon a par with his young countryman in ignorance of the world, and in ingenuousness of temper and feeling; his kindness was unbounded, but it was not always advantageous, and he who wanted a guardian over his own actions, such as the stern Johnson, was ill qualified to become Mentor to one whose natural tastes and national character were as easy and indiscreet as his own. Goldsmith was at that time in all the delirium of his passion for the theatre, where he had already brought out his charming comedy *She Stoops to Conquer*. He was intimate with the managers of both theatres, including Garrick, his earliest and fast friend; with Sheridan, his splendid countryman, as well as with the celebrated musical lessees of Covent Garden, Signor Giordani and Dr. Fisher. Goldsmith being an *habitué* of the green-room of both the Royal theatres, he occasionally and unnecessarily took his young countryman to those dangerous *foyers* of art and beauty which proved perilous to men of greater discretion than either of the two Irishmen. But danger awaited the younger man in a smaller and more intimate circle. Among the eminent artists of the day, who occasionally presented themselves in the highest classes of Dr. Worgan, was the then beautiful and celebrated Madame Weichsel, wife of the *primo violoncello* of the Italian opera, and mother of the greatest English vocalist of after times, Mrs. Billington. Madame Weichsel was the *prima donna* of His Majesty's Theatre, and was, or had been, the *prima donna assoluta* over the heart of the famous Duc de Nivernois, at that time ambassador from France at the Court of St. James. The foreign siren was no longer young, and perhaps was not the less dangerous on that account; her engagement at the Italian Opera House did not prevent her occasional performances upon the English stage, and her engagement to play the part of Mandane in Dr. Arne's *Artaxerxes*. She was induced to study that elaborate *rôle*, under the immediate direction of Dr. Worgan: in the duets between the Persian heroine and her lover Arbaces, the stage lover was frequently absent *without leave*, and his place was too readily supplied by Dr. Worgan's favourite young Irish pupil, Robert Owenson. Never was "Fair Aurora, prythee, stay," more passionately sung, and had old *Weichsel* been as apprehensive as the father of Cyrus, the Irish Arbaces would have given cause of uneasiness to that worthy gentleman, while the Duc de Nivernois might have applied at home for a *lettre de cachet* against his successful rival. This *liaison* had already lasted some time when Mr. Blake resolved on a journey to Ireland, refusing his young companion the permission to accompany him, for young Owenson had occasionally shown symptoms of the *mal de pays*. He was left, therefore, the unrestricted master of his own actions, and at liberty to follow his own devices in London.

During the absence of Mr. Blake in Ireland, as was thought, Madame Weichsel consented to "star it" for one night at Vauxhall. Young Owenson accompanied her thither. When she entered the orchestra, it was discovered that the singer who was to take part in the duet of "Fair Aurora" had not arrived. She insisted that her companion should take his place, and her request was too seducing to his vanity to be refused. He was in full dress; which was as indispensable then for Vauxhall as for the opera. He was announced as an amateur who had kindly offered to take the place of the original Arbaces, "who had been attacked by sudden indisposition," &c. "Fair Aurora" was sung *con amore*, applauded and encored. Among the audience, however, was one neither expected nor desired; it was Mr. Blake, who had suddenly returned home unannounced, and finding the house deserted except by the old *major domo*, who could give no account of the young viceroy who had been left over him, except that he had dressed and gone to Vauxhall. Mr. Blake, who followed his example, somewhat out of humour, arrived just as Arbaces was finishing his duet! The truant did not return to Great Russell Street till the third night of his absence; and then went back, never imagining that his patron had returned. He found his trunks in the hall, packed and corded; a letter from Mr. Blake was put into his hand by the butler, who sent out for a hackney-coach, had the trunks placed upon it whilst young Owenson read his letter, and then inquired whither he wished the coach to be driven? Too indignant to express surprise or irritation, he replied promptly, "To Dr. Goldsmith's," and drove off never more to cross the threshold of his offended patron. The letter was concise; in it Owenson was dismissed with unqualified decision, and it contained an order on Mr. Blake's banker for three hundred pounds, which he intended to be the last proof of his generosity. Young Owenson wrote a brief reply, accepting his dismissal, and returning the order with all the coolness with which it had been offered to him. Goldsmith received him with all the sympathy and kindness of his genial nature, and encouraged him in his scheme of independence.

Young Owenson had been more than four years resident in London, and had benefitted considerably by the instructions which Mr. Blake had liberally assisted him to acquire. An accomplished musician, he had also derived much advantage from those lessons in elocution, which young men, whether preparing for the stage or the pulpit, were then taking, at an epoch when declamatory recitation was indispensable to success in the sentimental comedies and high-flown tragedies of the day. The two cousins, putting their Irish heads together, pronounced in favour of the drama, as a profession best suited to the talents and personal deportment of the young adventurer who was now thrown upon himself. Goldsmith, although devoted to Irish music, and full of admiration for my father's musical talents, encouraged him in the idea that acting would be his forte, and tragedy his *spécialité!* Goldsmith had just made up a quarrel with Garrick, and he made use of the renewal of their amity to give Owenson a letter of introduction to that "abridgment of all that is pleasant in man," which he presented in person. The interview took place at Garrick's house in the Adelphi; the manager was gracious and favourable; and the son of Clasagh na Valla, in spite of his brogue, was permitted to make his first appearance in the high tragic part of Tamerlane! Tamerlane was, alas! a failure! as was only likely. It was declared by the critics to be not only bad, but absurd; and the bringing forward a *débutant* in that important part, a *débutant* who was a mere stripling, speaking with an Irish brogue, was declared to be one of the greatest insults ever offered to the town. The Irish Tamerlane, backed by his staunch ally, Oliver Goldsmith, begged for another hearing, and selected the part of Alexander the Great; but Garrick entirely declined to listen to the petition, flung the letter on the table, and Tamerlane retired for a short time into private life. This check did not, however, quench his spirit nor abate his hope. He made his next appearance as Captain Macheath in *The Beggar's Opera*. This character was more in accordance with his genius; he was received with applause;

which had the good effect of securing for him a permanent and profitable engagement for the next two years at Covent Garden, of which theatre the principal lessees and managers were Mr. Haines, Signor Giordani and Dr. Fisher, a celebrated composer and violinist of the day. The two latter gentlemen, whom Owenson had known at Dr. Worgan's, had evinced much kindness for him there and remained his friends. Years afterwards they were his guests and frequent visitors at his house in Dublin. He was now fairly launched in a profession, with a fair prospect of an honourable maintenance. The principal event which befel him during the next few years was his marriage with Miss Hill, the daughter of Mr. Hill, a respectable burgess of the ancient city of Shrewsbury. The brother of the lady had been a fellow student of Mr. Owenson in Mr. Eyle's classes; he had been charmed to infatuation with his companion's talents, and a friendship had sprung up between them, very ardent on Mr. Hill's part. On the occasion of his father being raised to the mayoralty of Shrewsbury, there was open house kept at Christmas, and young Hill invited his friend to come down and share the festivities. Miss Jane Hill, pious and prudent as the daughter of a substantial burgher ought to be—

"Sober, steadfast, and demure,"

was nevertheless not proof against the fascinations of the handsome Irishman. Nothing, however, came of it at that time, and the flame thus kindled might and probably would have died out, but that the sudden death of her sister obliged her to come to London to take charge of her brother-in-law's household for a time. This led to the renewal of her acquaintance with Mr. Owenson. Much as her brother liked him, he had no wish for a nearer connection, and the mayor's objection to receiving an actor for a son-in-law was insuperable. Miss Hill settled the matter by consenting to a clandestine marriage. The death of her father followed not long afterwards, leaving her the mistress of a moderate but independent fortune.

CHAPTER VIII.

MY FATHER'S STORY CONTINUED.

MARRIED, and twice a father of short-lived children, he was called upon for prudent consideration by the necessities of his position and the prudential suggestions of his wife.

She hated the stage although she loved the actor. Notwithstanding Mr. Owenson's brilliant success in Sheridan's Sir Lucius O'Trigger, and Cumberland's Major O'Flaherty, in both which he had been the substitute of Mr. Hirst and Mr. Mudie, who knew as much of Ireland as they did of New Zealand. Their English audiences, however, be it said, were satisfied, for they had not yet got beyond the conventional delineation of Teague and Father Foigarde, types of Irish savagery and Catholic Jesuitism. Cumberland and Sheridan both thanked my father for redeeming their creations from caricature; but in spite of their encomiums, he compromised with my mother's prejudices, and for the nonce gave up the stage for the church; that is, he became one of the best and most highly esteemed oratorio singers of the day, exchanging the boards of Covent Garden for the orchestra of Westminster Abbey.

Sacred music was just then the rage throughout England, especially in London, which had only a few years before slowly awakened to the merits of Handel, owing to the success of his "Messiah" in Dublin.

There were few cathedrals to which my father was not summoned when oratorios were celebrated. Sacred music was not then celebrated only in cathedrals, but in theatres, concert halls, and music rooms.

The pupil of Arne and W'organ, whose science was assisted by the noblest voice, obtained all the success he desired, and a good income, which he enjoyed in the best company, which favourable circumstances had procured for him. My mother was satisfied—but my father was not, for he wanted to return to the stage— "'tis my vocation, Hal!"

After a few years residence in England, an accident occurred which restored him for ever to the profession he liked and the country he loved.

Through the medium of his theatrical friends he had access to the green-rooms of all the metropolitan theatres, and he did not let his privilege lie idle, though he found there the charms which Johnson declared he had found it so difficult to resist.

Ireland had for the last half-century lent to the English drama, not only her best writers, but her best actors, and occasionally borrowed them back for her own theatres.

The patentee of the Theatre Royal, Crow Street,

Dublin, was at that time Richard Daly, Esq., of Castle Daly, a gentleman of high pretensions to birth and respectability, and above all to personal advantages. He had married a beautiful and fashionable actress, Miss Bersante. Being a younger son, he had no patrimony, but his family interest procured him the patenteeship of the Theatre Royal, in Cross Street, and as was usual, he came annually to London to recruit his company.

Mr. Daly had happened to be behind the scenes on the night when my father had been playing Major O'Flaherty, and had heard Mr. Cumberland say, shaking him by the hand, "Mr. Owenson, I am the first author who has brought an Irish gentleman on the stage, and you are the first who ever played it *like* a gentleman."*

Daly, who became a constant visitor at my father's house when in town, made him an offer to become a small shareholder in the Theatre Royal, Dublin, and deputy-manager; with the right of acting any characters he chose, in his own *répertoire*; Don Carlos, in the *Duenna*, and Careless, in the *School for Scandal* were added; the chief merit of both these parts being the songs, which he sang in perfection.

Mr. Daly had taken it into his head that my father

---

* One evening, at the Countess of Charleville's, the celebrated Mrs. Abingdon, talking to me when I was playing my own character of the Wild Irish Girl, inquired affectionately after my father, saying, "Of all the managers I ever had to deal with he was the most of a gentleman. I was present when Mr. Cumberland paid him the pretty compliment on his playing Major O'Flaherty."

would make a first-rate disciplinarian in a theatre where there had never yet been *any* discipline.

Of all this transaction my poor dear mother knew nothing till the articles were signed and sealed; but with a promise that she should return to England the moment she found Ireland unpleasant, my father found the means to reconcile her to his own views. *Ah! l'éloquence du mari!* it is worth all the logic in the world.

On her arrival in Ireland, my mother did her best to make her penal settlement supportable. My father took a pretty villa for her at Drumcondra, a lovely village, well known to the Stellas and Delaneys, the Monte Pincio of the Dublin dramatists and artists of the day.

My mother brought over with her an old Welsh servant maid; like herself, a disciple of Lady Huntingdon; a great comfort to her in her banishment to the land of potatoes and papists, both of which she hated with Christian inveteracy and culinary prejudice.

She wrote to an English friend, the wife of a Wesleyan minister, who had opened "a little concern of his own," at Portarlington, the asylum of Protestant refugees from France, to procure for her a maid to be about her own person, a pretorian guard in that land of idolatry.

My mother's friend sent her, in reply to her appeal, one of the children's maids from the great Huguenot school in Ireland, the well known Madame Terson, where I had myself the honour and happiness of being educated. The maid's name was Mary Cane, which my mother changed to Molly, because she would have no mariolatry in her family; and as Molly was a wit as well as a workwoman, and an excellent one, my father applied to her the pun of *Molle atque facitum*.

This passed into a *sobriquet* which degenerated into "Molly Atkinson." She was also called "French Molly," on the strength of a few words of bad French and an affectation of broken English. Servants in Ireland were at that time like the chorus in the Greek tragedy, and took that part in the household drama to which their sympathy and fidelity then entitled them.

Molly made her way with my mother by amusing her, and contrived, as is always the case, to introduce divers members of her family as "followers." One of these, and the only man servant in our establishment, gave himself the title of "James the Butler," and both Molly and he had been some time in my mother's service when she discovered that both were Catholics!!

As they had neither revealed nor concealed the circumstance, my mother dropped into their indifference, and accepted their good works without reference to their false faith.

In Celtic nations, CLANSHIP supersedes all other affections. Friendship sits lightly, and love more lightly, for both are generally the result of impulse; in Irish, "to fancy" means to love:

"All my fancy is for Nancy—hark, sweet tally ho!"

but feud, faction and faith are immortal. Dining one day at the hospitable table of the then member for Dublin, George Hampden Evans, I had the good fortune to sit next my friend the O'Connor Don, of Ballyna Gar, as legitimate a representative of the supreme kings of Ireland as any sovereign, on or off his throne, at this moment in Europe. I perceived him throwing looks, very like defiance, across the table, at our opposite neighbour and mutual acquaintance, the Honourable Mr. Ffrench, M.P., which induced me to ask, "Are you not on good terms with the Ffrench family?" "I have no *reason* to be, at all events. You, of course, know the way they have treated us." I pleaded ignorance, and he then entered on a long detail of grievances, public and private, of which the Ffrench's were the cause, to the O'Connor's. He was interrupted in the middle by Mr. Ffrench asking him to take wine, to which he courteously responded, and then resumed his story. "But when," said I, "did all this happen—lately?" "Well, not very long ago, in the last years of the reign of Queen Elizabeth." After dinner, Mr. Ffrench came to me, and said, "I am sure O'Connor Don was complaining of me." I said, "rather." "What did he accuse us of?" "Oh of robbing him, in the reign of Queen Elizabeth." "Well," said he, "and if we did, were we not robbed ourselves by the Cromwellians? I forget all about it, but I know there was an old grudge; and it is very odd, that though I forgive him he cannot forgive me?" Among the true Irish the language of praise and invective passed all bounds, and formed the leading traits of their parliamentary eloquence so long as they had a parliament in which to expend it.

After a friendship and intimacy of some years, my father and Mr. Daly broke off in a violent and sudden fit of temper and petulance. As there is no interest in such details, it is sufficient to say that he and Mr. Daly dissolved their partnership, and "all the counsel that they two had shared," was broken up for ever.

My father erected his flag before that time-honoured monument of past pleasures, the old Music Hall of Fish Shamble Street.

He flew to Mr. Byrne of Cabantely, one of the greatest proprietors and finest Irish gentlemen of the day, whose property the Music Hall was. My father had known him in London, both at Mr. Blake's and at Lord Clare's. Mr. Byrne endeavoured to dissuade him from his mistaken speculation; but persuasion has no hold over passion, and my father took a lease for ninety-nine years, with a pepper-corn fine, of a fabric that looked as if it would not last a month.

Here he hoped to realise the dream of his life, the restoration of the drama to its pristine importance and intent, in moral and social influence, as Mr. Sheridan, his eminent predecessor in theatrical management, had hoped yet failed to do some years before. One of my father's maxims was, that civilization would best be promoted by erecting theatres, like Martello towers, at regular intervals over the land for the protection and instruction of the national mind:

> "To hold as 'twere the mirror up to nature; to shew virtue her own
> feature; scorn her own image, and the very age and body of the time
> his form and pressure."

At a moment when Irish nationality was rising above the level of unavailing complaint; when Irishmen hawked their grievances as beggars hawk their sores; when the glorious body of Irish volunteers became the Prætorian bands of the land, not to impose, but to break her chains; my father snatched the epithet, and gave his theatre the name of "National." He was backed by some of the best men of the time; patriots, in the best sense of the word; and he set about his theatrical reformation with all the zeal and all the indiscretion of a true Irishman.

His family then consisted of his wife and two little girls, Sydney and Olivia, the elder under *five years*.*

My poor distracted mother gladly took refuge in her pretty country house at Drumcondra, leaving my father, "like Nature in her great works—alone."

She took the opportunity also of visiting her Wesleyan friend at Portarlington, in the hope of prevailing on Madame Terson, the head of the great French Huguenot school, to take the elder of her little girls, whose susceptibility of impression made her mother fearful of the influence of priests and players —those *bêtes noires* of her life. Madame Terson refused the infant pupil, as too young and too lively for her sober establishment, but promised to receive her when she should have attained her ninth year—a pro-

---

* The reader must exercise his own discretion as to dates.—ED.

mise she religiously fulfilled, though the anxious mother was not then alive to claim it.

Our maid Molly of course accompanied us to Drumcondra. These Irish servants of the family were a race by themselves.

Familiar as the Mascarilles, the Scapios, the Lisettes, and the Dorines of the French stage,—sometimes as witty, and always as humorous,—they frequently made a claim to participate in the affairs of the family, because they believed themselves *related* to the family. Dropping the "O" or the "Mac," which signified the chieftain of the sect, Pat Kavanagh could prove himself descended from the Kavanaghs, kings of Leinster; Thady Connor came lineally, "and that not fifty years ago," from O'Connor, king of all Ireland; and Dennis Brian, "if every one had their right," was the "ru'al O'Brian, prince of Thomond."

On the passing of the Emancipation Bill, several Catholic gentlemen who had dropped the suspicious cognomen, resumed it, without fear of being suspected to have any intention to resume the estates or principalities along with them. A Catholic friend of ours, dining with us one day, was addressed as usual, and asked to take fish; he moodily replied: "I'll trouble you for the *vowel* bit, if you please!"

If there is any merit in my delineation of Mac Rory, in *O'Donnel*, I owe it to the photographic impressions of some of the models in my own little domestic establishment who unconsciously sat to me.

The pride they take in their own country, even in

* See letter in the appendix from Pat Butler to Lord Ormond's agent.

its most unhappy times, comes out strongly when they accompany their masters to England or on foreign travel.

My husband and myself having received the honour of a command to dine with their Majesties of Belgium, at the palace at Brussels, I was followed to the antechamber by my Irish footman, Pat Grant (who figures in my novel of the *Princess* as Denis Fagan) to receive orders. I said as I was taking off my cloak, "This is a noble palace, Grant;" he answered with a look full of reproach and contempt, "Well, then, I wondher to hear your ladyship say that—you that has been at the Castle of Dublin."

CHAPTER IX.

MY MOTHER.

My Mother! there is something infinitely dear and tender in that name, and though all mothers may not be equally dear and tender, still it is the declared intention of Nature that they should be so.

I gratefully acknowledge the memory of my mother's worth, and early as I lost her, if there has ever come out in my poor nature a show of discretion and a scantling of that most uncommon quality, common sense, I owe it to her,—it is my inheritance from my excellent English mother.

A degree of common sense tempered down in me that exuberance of imagination which was the bane of my father's prosperity.

My mother came from her native land, an enemy of all slovenliness in habits, conduct, or mind.

She was disgusted with the dirty Dublin houses of that day, though in ostentatious finery they far surpassed anything she had ever seen in the old picturesque houses of Shrewsbury, with their black and white façades, and their pent-house roofs.

The society tried her as much as the houses; she was overwhelmed, offended and distressed at the style of conversation which then prevailed in company; the broad allusions to subjects which are now not mentionable to ears polite, but which were common enough in the days of the Swifts and Stellas, and were the delight of the Lady Berkleys and the Lady Betty Germains of the vice-regal court. She was utterly disgusted at the *double entente* freely introduced; she could not find either excuse or compensation in the wit they often brought along with them. The colloquial habit of what was then called "selling bargains," had not yet died out, the jest of which consisted in involving a person unconsciously into the utterance or the implication of some word or meaning, which placed the party in anything but a *delicate* dilemma.

Neither Catholic priest nor Protestant parson was spared; indeed, both parties bore the brunt of such jokes with an unblushing laugh, for the jokes usually alluded to their supposed success in gallantry,—an imputation which no Irishman of any profession can ever heartily resent.

The tendency to wit, or to its substitute—fun, had been a fashion in Ireland from the time of Charles the Second. Ladies of fashion played their game of equivoque, and

"Lips that not by words pleased only"

were sometimes desecrated by repartees which would not have been permitted in the *ruelle* of *Ninon de l'Enclos;* and one of the fairest daughters of the Irish peerage uttered epigrams in regal and vice-regal *salons*, which Woffington or Catlin would hardly have risked in the green-room or behind the scenes; and such as Kitty Clive would never have breathed in the chaste retreat of " Little Strawberry." My mother's matter-of-fact disposition and natural truthfulness were distressed and perplexed by the lively, brilliant exaggeration, which was the prevailing tone of conversation and of daily life.

She had received as much education as women of her class ever received in England—and no more. She had no accomplishments, no artistic tendencies, but she was a good English scholar, and was thoroughly well acquainted with the popular English literature of her time. She was familiar with the works of Pope, Addison (she had his *Spectator* by heart), all Shenstone's innocent pastorals, which she discordantly hummed and taught us to the music of Jackson of Exeter.

I can even now quote largely, and do so, no doubt, to the occasional *ennui* of my modern friends; but it is entirely owing to her instructions.

As a child I used to sing—

"With Delia ever could I stray,"

thumping on the table the accompaniment with a burlesque energy, imitating as well as I could the sounds of Jackson's drums and trumpets, to the amusement of my auditors.

"My banks they are furnished with bees,"

was a very favourite song of her's and mine.

Also one beginning—

> "I'm in love with two nymphs that are
> To the flowers in a garden those nymphs I compare."

This song my sister and myself used to drawl out with the solemnity of a requiem; my mother always substituting "Sydney" and "Olivia" for the original heroines of the Rose and the Myrtle.

She also taught us to chaunt that noble Psalm—

> "O come, loud anthems let us sing."

Much of my mother's life was of necessity passed in seclusion, for she avoided all society except that of a very few intimate friends; nevertheless, she had one great resource, in which she found both edification and amusement.

The habits of Irish cousinhood came forth very strongly under the influence of my father's supposed prosperity. Poor kinsmen from Connaught were numerous, and my father had not the heart to shut his door against them, nor my mother either. Sometimes they came to ask for a "shake down" at our house for a "few days," (the days were seldom less than weeks), whilst they were in search "of a place under Government," through the influence of some under-secretary's under-secretary at the Castle. They used to spend their days in pacing the "half acre,"* watching like detectives the exits and the entrances of their ideal patrons; but they always came home to Fish Shamble Street more hungry than they went out. I will call over the roll of our visitors during the

* The Upper Castle yard, the residence of the officials.

season which I best recollect, from the circumstance of the wonderful and celebrated boy-poet, Thomas Dermody, being one of the number. The first of these who most struck both my sister and myself, was the Rev. Charles Macklin, who some few years before had assisted at my christening; Fortune had not done much for him since that memorable epoch. My sister and myself were, one day, playing in the court in front of our dreary house, when a "noddy" drove up to the gates, and a person stepped out carrying a green bag, with some instrument in it, under one arm, and a huge book and a little portmanteau in the other. We ran on before him as he advanced, and the "noddy" man ran after him, holding an English sixpence between his thumb and finger, and crying, "Is it with a *tester* you put me off? and I come from Stoney Batter with ye! and that is worth the bould thirteen any day in the year! And you a parson, reverend sir!"

"I'll give you no more," said the "Reverend Sir," while we paused, with our hands behind our backs and our eyes raised to "the Parson."

"I'll give you no more," said his Reverence.

"Then I'll have ye before the Court of Conscience," was the reply, when his Reverence accidentally crushing the bag under his arm, a sound was emitted from a pair of bagpipes. Fearing the pipes were injured, he drew them from the bag and played a few notes of "Maloney's Pig," which struck the "noddy" man and the children as with magic music.

"Will ye give us a little more sir, of that, if you please?"

His Reverence complied; the children danced; the noddy man fell in, the servants rushed out, and began to dance too.

When the music stopped, the ecstatic charioteer held out the tester and said, "Here, plaize yer riverence, take it! By the piper that played before Moses I would not touch a farthing! sure, I would drive ye back again to Stoney Batter for nothing at all, saving a tune on yer beautiful pipes!"

The music which had so charmed the noddy man, attracted several passers-by from the streets. My mother threw up the window to see what was the matter; she dispersed the mob by calling out in a distressed tone, "Oh, Mr. Macklin, is that you? *pray* come in, and let the gates be shut."

Mr. Macklin, removing his clerical hat, displayed his bolt upright red hair, and gladly accepted the invitation.

On entering, he presented my mother with an Oliver Cromwell Bible, which he told her "was worth all the books in St. Patrick's Library;" shewing her, to prove its value, that the title-page of King James had been torn out in proof of the Low Churchism of its original proprietor.

My mother accepted the gift (or bribe) with reverential gratitude, and Mr. Macklin then informed her that he had come by special invitation from my father who had not led her to expect such a distinction.

"I suppose, ma'am, you know that Mr. Owenson is going to get up the grand mythological drama of *Midas?* and he wishes to take some lessons on the pipes, which Pan is to play at the trial between him and Apollo! Put me any where, Madam Owenson, only don't inconvunience yerself."

My mother inquired whether he had lost his late curacy, which had, with some difficulty, been obtained for him?

"Indeed, then, Mrs. Owenson, ma'am, I have— along of the villany of the honorable and reverend the rector, who dismissed me on hearsay on account of my playing my congregation out on my pipes one Sunday—tho' himself lives in Paris, and never comes near the church; and as to the congregation, Mrs. Owenson, it was just my own clerk, and Mrs. Mulligan, and her daughter, relapsed Protestants, and one or two others, all as one, as Dean Swift and his 'dearly beloved Roger.' The congregation was very much obliged to me; but somebody dirtily told the story, and I was turned out by return of post."

The story was scarcely told, when my father returned home. Mr. Macklin repeated it with such graphic humour as it would be impossible to throw upon paper; but its impression was indelible on all who heard it.

To Mr. Macklin, accident soon added another *locataire* of a very different description—a concealed Jesuit priest—whose order it was then proscription in Ireland to receive.

Molly, on her mission to the only restaurateur then living in Dublin, M. La Farrell, saw a tall, dark figure of very sinister appearance, pass through the shop. There was something priestly in his appearance, and the pious Molly inquired who he was?

"He is a poor Catholic clergyman," said, in a whisper, a little *gargotier* who was weighing some Bologna sausages behind the counter, "I think a Jesuit; he lodges in our four-pair of stairs, but master says he will give him notice to quit before long. I think he is starving, but he never buys nothing from us."

Molly, who was my charitable mother's almoner on all occasions, told her this piteous tale with many exaggerations. My mother sent him, by Molly, a small donation with a courteous note—a donation in money to a man who, perhaps, if the truth were known, could have bought the fee simple of the whole estate in which she lived!

He returned her an elegant note of thanks, with his name and address, and begged permission to call on her some evening when alone. She deemed him too unfortunate to be refused, and Father Farer became a frequent guest at her tea-table, to the entire satisfaction of my father, who was much pleased to set him at the Rev. Mr. Macklin, particularly as my mother greatly enjoyed their controversial synod.

To complete the group, Mr. Langley, of Irevecca, came on one of Lady Huntingdon's missions to Dublin, and spent much of his time at the Music Hall, bent on conversion and good dinners. My mother being the Protestant Pope among them all!

These "synods," which were held two or three times a week, interested her much; points of faith were freely discussed, and even the Catholic servants were sometimes permitted to stand at the open door and benefit by the discussions.

There was one, however, who seemed to derive a very particular amusement from these assemblies—it was my little *self!* My sister was duly sent to bed; but there was no getting rid of me. Not that I understood a sentence that was pronounced, but I was greatly interested in the expressions of triumph and defeat on the faces of each party. I saw everything from a pictorial point of view, as most children do; but the impressions that were made by these scenes, became, in after life, suggestive of inquiry and reflection. The group thus assembled in my mother's sober parlour, comprised within itself the *dis*union of religious creeds which still engages the minds of the religious world in Great Britain.

The violence of Protestant-Calvinism against the Irish Catholics, John Wesley at the head of the " Protestant Association," which he had founded, needed the genius, the wit, and the acrimony of Dean Swift to oppose and cope with them. The Catholics found their champion in Arthur O'Leary, whose caustic wit and brilliant Irish eloquence won the day.

These dissensions left a long train of religious disputation behind them, and my mother found her account in discussions which had become to her as her daily bread.

My mother was a little Lady Huntingdon in her way, and exercised a despotic influence to the full stretch of her very limited power. Before the season

was over, however, her connexion was dissolved, and
her relative from Trevecca was dismissed by my father
for ever, for the following cause :—Mr. Langley often
dined at our hospitable table, which was open to all
creeds; one day, however, to my father's infinite disgust,
the reverend gourmand drew from his pocket a
bottle of some very fine sauce which, after pouring a
little over his turbot, he re-corked and consigned again
to his side-pocket.

My father took no notice at the time, but when he
was gone he said to my mother, with an emphatic
phrase now proscribed, and which Lady Townley
used with difficulty "to gulp down" when she lost
at cards—

"Jenny, my dear, I'll be —— if that canting cousin
of yours ever puts his feet under my mahogany
again!"

And he never did.

For the rest of the connexion—the Spanish friar
resolved himself back into the mystery whence he had
come, and was never visible, at least in that form,
again.

The Rev. Charles Macklin was preferred to a curacy
through my father's influence with the celebrated Dr.
Younge, Bishop of Clonfurt, on the understanding that
he was not to play on his bagpipes in church.

But the dispersion of these quarrelsome saints was
followed by the advent of some lay visitors of a very
different description.

Two of my father's old London friends, joint lessees
of Covent-Garden, arrived in Dublin through the ne-

cident of professional life. One was Signor Giordani, the best cavatina composer of the time, and whose pupil, Madame Sistini, was the *prima donna* of a semi-Italian Opera in Dublin, where she lisped her Italian airs in broken English, which had a peculiar charm for the capricious amateurs of the day. Her part of Jessamy, in *Lionel and Clarissa*, was followed by the performance of Giordani's *Son-in-Law*, in which she played the principal part.

Giordani had come over to superintend his own work, and was so bewitched with the musical sympathies of the Dublin people, that he remained and established an Italian Opera in a small theatre in Capel-street, which had its rage for two or three seasons and then was heard of no more, but the *impresario* remained, with more pupils on his hands than he was able to attend to. My father's house was his house of refuge; it had many advantages for him—a table where he was always welcome, and a *piano-forte*, an instrument which had only recently, in Dublin, succeeded to harpsichords and spinnets.

Musical rehearsals in the morning or the evening, or whenever they could be performed, and a regular rehearsal every Sunday evening, led to the foundation of the Philharmonic Society in Dublin. By an odd coincidence, another lessee of Covent Garden, Dr. Fisher, the divorced husband of Madame Storaci, and the first violinist of the age, was tempted over to Dublin immediately on his return from his tour in France, Italy and Germany, and a long visit to that royal *fanatico per la musica*, Frederic the Great. He had come to Dublin to give a few performances at the Rotunda. Such musical *Giros* were very prevalent at that time, and this distinguished itinerant came in search of his old friend, at the Music Hall, immediately after his arrival, a scene at which I was present. My father's joy, my mother's horror, and the servants' astonishment made a tableau!

A foreign valet in showy livery, bearing a magnificent violin case, in crimson and gold, which he deposited in the middle of the room, was followed by the entrance of the great professor, who stepped in on tip-toe, dressed in a brown silk camlet coat lined with scarlet silk, illustrated with brilliant buttons, and a powdered and perfumed *toupée*, so elevated as to divide his little person almost in two. His nether dress was fastened at the knees with diamond buttons, and the atmosphere of the room was filled with perfume from his person. He kissed my father on either cheek, and my mother's hand with such fervour, that she was left in doubt whether the gallantry were profane or indecent.

With the tact of a man of the world, he opened his violin case and presented my mother with a *tour de gorge* of Brussels' lace, which some German princess had given him for his jabot. My sister and myself received each an embroidered aurora-coloured pincushion stuffed with bergamot. From this time, the two eminent *maestri* continued the favoured guests of my father, to the infinite disgust of my mother, who, knowing no foreign language, and hearing no other spoken at her table, took an earlier flight than usual to her house at Drumcondra.

Upon the occasion of these musical meetings, my sister and I usually crept in and hid under a table, in ecstasy at all we heard. Signor Giordani was so struck with our musical sensibilities, that he expressed his surprise to my father that he did not have us taught, young as we were. My father's answer I have never forgotten, and I am sure it had no inconsiderable influence on my future life.

"If," said he, "I were to cultivate their talent for music, it might induce them some day to go on the stage, and I would prefer to buy them a sieve of black cockles from Ring's End,* to cry about the streets of Dublin, to seeing them the first *prima donnas* in Europe." This sentence I understood later—and respected.

On looking back to this period, it seems to me, that our female visitors were few.

I only remember one theatrical family who belonged to our circle, that of Mr. Robert Hitchcock, an English gentleman, acting-manager of the Theatre Royal, and author of a history of the Irish stage, of great dramatic and historical interest. His accomplished and beautiful wife and daughter were received in the most respectable society of Dublin, particularly of the legal class. The young lady, in very early life, became the wife of an eminent barrister, Sir Joshua Green, who, as Recorder of Dublin in 1820, received George the Fourth on his first entrance into the second city of his empire.

Another of our lady visitors is at least memorable

* As famous for its cockles as Malahide for its oysters.

for the name she bore, though my mother used to stigmatize her as a "worthy dull woman," because she found neither charm nor temptation in religious controversy. She was Oliver Goldsmith's youngest sister. She resided with her brother, who was a respectable grocer in Aunger Street, at the corner of Little Longford Street; afterwards it was the residence of Moore's father, who carried on the same business in the same shop. I used to be called down when she came, with—"Sydney, come and see Miss Goldsmith." She is faintly sketched in my memory, as a little, plain old woman, always dressed in black, in a "coal-scuttle" bonnet, as it was then called, with a long tin case in her hand, containing a rouleau of the Doctor's,—portraits which she had for sale, and one of which handsomely framed, always hung over our parlour mantelpiece.

She delighted to talk of the Doctor to my father, of which my mother sometimes complained, for though she adored *The Vicar of Wakefield*, she always called the author a "rake."

Amongst other incidents which I recollect, was the mysterious visit of a lady, who was one day jolted up our court in a sedan-chair with close-drawn curtains; she was received by my father alone, for my mother withdrew and locked herself up in her bedroom until she went away.

This lady was no other than the celebrated Mrs. Billington, the daughter of Madame Weichsel—

"That light that led astray"

my father's early steps, which he could never afterwards retrace. Mrs. Billington was starring it in Dublin, where she enchanted all hearts and charmed all ears; she was the subject of a charming piece of poetry by Curran, as well as the object of his passionate though passing adoration.

A curious incident happened in connexion with Mrs. Billington's name. Soon after her departure from Dublin, it so happened that the officers of the Royal Barracks had got up *The Beggars' Opera travestie*, and they had prevailed on my father, who was a favourite guest at their mess, to act the part of Polly Peachum to the Captain Macheath of Mrs. Brown, one of the prettiest fairy-like little actresses in the world; my father stood six feet high in his petticoats, but so strong was his resemblance to Mrs. Billington, who had recently played the same part, that he was hailed with "three cheers for Mrs. Billington." If there was any foundation for the supposition which assigned to her a filial relationship, it would be curious to trace her fine voice in musical descent from "Clasagh na Valla."

Mrs. Billington married in very early girlhood and most unhappily. She died, however, full of years and wealth; her house in Brompton was the resort of musical amateurs, and her concerts were fashionable. The concert-room she built is still in good preservation.

Curran's lines "On Returning a Ring to a Lady," were addressed to Mrs. Billington—they are very beautiful and passionate; but, perhaps, the following "On Mrs. Billington's Birthday," are more appropriate to the present pages:—

1.

"The wreath of love and friendship twine,
    And deck it round with flowerets gay;
Touch the lip with rosy wine,
    'Tis Eliza's natal day!

2.

Time restrains his ruthless hand,
    And learns one fav'rite form to spare;
Light o'er her tread by his command
    The hours, nor print one footstep there.

3.

In amorous sport the purple Spring
    Salutes her lips in roses drest;
And Winter laughs, and loves to fling
    A flake of snow upon her breast.

4.

So may thy days in happiest pace,
    Divine Eliza, glide along;
Unclouded as thy angel face,
    And sweet as thy celestial song."

CHAPTER X.

THOMAS DERMODY—THE POOR SCHOLAR.

AMONG the fragments of Irish learning and Irish poetry, left floating upon Time, from the days of Tighearnach O'Brian, Abbot of Clonmacnois, who composed the annals of his native island in a mixture of Latin and Erse; from King Kimbaoth, three hundred and five years before Christ, down to A.D. 1088, there still remained, at the beginning of this century, a solitary fragment called the *Poor Scholar*. Some hapless and desolate boy inspired by Nature and taught by a hedge-schoolmaster, who exchanged his Greek and Latin, as well as a touch at the annals of the "Four *Maisthers*" for a consideration of a few sods of turf, eggs, or a "*sudan rhue*," (red herring). Such a poor scholar might have been seen on the Dublin road, the *via sacra* of every Irish country town, plodding his way from Ennis to the metropolis, a satchel tied over his shoulder containing a few tattered books, sibylline leaves from Homer and Horace, a few dirty MS. papers in the breast of his ragged jacket, an ink-horn dangling from his button-hole, and a pen stuck in the cord of his hat, which had long since parted with the greater portion of its brim, and which, with two shillings and one shirt, was all the personal property he possessed on earth. His name was Thomas Dermody; he had just entered his teens, and had been driven from the roof of his father, a learned schoolmaster in Ennis, but an incurable drunkard. Exhausted by " trudging along through thick and thin," his forlorn appearance led a carrier, on his way to Dublin, to offer him a lift on his car for the rest of the journey, which he repaid by reciting scraps of poetry and telling stories—the delight of the lower Irish. Such boys were welcome at every cabin door, and were lodged and fed at the outhouses of the great.

They reached the great western suburb of the metropolis—Thomas Street, of St. Thomas, his court—time immemorial the rendezvous of rebellion, both in ancient and modern time, and one of the gates of the city.

Here his good-natured protector dropped him, and he proceeded—

"Remote, unfriended, melancholy, slow,"

amidst the din and crowd, until attracted by the appearance of some books exposed on a cobbler's stall, which arrested his attention. The cobbler, with his eye fixed upon him, asked him what he wanted. The boy replied, "You have got an edition there, of Horace, of great value."

This observation induced the cobbler to ask him

into his stall, and discovering the utility the Poor Scholar might be of to him, engaged him to remain.

Here he worked for some months in various capacities; but chiefly as librarian. This stall was frequented by a certain Dr. Holton, who supplied the college boys with second-hand classics, which he picked up among the refuse of the scattered libraries of monastic times.

Dr. Holton took the boy home to his house, employed him in various ways, and exhibited him to his friends as a model of learning and ingenuity.

It happened, that the chief scene-painter of the Theatre Royal, frequented the library of the learned Doctor, and the Poor Scholar, ill fed and overworked, ragged and wretched, offered himself to the artist on any terms he might be pleased to give him. Here his condition was not much improved. He was constantly employed in the painting room, but the gaiety and bustle of theatrical life bewitched him. If he boiled size and washed brushes all day, he heard Shakespeare and Ben Jonson at night, and this awakened a poetic vein; he produced a characteristic poem on the performers which excited much mirth and applause in the green-room. It procured him, eventually, the patronage of Mr. Owenson, who desired him to come that evening to his own house.

It happened one evening, after dinner, when my father and mother, with my sister and myself sitting on a little stool at their respective feet, my mother telling Olivia a story, and my father humming a song of other times—the lament of "Drimindhu," or the man who lost his poor cow, a song which never failed to elicit my tears—when the servant announced that a ragged boy had come, by his master's order, from the theatre, by the name of "Thomas Dermody."

My mother looked rather scared. "Dermody! what a Papist name!" The servant was desired to wait awhile, and my father, turning to my mother, said in a deprecating tone—

"By-the-bye, Jenny, my dear, I have found the greatest prodigy that has ever appeared since Chatterton, or your own Pope, who wrote beautiful poetry at fourteen," and he gave her some rapid details which touched her feelings.

My mother was at once prepared to receive a guest so adapted to all her sympathies and tastes, and when James introduced a pale, melancholy-looking boy—shy and awkward—she pointed to a chair, and my father, filling him out a glass of port, cheered him up with many pleasant observations, while my mother listened to his story, artlessly told, with profound interest. The next day Dermody came to our house to make it his future home, and from that time forth he was treated as a child of the family. Well dressed, well cared for, his improvement in personal appearance and in spirits metamorphosed him into a very personable young gentleman. But before this happy change was altogether effected, Mr. Owenson introduced him to Dr. Young, afterwards Bishop of Clonfurt, and then Professor of Trinity College, Dublin.

Dr. Young pronounced him an excellent classical scholar; and his poetry—which was almost extemporised—to be, in sweetness of versification and copious and easy flow of expression, equal to Pope.

Dr. Young proposed to superintend his studies and prepare him for college. Meantime, Mr. Owenson presented him to Lady Moira, to Lord Charlemont, and several other persons of note and distinction.

A subscription was raised of some amount to support him in college and to lighten the burthen which my father had taken on himself. The Reverend Dr. Austen, then at the head of the first seminary in Ireland, took him into his classes.

Mrs. Austen, a leading woman of fashion, frequently summoned him to her assemblies, where he wrote verses *à commandment* and recited them with grace. The boy-poet was introduced, like the young Roscius of the day, to all the literary and fashionable society during the Dublin season; but his home was in the old Music Hall, and in the simple country house of Drumcondra.

It appeared, too, that he was there happiest; and though his occasional absences in the evening, among his fine friends, was very distasteful to the sobriety of my mother's habits and views for him, yet she was pleased by the distinction conferred on him, and she found in his society and literary conversation a resource against the tedium of those solitary evenings to which my father's absence devoted her.

Dermody undertook to teach the children to read and write, a feat which he accomplished, through our fondness for his society and his fun, with marvellous celerity and success.

He was the best of playfellows, and he was delighted with our early tendency to humour; he sometimes rolled with laughter on the floor at our drolleries.

He was passionately fond of music, and frequently made us sing beside him whilst he composed in the old spacious attic, which still bore the name of "the grove in the Music Hall."

He was a greater favourite with the servants than dependents usually are, and, perhaps, the two years so passed in "books, and work, and healthful play," were the happiest of his whole life, as certainly they were the most faultless.

He was just on the point of being entered on the College books when circumstances occurred which deprived him of the personal protection of his truest friend. Dr. Young being promoted to the bishopric of Clonfurt, the superintendence of Dermody's studies fell exclusively on Dr. Austen. The distance from Drumcondra, where we resided for eight months of the year, was pleaded as a great obstacle to his being in time to attend his studies, Dr. Austen residing at the other end of Dublin. It was resolved, therefore, that he should be placed in a respectable house in the neighbourhood of Dr. Austen's town residence, and near the College, for some part of the year; and, to the great regret of all parties, Dermody was removed, to lodge in the house of a Mr. and Mrs. Aichbone, in Grafton Street. They were rigid Wesleyan Methodists, and proprietors of a large glass and china warehouse.

They took great exception to Dermody's habits of life, and attempted his proselytism with no other result than to produce two or three very bitter epigrams against themselves on the part of their young lodger, which they found among his papers.

Unluckily, amongst these papers was an epigram of much greater importance, and quite as bitter as those against his stiff-necked hosts.

Mrs. Austen, the wife of the Rev. Dr. Austen, *très belle et tant soit peu coquette*, received the *élite* of the fashionable world at her house in Bagot Street. Among her guests she frequently numbered the young Marquis of Granby, the son of a former brilliant and well-remembered lord-lieutenant, who was quartered in the garrison. On the occasion of a *fête* given specially for him by Mrs. Austen, she commanded her young poet laureate to compose an ode in favour of the vice-regal reign of the Duke of Rutland, with a well-turned compliment to his handsome son. Dermody neglected the order—perhaps "accidentally on purpose"—he thought the desire fulsome, and he had become restive. Mrs. Austen, indignant at the negligence, considering it as the refusal of an upstart dependent, made use of some expression that struck his Irish pride on the life nerve; she ordered him to leave her house and never return, he accepted the command and did not reappear, in the expectation of being sent for. Whilst in the fever of his poetical dignity, he wrote a bitter satire, in which the foibles of his patroness were exaggerated into faults. This epigram was found by the detective Aichbone, and forwarded to Mr. Austen.

Dermody was *not* recalled; and the subscriptions

already received were returned by the indignant doctor to their respective donors as having been lavished on one whose ingratitude had proved him unworthy of their liberality.

Dermody was then flung upon the world, and after having for a time absented himself from all his friends, and even from my father's house, he was at last, through my father's kindness, taken under the protection of the Dowager Countess of Moira, who removed him from Dublin and placed him in the family, and under the tuition of the Rev. Mr. Boyd, who was then at work on his translation of Dante.

He sometimes wrote to my mother, but his letters, though full of affection and gratitude, were also full of complaint and discontent.

My mother's unexpected death, perhaps, bereft him of his best friend,—certainly of his wisest counsellor.

Lady Moira was all goodness and generosity; but persons of high rank and great wealth are too far removed from the accidents and incidents of wayfaring life to be able to understand the impatient peevishness of poverty and genius combined.

CHAPTER XI.

MY MOTHER'S DEATH.

My mother's death was the first touch of mortality that came home to my apprehension. It was my first affliction, as far as childhood can be afflicted, for coarser passions, rage, envy, jealousy may shake the nerves of expanding sensibility long before the deepest of all passions whilst it lasts sinks into sorrow or fades into regret, proportionate to the energy of its anguish.

It happened that early in spring my mother met with an accident which was attended by mysterious pains, which eventually terminated in gout in her stomach, and confined her to bed in the house at Drumcondra. Her frequent intervals of ease released my father from serious anxiety, and no one had any fear of a fatal result.

Early in June, the recurrence of the popular Irish festival called the "Riding of the Fringes," took place at the neighbouring village of Glas Nevin.

My father was in town on professional business, and the servants, taking advantage of the *relâche* from all authority, resolved "just to run down" to Glas Nevin to catch a peep at the "Fringes," taking my little sister with them, and leaving only a drunken gardener asleep in the kitchen, and myself seated in the open window of my mother's bedroom, reading and watching. My mother slept profoundly, and the setting sun shone through the curtains on her pale face. A deep-drawn sigh drew me to her bedside.

"Are you there, dear Sydney?" she asked faintly.

"Yes, dear mamma, and taking care of you."

"Kneel down," said she, "and give me your hand"—her's was cold and clammy. "Don't be afraid," she said, "you will soon be without your poor mother."

I burst into tears and sobbed bitterly.

After a pause my mother said:

"I leave you a blessing,—may you have as affectionate a child as you have been to me—you must replace me to your father, and take care of your dear sister."

I sobbed out:

"Oh, yes, mamma—oh, yes."

"And should your father give you another mamma,—as is most probable—you will be a good child to her, by duty and obedience."

I sobbed out:

"No, no, mamma; indeed I won't!"

She drew me to her, kissed my cheek, and said:

"Go, now, and receive your papa, and send Molly to me."

But, alas! there was no Molly. I was alone with my dying mother.

I was distracted, but I did all that circumstances suggested to me. I flew down to the road where some paviours were at work. I besought them to go and look for the servants.

They instantly complied, threw away their implements, and with looks full of sympathy, set off; but at that moment the servants and my father entered the house almost together.

His rage at their conduct was soon quenched in grief, as he hung over my mother and raised her in his arms. Two physicians were sent for to town; a messenger was also despatched for the rector of Drumcondra, but he was from home; and before any assistance, spiritual or physical, could arrive, my mother had breathed her last.

My father, unconscious of the event at the moment, was walking in restless agony up and down the drawing-room, with a child in either hand. The poor paviours were fixed in attention at the open windows. My father's lamentations were loud and even poetical, and in the Irish style of declamatory grief. The doctors arrived,—feathers were burned and musk scattered about the bedroom; the atmosphere was that of death, but we knew it not till Molly entered and presented my father with my mother's wedding ring,— the Irish mode of announcing the death of an Irish wife and mother.

Early the next morning, my sister and myself were sent to the house of a kind neighbour, who had offered to take charge of us till the funeral was over. She received us with strict charge that I was not to be let back till sent for; the difficulty of keeping me from my father was anticipated.

I was arrested twice on the point of making my escape; but at last I found the means after we had been there nearly a week. I got up one morning very early. I had discovered a hole cut in the coach-house door, which gave upon the road from Richmond to Drumcondra, to let the dog in and out; I availed myself of the discovery, squeezed myself through it, and never rested running till I found myself at the garden gate of our house at Drumcondra.

The road was strewed with hay and straw, and there were marks of carriages. The doors were all open,—the funeral had not long passed through—I entered the house. I looked into the parlour, the remains of the funeral breakfast was there. I went into the kitchen, but there was no one. I ran up the short stairs to my mother's bedroom, the door was open, and the smell of the musk seemed an atmosphere of death. Across the threshold old Sawney lay stretched, and scarcely noticed me.

I entered the drawing-room and there found my father lying back in a chair with his eyes closed. I sprung into his arms, and the embraces and tears that followed were a relief to us both.

He, however, chided me for coming.

"But papa," I said, "I promised dear mamma that I would take care of you, and I must."

A tingle at the bell at the gate called me down to attend to it, for there was no one else in the house.

A pale face was pressed against the bars at the gate: it was Dermody.

"Is it true," said he, "that I have lost my best friend?"

I said, "Yes, and I too, Dermody."

I took his arm, and we walked in together.

He flung himself at my father's feet, round whom he threw his arms, and from that moment, or at least for that moment, all was forgiven and forgotten.

Dermody returned that night to Dr. Boyd's; he remained there for a short time, but he then disappeared, and we heard no more of him for some years, except that once he sent on to my father a letter which he had received from Lady Moira, written in a strain of high displeasure.

CHAPTER XII.

AFTER MY MOTHER'S DEATH.

INCIDENTS in our little family were hurried on by circumstances of domestic importance.

My father let off part of the unlucky Music Hall, and the whole of our much-loved house at Drumcondra.

My sister and myself, by his goodness, forethought, and self-privation, were placed, in accordance with what had been my mother's earnest desire, at the best school in Ireland. I may add in the whole United Kingdom.

Madame Terson had long ago promised my mother that she would receive me when I should have reached my ninth year; my dear little sister was received along with me at my father's earnest request. At length, then, were we admitted within the portico of education, and for the next three years we had the benefit of the best instruction that the best masters could bestow, and we were subjected to a discipline which I firmly believe was the very best ever introduced into a female seminary in any country.

Portarlington had become a little foreign university, founded by some of the learned refugees who had been victims of the Revocation of the Edict of Nantes.

The Bonnivaux established an academy for youths and boys, and along with Calvinistic doctrines introduced a spirit of military discipline in their classes, which made it resemble the Ecole Polytechnique of modern times, more than the Sorbonne or Port Royal. At this school, many of the young Irish nobility received the rudiments of an education that was sometimes finished in the field with singular *éclat*:—among these were sons of the Earl of Mornington, then resident in Dublin, and young Bailey, who died Marquis of Anglesea.

At the period we entered her school, Madame Terson had been induced to remove to Clontarf House, near Dublin; her health required sea air, and this fine mansion, standing as it did on the brink of the bay, had many advantages, both for her pupils and herself, superior to what the crowded village of Portarlington afforded. The situation was as magnificent as it was historical, for the avenue leading to her house was terminated by the Castle of Clontarf, then, and I believe still, the residence of the Vernons, one of the most ancient Anglo-Norman families in Ireland.

The castle, which at that time was still in good condition, had been the residence of King John during his short sojourn in Ireland; and Brian Borrinhe, the last supreme King of Ireland, fought near its site the famous battle of Clontarf, which for ever deprived

Ireland of its national independence. This sanguinary contest with the Danes led the way to consequences of more importance to the happiness and liberties of the land than could be foreseen.

This our first step forwards in life, which broke all former associations, and separated us from the companions and habits of our secluded and singular social existence, was an epoch of great emotion and of new impressions. When my father led us into the reception room at Cloutarf House, holding one of us in either hand, in deep mourning, with tearful eyes and sad looks, followed by Molly, who took no pains to disguise her turbulent feelings,—Madame Terson, who met us at the door, was struck with the little picture of family despondency.

Madame Terson was tall, dark, and more conciliatory in her speech than in her looks.

She withdrew our hands from my father's and said, "Come, I must take you to two little girls who have not long since arrived, whilst papa gets his lunch."

My father wept and could not speak.

Madame Terson led us into a spacious room of very scholastic appearance, with desks, and books, and benches, backboards and stocks. The windows of the further end looked on the sea. There was no one in the room except two little girls,* apparently about

---

* These interesting little girls were the daughters of the illustrious Grattan; they had been left under the care of Madame Terson whilst their parents sought the baths of Germany for Mr. Grattan's health. The elder one, who was afterwards Countess of Carnworth, died some years since.

our own age, and curiously dressed, as though they belonged to some order. They sat with their hands clasped together at the farthest window.

Madame Terson put our hands into theirs and told us she would order some fruit and *bon-bons;* she said the young ladies who were now out walking, would soon be back and cheer us up. She then went away. The two little girls looked at us sulkily and shyly; the eldest haughtily.

We said nothing because we had nothing to say.

The eldest, at length, broke silence with the simple question, " What is your name?"

I answered, " Sydney Owenson."

"*My* name," continued my interrogator, "is Grattan—Mary Ann Grattan—and," looking very grand, *my* papa is the greatest man in Ireland. What is *your* papa?"

The question puzzled me, and I did not reply. On her reiteration of the inquiry, I replied, " My papa is free of the six and ten per cents."

The answer stunned her, for she understood it no more than I did myself, but probably thought it an order of unknown magnificence. We remained silent, after this, for some time, and then, having nothing else to do, began to cry! The entrance of a crowd of young ladies, active and noisy from their sea-shore rambles, by their numbers and mirth distracted our grief; there could not have been less than thirty or forty.

Meantime, Madame Terson had wisely sent our father away with Molly, and although we sobbed under the intelligence, we soon made acquaintance with some of the other little girls, who were less occupied with their family illustrations.

It was a holiday, for it was the 14th of July—the commemoration of the Battle of the Boyne. The ballad of this battle I had learned, for it was the Chevy Chase of Ireland; I had learned to sing it with great spirit from our servant James, and I communicated this fact to a Miss Susan Haslam, one of the impromptu friends I had just made, for the joy-bells, which were loudly ringing, had inspired me. I was called on by acclamation to sing it directly. I complied, and my dear little sister Olivia joined me, as a matter of course. As all my audience had been brought up with a wholesome fear of "Popery and wooden shoes," our song had a great success, and was encored.

This little talent, thus early put in practice, ensured

---

* I preserve a few lines of this once-popular ballad, one of the many composed for the same occasion:—

"Twas on the fourteenth of July,
    There was a grievous battle;
The musket-balls about did fly,
    And the cannons they did rattle.

"King James his bomb-shells did fling in,
    To set us all on fire;
William of Nassau banged him well,
    Which made us all admire."

It is to be observed, that King James, although a Catholic, and of Irish descent, into the bargain, was very unpopular even with the most faithful of his followers, who fought for their faith far more than for the faithless Stuart. They gave him a *sobriquet* which stuck to him, for to this day he is remembered among the lower classes by the

our future popularity. When our supper of bread
and milk was brought in there were many calls of
"Come and sit by me;" but nothing could soothe our
regret for the less orderly home we had left.

The solemn prayers read in French by Madame
Terson, with a very nasal accent; the solemn curtsey
she made as we retired to our dormitories; the strange
face of the French *femme de chambre* (the successor of
our own poor Molly), who put us to bed in little cribs,
on flock mattrasses; and the solemn injunction of "Silence, Mesdemoiselles!" by which we were expected
to go to sleep by commandment, for after that not a
whisper was allowed, broke our hearts, and we wept
ourselves to sleep.

Madame Terson piqued herself upon her school
being founded on the discipline of St. Cyr, so far as
a Huguenot establishment could be compared to one
founded by "that fatal she," whose influence let loose
the Dragonades on the professors of her own early
faith, and deprived France of the best and noblest of
her subjects. Madame Terson's school was divided
into four classes; each sat round a large table with a
governess at either end. In these classes were taught
foreign languages, grammar, geography, writing, arith-
metic and drawing. The hours were regularly marked

style and title of "Shamus a haughna," or dirty James. His flight
from the Battle of the Boyne to Dublin, and thence to Lismore Castle,
the seat of the present Duke of Devonshire, covered him with infamy
in the eyes of the Irish, and well merited the witty and spirited reply
of the Duchess of Tyrconnel, who, when he said, "Madame your Irish
subjects have lost the battle," replied,

"Sire, you are the *first* who come to tell us!"

by a tolling-clock in the schoolroom for each particular study.

Madame Terson sat apart, walking occasionally up and down the room, taking cognizance of everything. The hours of rising were six in summer and seven in winter. When the weather and the tide served, the pupils issued through the garden door to the seashore, where bathing-machines were waiting for them. On one of these occasions the fragment of an adventure befel me. Having got the start of my companions in the race for a bathing-machine, I rushed into one, and found it occupied by a man dressed like a gentleman, who was asleep on the floor!

Awakened, even by my light footstep, he started up with a look of terror, sprang into a little boat which was undulating up and down in the water, seized an oar, and was out of sight in an instant among the winding of the sheds.

The next day the *Hue and Cry* announced the escape of the celebrated highwayman, Barrington, who had been traced as far as the sheds of Clontarf.

He was captured a few days afterwards.

On our return from bathing, prayers were read; then the English lessons of the day, grammar and geography, were got through before breakfast, with clear heads and empty stomachs!

Breakfast was then served—bread and milk—after which the whole flock were turned into the gardens and shrubberies belonging to the house for recreation and exercise. A simple toilette followed, and before twelve o'clock the pupils had taken their places for the day, and remained at their studies till three, when they were permitted to refresh themselves for half-an-hour whilst the rooms were cleared out and the tables laid for dinner (a basket of dry bread having been left for the hungry during the morning).

The diet, though plain, was wholesome and good, and particular care was taken to teach us *l'etiquette de la table*. All conversation was carried on in French.

After dinner, we were let loose upon the sea-shore or the shrubberies, under the surveillance of governesses, or we were allowed to walk in the grounds of Clontarf Castle, whose owner's beautiful little daughters were among our fellow pupils.

Our tea, or milk supper, for we had our choice, followed at seven, after which we prepared our lessons for the following morning. At nine o'clock, prayers, and to bed.

A life more healthful or more fully occupied, could not well be imagined for female youth between twelve and fifteen—the latest age at which Madame Terson would retain.

Among the pupils were many girls of rank and some of distinguished talent; one, I well remember, was Miss Marly, the niece of Dean Marly, afterwards Bishop of Clonfurt, immortalised by Goldsmith in *Retaliation*, and one of the immortal Club over which Johnson presided.

Among the governesses, one also left her impression on my memory. She was an old maid; a sister of the then celebrated General O'Hara. She had known Goldsmith intimately; adored his works, which she taught us all to admire and to recite. She selected his beautifully-written *History of England* for our prescribed historical study; what I then learned of his poetry I have never since forgotten, and his *Vicar of Wakefield* I still know by heart.

So much for our governesses, and lessons, and the programme of our life, varied by our "balls" once a month—to which, however, no one was asked but ourselves—when we put on our best dresses and went through all the formalities of a regular "drum."

It may here be observed, that the dispersion of the French Huguenots who, for reasons very assignable, settled in great numbers in Ireland, was one of the greatest boons conferred by the misgovernment of other countries on our own. Eminent preachers, eminent lawyers, and clever statesmen, whose names, not unknown to the literature and science of France, occupied high places in their professions in Dublin; of these I may mention, as personal acquaintances, the Saurins, the Lefanus, Espinasses, Faviers, Corneilles, Le Bas, and many others, whose families still remain in the Irish metropolis.

It may be, that this draining of the life blood of all that was best and worthiest of France (for men must have stamina of character who suffer for their convictions of truth) left the moral calibre of the men brought to the surface in the first French Revolution, so much below the grave religious character of the men of our own Revolution. The execution of Louis the Sixteenth is a stain on French annals in the estimation of the world; whilst the judicial trial and execution of our own Charles the First, raised the character of England, and enforced respect as an act of retributive justice,—which took it out of the category of political crimes.

The pure air, well-regulated habits, and frugal but wholesome diet, must have had a beneficial influence, in after life, on the mental and physical constitution of those who were subject to it, and which no home education could have given.

My father's visits were as frequent as the circumstances of his life would allow, and though all the masters were very expensive, he subjected himself to personal privations, that we might have the advantage of the tuition of the first masters of the day. I remember once, our music mistress, Miss Buck, complained to my father of our idleness, as he sat beside us at the piano, whilst we stumbled through a duet from the overture to *Artaxerxes*. His answer to her complaint was simple and graphic,—for drawing up the sleeve of a handsome surtout great coat which he wore, he showed the shabby threadbare sleeve of the black coat beneath, and said, touching the whitened seams, "I should not be driven to the subterfuge of wearing a great coat this hot weather to conceal the poverty of my dress beneath,—if it were not that I wish to give you the advantage of such instruction as you are now neglecting." This went home; and Miss Buck had nothing to complain of during the remainder of our tuition. Religion was "taught us," as the phrase goes, in all the purity of the Reformed Church of Geneva, and with, perhaps, fewer of the external forms and formulas of that eldest daughter of St. Peter—the Church of England. We kept no fasts or festivals, and I don't think we learned that "malignant riddle," the Athanasian Creed. We repeated the Catechism on Saturdays, and bore testimony to the false vows of our godfathers and godmothers. On Sunday morning we went to the parish church; and on Sunday evening we had Bible-reading, expounded by one of the governesses, to the best of her knowledge and ability. We, therefore, got nearly through the Bible in the course of the year, and if our edification was not always in proportion, at least our memories were stored by the text.

Children are affected by what they read according to their temperament and physiological tendencies, to which that vain-glorious faculty called Reason must submit.

The mischievous girl who had been found like the rude boy in *The Universal Spelling-Book*—stealing apples, and who had been severely punished in consequence, shuddered before the history of the "Tree of Knowledge," and I selected the history of poor Hagar and her desolate boy (of whose relationship to the Father of the Faithful I was ignorant) for the subject of a tale, which painted my horror of such injustice.

Madame Terson heard my paraphrase but did not approve of it, and threw the MS. in the fire, the usual proceeding on such occasions of orthodox authority; she warned me mildly at the same time, not to meddle with such sacred subjects till I was better able to understand them. Her admonition, and the *sine die*, to which she adjourned my "understanding," recalled to my mind my controversy with my mother on the subject of "Ginger" the cat, and I wondered when I should be able to understand anything. I likened myself to the poll parrot that hung in the hall, which repeated incessantly, "*à vos classes mesdemoiselles.*" I continued, however, all the same — *voulant savoir le pourquoi de tout*, till it landed me on the index expurgatorius at Rome, where I have seen my name in red letters at St. Peter's.

This, my first attempt at a bit of authorship at school, was followed by others of a more local and personal tendency. I imitated Goldsmith's *Retaliation*, converting the illustrious names into those of my schoolfellows; it was tame and servile as an imitation could be, but it won me great popularity in the school, and brought me an immense *clientèle* in the way of letter writing, for girls who could not get over the asses' bridge of "My dear Father and Mother—In compliance with your commands I sit down to fulfil your request!"

The third year of our residence at Clontarf House was in progress, and among the best things we had acquired there, was a respect for punctuality and the fear of doing wrong, the disgrace of which was substituted for punishment. There is a sort of public opinion established in schools which domestic education can never give,—and a public spirit which domestic circumstances rarely call out.

I had now entered my teens, and my father was in anxious doubt what to do with two motherless girls at our perilous age, when at this precise epoch Madame Terson was seized with asthma, a malady to which the sea-air is fatal. She resolved to retire from her arduous situation, which her means enabled her to do. She retired, accompanied by her beautiful daughter and only child, to the pretty little village of Ranelagh, then part of the large estates of the lords Ranelagh, and remarkable for the large convent which still flourishes there in unrivalled prosperity, as an affiliated branch of the *Sacré Cœur*. She had the great kindness to carry my sister and myself along with her as visitors, until she could find a suitable successor.

She was not easily pleased—neither was my father; but at last she placed us in the fashionable "finishing school," as it was then called, of Mrs. Anderson. The lady at the head of this establishment had been governess for many years in the family of the Marquis of Drogheda, whose accomplished daughters, the Ladies Moore, were her best recommendation. Her school was within a few doors of Drogheda House, one of the many palaces now turned into public offices. The transition from the sea-shore of Clontarf to the most fashionable and fussy part of Dublin, was not pleasant to us. The change was a shock—even though we were soothed by our self-conceit, that whispered we were superior to those around us!

We at once perceived that there was not the selectness in the school that there had been in the one we had left. The French was school French, and the English by no means classical.

The pupils were the daughters of wealthy mediocrities, and their manners seemed coarse and familiar after the polished formalities of the habits of St. Cyr. Our instructors, too, were changed, with the exception of M. Fontaine, the professor of dancing; but still the school in Earl Street had its advantages, for it brought us constantly in contact with our dear father, who walked out with us every Sunday on the Mall in Sackville Street, where the fashionables of Dublin most did congregate, who seldom passed us without the observation, "There goes Owenson and his two dear little girls!"

We were, indeed, very *dear* to him, for our toilette was proportionably expensive as our school; and the beauty of my sister contributed not a little to this audible admiration, and I had a certain little jaunty air of my own, peculiarly Irish, which my old acquaintance, Leigh Hunt, celebrated in his charming poem some forty years later:—

> "And dear Lady Morgan, see, see when she comes,
> With her pulses all beating for freedom like drums,
> So Irish; so modish, so *mirtish*, so wild;
> So committing herself as she talks—like a child,
> So trim, yet so easy—polite, yet high-hearted,
> That Truth and she, try all she can, won't be parted;
> She'll put on your fashions, your latest new air,
> And then talk so frankly, she'll make you all stare."

Whether this is a portrait or a caricature I am not the one to decide; but there is a national idiosyncrasy about it which I cannot deny—and which perhaps places it between both.

My father took us occasionally to the theatre, where we saw for the first and last time Mrs. Siddons. I may also mention, that we saw Miss Farren as Susan in the *Marriage of Figaro*,—I believe her last performance before she married the Earl of Derby. In taking leave of her, my father observed, " Your good fortune is, after all, the result of your good conduct as well as of your great talents."

"Oh, that is all very well, my dear Owenson," she said, "but observe, I am just making my exit in time, as the dangerous age of indiscretion is approaching!"

My father said, he thought she was then forty.

Notwithstanding my father's denunciation against music as part of our education, we had the distinction of becoming the pupils of Giordani, who was still teaching in Dublin, but who refused any payment for our tuition, and took an almost paternal interest in our progress.

CHAPTER XIII.

KILKENNY.

Towards the close of our first year at Mrs. Anderson's, an event occurred which overwhelmed us with joy. My father took us with him to Kilkenny, during the long summer vacation, longer in Ireland, I believe, than in any other schools in the world.

His own residence there, and the circumstances connected with it, had considerable influence on the after life of my sister and myself.

It may be recollected, that it was stipulated in my father's agreement with Mr. Daly, that no *paid* actor nor actress should appear on the boards of the Music Hall Theatre; but, after some time, this article was violated by the engagement of Miss Gough, the rival of Mrs. Siddons for the time, the Honourable Mrs. Mahon, the "Bird of Paradise," Miss Poole, the great English vocalist of the day, Miss Campion, afterwards Mrs. Pope, and other eminent professional actresses, by the noble amateurs to whom he had let his theatre, and my father was made liable to the forfeiture of all the benefits of his agreement.

A lawsuit ensued, which my father lost. The noble *dramatis personæ* of the Music Hall were anxious to make him what reparation they could, and Lord Thurles (afterwards Marquis of Ormond) and other of the nobility and gentry of Kilkenny, who belonged to the company, proposed that he should build a theatre in Kilkenny, then, in point of fashion and rank, the Versailles of Ireland, and where a number of stage-struck young lords, and hyper-critical old ones, were desirous to establish upon a theatre such principles of dramatic perfection and aristocratic respectability as should form a distinguised epoch in the theatrical history of Ireland. This proposal, which promised to realize all my father's ideas of theatrical perfectibility, he gladly accepted.

Lord Thurles was at the head of the Committee, and invited my father at once on a visit to the Castle at Kilkenny, to settle preliminaries and to take observations for the best site on which to erect the new theatre.

Lord Ormond was anxious to promote any plan which might induce his brilliant but dissipated son to remain on his ancient estate, and to reside more frequently at the most historical castle in Ireland; for Lord Thurles had been the chief of those terrible "Cherokees" who were so long the terror of the Dublin dowagers of both sexes. Lord Ormond, therefore, forwarded to the uttermost the wishes of the amateurs.

He seemed to conceive a personal partiality for my

father, in proof of which he made him a present of a valuable piece of ground, immediately opposite the Castle gates, on the Parade—the Corso of Kilkenny—for the erection of his theatre, and put down his name for fifty pounds as a subscription to the fund. One half of the expenses was to be paid by subscription, and for the other my father was to be responsible.

Names to the list came in fast, but subscriptions so slowly, that Lord Ormond remained for a long time in solitary dignity at the head of a list where so few followed him.

This beautiful little theatre rose with a rapidity like magic, for the workmen were paid high wages, and were paid punctually. It was mortgaged for five hundred pounds, before it was finished, to a Mr. Welsh, a wealthy and fashionable attorney of the day.* Ad-

---

* Apropos of "fashionable attorneys," the late well-known Pierce Mahony, who came under this head to the very extent, and who was, besides, an excellent and worthy gentleman, when presented to Lord Wellesley, at the levee, his Excellency, with one of the *banalités* of royalty, said,

"Of course, Mr. Mahony, you are of one of the liberal professions? At the bar, I suppose?"

"Well, almost, my Lord—that is, my estates are in Kerry; but I employ my leisure hours, when in town, with the profession of an attorney."

Every body in Ireland was then ashamed of following any profession that could not come under the category of "liberal."

We happened to have a very equivocal-looking house next door, when we lived in Kildare Street, and a neighbour of suspicious appearance having come into it, Sir Charles sent for him in to make a little inquiry as to his mode of life, and asked him what he was?

After some hesitation, he answered, "Well, Sir Charles, I *should* say, that I am rather what may be called in the—tailoring line!"

vances at a high interest had been obtained, also, from other quarters, but no subscriptions came in except those of the Ormond family and Colonel Wemyss.

Performers of the first class were brought down, at large salaries, from Dublin and London, and in the summer which folowed the laying of the foundation, the beautiful Kilkenny Theatre (afterwards to be so celebrated for its private theatricals) was opened with great *éclat*, and filled nightly to overflowing, with a fashionable crowd from the town and neighbouring seats.

It was at this point that my father brought us down for our six weeks' holiday. We were lodged in a delightful old house, the residence of a delightful old lady, who remembered the Great Duchess of Ormond going to take the air in the streets of Kilkenny in a coach and six, with two running footmen before her.

Our old lady was the grandmother to a charming family; her only daughter had married a *gentilhomme de la chambre* to the King of Sardinia—a contemporary of Louis XV.—his name was O'Rigan, and he was a native of Kilkenny; but he had dropped the vowel that marked his rank. He had succeeded to a large fortune, and returned to his native country to live as an Irish gentleman, and sport his cross and ribbon to an extreme old age. The young people were highly accomplished; we became their intimates and associates, and our long walks on the banks of the Nore were amongst the most delightful recreations of our holidays.

Goldsmith's tender lines to his mother and his home, in his *Traveller*—

> " Where'er I roam, whatever climes I see,
> My heart still fondly turns to home and thee,"

is beautiful enough as a sentiment, but perilous as a practice. Change of scene, circumstances and society, is the true " royal road to education," and cuts short the tiresome stages of school discipline. Every step forwards from the dear early home of our childhood, was a page in the history of our mental development.

Kilkenny itself, with its historical Castle, where Parliaments had been held and sieges resisted, was still in the highest state of preservation. The picturesque ruins of its innumerable abbeys, each with its legends and traditions, especially that of the Black Abbey— the after scene of many interesting events in modern poetics, was the first.

But above all was the picture-gallery of the Castle of Kilkenny, where I first became acquainted with that master mode of expressing the human form divine in all its phases! This was my first contact with high art, and awakened a passion for its noble powers which in after life broke forth in my *Life of Salvator Rosa*—of all my works the most delightful to myself in its execution.

I had lent to me the *Lives of the Great Painters of the 16th and 17th Century*, and I actually thought of executing a life of Rubens, about which Moore has made an amusing anecdote in his *Diary*. The gallery of Kilkenny Castle was rich in the works of Lely, and was irradiated by the gallant bearing of the handsome men and beautiful women of the naughty court of Charles the Second.

The sons and daughters of the House of Ormond were amongst the most distinguished of the originals of these beautiful portraits, which furnished forth the pages of the pleasantest book that perhaps ever was written, The *Mémoires de Grammont*, by Anthony Hamilton, nephew of the then great Duke of Ormond, pages of which might have been written in this very gallery when gazing on the portrait of his idol—Elizabeth Buller, Countess of Chesterfield.

The occasional presence of some of the officers of the Irish Brigade, the descendants of the Dunois and Bayards of the Battle of the Boyne, who were then drafted back in poverty to their noble families in the neighbourhood of Kilkenny, with whom they had sought refuge after the French Revolution, contributed to give a tone of elegance and refinement to the society. They spoke the French of the Academy, and English with an unmixed brogue, which was all that war and adversity had left them from their brave ancestors.

Many years afterwards, I was indebted to them for furnishing forth the story and character of my novel of *O'Donnel*.

Of their names I still remember the Honourable Captain Southwell, General Conway, Colonel Eugène Macarthy (of Spring House, and of course a cousin twenty times removed from my Florence Macarthy). Of course these charming and accomplished gentlemen, with the inevitable gallantry of their country and calling, struck me as being very different from the pastors and masters of our school society; still, the impression they left was more on the imagination than on my less developed feelings, and that I was saved from a premature indulgence of a sickly sentimentality, which is so frequently nothing more than the result of gratified vanity; the only permanent influence they had on my character was, that years afterwards I turned them to account in the pages of *Florence Macarthy*, *The O'Brians* and *O'Flaherties*, and *O'Donnel*; where they certainly stood as types for the heroes, and thus helped me on in advocating the great principle of Catholic emancipation.

An old diocesan library was placed at my disposal, and I took the opportunity of fluttering over a quantity of genuine old Irish books; which study engendered a taste for Irish antiquity, which never afterwards slumbered, and which circumstances in after life greatly favoured.

My father's paternal vanity had induced him to print and edit a little volume of my verses, which he called *Poems by a Young Lady between the Age of Twelve and Fourteen*. They had all the faults of tiresome precocity, which is frequently disease, and generally terminates in dulness.

My head, however, was teeming with thick coming fancies, and when I have been complimented on the works I have written, I might answer with Rousseau,

"Ah, if you had only seen those I have *not* written!" Amongst others, I began a tale called the *Recruit*, of which Dermody's misadventures furnished the story.

Never were three months more occupied or more enjoyed; but the "coming event" of school cast its shadow before us, and our departure was hastened by a calamity of which we were kept in ignorance until ignorance was no longer possible.

Mr. Welsh foreclosed his mortgage suddenly, and bills to an enormous amount were presented.

The season of the Kilkenny theatricals came to a close, and my father carried us back to Dublin, where our maid, Molly, had arrived a few days before. She had taken lodgings for us opposite the Round Church in St. Andrew's street.

Although we were not aware of facts, which, perhaps, we should not have understood, yet we were much grieved with the appearance of embarrassment, melancholy, preoccupation; visits from strange men, and the total change in my poor father's habits and manners. His sudden departure for the south of Ireland, and his promise either to come back soon or to send for us, pacified us for the moment, though we were far from happy at being left by ourselves.

We knew but very few persons, and those chiefly the families of our school-fellows who resided near us, and those of our excellent preceptors.

The facts, as they afterwards came to my knowledge, were these:—A statute of bankruptcy was in process against my father. Our cousins, those sage, grave men of Bordeaux, with every inclination to be indulgent, were obliged to proceed in the way of business. In spite of "the freedom of the six and ten per cents," my father's wine business had not benefitted by the Kilkenny Theatre, nor his theatrical speculations by the wine business, for he had more custom than receipts. Whilst the process of bankruptcy was going on he was advised to avoid the crash and get out of the way until the final meeting of his creditors. He therefore accepted the kind invitation of a friend in Limerick, and left us with Molly until school should re-open.

An accident, in the interim, put me in possession of circumstances which my feelings rather than my intelligence enabled me to understand.

Opening, one day, one of my father's old theatrical books, the *Memoirs of Mossop*, I found the following paragraph:—

"Mr. Mossop appeared before the Commissioners of Bankruptcy at Guildhall, being the third meeting, when he passed his examination and delivered up his effects, which were thirteen hundred pounds in cash, a forty-pound bill, and a ten-pound bill, and his gold watch, which the creditors humanely gave him back, as well as the bills. Mr. Garrick attended, and proved a debt of two hundred pounds," &c.

This enlightened me as to the meaning of bankruptcy, and also accounted for the fact that Molly had shortly before unhooked my poor mother's watch and chain, which I wore at my side, to which was appended a valuable chatelaine, consisting, strange to say, of two miniatures of Abelard and Heloise, and an enamelled egg-shell filled with musk. I think I smell it now! She made the pretence that it needed to be cleaned, but the tears were in her eyes as she unhooked it.

Under these circumstances, my character seems to have developed itself rapidly, for adversity is a great teacher.

My father's last words before his departure, were, that we should write to him daily, a command I took on myself to obey with great alacrity, trusting to chance for *franks*. I was already passionately fond of writing about any thing to any one.

CHAPTER XIV.

EARLY GIRLHOOD.

"What can we argue—but from what we know?"—Pope.

Some copies of old (or rather young) letters were preserved by our poor old servant Molly, from my school days up, and found in her Pandora's box, after her death, with many curious relics. They are thus noted on the defaced and dirty covers:

"Letters from Miss Sydney Owenson to her father, during her last school holidays. God pity her!"

St. Andrew's Street, Dublin.
Sunday night, 9 o'clock.[*]

My Dearest Sir and most Dear Papa,

You see how soon I begin to fulfil your commands, for you are not many hours gone. But you bid me not let a day pass before I began a journal and telling you all that happens to your two poor loving little

[*] The year is probably 1796.—Ed.

girls, who never were so unhappy in all their lives as
when they saw the yellow chaise wheels turn down
the corner of Trinity Street, and lost sight of you.
There we remained with our necks stretched out of the
window, and Molly crying over us, " Musha, Musha!"
when, looking up, she suddenly cried out, "See what
God has sent to comfort ye!" and it was indeed remarkable that at that very moment the heavy clouds
that rested over the dome of the round church just
opposite, broke away, and, in a burst of sunshine, down
came flying a beautiful gold-coloured bird, very much
resembling that beautiful picture in the picture-gallery
in Kilkenny Castle which we so lately saw. Well, Sir,
it came fluttering down to the very sill of the window,
Molly thinking, I believe, it was a miracle sent to comfort us, when, lo and behold, dear papa, what should
it turn out to be but Mrs. Stree's old Tom pigeon,
who roosts every night on the top of St. Andrew's, and
whom her mischievous son *had painted yellow!*

Olivia made great game of Saint Molly and her
miracle, and made such a funny sketch of her as made
me die laughing, and that cheered us both up. After
breakfast, Molly dressed us "neat as hands and pins
could make us," she said, and we went to church; but
just as we were stepping out of the hall door, who
should come plump against us but James Carter, and he
looked so well and handsome in his new college robe and
square cap (the first time he had ever put them on), and
a beautiful prayer-book in his hand, that we really did
not know him. He said he had forgotten to leave a
message for us on his way to the college chapel, from

his grandma, to beg that we would come in next door and dine with her, as we must be very lonely after our father's departure, which offer, of course, we accepted; and he said with his droll air, "If you will allow me the honour, I will come in and escort you at four o'clock." "No, sir," said Molly, who hates him, and who said he only wanted to come in and have a romp with Miss Livy, "there is no need, as your grandmamma lives only next door;" and so we went to church and Molly went to Mass; and all this diverted our grief though it did not vanquish it. Well, we had such a nice dinner! It is impossible to tell you how droll James Carter was, and how angry he made the dear old lady, who put him down constantly, with, "You forget, sir, that you are now a member of the most learned university in the world, and no longer a scrubby school-boy." Well, the cloth was scarcely removed and grace said by James (by-the-bye with such a long face), when he started up and said, "Come, girls, let us have a stroll in the College Park whilst granny takes her nap." Oh, if you could only see granny's face. "*No, sir*," said she, "the girls, as you are pleased to call the young ladies your cousins, shall *not* go and stroll with you among a pack of young collegians and audacious nursery-maids. Now that you are a member of the most learned university in the world, you might stay quiet at home on the Lord's day, and read a sermon for your young friends, or at least recommend them some good book to read 'whilst granny takes her nap.'" All this time Jem looked the image of Mawworm in the play, and then taking two books off the window-

sents, he gave one to each of us, and said, "Mark, learn, and inwardly *digest* till I return. The next moment he was flying by the window and kissing hands, and so granny and the old black cat purring together, fell fast asleep, and we took up our books and seated ourselves in each of the parlour-windows. Now, what do you think, papa, these books were? Olivia's was *Sheridan's Dictionary*, and mine was an *Essay on the Human Understanding*, by Mr. Locke, gent. I was going to throw mine down, but struck by some anecdotes about children, which brought me back to my dear old days at Drumcondra, I began at the beginning and read on for a full hour and a half. How it set me thinking from the moment when I had not a thought or an idea, which was the case in my infancy, for it is clear that we have no innate ideas when we are born, which certainly never struck me before; and this set me thinking upon what I could longest remember, and *I think it was the smell of mignonette*, for I can remember when I first smelled it, and the pleasure it gave me, and above all, your singing "Drimindu," the Black Cow, which always made me cry. But when we meet, please God, we will talk over all this; meantime I shall make extracts, as you know I always do of what I read; for James has lent me the book, though it was his school prize, and very handsome, saying, rather pertly, "Why, you little fool, you won't understand a word of it." But I convinced him to the contrary at tea, to granny's amazement, who said, "You might have found a better book to put into her hands on the Sabbath day."

Now, dear Sir, good night; Molly is so teazing with her yawning, and saying, "After being up at six o'clock, one may, I suppose, go to bed before midnight." I forgot to tell you that good Mr. O'Flaherty has been here, and told Molly that he was very glad you were gone off and out of the way of the Philistines, and that he would bring us Castle franks twice a week from his friend Mr. Irk, who was in the Treasury, that would hold a house! so I shall have no conscience in writing to you on the score of postage. You are to direct your letters under cover to Mr. O'Flaherty to G. Irk, Esq., Castle, Dublin.

Your dutiful daughter,
SYDNEY.

To Robert Owenson, Esq.

ST. ANDREW'S STREET, DUBLIN.
Monday Morning, 9 o'clock.

DEAREST PAPA,

Molly told us last night when we were going to bed, that she had something to relate to us which would surprise us, and so, indeed, it has, here it is:—Whilst we were dining next door, Molly, as usual, looking out of the windows, a young gentleman passed and repassed under the walls of St. Andrew's Church, whom she at first took for one of the Irish Brigade officers whom we knew at Kilkenny last year, for he was dressed in uniform, blue and crimson; but at last he stepped across the way and took off his hat to her. You will never guess who it was—What do you think of *Tom Dermody?*

Molly run down stairs. You know how fond she always was of him, and asked him into the drawing-room. She hopes you will not be angry. He told her all his adventures "since you threw him off," those were his words; "you his best and only true friend," and he had never heard or seen anything of us since he went to school, until he saw a little book of poems by a young lady between twelve and fourteen, with my name to them; he then went to the printer's, and found out where we live only the night before, and he begged so hard to see us before he left Ireland, —for he is going off to Cork to join his regiment on Tuesday,—that he persuaded Molly to let him come to-day. He said he thought he could clear up a great deal of what you had been made to consider to his disadvantage.

Monday Evening.

Well, dear papa, Dermody has been! He came according to Molly's permission this morning. He was quite surprised at the change that had taken place in us and was most gallant about it. He has, I think, been most hardly used.

You know how ill Dr. and Mrs. Austen behaved, on the plea of old Aichbone, when he lodged in Grafton Street, showing a little bit of fun he wrote about Mrs. Austen; and how Dr. Austen returned all his subscriptions, and how he was obliged to write for his bread in the magazine *Anthologia*. Mr. Berwick, Lady Moira's chaplain, was so delighted with his poem that he brought it to Lady Moira, who immediately sent him to Dr. Boyd, the translator of Dante, to pursue his studies till something could be done for him. His years he said were lost in this way, and he thought Dr. Boyd wanted to retain him for the purpose of working at the translation and copying it for him; so he wrote to Lady Moira to request she would extend her patronage when he could earn an independent livelihood; so after some time Dr. Berwick wrote to him, that Lady Moira had an opportunity of placing him with Mr. Miller, a great bookseller in London as an apprentice—but just think! with his usual impetuosity he wrote to *decline* the offer, and expressed his mortification at such a position being allotted to him. Lady Moira desired Mr. Berwick to send him twenty pounds, with an order never to let her see or hear of him again. So he returned to Dublin and commenced writing again for the *Anthologia*, but could not make bread to support him, and in a fit of despair he one night enlisted, and was draughted off for his regiment in England a few days afterwards, where he served a year as a common soldier. Being one day on parade, the colonel of the regiment, who was walking up and down in front of the men, was joined by a very noble-looking gentleman, who every time that he passed fixed his eye on Dermody, who at last recognised him to be the Earl of Moira. You may suppose Lord Moira was a little shocked and surprised, as Dermody had frequently dined with him at Moira House.

The next day his sergeant came to him and said Lord Moira wished to see him. He went to his hotel and was received rather coldly, but without further reproof Lord Moira said, he did not wish to see one who had sat at his mother's table in the lowly condition to which his follies had reduced him; and, therefore he had used his influence to get him an ensigncy in the commissariat; that he would have his release on the following day and have an appropriate uniform for his new condition, when he must go immediately to join his corps in Dublin on its way to Cork, whence they were to sail for Flanders. He was, poor fellow, to sail on the following night.

Well, papa, never was anything so altered! He is a very handsome young man, and has lost all his shyness. He said he had been looking us out every where, ever since he arrived, and had been at the Theatre Royal for you, but could get no information. Seeing a little book by a young lady "between twelve and fourteen," at a little shop in Werburgh Street, inscribed with my name, he entered and got our address, and here he was that very evening! His gallantry was beyond anything in talking of the improvement we had made since we were at Madame Terson's school, and above all, his astonishment at my poetical productions.

The next morning I received a note by the penny post, with a poem which I should be ashamed to show you, dear papa, it is so very flattering, if it were not to prove that he has lost nothing of his art of poetry.

He will write to you from Cork, and begs mercy at
your hands, who, he says, with dear mamma, were the
only true friends he ever had; and so, dearest papa,
good-bye and God bless you; my fingers are quite
cramped with writing.

SYDNEY OWENSON.

To Robert Owenson, Esq.

LIMERICK.

MY DEAR PAPA,

Olivia and I are rather uneasy at your silence, and
hope you have not run the risk of breaking your
other leg in a frolic, as you did the other one in
Cork,—I don't mean a cork leg,—but the city of Cork.
You need not pity us at all, as we really are very
comfortable. I have opened a new mine of study
which will last me for life. We go every evening as
usual to tea at Dr. Douglas's, where there is at present
a very celebrated gentleman, a Dr. Higgins,* a
great chemist; and Dr. Douglas has built a beautiful
laboratory in his garden, where Dr. Higgins does the
most beautiful experiments that ever were performed;
assisted by young Mr. Cadenus Boyd,† Mrs. Douglas's
nephew, who is a pupil of the Doctor's. Now, dear
papa, observe, I never heard the word "chemistry" at

---

* This is the Dr. Higgins who, in one of his lectures observed, that
Roger Boyle was the father of chemistry and son to the Earl of Cork.
Moore has perpetuated the joke in his play of *The Blue Stocking*.

† Cad or Cadenus, was a name frequently given to children in Ireland, in memory of Dean Swift, and after "his Cadenus and Vanessa."

school, nor did I know what it meant, till Dr. Higgins took the trouble of informing me; for you must know that we walk home every evening by moonlight, accompanied by the whole party, and I always fall to the Doctor's share, who says my questions are very suggestive; a word, by-the-bye, I never heard before, and that one day he would not wonder if I was another Pauline Lavoisier. Now, I dare say, you never heard anything about her. Well, Lavoisier was the greatest chemist in France, and the greatest philosopher, and his beautiful wife Pauline cultivated chemistry with the greatest zeal and talent; and I would rather be the wife of such a man as Lavoisier, than any queen I ever read of.*

Dr. Higgins has lent me the *Memoirs of Lavoisier*, and I sat up reading them till one o'clock in the morning, Molly scolding or snoring all the time. And now, dear papa, I have a terrible thing to tell you, and hope you won't be angry, as it was only meant in fun. Well, one of Cadenus Boyd's experiments was, writing

---

* Lavoisier, the most illustrious chemical philosopher of France, and the most original expositor of the scientific philosophy of his age. His discoveries obliged a new chemical nomenclature which became a stumbling-block to older chemists, and was much complained of by our own celebrated philosopher Kirwan. His admirable financial work, *Les Richesses Territorielles de France*, had the distinction of being published by order of the National Assembly in 1791, and in 1704 this honour to his country and to humanity was dragged to the guillotine. His beautiful and gifted wife shared her husband's studies and pursuits; she not only cultivated chemistry with zeal and success, but engraved with her own hand the copper-plates for his last great work. She married the celebrated Count Rumford, and was living in Paris in 1847, when I had the gratification of seeing her.

words with phosphorus on a dark wall; he gave us a
bit of this in a bottle of water, so, after we were all in
bed and Molly fast asleep in her adjoining closet, we
got up and made a noise to awaken her, so she came
out and what should she see, but, written on the wall
in flame, "*Molly, beware!*" She screamed out, "Lord
Jasus, preserve us!" and we laughed so that I let
fall the phosphorus, which burned through the table,
and even the floor, and my left hand too, which
brought up Mrs. Shea in her night-shift; you never
saw such a figure, and she and Molly instantly set
into a row as usual. As soon as it was daylight, I was
in such pain I was obliged to go to Dr. Douglas's with
my arm, and Mrs. Shea said, she wouldn't let young
ladies stay in her house, who risked setting it on fire
with their tricks. However, we are both full of repentance for indulging in such childish pranks, and
will endeavour to remember what you so often remind
us of, "that we are no longer children," and which is
above all applicable to *Miss in her Teens*—myself; so
from this time forth I promise to be more considerate
and serious, but I never can be more in all duty and
respect to you, dearest papa, whose most affectionate
child I am, Livia included,

SYDNEY OWENSON.

ST. ANDREW'S STREET.

DEAREST PAPA,

You see I have let two days pass since I wrote last;
but Olivia sent you, I know, a very funny letter, with

a caricature of Molly answering to her call—"'Tis I,
my lord, the early village cock"! I have nothing so
amusing, dear papa; but I have made up my mind on
a subject which I trust you will not oppose; for
there is no use in opposing it. I have made up my
mind, once and for all, and I am so convinced I am
in the right, that though it would break my heart to
disobey you, should you differ from me, still, I will at
least try the experiment of what I have hit on, for, I
hope, all our benefit. Mr. O'F—— has been here;
he has told me all; and I have seen your name on the
list of Statutes of Bankruptcy. He said it was the
best and honestest, indeed, the *only* thing that could
be done, and that you will come out of this terrible
dilemma as well considered and respected as you have
hitherto lived; but that time, and great economy, and
your resuming your theatrical position with Mr. Daly,
at the Theatre Royal, were indispensable. Now, for
all this, dear Sir, we must relieve you from the terrible
expense you have been at for our education. Of
this, I am resolved to relieve you, and to earn money
for you, instead of spending the little you will have
for some time to come. *I will not go to any school—*
where they can teach me nothing I did not know before!
I was at the head of my classes at Madame
Terson's, and as for Mrs. Anderson — the vulgar
creature!—she is not worth mentioning. *Now, dear
papa, I have two novels nearly finished!* The first, is
St. Clair; I think I wrote it in imitation of *Werter*,
which I read in school-holidays, last Christmas. The
second is a French novel, suggested by my reading

The Memoirs of the Duc de Sully, and falling very much in love with Henri IV. Now, if I had time and quiet to finish them, I am *sure* I could sell them; and observe, Sir, Miss Burney got three thousand pounds for *Camilla*, and brought out *Evelina* unknown to her father; but all this will take time. Meanwhile, I want an asylum both for myself and Olivia. *Her* education is certainly not finished, and she has none of my pursuits; droll, and witty, and musical as she is. Now, Madame Dacier, who was head governess at Mrs. Anderson's, left that school in disgust, and has set up in a school for herself, in a beautiful place, at Richmond, near Ballybaugh Bridge, where she means to take twelve pupils to educate with her own family. Now, she is most desirous to have Olivia; and her terms for everything are only twenty-five pounds a-year; she is particularly protected by our dear friends and masters, Signor Pellegrini and Monsieur Fontaine, and she will take Molly as children's maid to the school. Now, dear Sir, you see there is *so much* of the family disposed of—now for me. I, yesterday morning, opened my heart to Dr. and Madame Pellegrini, who approved of everything I said, though they earnestly asked me to come to them and stay for six months, having neither chick nor child but dear little Alphonsina; and the Doctor, on his return from the *grand tour*, with a rich young Mr. Dick, has been appointed Professor of Italian and Spanish at Trinity College, Dublin, with a very handsome income, and is very well off in a charming house near Merrion Square, where I

drank tea, last evening, with the Vice-Provost's family
(the Fitzgerald's), and a most astonishing creature,
Miss Emily Curran, the daughter of the celebrated
Mr. Curran, Olivia having gone to the play with the
Douglasses. Well, Dr. Pellegrini approves of my
intention, which is, simply for the present, to go as
instructress or companion to young ladies. My books,
against which he says there is nothing but my youth—
but that will soon cure itself—won't be ready for
a year to come. He says, he really thinks at this
moment he knows of two families, pupils of his own,
who would be delighted to have me; the one, Mr.
Sheridan's, the Secretary of War; the other, Dr.
Dickson's, the Bishop of Limerick. Should the latter answer, I should prefer, as it would take me out
of Dublin and all former acquaintance, not that I am
ashamed of what I am about to do, but then I think
you will be, with your Irish pride; and as for Olivia
and Molly, I am afraid to break it to them. But I
am RESOLVED. I know I shall go through my appointed task right well, and, as Shakespeare says, "All
my corporal faculties are bound up to the purpose."
I will not say more, dear papa, at present; but I hope
to have everything settled by the end of next week,
when we *must* give up these expensive apartments,
happen what may.

      Your own old
        SYDNEY.

PS. Captain Earl and Captain White Benson, of
the 6th, whom you may remember at Kilkenny, al-

ways running after us, called yesterday; but Molly
would not let them in, which I think was rather impertinent of her. However, as things are at present,
I believe it was all for the best.

ST. ANDREW'S STREET, 18—
DEAREST SIR,
It breaks my heart to annoy you; but what
can I do without your advice? I wrote to odious
Mrs. Anderson to say, that though we knew she
would not open school till after next week, yet you
would be obliged by her receiving us a few days
earlier than the time appointed, as your return to
town is uncertain. I will not afflict you by enclosing
her insolent answer; besides, it is not my frank-day; but the sum of her impertinence is, that she
will not receive us at all until our last half-year's bill
is paid up; and that she will not have Molly on *any*
terms! Now, dear papa, with respect to the items of
her shameful account; in the first place, half-a-guinea
a lesson to Dr. Pellegrini! when he distinctly said to
her, before me, "These two little girls are not *school*
pupils, for I don't give lessons in schools, but as the
friends and playfellows of my little Alphonsina. I
told their good father I would read a little Italian with
them whenever I came to give Alphonsina her lesson."
Now, as to a guinea a month to darling old Fontaine,
as he was your *maître de ballet* at the theatre, he would
not hear of payment, or, at least, he would settle with

you himself. Well, dear sir, while we were all agitated and annoyed by this letter, up comes Mrs. Shea, to say we could not have the apartments after next week, because Councillor Costello, who has them by the year, is coming to town on business, and will want them! Molly says this is all a pretence, as councillors don't come to town at this season of the year; and, would you believe it? when Mr. Lee sent his men from College Green for the piano, as I told him to do, the month of hire being up, Mrs. Shea would not let it go, but bid them come back for it the week after next; and then she and Molly had a row, which really frightened poor Olivia and myself, for we thought they would have come to cuffs. Well, when all was quiet, we all sat down and had a good cry, and in the midst of all this, Monsieur Fontaine drove up in his new carriage, going to the Castle, where he has been appointed Master of the Ceremonies; well, poor darling old gentleman, I thought he was going to cry with us (for we told him everything), instead of which, however, he threw up the window and cried out, "Montez donc, Martin mon fils, avec votre petit violin;" and up comes Martin, more ugly and absurd than ever, with his little "kit," and what does dear old Fontaine do, but put us in a circle that we might dance a *chasser à la ronde*, saying, "Egnyez vous mes enfans il n'y a que ça de bon;" and only think, there we were; the next moment we were all of us—Molly, Martin, and Monsieur included—dancing away to the tune, "What a beau your granny is," (the only one that

Martin can play), and we were all laughing ready to
die until Livy gave Molly, who was in the way, a
kick behind; she fell upon Martin, who fell upon his
father, who fell upon me — and there we were, all
sprawling like a pack of cards, and laughing; and then,
dear papa, Fontaine sent off Martin in the carriage
to the confectioner's, in Grafton Street, for some ices
and biscuits, so that we had quite a feast, and no time
to think or be sorrowful. Well, *pour comble*, M. Fontaine, before he went away, showed us a card of invitation from the Countess O'Haggerty for that evening,
"*pour M. Fontaine et ses amis*," music and recitation
by M. Tessier; and he had really come to say he
would take Bessie and ourselves there, but that our
crying had put it out of his head, and that they would
come for us at eight o'clock, and that we must put on
our best *toilette*. So Molly shook out our school dancing dresses, which, as you know we did not take them
with us to Kilkenny, looked quite fresh when they
were ironed, and then, dear papa, away we went at
eight o'clock, sure enough, to Stephen's Green. And
whose house do you think the O'Haggerty's are
lodged in ? Why in your old cousin's, Mrs. Molloy's,
where we used to walk every Sunday. I knew it the
minute I got into the hall by the bust of Cicero, with
his broken nose! It was scarcely daylight, and when
we entered the large front drawing-room there was
only one candle lighted — and such a scene! I am
sure I shall never forget. On the old red damask
sofa, at the bottom of the room, stood up an elegant
young man in his *robe de chambre*, fixing wax candles

in the old girandoles, which he took from a pretty young woman who stood below with a basket of wax candles, handing them up; but I observed they were all partly burned, and supposed they were "Castle Butts." At the end of the sofa, in an arm-chair, sat a nun! the very moral of the nuns of Ranelagh Convent, but far handsomer than any nun *I* ever saw, and quite elegant. At a little distance was such a charming little *rondelette* lady, tuning a harp, but exclaiming, addressing a little *espiègle* looking boy, "Qu'as tu done fait de la clef de ma harpe, Hyacinthe?" "Je ne sais où je l'ai posé." Now, dear papa, I never heard that word "*posé*" before; at school, we should have said, "où je l'ai laissé." I shall not forget it, I can tell you. Well, then came in one of the finest looking gentlemen I ever saw, and so like Count Eugène Macarthey that I almost thought it was he; but you know you used to say, that all the Irish brigade were stamped from the one type—and he had a violoncello in his hand. This was General Count O'Haggerty!

Monsieur Fontaine presented us to them all as his little *protégées*, and *élèves*, and they were all so delighted to see dear old Fontaine; but as for me, I had no eyes for any thing but the beautiful nun, who, seeing my attention rivetted on her, beckoned me towards her, and made me sit down beside her, and while the rest went to draw off their *robes de chambre*, and Fontaine made little Hyacinth go through his five positions, not to lose time, and then do his *battemens* while Bessie played the piano, I had this little conversation with the nun, which I will give you, first in her pretty broken English, which, however, she spoke with the true Munster brogue, though she never was in Ireland before, and then in French, which she said I spoke "Merveilleusement bien."

Nun. I suppose you never saw a live nun before?

Me. Oh, yes, ma'am, often; but never one so charming.

Nun. Ah! you have rubbed your tongue against the blarney stone! You see I know something of Ireland.

Me. Are you Irish, ma'am?

Nun. Yes, and from Cork, too; where I am going to resume my convent life.

Me. I beg pardon, ma'am; but may I ask you why you left France?

Nun. Because I should have been killed had I remained there. Our convent was destroyed, and only for my cousins, the dear O'Haggerty's, who carried me back to my own country, I should have been destroyed too.

Me. But who was the Countess O'Haggerty? Irish too?

Nun. That is the Countess O'Haggerty there. That pretty little dodu lady at the harp. She was the finest harpiste in France, after the Countess de Genlis, a great friend of her's.

Me. Oh, I know, I have read her *Veillées du Château.*

Nun. That tall gentleman is the Count, and those two young persons who were putting up the candles are the Vicomte and Vicomtesse, all great personages in France. The General was Master of the Horse to the Comte d'Artois; the two ladies had places at court, and the Vicomte was Colonel in the *Garde de Corps*. They escaped from France with life and honour—nothing more; and they are now earning their bread and supporting their families by the exertion of those beautiful talents which were once the delight of the court and the best circles in Paris; and as their noble spirit of independence is compensated by high respect and wonderful success, I really believe they are as happy as they ever were. But they are a fine lesson for young people of your age. Self-support is a gift from God and alone to be depended on, and wear this upon your heart, "*Aide toi et Dieu t'aidera.*"

In spite of myself the tears would come into my eyes, and I shall never forget *that* maxim, "*Aide toi et Dieu t'aidera.*"

She asked me if I were a Catholic, and many other questions, and seemed quite to take an *engouement* for me. We talked on till the company came in, when she instantly darted off into the back room and appeared no more.

From the time the *beau monde* came in, all was *buzz*, and Olivia and I tucked ourselves into a corner by the piano, where we could hear the music, and could see everybody and nobody see us, while dear old Fontaine was running about kissing the hands of all the fine ladies, who all seemed delighted with him—he told me he had taught all their mothers to dance. The music opened with that charming quartett of Pleyel's, which Livy and I played, as you remember, with Dr. Fisher.

We were enchanted. Then the Countess played a solo on the harp, by Krompoltz, very difficult; but, oh dear, daddy! *entre nous*, the *Irish* harp is a very poor concern compared to the French; at the same time, the working of the pedals was very disagreeable, making a noise like a kitchen-jack. Then M. de Tessier read a scene from *Les Précieuses Ridicules* of Molière. Now observe, we were never allowed to read Molière at school. I never laughed so much in my life nor heard such French reading. Then two young ladies, pupils of Madame O'H., sang a duet, "Rise, Cynthia, rise," very badly, *I* thought; but what do you think, dear papa, M. Fontaine, in his partiality for us had the cruelty to tell some of the company we were wonderful little musicians, and, for all we could do, we were obliged to sing a duet too. So we sung our old duo of "Nous, nous amions dès l'Enfance," with Olivia's beautiful second, and Madame O'Haggerty's *arpèggio* on the harp. We were encored and applauded till we were almost ready to cry, and made to sing an English song, which we did, "In Infancy our Hopes and Fears were to each other known," from your own *Artaxerxes*. Well, we were drawn out, and introduced and caressed, and I don't know what; but there was one lady who interested me more than all the rest. She sat in the centre of the room, surrounded by *beaux*, one of whom leaned over her chair the whole of the night like a *vignette* in one of Marmontel's tales. Now, *who* do you think this was? Do you give it up? Well, the sister of the great Mr. Sheridan, the author of your own Sir Lucius O'Trigger — Mrs. Lefanu;

her other brother is secretary at war here; and Monsieur Fontaine told us, going home in the carriage, that her house was the resort of all the literary people, and foreigners in particular. He is to take us to see her some evening, for she invited us very cordially, and said she knew *you*, dear papa, very well. Well, we got home very late, but *too* happy, and I never slept the whole night; what wearied me was that I went through all the scenes to the tune of Pleyel's quartett, and the nun always before me, while Olivia slept like an angel, and Molly snored like a pig in the next closet; so I rose at peep of day and wrote all this for your amusement, as this is Mr. O'Flaherty's *frank*-day: but, to use Job's words, "I rose from visions of the night" quite another creature. Great thoughts have come into my mind, which I will tell you in my next; but the sentiment uppermost is, "*Aide toi et Dieu t'aidera*." So God bless you, dearest papa, I am going to try to sleep.

Your own
SYDNEY.

ST. ANDREW'S STREET.

DEAREST DAD,

Your letter and the enclosure were most welcome and most gratefully received. To show you how much I am up to business, I accompanied Molly to Sir William Newcomen's Bank in Castle Street, and presented my twenty-pound cheque with the air of one who knew what she was about, though I never was so confused in all my life. Oh, dear papa, if you were never in a bank you have no idea what it is. Just paint to yourself, sir, if you please, a great hall, with a counter running from one end to the other, with about a hundred young men behind it, all fluttering and flying about with papers, like kites, in their hands. We were directed to the "paying desk," but, as Molly observed, "nobody asked us to sit down," so I delivered my cheque for £20, Irish, and wrote my name in a book, and may be, when we got home, I did not walk into Mrs. Shee's dirty back parlour, and throw down seven golden guineas, Molly crying out, "We will trouble you for a receipt to *that*, if you please!"

Mrs. Shee looked surprised, and asked Molly to tea in the evening. Coming home, through Dame Street, we stopped at Mr. Lee's music shop, and I asked him for his bill for the hire of the piano, and begged he would send for it immediately. He said very politely that he would send for the piano, but he begged we would accept the hire, as you had been one of his best friends, and had ordered above a hundred pounds worth of music from him for the Theatre Royal, but that everything was changed now, and there was no longer any taste for music. I asked him if he would lend me a copy of the *Beggars' Opera* and the *Padlock*. He sent them to me in the evening, with a pretty note, begging my acceptance of them; and as we had another night out of the piano, may be Olivia and I did not sing them from one end to the other! "The Miser who a Shilling sees," makes the most beautiful duet in the world. I am sure it is Irish.

Well, sir, on arriving home what should I find but a note from Dr. Pellegrini relative to my intentions, which, to tell you the truth, I had explained to him, saying that the Rev. Mr. Peter Lefanu, a celebrated preacher, would call on me at one o'clock the next day. He had given him a commission to find a young lady who would act as something between a governess and a *dame de compagnie* to two young ladies, daughters of the Right Honourable Charles Sheridan, Secretary-at-War for Ireland, and the husband of that beautiful woman who, you may remember, put out the fire of the curtain of her box at the theatre last winter, when the whole house rose up to applaud. Well, the idea of this visit from Mr. Lefanu frightened me beyond everything, I was so utterly unprepared for it; and Olivia positively refused to be in the room. However, I was dressed very nicely, and seated on the sofa all in good time, and I took up *Locke*, "to call up a look," as Lady Pentweasle says, when I heard his knock at the door. Molly announced him—" The Rev. Mr. Peter ——," but could get no further. She was in such a rage. Well, now, dear papa, who do you think he turned out to be? Why, the clergyman who preached the charity sermon at the Lying-in Hospital last Christmas, and that we all cried at hearing, and you said, "That man is a regular pickpocket, for I have given a crown and I did not mean to give half." Well, he took my hand, and we sat down. He looked very earnestly, and said:

"Are you the young lady of whom Dr. Pellegrini

was speaking last night as wishing to enter upon a very important situation?"

I said, "Yes, sir, I believe so."

"Are you Miss Owenson, my dear—daughter of my old friend Mr. Owenson of the Theatre Royal?"

I was ready to burst into tears, and could only answer, "Yes, sir."

"But you are very young, my dear; I should say you were fitter to go to school than to commence instructress."

"Perhaps so, sir; but great misfortunes have come upon poor papa unexpectedly, and ——"

Here I was obliged to cover my face with my handkerchief. I suppose to give me time to recover, he gently drew Locke out of my hand, and appeared to be looking through it.

"Upon my word," said he, laughing, "this is a very grave study for so young a lady. Now," said he, "let me hear *your* definition of an 'innate idea.'"

He looked so comical that I could not help laughing, too.

"Oh, my dear, don't hurry yourself, it is a question might puzzle a conjuror."

"Well, sir," said I, "I had no idea of *you* until I saw and heard you preach your beautiful sermon for the poor women of the Lying-in Hospital; but having seen and heard you, I have an *idea* of you which can never be removed."

He actually threw himself back in his chair, and took my hand, and, would you believe it, papa, kissed it. He is of French descent, you know.

"Well," said he, "you are the most flattering little logician I ever coped with." He then took a serious tone, and said, "My dear little girl, I respect your intentions; and from what Dr. Pellegrini tells me, your acquirements fit you for the situation you are seeking, but you have at present one great fault. Don't be frightened" (I suppose I looked so)—"it is one will mend but too soon. The Misses Sheridan are, I should think, much about your own age, and the worst of it is, there are two rascally boys, Charles and Tom, who have the bad habit of running into their sisters' study when they come home for vacation, and making a terrible row there. However, I shall meet Mr. and Mrs. Sheridan at dinner to-day at my brother's, Mr. Joe Lefanu's, who is married to their sister. We will talk over this, and you shall hear from me early to-morrow."

He now rose, and as he deposited Locke on the table, he took up a dirty little volume of my poems, which lay beside it.

"Pardi!" said he, in some surprise, "You are a poetess, too, are you?"

And then he read aloud, and most beautifully, my little stanzas to you on receiving your picture, and then rolling up the book put it into his pocket without ceremony; and, with a cordial shake of the hand and a "*je me sauve*," disappeared—and so ended this awful visit, which, though it left me agitated, left me delighted with what I had done, and so will *you* be some day, dear papa.

I am so tired I can write no more to-day; but we are

both well, and both in love with the Rev. Mr. Lefanu, for Olivia had her head through the door of the back drawing-room all the time making faces at me!

Dear Papa—The Sheridan scheme is all ended. The beautiful Mrs. Sheridan would not have me, and I am glad, as on consideration, I see it would not do, but I have got something to console me, I think.

This morning, at nine o'clock, Mr. Lefanu's servant was here with a note,—I send it to you:—

"My dear Miss Owenson—The Sheridan scheme won't answer—something better has just suggested itself. Dr. Dixon, the Bishop of Limerick, who has come to town to be present at a charity sermon this day, to be preached before the Lord-Lieutenant in St. Anne's Church, sent me a note last night from his lady, desiring that I would find an accomplished young lady to take charge of her daughter, a little girl of ten years old, and that I would let the Bishop see the person before he left town, which he does on Monday morning. I must beg you, therefore, to come to his house in Molesworth Street, at ten o'clock this morning. I will be there to receive and present you. They are charming as well as excellent people.

Yours, &c., &c., P. LEFANU."

And so, sir, Molly and I started at half-past nine, and hustled our way as we could through the crowds that were parading towards St. Anne's Church, which you know always fill the streets when the Lord-Lieutenant goes in state, and soldiers on horseback included. It is but a short distance, but still a disagreeable walk. We soon discovered the Bishop's house by two tall footmen in purple liveries, and gold-headed canes as tall as themselves, before the door. You know at the top of the street is Leinster House; the gates were all open, and the carriages were parading round and round the beautiful court. An old housekeeper took Molly into a parlour, and when I gave my card to a footman he was conducting me upstairs, — when, dear Mr. Lefanu came forward, and drew my arm through his, and led me into a beautiful front drawing-room where the Bishop was at breakfast, the sun shining full on his face; his pale, conceited-looking chaplain was making tea, a regular maccaroni, who soon got up and went to the window, leaving us to do our business.

Nothing could be more cordial and kind than the Bishop. He slightly alluded to the original objection of youth, and said he could not give any positive answer till he had seen Mrs. Dixon, and that he would not lose a moment in writing to my friend Mr. Lefanu. He said he was sorry he was so hurried for time, but he was obliged to be back on diocesan business the following day; but he should carry away more than one agreeable impression of me;—and only imagine! he then took up a ragged book lying beside him,—my poems again, which that darling Mr. Lefanu had brought him,—and the stanzas to you turned down.

"These are very pretty stanzas," said he, "as to

poetry, and charming as to feeling, which I believe is the best ingredient of all poetry."

After a little more conversation, the beau chaplain drew in his head from the window, and said, "My lord, the Duke of Leinster's carriage has drawn up, and the 'bidding bell' has begun to ring." The Bishop started up. The chaplain presented him a pair of white gloves fringed with gold, and his square cap. Of course I rose in a flurry. The Bishop wished me a cordial good-bye, and Mr. Lefanu said, "You will hear from me immediately." So then I was just hurrying down to join Molly in the housekeeper's room; but Mr. Lefanu, running upstairs to meet me, said, "Stay here, my dear, the Bishop will send back his carriage for you in five minutes, the streets are so crowded;" and then he sprang into the Bishop's coach and was out of sight in a minute. I was waiting in the parlour for the carriage to return when it rolled up. I ran out to get in—the steps were let down slap dash—the footmen standing on either side, when to my surprise Molly sprang in after me! the footmen grinning from ear to ear. Away we drove! Molly's head a mile out of the window, bowing to every one she knew and every one she did *not* know; but, oh, papa! I wish you could have seen the scene at Mrs. Shee's hall door! The thundering knock brought all the house to answer it, Mrs. Shee at their head; but, oh! when she saw *Molly* handed out of the Bishop's carriage, she looked as if she would die of surprise and envy—Olivia, with her head half out of the window, ready to fall out of it with convulsions of laughter;

and so, dear papa, for the present has ended my episcopal visit; but with or without other result it has been an incident of which I am proud, and I conclude with your own favourite Irish sentiment—

"Foglan foh—Wait awhile."

SYDNEY OWENSON.

Just as I was sealing up this to send for my Castle trunk, a note from Mr. Lefanu arrived. Mrs. Dixon has been ordered abroad for her health; consequently the settlement about a governess is postponed. So dearest papa, good-bye and God bless you, my fingers are quite cramped with writing.—S. O.

ST. ANDREW'S STREET.

MY DEAR PAPA,

I write to tell you what has offered for our darling Olivia.

You know, with all partiality, that she needs a good deal of finishing, though she has left me far behind in music and drawing.

Madame Dacier paid us a visit yesterday, and said she would be happy to receive Olivia whenever she could come; and, what has pleased me much, she has offered to take Molly as upper children's maid to the establishment, so she will be returned to the situation which dear mamma took her from when she was at Madame Terson's and she will not be separated from her darling nursling. Molly is cheered up, for she has been very sulky and cross for some time past, and said, "She supposed she was to be thrown over, and that it was no matter what became of old servants," &c., &c.

I have some good news which I shall reserve for another letter, as I want to save the post; but I just ask you if you ever heard of an old lady of the name of Steele; or a family of the name of Featherstone? they are friends of Dr. Pellegrini and Mr. Fontaine.

God bless you, dear papa, you shall hear again soon, don't be uneasy if not for a few days.

SYDNEY.

[The family of Featherstone, or Featherstonehaugh, became of great importance to Miss Owenson. The name is spelt either way: by the lady—Featherstone; by the gentleman—Featherstonehaugh. Under each of these forms the reader will recognise the same family. ED.]

CHAPTER XV.

AT BRACKLIN.

CASTLETOWN, DELVIN, WESTMEATH.

DEAREST SIR,

The reason I have not written to you for some days is that I have so much to say, and so much that I was afraid of saying, that I thought it better to say nothing at all; which "all," I think, will surprise you —and for myself *je n'en reviens pas!*

Well, last Thursday, Mr. Fontaine enclosed me a note from a lady, Mrs. Featherstonehaugh, of Bracklin Castle, intimating her desire to have just such a charming young person as myself! as governess or companion to her two daughters; the eldest just returned from a great finishing school, Madame Lafarrelle's, and the younger who has never left home.

Mrs. Featherstone was for a few days at her mother's, the Dowager Lady Steele's in Dominic Street, but anxious not to lose a moment, and would send her carriage for the young lady M. Lafontaine had mentioned in his letter (Miss Owenson) if he would send her address. And so he did, and so the carriage came—and so I went—rather downhearted from my former disappointments.

You know what a fine street Dominic Street is, and so close to my old school. Well, a handsome mansion, two servants at the door, my name taken, and I was ushered at once into a large and rather gloomy parlour, in the centre of which two ladies were sitting at a table. The one at the head of the table, a most remarkable figure both in person and costume, but who bore her ninety years with considerable confidence in her own dignity. She sat with her head thrown back, her little sharp eyes twinkling at me as I entered, and her mouth pursed up to the dimensions of a parish poor-box. She wore a fly-cap (of which I have taken the pattern), on her silver but frizzled hair,—her very fair face was drawn into small wrinkles, as though engraved with a needle over her delicate features, and when I tell you what I have since heard, that she was the rival and friend of the beautiful Lady Palmer, the belle of Lord Chesterfield's court, and the subject of his pretty verses which you used to recite so often,—you will allow that she had every right to wrinkles and the remains of beauty.*

* The occasion was this :—At the court of Lord Chesterfield, when religious party spirit was symbolized in Ireland by the colours white or orange, as the wearer was Williamite or Jacobite, Lady Palmer, a reigning beauty and a Catholic, appeared at one of the drawing-rooms

Seated near her at the same table, and writing, was a sweet, charming, good-humoured-looking lady, who got up to receive me in the most cordial manner, whilst two nice girls, the eldest already apparently in her teens, struggled to get me a chair, and then stationed themselves one each behind their mamma and grandmamma.

Mrs. Featherstone opened the conversation by telling me that she had been a pupil of Mr. Fontaine's as her daughters were now, and that he was the best of human beings.

"That is nothing to the purpose!" said the old lady sharply, "Come to the point with this young person, as you know you have no time to lose;" and turning to me, she said, "You are very young to offer yourself for so important a situation."

The two girls looked at me as much as to say, "Don't mind grandmamma," and Mrs. Featherstone added,—

"Dear mamma, now, you must leave Miss Owenson to me," and then she said to me, "I assure you, my dear, I am much prepossessed in your favour by all that our good Fontaine has told me of you; and your being so merry and musical as he tells me you are, is

---

with an orange lily in her bosom. Lord Chesterfield, having kissed her fair cheek, took out his tablets and wrote the following stanza—

> "Thou little Tory! where's the jest,
> To wear the orange on thy breast,
> When that same lovely breast discloses
> The whiteness of the rebel roses!"

very much in your favour with us, for we are rather
dull and mopy."

"But to begin," interposed Lady Steele again,
"What will this young person expect? she cannot
offer herself as a regular governess, she is so very
young."

The girls winked at me and grimaced again.

"She shall first offer herself as my visitor at Bracklin Castle for the Christmas holidays," said Mrs. Featherstone, kindly, "and then we shall see how we get
on and suit each other, which I am sure we shall very
well."

The old lady said, knocking her hand on the table,
"I never heard such nonsense in all my life!"

At this moment the footman came in to announce
that the carriage was at the door, followed by a handsome jolly-looking woman, the lady's maid, with Mrs.
Featherstone's cloak and bonnet.

Mrs. Featherstone said, "Come, my dear, and I will
set you down, and we will have a little talk by the
way, for I have an appointment which hurries me
away at present. The two girls ran after us and said,
"Do come to us, we shall be so happy at Bracklin,
and never mind grandmamma,—nobody does," and
with this dutiful observation they shook hands cordially with me, and I drove off with my bran new
friend. What was amusing in all this was—that I
never opened my lips till I got into the carriage, when
I thanked Mrs. Featherstone for her kind reception,
and accepted cordially her invitation to Bracklin. In

short, there was a mutual sympathy between us; the result, I believe, of mutual good humour and good nature.

As we went along I settled a few points relative to my journey to Bracklin; but I was dying to ask her if this Lady Steele was any relation to Sir Richard Steele of the *Spectator*, which was the thought uppermost in my mind all the time.

At last I did, and she said, "Oh, yes, my father, the late Sir Richard Steele of Hampstead, was second cousin to *your* Sir Richard; but being of the elder branch he succeeded to the estate, as his poorer cousin did to the wit of the family. My nephew, the present Sir Richard Steele, is now the representative of the family and the possessor of the property."

Well, it was finally arranged, I was to start for Bracklin on the following Monday (this was Friday) by the mail, which would take me as far as Kinigad, where the Featherstone carriage, horses and servants would meet me; but as the mail reached Kinigad at an awkward hour, I was not to leave that place till daylight. In short, I never met any one so kind as this dear lady.

Olivia and Molly heard all this with astonishment, but agreed that it was quite right; as did also Dr. Pellegrini, who came with Madame and carried us off to dinner.

The next morning I took my darling Olivia to Madame Dacier's—

"Some natural tears we dropped, but wiped them soon,"

full of the hope of meeting next spring.

Molly came back with me to prepare all my little arrangements, towards which we changed our last bank-note. And having next day received all details in a letter from Mrs. Featherstone from Bracklin, written the night she arrived, I accepted a farewell dinner and a little dance after, which Mr. Fontaine called a *petit bal d'adieu* for the night of my departure; he said, "the mail goes from the head of this street; it will blow its horn when it is ready for you, and we will all conduct you to your carriage."

Well, papa, this was all very nice, for I wanted to be cheered, so I dressed myself in my school dancing dress, a muslin frock and pink silk stockings and shoes. Molly had my warm things to change in time for the mail.

Well, dear papa, we did not exactly mind our time, and the fatal result was—that I was dancing down "Money in both Pockets" with a very nice young man, Mr. Buck, the nephew to Miss Buck, when the horn blew at the end of the street! Oh, sir! if you knew the panic! All that could be done was for Molly to throw her warm cloak over me, with my own bonnet and my little bundle of things, so that I might dress when I got to Kinigad.

One of the young gentlemen snatched up my portmanteau, and so we all flew along the flags, which were frosted over, and got to the mail just as the guard lost patience and was mounting, so I was poked in and the door banged-to, and "my carriage" drove off like lightning down College Green, along the Quays, and then into some gloomy street I did not remember.

As for me, I was so addled, I did not know where I was. At last we drew up before some ponderous gates and a high wall.

A sentinel was pacing up and down with a lantern flashing on his arms, which reminded me of the castle of Otranto. The guard blew his horn, and the next minute I heard an awful shout and uproar, and singing and laughing, and the gates opened and there appeared a crowd of officers and gentlemen, who were shaking hands with one person, with "Good-bye, old boy, and let us hear from you soon," and other phrases.

The coach door was opened, and the gentleman asked the guard, "Is there any one inside?"

And the guard answered, "Only an old lady, sir, as far as Kinigad!"

"Oh, by Jove!" said the gentleman, retreating. "I say, coachy, I'll take a seat by you." So the door slapped-to, up he mounted, and the horn blew, and we were off in a minute.

Oh-h, sir, it takes away my breath only to think of it now!

Well, we were soon out of Dublin; the moon rising over the beautiful Phœnix Park, the trees of which were hanging with frost and icicles; the Liffey glittering to the left, and lights glittering in the Vice-regal Lodge as we passed it on the right.

If my heart had not been so heavy, this would have been a scene I should have delighted in. And so we galloped on, changing horses only once, when I was much struck with the interior of the stable, which was lighted only by a lamp, but very picturesque; something one would like to paint or describe.

Our next stage was Kinigad; but it was a very long one, and we did not arrive till three in the morning.

Such a picture as the inn was! The ostler, half-dressed, coming with the horses, and roaring for a waiter, or Caty, the chambermaid, to come down; and then the officer sprang down from the coach-box and came to rummage in the coach for his hat just as I was stepping out, assisted by the dirty ostler. I suppose the officer was struck with my pink silk shoe, for he laid hold of my foot, and pushing back the ostler, he said,

"What! let such a foot as *that* sink in the snow— never!" and he actually carried me in his arms into the kitchen, and placed me in an old arm chair before a roaring turf fire! and then, ordering the chambermaid and Mrs. Kearney (the landlady I suppose) "to get up and get tea, and everything for the young lady," to which everybody answered,

"Yes, Major; to be sure, sir; everything your honour orders. Your gig, has been here, sir, this hour."

In short, he seemed the commandant of the place.

He then came up to me and said,

"I had not the least idea who was in the carriage. The guard said it was an *old lady*; in short, you must let me make amends by offering my services in this wretched place. I hope you will command them now. I am quartered here, and know its few resources. You are not going further to-night, I suppose?"

I was dreadfully frightened and confused, but I answered,

"No, sir; not at present. I am expecting a carriage and servants to take me on to Mr. Featherstone's of Bracklin."

He took off his hat, made me a low bow, but seemed stunned with the information. He again called the landlady and said,

"I would prescribe some white wine negus, for you are chilled."

The waiter now appeared, and said, that Mr. Featherstone's carriage and servants had arrived an hour before; but had put up the horses and gone to lie down, as they would not proceed till after daylight. The chambermaid now came, and said she had a room prepared and a good fire up stairs. This was a great relief to me; but the young officer seemed to deplore it. He said he knew Mr. Featherstone, and would take the liberty of coming to inquire for me.

So I went to my smoky room; but on inquiring for my bundle and portmanteau, I found they had gone on in the Kinigad mail!

Fancy, dear papa, my dreadful situation! My whole stock in trade consisted of a white muslin frock, pink silk stockings, and pink silk shoes, with Molly's warm cloak and an old bonnet!

Well, sir, you know I had nothing for it, so I took my glass of hot white wine negus, threw myself on the bed, and was warmly covered up by the fat chambermaid, who had neither shoes nor stockings on, and I fell fast asleep; "but in that sleep what dreams!"

papa; from all of which I was roused by the fat chambermaid coming to tell me that Mr. Featherstone's coachman could not wait any longer; so I rolled Molly's cloak round me, and proceeded to Bracklin.

The dreary Irish road from Kinigad to the pretty village of Castledown Delvin—an appendage to the domain of the Earl of Westmeath—brought me to the approach of the pine-sheltered avenue of Bracklin, which pines, green and formal as they were, screened out the black bog behind them, where the wood of ages lay buried, from among which "the mere Irish" could never be taken by their Saxon invaders "when the leaves were on the trees!"

The approach to the domain was announced by a civilized-looking lodge; large, beautiful iron gates, opened by a fairy child, and all that lay within was cultivated and promising, leading to a large, handsome mansion of white stone—two carriages were rolling before the door, at which stood two footmen, who at once ushered me into a handsome drawing-room, to a party of ladies, muffled in carriage dresses, who stood in a circle round the fire. Pinched, cold, confused, and miserable, as you may suppose, dear papa, I must have been—in my pink silk shoes and stockings—I perceived that my appearance excited a general titter; but dear Mrs. Featherstone and her girls came to my relief, and welcomed me and kissed me; but Mr. Featherstone—a grave, stern-looking man, who sat apart reading his newspaper—he just raised his eyes above his glasses, and I read in his glance condemnation of his lady's indiscretion in bringing *such* a being for *such* a purpose as I had come.

Mrs. Featherstone inquired how I had come to travel in so light a dress; and so, dear papa, I thought I had better just tell the story as it happened—and so I did—from the little *bal d'adieu*, at dear old Fontaine's, till I reached Bracklin gates, not forgetting the portmanteau and little bundle left behind. Well, you have no idea how it took! they screamed at the fun of my details, and I heard them mutter, "Dear little thing—poor little thing!" The two girls carried me off from them all, to my own rooms, the prettiest suite you *ever* saw—a study, a bedroom, and a bathroom—a roaring turf fire in the rooms, and an open piano and lots of books scattered about!

Betty Kenny, the old nurse—the "Molly" of the establishment—brought me in a bowl of laughing potatoes, and *such* fresh butter, and gave a hearty "much good may it do ye, miss;" and didn't I tip her a word of Irish which delighted her. Pen, ink, and paper were brought me, and I was left to myself to rest and write to dear Olivia a line just to announce my arrival here, which was sent to the post for me.

The girls brought me, I believe, half their mamma's and all their own wardrobe, to dress me out; and as they are all little, it answered very well. Well, sir, when I went down, the carriages and party had drawn off to spend two days at Sir Thomas Featherstone's.

Our dinner party were mamma and the two young ladies, two itinerant preceptors—Mr. O'Hanlon, a writing and elocution master, and a dancing master, and Father Murphy, the P.P.—such fun! and the Rev. Mr. Beaufort, the curate of Castletown Delvin.

Now I must just give you a picture of the room. A beautiful dining-room—spacious and lofty; a grand benufet and sideboard; before it stood Mr. James Moran, the butler—the drollest fellow I ever met, as I will tell you, bye-and-bye—and two footmen.

The dinner, perfectly delicious!

Well, I was in great spirits; and Mrs. Featherstone drew out the two tutors, I think on purpose. She made Mr. O'Hanlon—a most coxcomical writing-master—tell me his story; how he was the prince of nearly all he surveyed—if he had his rights, being descended from the Princes O'Hanlon. Now, papa, you know if there is anything I am strong on it is Irish song—thanks to you—especially "Emunch ach Nuic," (Ned o'the Hills) which song I sang for them afterwards, by-the-bye, and did I not take his pride down a peg and get him into such a passion! The servants laughed and stuffed their napkins down their throats till they were almost suffocated. James Moran, the butler, winking at the priest all the time, who enjoyed the joke more than any one, except the dancing-master, his rival, who is a very clever man, I am told, and teaches mathematics besides, and put me very much in mind of Marcus Tully. Well, sir, we got so merry, that at last Father Murphy proposed my health in this fashion—which will make you smile. He stood up with his glass of port wine in his hand, and first bowing to Mrs. Featherstone, said, "With your love, madam;" and then turning to me, he said, "This is a hearty welcome to ye, to Westmeath, Miss Owenson; and this is to yer health, mind and body," which made them all laugh till they were ready to fall under the table.

Well, after dinner I sang them "Emunch ach Nuic," and "Cruel Barbara Allen," which had an immense effect.

After tea, James Moran announced that the piper had come from Castletown "to play in Miss Owenson," upon which the girls immediately proposed a dance in the back hall; and when I told them I was a famous jig dancer, they were perfectly enraptured. So we set to; all the servants crowding round two open doors in the hall.

I, of course, danced with the "Professor," and Prince O'Hanlon with Miss Featherstone, and Miss Margaret with the Rev. Mr. Beaufort. It is a pity we had no spectators beyond the domestics, for we all really danced beautifully; and, considering this was my first jig in company, I came off with flying colours, and so ends my first day in Bracklin. And I think, dear papa, you have no longer any reason to be uneasy at my position or angry with my determination, and so God bless you. I shall write to you now once a-week, loving you better and better every day,

Your own
"SYDNEY."

Public for public! It may be worth while here to contrast my last jig in public with this my first out of

the schoolroom. During the vice-royalty of the Duke
and Duchess of Northumberland—by whose attentions
I was much distinguished, as indeed were all my
family—it happened that Lord George Hill came on a
little embassy from her excellency, to beg that I
would dance an Irish jig with him, as she had heard of
my performance with Lady Glengall in a preceding
reign. He said if I would consent I should choose
either the Castle or the Vice-regal Lodge for the exhibition, and that his brother, Lord Downshire, would
write to Hillsborough for his own piper, who was then
reckoned the best in Ireland. As it was to be a private and not a court exhibition, my husband permitted
me to accept the challenge from the two best jig
dancers in the country, Lord George himself and Sir
Phillip Crampton. I had the triumph of flooring my
two rivals. Lord George soon gave in, and the sur-
geon-general "felt a twinge of gout," he said, which
obliged him to retire from the lists.

S. M.

CHAPTER XVI.

BRACKLIN CONTINUED.

I soon fell into my new position, not only with ease, but avidity, for I found that "'twas my vocation, Hal!" It was so new to teach and not to be taught—to assume authority and not to submit to it—to snatch some hours from congenial duties for voluntary pursuits as pleasant as they were habitual—to be petted like a child and to govern like a mistress. Fine air, great exercise, spacious rooms, and abundant and wholesome living produced an immediate effect on my spirits and my health. As my conscious independence influenced my mind, which was now breaking forth at various points, I seized with avidity the reasonable observations of Mr. Featherstone, a sensible and excellent man, who, in his grave tones resembled the *raisoneur* of a French comedy.

The order and propriety which marked the economy of the house, the regular and easy hours gave me impressions of domestic discipline which are not yet effaced from my life and practice.

It was just the epoch when "the tide in the affairs of man" had taken that turn which introduced a high domestic civilization into the houses of mere country gentlemen unknown to the Irish nobility of other times.*

And so in health and spirits, labour and amusement, flowed on sunny days and seasons, which dear Dr. Watts himself would have considered as coming up to his own ritual of

"Books, and works, and healthful play;"

whatever the *collés montés* of to-day or yesterday may have thought of me.

My intimacy with my young friends prolonged the epoch of my own adolescence, and as a few hours sleep

---

* Speaking of this one day to the late Earl of Rosse, so eminent as Sir Lawrence Parsons in earlier days, he assured me that he remembered in his boyhood, in the country houses of remote provinces, habits not far removed from semi-barbarism, and which would startle credulity now. At festive seasons, when the country houses were thronged beyond even their expansive power of accommodation, the "Barrackroom," the room appropriated to all late comers, had a hearth in the centre, and an opening in the roof for the emission of smoke (such as still exists in the castle of the Sydneys, near Tunbridge), where they all lay down on the floor, with their feet to the fire, in a ring, and their heads on their portmanteaus.

A few years back, during my residence at Kissingen, the Princess Esterhazy, with whom I had been associated in my first travelling life, and who renewed our acquaintance at the German baths, pressed my husband and myself to pay her a visit at Esterhazy, adding, "The style of the place I think will interest you. If you ring your bell in the morning for hot water for your toilette, I won't promise that you will get it. Accommodation is not the character of German castles; but *ea revanche*," she added, laughingly, "your toilet table will be of solid silver, and the dressing-boxes studded with gems."

Domestic civilization in Austria, and what it was in Ireland a century ago, seem much on a par, *le superflu mais non pas l'essentiel.*

sufficed then—as, alas, now—I had always the start of the rest of the family, and rose and rambled with the sun, and often got into *escapades* which brought me to the verge of disgrace with dear matter of fact Mr. Featherstone.

Here is one as an illustration:

Looking from "my bower window," one fine morning, I saw the "water-cask boy" on his way with the cart to a pure spring, a mile off, which supplied us with water; for Bracklin owed its name to its "Brack Lynn," or the muddy stream: that was all the water *then* on the grounds.

Miss Matty Reynolds, an old vestal of high family and great agricultural celebrity in the county, had in her domains a fine spring of water, to which the whole neighbourhood resorted for their supply.

It struck me that it would be charming to have "a drive" before the duties of the day began, and that I could think of my novel as I went along. I was then in the midst of St. Clair.

So I perched myself on the hogshead behind "little Pat Lester," the lodge-keeper's son. Miss Matty Reynolds was standing at her gate, "tall and straight as a poplar tree," when we arrived. She received me with Irish welcome, insisting that I should come in and breakfast on "a griddle cake" and fresh-churned butter, "and an egg that was not laid yet, but would be in a minute."

I yielded, and so did little Pat Lester, for, instead of filling his hogshead, he went down to the kitchen to have his breakfast on potatoes and ale.

We both alike outstaid our time, and when I was reseated on my cask and little Pat on his donkey, flurried and hurried, we neither of us perceived that the bung had flown out of the hogshead, so that by the time we reached the castle gates I sat dripping

"Like a mermaid just risen from the say,"

and those gates were opened by Mr. Featherstone himself, who exclaimed with grave astonishment,—

"Miss Owenson, is that you? We were afraid something had happened to you!" and so certainly there had.

He said no more, but stalked before me into the house.

The girls were ready to die with laughing when I appeared, but Mr. Featherstone declared his intention of "writing to my father;" dear Mrs. Featherstone "championed me" to the uttermost, and an Irish song with "Barbara Allen," in the evening, settled the account, and the next day I was taken back to favour on the promise to be more circumspect for the future.

The most striking events in the first year of my residence with the Featherstones, was the death of the Dowager Lady Steele, and the inheritance of her house and property in Dublin, by her most amiable daughter. I was all but present at the death of the eccentric belle of Lord Chesterfield's court. Pope never drew anything more characteristic of the master passion strong in death; and that charming description of the dying coquette was not more illustrative of the intensity of original confirmation than the almost last words of Lady Steele, who, hearing a fish woman cry in the streets " Fresh oysters," said, " That's a lie!" in memory of some stale fish the same voice had announced to her some days before.

A frequent occasional residence in Dublin was the result of our getting the fine, old-fashioned furnished house in Dominic Street, which preserved in the costume of the eighteenth century a study for me of infinite delight.

The " best drawing-room " had not been entered for some years, and on opening the doors there was a rent in the tapestry of cobwebs, which was quite suffocating.

The curtains lined, and wadded and "finished" at the bottom with leaden weights to regulate their drawing up, were of rich crimson satin damask, and the fact that a crimson silk stocking filled with money fell down from the cornice on the first attempt to move them, was not the least interesting incident connected with them. The careful old lady had various such hiding places for her money.

The beautiful marble chimney-piece, finely sculptured, reached half way to the ceiling, and was surmounted with a range of Etruscan vases. The ponderous chairs and settees, as the sofas were called, were regimented against the wall, and intermingled with cabinets inscrutable from their dust. A large table in the centre of the room was covered with folio books, and here I must record the delight with which I first opened a volume of Cowley. Chinese paper was on the walls and Turkey carpet on the floor;

it had no other decorations than girandoles for lights. This antique splendour was replaced by the style of furniture then in vogue by the most fashionable upholsterer in Dublin, from whose "taste" there was no appeal—

"The dæmon whispered, Timon have a taste,"

and the " taste" was—lemon-coloured calico hangings, highly glazed with dark chintz borders; the Etruscan vases were replaced by ornaments of Derbyshire spar, and pier tables painted and gilded; under the mirrors were tables covered with filligree ornaments painted by me, which passed for works of art!

Such was the result of the frippery influence of Carlton House on the taste of the day.

Taste is truth, the truth of Nature in art. All transition states are the doubts between habit and experiment, impeding present progress even whilst they recognise past mistakes. The regency of England was in its season perilous as that of France. Both of them were under the guidance of men well gifted, but profoundly corrupted by the selfishness induced by their position, and the vulgar illiteracy of their bringing up.

During the interregnum between the removal of the sumptuous old furniture and the advent of the lemon-coloured calico, this precious old room was entirely consigned to my care and occupation, and there I pursued my own studies among the old folio books on the table.

I had never read Cowley before. I was enchanted,

and the greatest indulgence that could be granted to me was to be left at home in this dear room, whilst my darling charges were in an adjoining room taking lessons from Sir John Stephenson or other high class masters.

I think it was about this time that a demand being made by the butler for paper to put round his candles, which Lady Steele's *femme de ménage* had hitherto supplied from a coffer filled with old papers in the garret, I was requested by Mrs. Featherstone to see if there were any left.

I gladly undertook the *fouille*; and when some few years afterwards I was present at the digging up of a priestess, whose statue had been long looked for in Pompeii by Neapolitan antiquaries, my excitement at the process was scarcely more than what I felt when, as I stooped over the old trunk, I read the name of "Alexander Pope" appended to one old yellow letter and "Jonathan Swift" to another! I left the butler to help himself, and ran down with my treasures to Mrs. Featherstone, who merely said, "Well, my dear, you are heartily welcome to them."

My first impulse was to enclose Pope's letter to Lady Moira, because it was my first opportunity to acknowledge her literary patronage in general and her kindness to myself and my father in particular. A few days afterwards she sent a gentleman to pay me a visit, the Rev. Mr. Gouldsbury, who was also a friend of the Featherstones; he was the bearer of a very gracious letter from her noble self. Of course I communicated her letter to my father, who wrote to thank her Ladyship for her great condescension, and gave expression to wishes in which there was more parental vanity and ambition than discretion.

My father's Irish pride still rose in revolt against my position in Mrs. Featherstone's family. He wrote me word that he hoped soon to place me under the protection of some of our Connaught cousins. But I hated the idea of Connaught cousins, and my pride revolted from idle dependence. He sent me Lady Moira's answer to him, which ran as follows:—

Moira House, Dublin.
March 26th, 1800.

I have just received Mr. Owenson's letter dated the 24th; and though my eyes are still weak from the effects of a late inflammation in them, I do not delay the acknowledgment of it, lest the many trifles which often intervene to prevent one's intentions, that are neither foreseen, nor can be avoided, should arrive to prevent my quickly assuring him, that I feel sensibly his paternal anxiety, and shall be very happy at any time to be serviceable to his daughters; and the pains he has taken in their education and the success of it, are points that I am well acquainted with. My friend, Mr. Gouldsbury, I have the pleasure to assure you, thinks extremely well of your literary daughter, and as a very sensible, worthy and an informed personage, Mr. Owenson will be persuaded he has a strong advocate with me for that daughter; but, unfortunately, it must be confined rather to my inclination than power to serve her. The change that has taken place in my circumstances (one that must take place with every woman whose lot it becomes to exchange a large property for a jointure) does not permit me to expend what I did when I patronized Dermody out of my pin-money. That eccentric being owed everything to you, and even my notice of him; I in no degree regret my assistance of him; he had talents, and he might, with the friendship he experienced from you, and through your kindness in procuring for him the protection of others, have done well. He got an ensigncy through the favour of my friend, which, when the corps was reduced, left him on half pay; yet that was sufficient to support him whilst he employed his talents, but he sold it, and the last I heard of him was from a letter he wrote to me, stationed then as a common soldier. Several individuals whom I formerly had it in my power to educate, from appearing to me to be possessed of natural genius, and these depressed by the want of means to cultivate them, have been successful in life; some have proved ungrateful, but others highly the contrary, and one who may have benefitted by my aid is sufficient to repay the failure of others, were they never so numerous; therefore I have not any reason to complain; I only lament that it is not now in my power to give to others a like chance of profit, or ingratitude, by rendering them assistance. Your daughter is perfectly welcome to dedicate her work to me. But I live so much secluded, that I can be of little, if of any, service to her, —and I would have her and you to reflect, if some other individual who lives more in the world may not be more serviceable to her, in getting for her subscribers. If so, let her decide for those who may be thus useful preferably to me. My good wishes for her, you, and the rest of your family, shall in that case, equally attend you, and I desire Mr. Owenson to believe me at all times his and their

      Very sincere friend,
    E. MOIRA HASTINGS, &c., &c.

For Mr. Owenson.

My eyes remain still so weak that I have with some trouble written these almost illegible lines.

Having read this epistle from Lady Moira, I wrote the following:—

      DOMINIC STREET.

MY DEAREST SIR,

A thousand thanks for sending me Lady Moira's amiable letter, but I am so sorry, dear papa, that you wrote to her on my account.

The idea of *my* being *dame de compagnie* to so great a lady is *too* presumptuous, and a "humble companion" I will NOT be to any one. I could never walk out with little dogs or "run little messages" to the housekeeper's room, as poor Miss Harriet Ronker told me *she* was obliged to do at Lady Shannon's, although she, Miss Ronker, is of one of the best French families that emigrated at the Edict of Nantes.

What objections *can* you have to my occupying a position as teacher to the young? It is a calling which enrols the names of Madame de Maintenon,

Madame de Genlis, and I believe, at this moment, even of the young Duke of Orleans; Dr. Pellegrini saw him at a school in Switzerland when he (the Dr.) was making the grand tour with Mr. Quentin Dick; and I believe Dr. Moore is the tutor to the Duke of Hamilton,—by-the-bye I have just read his delightful book *Travels through France, Italy and Germany*. It strikes me that we asked *quite* enough of Lady Moira when we asked her to give her name to the dedication of my poems, and to which she has so kindly acceded.

      Always your old dutiful
          SYDNEY.

CHAPTER XVII.

FROM BRACKLIN TO DUBLIN.

Sir John Stephenson was, at that time, the Coryphœus of the Musical Society of Dublin. The music of Bach, Handel, and Lord Mornington, which had charmed the preceding generation of musical judges, was giving place to a new school, at the head of which was Sir John Stephenson. The Irish people were not easy to convert from their old favourites; when they took a fancy to a song or an air, they were constant to it. Enamoured of Kelly and Crouch's singing of the air, "Oh, thou wert born to please me," they could not listen with patience to the fine opening duo in *Artaxerxes*, "Fair Aurora, prithee stay," and one of the impatient audience cried out, with a loud yawn, "Ah, then, will ye give us, 'Oh, thou wert born to *plaze* me,' instead!" But under the influence of Sir John Stephenson, even "Carolan and the bardi tribe" were forgotten. His school was vocal, not instrumental; and Dublin, at that time abounded in fine voices, both professional and amateur. The composi-

tions of Sir J. Stephenson all tended to emphasis and
expression. Ossian himself was not more graphic in
his poems than is Sir J. Stephenson in the music with
which he illustrated many of them; "The Maid of the
Rock," for example. The choir of St. Patrick's Cathedral, of which Sir John was the chief director, had acquired the *sobriquet* of "Paddy's Opera," from the
fashionable attendance which crowded the aisle when
the grand anthem was sung. Another musical society
of a different kind, was the "Beef-Steak Club," founded
by Mrs. Woffingdon, and presided over by her. She
enjoyed the patronage of Dr. Andrews, Provost of
Trinity College. The splendid vocalization of this
club always drew the attention of the Viceroy and his
Court, and most of the nobility of Ireland were en-
rolled among its members. But a young amateur,
and an intimate friend and disciple of Sir John Stephenson, *Thomas Moore*, superseded in his own *spécialité* of passion and sentiment, better singers and more
learned musicians.

Sir John Stephenson knew my father well; and he
was extremely kind to me on the occasions of his
professional visits to the family, and often would remain, after his highly-paid hour had expired, to sing
for me, or even with me, and always to my benefit
and delight.

One day he happened to play a piece of music, just
then come out, which he had brought for his pupils.
I was charmed. He then said, "Oh, you shall hear it
with Moore's words," and he then sang,

> "Friend of my soul this goblet sip,
>   Twill chase away thy tear;
> 'Tis not so sweet as woman's lip,
>   But oh, 'tis more sincere!"

I was enchanted; a new musical sensation seemed to be developed in me.

Sir John said, "Oh, what would you think of it, then, if you heard the author sing it!"

I had not then even heard of Moore, and if he had told me it was by Sir Thomas More, or "Zelucco" Moore, I should have taken it for granted.

Sir John, amused by my enthusiasm, said, "Would you *like* to hear him sing? He is too great a man to be brought here, for never was a man so run after in my days."

He then proposed to bring me an invitation from Mr. Moore's mother, who was giving a little musical party the following week; and as he was to take his own little girl with him, he offered to call and pick me up.

It was among the delights of my residence in Dominic street, that I was within half an hour's drive of the village of Richmond, where my beloved sister still resided with Madame Ducier. Mrs. Featherstone's kindness to her was beyond measure—she generally passed her holiday from Saturday till Monday with us—so I resolved she should share the pleasure of this proposed music party, which she, of all others, was calculated to appreciate.

Moore had just returned after his first or second expedition to London, I forget which; he had come back, as we read in the papers, "the guest of princes, the friend of peers, and the translator of Anacreon!"

From royal palaces and noble mansions, he had returned to his family seat — a grocer's shop at the corner of Little Longford Street, Augier Street. The Palace Borghese, at Rome, was called the "Cymballo," from its resemblance to a harpsichord in shape, and, certainly, the tiny apartment over the shop where Mrs. Moore received us, might be described by the same epithet both for size and shape.

Moore's sisters, Kate and Ellen, and their nice *dodu* mother—who looked like Moore himself in petticoats—received us with cordial kindness, and formed a strong contrast, with their dark heads and complexions, to the beautiful little Olivia Stephenson, whose loveliness is not yet effaced from the records of London fashion, as the beautiful Marchioness of Headfort, immortalized by the admiration of Lord Byron, and in after times one of the great ladies to whom Moore dedicated one of the books of his *Irish Melodies*.

The women present were few, but all pretty; and the men eminent for their musical talent. I remember them all; Doctors Warren Ray, Wesley Doyle, and Mr. McCusky (the finest basso, except Lablache, I ever heard). At first it threatened to be the old story of the *Beggars' Opera* without Captain Macheath, for alas, there was no Moore! But late in the evening Moore came in from dining at the Provost house, with Croker, and some other pets of the Provost's lady, for she was the queen of the Blues, in Dublin, at that time, though Mrs. Lefanu, Sheridan's sister, reigned vice-queen under her.

Moore announced, at once, that he was on his way to a grand party, at Lady Antrim's, but sat down to the piano as though to execute the sole purpose of his mother's bidding. At Sir John's request, he first sang "Friend of my Soul." My sister and myself, two scrubby-headed and very ill-dressed little girls, stood niched in a corner close to the piano.

My sister's tears dropped like dew—

"Not touched but rapt, not wakened but inspired."

Moore perceived our enthusiasm, and was, as he ever was, gratified by the musical sensibility of his audience. His mother named us to him; he bowed, and sang again, "Will you come to the bower," a very improper song, by-the-bye, for young ladies to hear—and then rising from the piano, rushed off to the bowers of the jolly, handsome, and very popular Countess of Antrim, a wealthy peeress in her own right, who "gave to love and song" what worldly honours "could never buy," for she married an accomplished professional *artiste* of the Dublin orchestra, Mr. Phelps, who, with a nobility of nature beyond what mere birth or rank could bestow, was known and respected in London under the name of Mr. Macdonald; a name granted him by patent royal—it was the patronymic of the Antrim family.

Mrs. Featherstone sent the carriage and footman to fetch us home, and we both went to bed in delirium, actually forgetting to undress ourselves. We

awakened each other by singing, "Friend of my
Soul!"

My sister rose to draw Moore's picture, which
looked more like a young negro than a young poet,
and I set down the first inspiration for my *Novice of
St. Dominic*, in the description of the minstrel under
the windows of the Lady Magdalen.

Moore vanished; and my vocation for authorship
as a means to relieve my father from his embarrassments, became a fixed idea, originating in the one
strong instinct of my nature—family devotion—a very
Irish one, and not the one least creditable trait of
Celtic idiosyncracy. I think it was quickened into
development by the success of Moore, the grocer's
son, of Little Longford Street.

I had already completed my first novel, *St. Clair*,
unanointed, unanneled, and unknown to everybody.

The Featherstone family were shortly to leave town,
and I resolved on the desperate step of publishing my
novel, though I did not know the difference between
a bookseller and a publisher, and I intended to take
my chance of finding one in the streets of Dublin.

I had observed that the Dominic Street cook, a
relic of the Dowager Steele *régime*, was in the habit
of hanging up her market-bonnet and cloak in the
back hall. I slipped down quietly one morning early,
put on the cloak and bonnet, and with the MS. tidily
put up under my arm, passed through the open hall-
door at which a milkman was standing, and started on
my first literary adventure

I wandered down into Britain Street, past the noble

edifices of the Lying-in Hospital and the Rotunda, quickened my steps down the aristocratic pavement of Sackville-street, then occupied by the principal nobility of Ireland. When I got to the bottom, with Carlisle Bridge and the world of trade and commerce "all before me where to choose," I was puzzled; but as chance directed, I turned to the right into Henry Street, proceeding along frightened and uncertain. To the left rose the church of St Peter, where I had gone to be confirmed; opposite to it, were Stella's lodgings, where she and Mrs. Dingley held their *bureau d'esprit*; at the other end of the carefour, and on a line with the church, and on the same side with it, my eyes were dazzled by the inscription over a door of,

"T. SMITH, PRINTER AND BOOKSELLER."

As I ascended the steps, a dirty-faced boy was sweeping the shop, and, either purposely or accidentally, swept all the dust into my face; he then flung down the brush, and springing over the counter, leaned his elbows on the counter and his chubby face on his hands, and said:

"What do you plaize to want, Miss?"

I was stunned, but after a moment's hesitation, I replied:

"The gentleman of the house."

"Which of them, young or ould?"

Before I could make my selection, a glass door at the back of the shop opened, and a flashy young yeoman, in full uniform, his musket on his shoulder, and whistling the 'Irish Volunteers,' marched straight up to me.

The impudent boy, winking his eye, said:

"Here's a young Miss wants to see yez, Master James."

Master James marched up to me, chucked me under the chin, "and filled me from the crown to the toe, top full of direst cruelty." I could have murdered them both.

All that was dignified in girlhood and authorship beat at my heart, when a voice from the parlour, behind the shop, came to my rescue by exclaiming:

"What are ye doing there, Jim? Why ain't you off, sir, for the Phaynix and the lawyer's corps marched an hour ago."

The next moment a good-humoured looking middle aged man, but in a great passion, with his face half-shaved, and a razor and shaving-cloth in his hand, came forth, and said:

"Off wid ye now, sir, like a sky-rocket."

Jim accordingly shouldered his musket "like a sky-rocket," and Scrub, leaping over the counter, seized his broom and began to sweep diligently to make up for lost time.

The old gentleman gave me a good-humoured glance, and saying:

"Sit down, honey, and I will be with you in a jiffey," returned in a few minutes with the other half of his face shaved, and wiping his hands with a towel, took his place behind the counter, saying: "Now, honey, what can I do for you?" This was altogether so unlike my ideas of the Tonsons, the Dodsleys, and the great Miss Burney, that I was equally inclined to laugh and cry. So the old gentleman repeated his question, "Well, what do you want, my dear?"

I hesitated, and at last said:

"I want to sell a book, please."

"To sell a book, dear? An ould one? for I sell new ones myself. And what is the name of it—and what is it about?"

I was now occupied in taking off the rose-coloured ribbon with which I had tied up my MS.

"What," he said, "it is a manuscript, is it?"

"The name, sir," I said, "'St. Clair.'"

"Well, now, my dear, I have nothing to do with church books, neither sermons nor tracts, do you see. I take it for granted it is a Papist book, by the title."

"No, sir, it is one of sentiment, after the manner of 'Werter.'"

He passed his hand over his face, which left the humorous smile on his face unconcealed.

"Well, my dear, I never heard of 'Werter;' and, you see, I am not a publisher of novels at all."

At this announcement—hot, hungry, flurried, and mortified, I began to tie up my MS. In spite of myself, the tears came into my eyes, and poor, good-natured Mr. Smith said:

"Don't cry, dear,—don't cry; there's money bid for you yet! But you're very young to turn author, and what's yer name, dear?"

"Owenson, sir," I said.

"Owenson?" he repeated. "Are you anything to Mr. Owenson of the Theatre Royal?"

"Yes, sir, I am his daughter."

"His daughter? You amaze me!" and, running round the counter with the greatest alacrity, he said, "Come into the parlour and have some breakfast, and we will talk it over. Why your father is the greatest friend I have in the world."

"Oh, no, sir, impossible; I am expected to breakfast where I live—I must return."

"Well, then, what can I do for you? Will I recommend you to a publisher?"

"Oh, sir, if you would be so good!"

"To be sure I would?" He then took a sheet of paper, wrote a few lines, rapidly tossed a wafer about in his mouth for some minutes, sealed his letter, and directed it to Mr. Brown, Bookseller and Publisher, Grafton Street. "Now, here, my dear; Mr. Brown is the great publisher of novels and poems. 'Twas he brought out Counsellor Curran's poems, and Mr. O'Callaghan—a beautiful poet, but rather improper. Now, dear, don't lose a minute, this is just the time for catching old Brown; and let me know your success, and what I can do for you." And so with curtseys and blushes, and wiping away my tears, I started off for the other side of the water, and ran rather than walked, to Mr. Brown's of Grafton Street.

A neat and rather elegant shop, and a door with a bell in it, admitted me to the sanctorum of Mr. Brown the publisher: an old gentleman in a full suit of brown and a little bob wig, looking over papers at the counter, answered my inquiry whether I could see Mr. Brown, by saying:

"I am Mr. Brown."

I presented him the letter, and while he read it I cast my eye into the interior of the shop-parlour, where sat an elderly lady making breakfast, and a gentleman reading beside her. My patron Smith's note seemed to puzzle him, and to *impatienter* the old lady, who came forwards and said:

"Mr. Brown, your tea is as cold as ice!" She looked at me earnestly, and then drawing Smith's note out of her husband's hand, said, "What is it?"

"A young lady who wants me to publish her novel, which I can't do—my hands are full."

I put my handkerchief to my eyes, and the old lady said, in a compassionate voice:

"Wait a little, perhaps Mr. J—— will look it over and tell you what it is about," (that was the gentleman in the back parlour). Turning to me, she said, "This gentleman, who is our reader, will give us his opinion of your book, my dear, and if you will call here in a few days, I am sure Mr. Brown will be happy to assist you if possible."

I could just answer, "Thank you, madam," and depositing my MS. on the counter, I went out of the shop, getting back to Dominic Street in time to hang up the bonnet and cloak in the cook's hall undetected, and to wash my hands and face and make my appearance at the breakfast-table, my absence being only noticed by Mrs. Featherstone's remark:

"You have been taking your early walk, Miss Owenson. I am glad you did not call on the girls to go with you, for the heat is very great."

The next day we departed for Bracklin, and I abjured, as I then thought, for ever, authorship, its anxieties and disappointments. I heard nothing of my book:—one reason, perhaps, was, that I had left no address, though I did not think of it then.

This was the last portion of her autobiography which Lady Morgan dictated.

CHAPTER XVIII.

ILLUSTRATIONS OF THE AUTOBIOGRAPHY.

AMONG the papers which refer to the period covered generally by the foregoing autobiography, is a packet of letters tied together, and endorsed in Lady Morgan's own handwriting:—"Youth, Love, and Folly! from the meridian of sweet fifteen to the freezing point of matrimony."

This packet contains the records of many incidents which illustrate at once her history, her character, and the manners of the time when they were written. Some of the letters are interesting for their own sake, all of them are endowed with that questionable interest which attaches to the unadorned records of those "very privatest of men's affairs," about which every one likes to hear, but about which scarcely any person ever tells the truth.

The packet has two lines by way of epigraph:—

"Que l'amour est beau et son commencement joyeux
Mais il n'y a point d'éternel amour."

Under date of 1823, there is a memorandum:—
"This whole farrago I lay at the feet of my dear husband, with whom love began (true love, *pair parenthèse*), folly ended, and youth has already passed away in the enjoyment of the purest happiness."

All who knew Lady Morgan know that this assertion is quite true.

The letters written to her father during her stay at Bracklin, give no indications of correspondence with any one else; but the following letters found in the above-mentioned packet, are addressed to Miss Owenson at that time. In spite of the prudent counsels of her father (and as regarded good advice he gave the best possible counsel to his daughters), and in spite, too, of her own prudence, which was early called into exercise and never called in question—it will be seen that she did not escape the natural fate of young women who are witty, agreable, good humoured and—good looking. She drew adorers to her side, whom she did not altogether discourage.

The activity of her mind, her passion for self-improvement and self cultivation; her ambition to help her father in his embarrassments, an ambition that came before the desire of personal distinction had made itself felt, were so many guardian spirits which took her thoughts out of the enervating and dangerous course of day dreams of love, marriage and eternal felicity. In writing her novels, she found a channel for her imagination, which turned to profit a warmth of sentiment which would otherwise have gone into love affairs, and have brought neither comfort nor credit to her life. The fact of writing novels which abound in scenes and descriptions of the most ardent love was her salvation; this kept her out of all sorts of mischief, to which her exposed and unprotected situation left her open. Her conduct in circumstances of great difficulty, when left quite a girl with a younger sister, alone in Dublin, with no guardian but an old servant, was marked with the good sense which makes the prosperity and success she attained in after life easy of explanation. Lady Morgan's success was not owing "to strokes of fortune," nor to that Irish divinity "good luck," but to her good conduct and good sense, developed, strengthened and disciplined by early difficulties.

Captain White Benson and Captain Earle were two young officers quartered in Kilkenny, during the period when Mr. Owenson had his daughters with him whilst his theatre was being built. She refers to the young men in one of her Dublin letters to her father, telling him that they had called, but that "Molly would not let them in."

Molly was a very dragon of discretion, and the two girls might have had a worse guardian. Lady Clarke often told of the Kilkenny days, when she, "an unformed lump of a girl," whose greatest delight was to go rambling about the fields "armed with a big stick, and followed by a dog," once returned from her rambles covered with mud, and her frock torn from scrambling over hedges and ditches; her hair all blown over her face (she had the loveliest long golden hair that ever was seen) and found her sister Sydney, and

these two officers, sitting in the parlour talking high
sentiment, and all the three shedding tears.

Molly came in at the same moment to lay the cloth
for dinner, and thinking they had staid quite long
enough, said, in her most unceremonious manner,
"Come, be off with yez—an the masther will be
coming in to his dinner, and what will he say to find
you here fandangoing with Miss Sydney?"

Olivia, who had no patience with sentiment, fell on
them with her stick, and pelted them with the apples
she had picked up in her ramble. Sydney, who the
moment before had been enjoying her sorrows, burst
out laughing at this sally, and shaking her black curly
head, danced away like a fairy. In early girlhood
her figure was slight and graceful; there was little or
no appearance of the curvature which, in after life,
became apparent. It was developed by the habit of
leaning to one side over her writing, and playing upon
the harp.

These letters require no explanation.

White Benson to Miss Owenson.

YORK, *May* 16, *(date torn off,
but the post-mark is* 1798.)

To address you perhaps from the most selfish of all
motives, as I once resigned the correspondence you
honoured me with from one of all motives the least so,
I begin enigmatically; but I shall unravel as I go on,
and if you then doubt me I shall at least have the
consolation of your pity. You will at least give me

that when I tell you that our dear, our invaluable friend Earle, is no more. If this melancholy intelligence has not yet reached you, I see you, in my mind's eye, again taking it up to convince yourself, and wipe away the tears that fall to his memory.

To say that I have been unhappy since these afflicting tidings were conveyed to me, would be to say nothing. I have incessantly mourned a loss no circumstance can efface, no time repair, and the only act of alleviation I can now have recourse to I have thought of often, and at the distance we now are it is, perhaps, no longer liable to the objection that once influenced me—at least, *should* it again become dangerous to my peace of mind,—it is impossible I should feel an added weight of sorrow to that I have so long endured. Yes, my dear Sydney, dangerous it is too true, I repeat the words, dangerous to my peace of mind. I anticipate your incredulity; it is, nevertheless, too true; I renounced your correspondence, I sacrificed the first wishes of my heart when I found wishes springing up in which I durst not indulge, and I determined to listen no more to the voice of the charmer. I was not true to that friendship I once pledged to you — I dared to violate the brotherly affection I fear I never truly felt for you; but it was not till the receipt of your last letter, when you defined so beautifully the nature of your sentiments towards me, when conscious *those* sentiments were not mine, it became me to declare what they *were*, or to be silent for ever. I will not now suppose what might have been the effect of such a declaration; I will not now state to you whether I then sanguinely for a moment indulged in hopes, on the gratification of which future sorrow and a life of misery were evidently entailed, or whether I abandoned them from the consciousness of the fate of such a declaration. It is sufficient that I now again, perhaps, subject myself to the endurance of sensations I have hitherto, not without the exertion of fortitude, succeeded in some measure to repress. Yes, my dear Sydney, I then loved you! I fancied it was friendship; but I beheld you also, in fancy, the wife of another—the wife of my best friend—and I felt I could not calmly reflect on such a circumstance. Nay, instead of feeling sentiments of admiration and esteem for such a man, I was conscious that I could have no emotion save hatred for the man who had made you happy. This declaration, you will say, I ought, at that time to have stated to you. True, I might have done so. I ought heroically to have declared to you my intentions; yet had I met you during the month I staid in Dublin, I should have felt authorized by having once written to speak to you on the subject, and the resolution I had at a distance to contend with the wishes of my heart, would have vanished before you, and the lover only would have remained.

What absence and the distance we are now at may have done I will not describe to you; I will not be guilty of a falsehood in saying I have either forgotten you or that I remember nothing of the sensations I have felt for you; on this subject, indeed, I dare

not dwell. I have too long selfishly indulged in this strain. I need not, surely, describe to you what I have already possibly described too much. I wait for the moment when you in return will speak only of *yourself*, for will you not at least afford your poor *friend*—I cannot yet say *brother*—consolation? [here much of the letter is effaced.] Selfish as the idea is, we still love to have sharers in our affliction, and I feel that if you mingle your tears with mine on this sad occasion, that my heart will be lightened by your sympathy. Farewell, my dear Sydney. You may have learned that I resigned and quitted the 6th. The sale of my commission, I am in great hopes, will bring me again to Dublin. Should I then see you—! At present both my father and mother are in a wretched state of health. Gloomy as my present thoughts are, it may perhaps not be wondered at when I fear I may lose them also. * *
[End missing—torn away.]

Miss Owenson wrote an elegy on Captain Earle, in which real feeling shows itself in spite of phraseology which reminds the reader of the marble ladies bending over marble urns, which seem *de rigueur* in monumental tablets.

White Benson to Miss Owenson.

York, *June 8th (post-mark,* 1798).
A second time I address you—in what manner I ought to do it I know not. I have offended you, I

know. Your friendship, it would seem, is lost to me for ever; but I entreat you to pause ere you banish from your remembrance one who has always, amid apparent neglect, and in your eyes, perhaps, unjustifiable ones, preserved that affection for you his heart is proud in the possession of.

I wrote to you, Miss Owenson, last month; I conjured you, by the remembrance of our lost friend Earle, to give consolation to one who, labouring under the most poignant sorrow for the death of his only friend, felt some degree of alleviation in the idea there was on earth still one who could feel and relieve the affliction of his soul.

I offended you, perhaps, in daring to transgress the sacred rule of friendship you only authorised me to preserve. If so, let me perhaps be more daring in saying, I ought to be forgiven. I have prescribed to myself limits of affection over whose boundaries it were wrong to pass. You conceive, perhaps, it is imprudent in you to continue a correspondence with a man who has said that he once *loved* you. Be it so, I pledge to you my word of honour to mention the subject no more; I pledge you my promise never to violate that friendship I have so repeatedly professed for you, and to remember only the *sister of my heart*. If, from any circumstance whatever that has occurred since I first knew you, of whatever nature it may be, you are convinced it will not be the least gratifying to you to hold any communication with a man you certainly once honoured with some degree of regard, at least *say so*, leave me not in cruel ignorance whether you may not, at this moment, perhaps, be also numbered with the dead. Oh, Sydney Owenson, you have it (I hope you have it) in your power at this moment to secure me from a weight of sorrow which the idea that you also may be lost to me occasions. Remember, that I ever loved your sister; suffer her, at least, to tell me that you exist, and that you are happy.

WHITE BENSON.

These two letters are much worn and torn, as though from frequent reading and handling; very different to the condition of the other letters in this packet. On the back of the above letter is written, "This elegant-minded and highly-gifted young man drowned himself near York, a few months after I received this letter!"

The unfortunate young man seems to have served for the model of *St. Clair*, or, at least, to have furnished some of the characteristics.

One advantage that artists possess over the rest of the world is, that although they suffer keenly, they have the faculty of turning their emotions into knowledge, and of finding consolation in the very act of using this knowledge as material for their art.

In spite of her natural heterodoxy, Lady Morgan had always a penchant for bishops and church dignitaries, who, in their turn, seemed to have reciprocated the good will. She was always a good tough subject for conversion, and offered the attraction of an unsolved problem; here, however, is a bishop's letter to Mr. Owenson, about his daughter, when, as yet, she had only published her *Poems of a young Lady*. It contains advice, good and sound as regards infant prodigies in general, and shows much kindly feeling. It is endorsed by Lady Morgan:

From Dr. Young, Bishop of Clonfurt, to my Father,

December 17, 1800.

DEAR SIR,

I received your kind letter, and it gave me very sincere satisfaction to find that you were blessed with a child whose talents and good disposition were likely to prove so great a comfort to you. I need not tell you how necessary it is, at the same time that you foster her genius, not to feed her vanity, which is so apt to keep pace with reputation. Neither need I tell you that vanity is one of the most dangerous passions in the female breast. I have been in Dublin these six weeks, under the hands of the surgeons, confined to a sick room, and therefore little qualified to forward your wishes respecting her publication. I hope that I shall not always be a prisoner; but the first effects of my liberty will be to return to the country, where alone I can hope to perfect my recovery. When I return to town, both Mrs. Young and I will have great pleasure in forwarding the publication of your young poetess. I hope your friend received the pamphlet on sounds, which I sent to Henrietta Street, directed to him in the manner you desired,

I am your very sincere servant,

M. CLONFURT.

The next letter in the packet is from Dermody, and like to the love-letters of other young poets, is more concerned with his own vanities than those of the lady to whom it is addressed :—

From Thomas Dermody to Miss Owenson.
London, Feb. 2nd, 1801.

I received your very affectionate letter with the sincerest transport, and take the earliest opportunity of answering it. Though of late not unused to general adulation, when I pictured that angelic semblance I had once seen, writing my encomium, the flattery, I confess, was of the most pleasing kind. Did I not know your taste and accomplishments, indeed, in my opinion unrivalled, the pleasure would be less. Why not mention my dear Olivia? Why not tell me more of your, I may say my, father, for as such I shall ever respect him. I have a thousand things to say, so expect nothing but incoherency. First for the army :— I am not now in commission, being put on half-pay after the reducement of the corps. I have lost the use of my left hand, and received two wounds more, being in five different engagements; however, I do not know but I shall be promoted, having lately had a line from His Royal Highness the Duke—of this you shall hear more. Now for literature; besides the little volume you have seen, there have been two satirical poems of mine, published under the signature of "Mauritius Moonshine;" one, the *Battle of the Bards*, the other, *More Wonders*, besides a variety of biographical and critical pieces in the monthly publications. I have just transcribed another volume of

poetry for the press, which will be immediately printed.
I have now commenced my own memoirs, where some
of my acquaintance will not find me *neglectful*. I am
not sure if a certain affair takes place, but I shall be in
Dublin about June next. Your father knows Grant,
alias Raymond, the performer; he is here, but no genius. Cooke is a constellation, the everything, the rage.
Curse fame! I am sick of it for my share. I had more
rapture in dropping a tear on the tomb of Abelard, in
Normandy, than in the plaudits of all the reviews. I
have grown very much since you knew me, and, except a scar or two on my face, am altered much for
the better. You will see my picture in the next
poems. I request you speedily to write, with every
domestic circumstance of moment. Your father is
certainly too sensible to deem me ungrateful. If this
letter had been as I first meditated, it would be all
poetry, for, I assure you, my heart was touched. I
remember distinctly the last time I saw *you*; it is a
long, long time since. How could you remember me?
I hope I shall yet see *some* of my dear friends here,
all is impossible. I have been melancholy since I got
your letter. No stranger is to see this letter, it is a
miserable production for an author, but it is sincere.
Mind my injunctions, and pray answer me soon.

   My dear and respected Sydney,
     Yours ever,
       THOMAS DERMODY.

Your epistle is much more poetical than some
modern compositions in rhyme. Direct to me,
 "No. 28, Stratton Ground,
  "Westminster, London."

From the same clever but foolish young poet, there is a letter to Miss Owenson's father.

Mr. Dermody to Robert Owenson.

London, April 17, 1801.

MY VERY DEAR SIR,

I received your letter this moment, and waive all other business to accelerate the answer. I shall not take up your time with professions of gratitude, which you know I owe you ever, and will therefore excuse. I have been very fortunate since I had the pleasure of Miss Owenson's last letter, which I intended to answer when I could, with most news and propriety. A certain great man of literary celebrity coming accidentally acquainted with some things of mine, has nearly freed my fortune. One poem of mine has been applauded *as the finest in this age*, in which are the venerable names of Cumberland and Arthur Murphy. This poem, with others, will be published in the most splendid style, by subscription, which is expected to be very large. His Majesty, the Duke, and Princess Amelia, are among the first. In this volume will be a poetical epistle to my sister competitor, Sydney, which proves I need no other incentive, even at this distant period, but my own sensibility of your goodness, to render our friendship immortal. The lines are very beautiful, but it is impossible to give you any adequate extract. I have had some lines from Sydney which are eminently charming, but how she has arrived at such excellence I cannot well imagine.

I have not yet seen her poems here, but will inquire among the booksellers for them. Are you certain they have been sent here? When I can find a copy I will be their reviewer *myself* in three monthly publications —viz., the *London Review, Monthly Review,* and *Monthly Magazine.* Though unconnected with newspaper *editors,* I will likewise observe what you mentioned with regard to *them.* The *Monthly Mirror* is what I publish most poetry in (which is very little, for some reasons), and I therefore shall send some verses, on the appearance of these poems, to it. Pray let me manage the affair in my own way. Two satirical poems of mine, under the signature of "Mauritius Moonshine," have made a great noise here; but I shall pursue that path no further. You may be dreaded and admired, but never loved for such productions. Who is the *Mr. Moore* Sydney mentions? He is nobody here, I assure you, of eminence. Let me have no strictures on some little vanity I have been forced to indulge in, describing my literary prospects; pardon likewise this illegible, unauthor-like scribble, and ever believe me,

Your most obedient and obliged,
THOMAS DERMODY.

" No. 28, Stratton Ground,
 " Westminster, London."

I had like to have forgot your remembering me to my dear Olivia, and all old acquaintances.

CHAPTER XIX.

PERIOD OF 1801.

The autobiography, it will be remembered, closes abruptly with Miss Owenson's adventures in search of a publisher. On her return to Dublin, with the Featherstone family, she one day accompanied Mrs. Featherstone to visit a friend, who was an invalid. Whilst Mrs. Featherstone went upstairs to the sick room, Miss Owenson was left to amuse herself in the parlour. Seeing a book lying in the window-seat, she took it up and found it to be her own *St. Clair!*

The publisher excused himself for not having communicated with her, by reminding her that she had left him no address. He presented her with four copies, which, for that time, was all the remuneration she received. Afterwards she re-wrote the work, and it was published, improved and enlarged, in England.

Her father, at this period, 1801, was for some time stationary at Coleraine, and he wished to have both his daughters with him—he had been a long time separated from Sydney. He had never cordially liked the idea of his daughter going out as a governess to earn her living; or, as her imagination presented it, "to make her fortune," though his necessity had consented to it. For the present, at any rate, he had a home to offer her, and he wished her to give up her engagement.

In the latter end of April or the beginning of May, 1801, Sydney Owenson left the Featherstones, who, through life, continued her constant admirers and attached friends.

The following letter, addressed to Mrs. Featherstone, tells its own story:

Sydney Owenson to Mrs. Featherstone.
COLERAINE, *May 4th*, 1801.

Here I am, dearest Madam, safely and happily arrived on the shores of the vast Atlantic, after a journey, tedious indeed, but amusing from its novelty, and comparatively delightful from the unexpected circumstance which attended it, namely, my father and Olivia meeting me sixty miles from Dublin. Just as I had given Colonel Lindsey (who was extremely pleasant and attentive,) warning not to be frightened at the sight of a withered duenna, he saw me leap into the arms of a man six feet high and armed at all points for conquest (for my father never travels without the apparatus of the toilet); he looked as if he thought this the most *extraordinary duenna* that ever waited to give a young lady *convoy*. I found these dear beings perfectly well, never looking better, and my father at least ten years younger than when I parted with him. After a survey of the beauties and curiosities *natural* and *artificial* of Ardmagh (where we met) we proceeded to Coleraine. After a journey through a country in some respects the wildest and most savage, nothing can appear more delightful than the situation of this town, which is in the highest degree picturesque and romantic. I cannot say much for the town, less for the town's people. They are almost all traders; rich and industrious, honest and methodical; these are not the result of my own experience or observation, but are taken from the experience and observation of others. The military and their families form the only society worth cultivating, and even for these there is not much to be said. But *you* know *that* is a subject on which I am not easily pleased. Now for matters more substantial: meat and bread are at Dublin prices; fish of the finest and choicest kind almost for nothing; poultry *very, very* cheap; and vegetables scarce altogether; notwithstanding being reduced to *one* course, I contrive to live, and still bear such visible *testimonies* of your good table as will enable me to keep up a good appearance for a *month* at least. And now, my dearest madam, having so long pestered you with myself, let me speak a little of my kind friends in Dominic Street. Neither my restoration to my family, my present happiness, nor the distance which divides us can soften the regret I felt at parting from your good family, nor obliterate the remembrance of the many happy hours I spent in it, or the kindness and affection which I experienced from every member of it. Though my many negligences and those faults inseparable from human nature, must have frequently excited your disapprobation, yet the interest I felt for you and my little friends was always unvariable, and always more than I could or *would* express—and this interest promises to exist when probably she who cherishes it will no longer live in your remembrance. The benefits I derived from my residence with you were many, but they never exceeded the gratitude they inspired, nor the sincere attachment with which I remain,

My dear madam,
Your very sincere friend,
S. OWENSON.

PS.—I must say a word to you, my dear little girls, though but to tell you I dream of you every night; that I long to hear from you, that I request you will coax *mamma* to write to me, and remember me most affectionately to the *boys*. Olivia thanks mamma a thousand times for her present, of which she has just made a handsome cap. I am in hopes of getting a piano from Londonderry, which will save me great expense in the carriage. You will have the goodness to mention this, that I may not prevent him selling his.

Although Mr. Owenson was a true Irishman in the art of getting into difficulties, he was a careful parent in all that concerned his daughters. He had made great efforts to give them both the education of gentlewomen. He had kept them carefully from all contact with whatever was undesirable in his own position and environments as an actor. In his own manners and bearing he was, by the testimony of all who knew him, a polished Irish gentleman. But, though full of the social talents which made him a delight at every mess-table and barrack-room of the places where he played, he had always been very careful with whom he allowed his daughters to associate. As children, he seldom allowed them to go to the theatre, and was strict in obliging them to go regularly to church, whether he accompanied them or not; he considered it a sign of steady and correct deportment, which showed they had a proper pride in themselves. In spite of his constant embarrassments about money matters, he had fine rollicking Irish spirits and was full of fun and geniality. For some time past he had contrived to keep his youngest daughter with him under his own eye, and under the guardianship of the faithful Molly. So far as he knew how and was able, he had always taken great care of her.

There never was the most passing thought of allowing either of his daughters to go upon the stage. So far as Sydney was concerned, with all her cleverness, she was incapacitated by the total want of what is called "study;" she could invent, she could improvise, she could play all manner of droll pantomime of her own invention, but she could not commit to memory anything out of a book beyond an epigrammatic quotation.

St. Clair had some success. It was translated into German with a biographical notice prefixed; a remarkable production, which asserted that the authoress

had strangled herself with an embroidered cambric
handkerchief, in a fit of despair and disappointed love!
In spite of faults and absurdities, *St. Clair* contains
the promise of better things. *The Sorrows of Werter*
was her model, but there is an idea of drawing characters and inventing situations far from hackneyed or
conventional; and, in spite of the pedantry, there is
an eloquence and passion which redeems its impossi-
bility. The characters are shadows of ideas and utterly unlike human beings, but each personage has
a character and supports it; the work abounds in
high-flown discourse and discussion upon the topics of
love, music, poetry and literature in general. The
authoress talked out her own impressions and opinions
of the books she had read, and though the display of
her reading hinders the action and spoils the story,
there is a freshness and enthusiasm which only needed
time and practice to turn to profit. The extent of
her reading is quite wonderful for so young a girl; it
consists of solid works and standard authors, requiring
careful and painstaking study. She had a strong passion for acquiring knowledge, stronger even than her
love of displaying it. She revelled in allusions to her
favourite books, in quotations, and in fine-sounding
words. In all her early works, her heroes and heroines indulge in wonderful digressions, historical, as-
tronomical and metaphysical, in the very midst of the
most terrible emergencies where danger, despair and
unspeakable catastrophes, are imminent and impending. No matter what laceration of their finest feelings they may be suffering, the chief characters have

always their learning at their finger ends, and never fail to make quotations from favourite authors appropriate to the occasion!

It is easy to laugh at all this; but it were devoutly to be wished that the young authors of the present day would read a little before they begin to write so much.

Sydney Owenson's reading was truly miscellaneous—pursued under every circumstance of difficulty and disadvantage. She never had any one to guide or direct her—in all things, intellectual as well as practical, she was left entirely to herself.

A home picture when she returned for a short time to her father and sister after leaving Bracklin, may be extracted from a scrap-book in which she made her multifarious extracts from the works she read, wrote out the rough draughts of poems, and entered (very sparingly) her own thoughts and impressions:—

"*September* 12*th*.—Indisposition confines Olivia to her room; it is, thank God, but slight, yet sufficient to awake my anxiety and tenderness. We are seated at our little work-table, beside a cheerful turf fire, and a pair of lights; Livy is amusing herself at work, and I have been reading out a work of Schiller's to her, whilst Molly is washing up the tea-things in the background, and Peter is laying the cloth for his master's supper—that dear master!—in a few minutes we shall hear his rap at the door and his whistle under the window, and then we shall circle round the fire and chat and laugh over the circumstances of the day. These are the scenes in which my heart ex-

ponds, and which I love to sketch on the spot. Ah!
I must soon leave them."

The following commentary on that universal text—
Love—is curious as coming from a girl. It comes
from the same scrap-book, and bears her initials after
it:—

"Burns says, 'If anything on earth deserves the
name of rapture or transport, it is the feelings of
green eighteen in the company of the mistress of his
heart, when she repays him with an equal return of
affection.'

"I do not agree with Burns; at eighteen the passion is but a simple sensation of nature, unmingled,
unenriched by those superadded ideas which constitute its purer and more elevated charms. Other sentiments mingle with love, as other metals amalgamate with gold—the sympathy of congenial tastes—
the blandishments of the imagination—the graces of
intellectual perfection—the exaggeration of fancy,
glowing with poetic images, and the refinement of
taste to apply them to the object beloved—all these
heighten and sublimate the passion which has its origin in Nature.

"S. O."

The indomitable energy and indefatigable industry
which characterized her both as Sydney Owenson and
Lady Morgan, are even more remarkable than her
genius, and gave her the coherence and persistence

essential to success. Her tenacity of purpose through life was unrelaxing—whatever project of work she had in hand nothing turned her aside; with her, the idea of Work was the first object in life. All other things, whether they appertained to love, amusement, society, or whatever else, were all subordinate to her work. Intellectual labour was the one thing she thoroughly respected and reverenced. She never wasted a moment of time, and wherever she went, and whatever she saw, she turned it to practical use in her profession.

In spite of her romantic love for her father, and her sincere attachment to her sister, the beautiful illusion of living a domestic life with them soon wore off.

Accustomed as she had so long been to the plentiful comfort and regularity of the Featherstones' well-ordered household, she felt the difference between that and the scrambling poverty and discomfort of life in an Irish lodging. Her father's financial difficulties increased rather than diminished. Sydney's virtues were not of a patient, home-staying, household kind; she could go out into the world—she loved the adventure of it. Whatever she saw, or did, or said, was always to her like a scene in a novel, the *dénouement* of which could not be foreseen. She was capable of working hard in her own way, and she worked from the honest stimulus of wishing to earn money to help her father out of his difficulties; but she *could not* endure dulness or discomfort.

In the course of a very few months after her return

to her father and sister, she quitted them to take another situation as governess in the family of Mr. Crawford, at Fort William, in the North of Ireland. The following is a fragment of a letter addressed to her sister from her new home; the first few lines are torn off :—

—— "After all, I can meet with nothing to recompense me for the loss of your's and papa's society, nor would I hesitate a moment to return to you were I to consult happiness only. You do me great injustice in supposing I was not happy when last with you. It is true, my spirits sank beneath the least appearance of discord, and I have hitherto glided on through life so much at peace with all the world, that it would give me pain to excite ill-temper or ill-humour in the most indifferent person in existence; and though I was not so fortunate as to please *every* member of my own dear family, you best know with what heart-breaking regret I left it.

"Here I am, almost an object of idolatry among the servants, and am caressed by all ranks of people. You know one of my maxims is, never to let anything in the world ruffle my temper, and by this means I continue to keep others in good humour with me.

"Accept my compliments of congratulation on your cloak. I have a correspondent in Dublin (Miss Harrold), who wrote me a long letter to-day, full of the fashions. I wrote to her for a cloak, for I have still some of the money left that papa sent me. The cloak is made like a Spanish cloak, of lace, and trimmed with the same; some of them with full sleeves—plaids all the fashion. Mrs. Crawford has given me a very pretty plaid handkerchief and ribbons, and a gold ring—which I mentioned before. Crops are *all the rage*, as savage as possible—you never saw such a curly-headed little rascal as I am. Margaret Ryan sent me a plait of her hair, a yard long, for a locket string; the most beautiful thing I ever saw, and the most admired—it is as broad as a fourpenny ribbon. We had a very pressing invitation sent us for a ball at Clough-Jordan, given by a club there—mine was, as usual, *separate*, but Mrs. Crawford would not go; it is the third she has refused—is it not provoking? Be content with your situation. You are young, you are beautiful, you are admired, and foolish women do not torment you. Work well at your music—music is a *passe-partout*. Be economical. The people here, I believe, love me with all their hearts, and I am well and happy.

"I wish you would read history. My little folks are going on charmingly; they are the dearest children in the world, and dote on me as I do on them. They would amaze you at geography, and history, and music. Write soon. S. O.

"We are expecting the *handsome, fat* Count d'Alton here, every day."

From Thomas Dermody to Sydney Owenson.

MY BEST SYDNEY,

I have just come to town, and sent your father the answer to his commands. Your letter was highly interesting, and your lines to the Quaker, "Ah! why do I sigh?" extremely beautiful. You are, indeed, my Anthenœ, and let the following verses convince you. My poems are printing at Bristol in a most elegant style—this makes one of them.

> "There lurks within thy lyre a dangerous spell,
>   That lures my soul from Wisdom's dauntless aim;
> Yet if I know thy generous bosom well,
>   Thou would'st not dash me from the steeps of Fame.
> Trust me, thy melting, plaint, melodious flow,
>   Could animate to love the icy grave;
> And yet, if thy pure feelings well I know,
>   Thou would'st not sink me to an amorous slave!
> Graced with no vantage, nor of birth nor wealth,
>   That to Ambition's happier sons belong;
> E'en at the price of my sole treasure—health,
>   I own that I would be renown'd for song!
> For this I wander from the world aside,
>   Muttering wild descants to the boiling deep,
> 'Mid the lone forest's leafy refuge hide,
>   And slight the blessings of inactive sleep."

Now, considering that this comes neither from a "very old" nor "very ugly fellow," you might excuse some warmth of colouring. To use another quotation of my own—

> "Why, though thy tender vow reveal another,
>   May not my rapt imagination rove,
> Beyond the solemn softness of a brother,
>   And live upon thy radiant looks of love?"

In reply to your desire of knowing why I thought *Moore intended you*, I can only repeat that it was mere supposition, founded on the idea that he could not be in your company without poetic emotion. But on my soul, I think you are be-rhymed enough for one lady!

Thomas Dermody appears to have been something more than a poetical lover. He loved Sydney Owenson, as well as so wayward and egotistical a fellow could love anything except himself.

In the midst of his reckless life he retained for her sentiments of respect and attachment; and he cherished the memory of Mrs. Owenson as his best and tenderest friend.

To Miss Owenson, when at Fort William, he again wrote:—

My volume is already in the press, and I hope will soon be published, for I abhor correcting proofs. Let me inform you how far you are connected with it. The sonnet to you is to be published with a note, and another long, and perhaps not despicable poem, called "An Epistle to a Young Lady after many years Absence." I did not think it might be agreeable or prudent to affix your name. I will also confess that in writing the verses to Anthenæ (a Greek name of my own, signifying flowery, and in a figurative sense amiable,) you were not entirely absent from my imagination. Between friends, this is my *chef-d'œuvre*, and I have no small hopes of its future success, with a little patience. I feel a sensible and refined delight in

paying this tribute of the purest affection to an object
so worthy of every emotion, and mostly on that account I should be elevated with the applause that
must consequently be shared. I had the honour of a
letter from Mr. Addington (the Prime Minister) on
receiving a copy of my ode—he has behaved well and
promises much. You see I am a little favoured by
the great as well as by the fair. You are mistaken if
you imagine I have not the highest respect for your
friend Moore. I have written the review of his poems
in a strain of panegyric to which I am not frequently
accustomed. I am told he is a most worthy young
man, and I am certain myself of his genius and erudition. Did you not laugh at and think some of my letters extremely romantic? They were so, I allow, but
on my soul it is impossible to write to my dear sister
without being so. I would willingly not increase the
crowd of idle flatterers that surround a young woman
of sense, and accomplishments and beauty; however, I
should not be displeased that you could conceive how
much I value you. I often converse with you in
fancy, and feel my heart lighter and better after this
imaginary *tête-à-tête*. I am not often in the company of females, and when I am, I turn with disgust
from their odious affectation and insensibility, to the
" celestial visitant" which my own rapturous melancholy forms. I certainly esteem, I may almost say
love, you more than I actually should in your presence.
Absence so softens and breathes such a delicious languor over the truly tender heart! I remember a time
(excuse me, lady,) when I thought you affected,

haughty and unkind! Do I think you so now? No! I undoubtedly place your single approbation above all the vain trophies which mortals hoard, " by wit, by valour, or by wisdom won!" and your unimpassioned and delicate attachment with "glorious fumes intoxicates my mind." But how is our father? I need not inquire, you would have told me had there been any material occurrence. Happy evenings! I cannot but remember such things were most dear to me. Miss *Lizy* (what an historical abbreviation!) and Miss Sydney too (how heroic!) might have spared their laughter,—beneath the dignity of a Laura or a Stella. You had no determinate description of the sylph to animate your pencil; try this subject at your leisure, though I fear it is too wild and horrible. My Car of Death is finely dreadful, but my only copy is with the printer. It is in the "extravaganza."

Conceive how I idolise your remembrance. Were you Venus I should forget you; but you are a Laura, a Leonora, an Eloisa, all in one delightful assemblage! My idea of your literary merit is very exalted indeed; this in a woman, a beautiful woman, whom I must ever esteem, what magic can be so irresistible in this world!

Pray did you not mistake my meaning in some passage where you say I seem to boast of an affected libertinism? certainly, my fair monitress, you did.

I have been a libertine but never a hypocrite, for which reason my failings have been more noted than my few deserts. I detest and despise the false taste and false wit of modern infidelity. I have written

some very pretty lines to a "Brown Beauty;" you
will see them in my volume. There are two imita-
tions of Spenser which I am sure you will like; besides the extravaganza, which is entirely in obsolete
English, and on which rests my reputation. But,
perhaps, you would rather have some of "my dear
prose" than my d—d poetry!

When the publication of this volume is complete, I
am determined to have one month's happiness in Ireland; but it *must* be when you are at home. What a
meeting it will be, if I do not deceive myself! Then
I may share (another quotation of mine from the epistle to you by name):—

> "the exalted power
> Of social converse o'er the social hour."

How I long for you to read my next volume; you
make so sweet a part of it yourself. It is my pride to
be publicly allied to you in fame as I am privately in
the fondest friendship. Adieu.

THOS. DERMODY.

September 14th, 1801.

This roving, clever, inconsequential and rather silly
young gentleman died of consumption in July of the
following year. Sydney Owenson felt a good deal for
him—not in the way of love, but of old fellowship and
pity. She thought highly of his talents; too highly,
no doubt; but the weakness was in her very natural
and commendable. She was as warm a friend to him
when he was gone as she had always been to him

when he was living; and her friendship was, in fact, very much required.

It must be borne in mind, that Thomas Dermody and Sydney Owenson wrote their poetry before Lord Byron had introduced a more direct and rigorous style. Women were then "nymphs," who were "coy," "cruel," "unkind," "disdainful;" and men in poetry made believe to be "shepherds," "swains," adoring the charms of their mistresses with a freedom of expression which would be deemed highly indecorous, but which the nymphs in question took as a matter of course. Dermody got very little mercy from the reviewers; but, in strict truth, he was no more a poet than Sydney Owenson was a poetess.

The days of Sydney Owenson when she was an instructor of youth did not pass over in sadness nor in looking at the world out of back windows. Her genius and spirit made her a fascinating acquisition in a country house. Few governesses have her social talents, and possibly in a steady-going English family they would scarcely be allowed the scope for displaying them, if they had them. Her experiences are in curious contrast to poor Charlotte Brontë's; but Sydney Owenson knew how to make herself agreeable. She was always grateful for kindness, and she possessed the rare gift of knowing how to accept kindness gracefully, so as to make it a pleasure to the bestower. She was not prone to take offence—she took benefits as they were intended, and she brightened all that surrounded her with the sunshine that emanated from herself.

The following letters to Mrs. Featherstone contain all that is known of Miss Owenson in the year 1802. The first letter refers to Dermody's death:—

Miss Owenson to Mrs. Featherstone.

       Fort William,
         Oct. 8th, 1802.

It is well if even *this original scribble* will serve to call to the minds of my dear Bracklin friends, that *little body* who often thinks on them with many pleasant recollections.

On my return from Enniskillen I wrote you, my dear madam, a long letter, with a *full* and *true* account of my northern expedition, and all the Dublin chit-chat I could collect. This was two months back, and yet not a line from Westmeath. I will, however, gladly compound for a little *neglect* and *unkindness*, provided no domestic misfortune has prevented me hearing from you. If Mr. Featherstone and the dear little ones are well and happy—I shall pout a little to be sure—but a line from you will settle all difference between us. I must, however, say, I think the girls both *unkind* and *ungrateful*, but I know the world *too* well not to be more *hurt* than surprised at it. I believe I often told *you* it was what I expected, nor was I a false prophetess. Let me hope, however, that your and Mr. Featherstone's friendship is still in my possession, and I shall be satisfied. I saw Mrs. Praval very often when in Dublin—as *stiff* as ever. I met also the

M.'s, O.'s, and B.'s. The country is a pleasant security to me, and I was not sorry to return to it. My little girls are going on charmingly; they really astonish me at music; they read it almost at sight, yet they barely knew their notes when I came to them. My situation becomes daily more pleasant. I never was more my own mistress, at the same time I am exceedingly anxious to return to my father; but when I mentioned it there was so much persuasion and kindness to induce me to change my determination, that, for the present, I gave it up. At all events I will go and pay him another visit as soon as I can, and will so arrange it to go to town when I shall have a chance of seeing you; and if you have a spare *garret* that you could *bundle* me into for a night or two, I will *invite myself* to spend a couple of days with Mr. Featherstone, if he has no objection.

My novel is publishing this month back, in Dublin, and will be out early next month. You will be surprised to hear the work I composed at Bracklin I have given to oblivion, and that this one I wrote in the evenings of last winter, though I went out a great deal. It is inscribed to Lady Clonbrock, and its title, *St. Clair, or First Love.* You will probably see it in the papers. I have already disposed of every copy, except a few books I have kept for my own immediate friends. My poor friend Dermody, the poet, died last July, of a rapid decay, at *five-and-twenty.* We corresponded constantly for two years previous to his death, which affected me and my *father* very sensibly. We have got his picture (done a few hours before his death),

There is a life of him published in last month's magazine—every syllable FALSE. I am told his life and works are now publishing in London, by subscription, in a very splendid style. Adieu, my dear madam; pray let me hear from you soon, and give me a circumstantial account of the *little boys*. Take the trouble of presenting my best respects to the Riversdale and Grange families, and to believe me ever yours,

SYDNEY OWENSON.

Miss Owenson to Mrs. Featherstone.

FORT WILLIAM, NENAGH,
December 29, 1801.

Many happy Christmases and New Years to all the family of Bracklin, and very many thanks to my dearest Margo for her welcome and charmingly written letter, which nearly equals C.'s in style (who, however, promises to be the Sevigné of the family), and surpasses it in writing. Here we are, singing, playing, and dancing away as merry as crickets, and ushering in the seasons with all due merriment. So now for some little account of our festivals. The other day we had upwards of forty people to dinner; among others, Lord Dunally, Lord and Lady Clonbrock, Honourable Miss Dillon, the Vaughans, of "Golden Grove," whom I think I heard mamma mention to a great many other fine people. We began dancing, without the gentlemen, almost immediately after tea. I had the felicity of opening our female ball with Miss

Dillon—the nicest girl I have seen anywhere—gentle, humble, and unaffected. I was most heroically gallant, and played the beau in the first style. We sang and played a good deal too, and the night finished most pleasantly with my Irish jig, in which I put down *my man* completely. This has produced an *ode to a jig*, which I will send, when I can get a frank, to your papa; for I know it will please him. Well, the other night we were at an immense row at Lady Clonbrock's, to whom I owe so many obligations for her marked attention to me since my residence here that I am at a loss how to mention them. It was quite a musical party, and (give me joy), on the decision of Lord Norbury (who was of the party), I bore away the palm from all their Italian music by the old Irish airs of "Ned of the Hills," and the "Coolcen," to which I had adapted words, and I was interrupted three times by plaudits in "The Soldier Tired." Now, I know you will all laugh at me, but the people here are setting me mad, and so you must bear up with the effects of it for a little while, until I become accustomed to the applause of the great. This is the *Athens* of Ireland, music and literature carry everything before them; and Lady Clonbrock who is one of the leading women here, is an enthusiast in both. It is to this, I believe, as well as to the conduct of Mr. and Mrs. Crawford that I received such kind attentions from all the first people here. My invitations are always separate from theirs, and I have long been forced to consider myself as their child and friend. Miss D. draws nicely, and has just sent me some transparent screens to copy, which I wish you had. At present there is staying with them an old friend of mine who spends many of his mornings here—a Mr. Wills, you have heard me mention him and his sisters as being among my earliest friends.

Nothing can be pleasanter than our life at present; to-morrow we are to have Lord Norbury, and all the world to dinner, and music in the evening. We got a delightful piano and tambourine, and I do nothing but sing and play, and am much improved in voice and singing since you heard me. Do you know our house is not much more than half the size of Bracklin—everything in the simplest style; neither can I say much for Lord Clonbrock's mode of living—there was a thousand times more show at Bracklin on a gala-day than we had at *Latteville.* My little girls are the best and most attentive creatures in the world, and if mamma and papa do not flatter, are making a wonderful progress; but you shall see them in spring, for we all go for two or three months to Dublin, from that to Ballyspellin Spa, and then make a tour to Killarney, and so back home; such is the plan laid down for the present; but give me Fort William, and I am content. Why do you force me to tell you my pupil's names, or why cannot I answer you by writing Rosabella or Angelica? Alas! no, I must stain this sublime epistle by confessing their names are —— Miss Bridget and Miss Kate: after that can you ask me to write more than that I am,

Dearest Margo's attached friend,
SYDNEY OWENSON.

CHAPTER XX.

STILL A GOVERNESS.

THE two letters which follow would appear to have been written by Miss Owenson to Mrs. Lefanu, but there is no address upon them. The other letters had their proper addresses.

January 12th, 1803.

"*L'union de l'esprit et du corps est en effet si forte qu'on a de la peine à concevoir que l'on puisse agir sans que l'autre se ressente plus aux mains de son action,*" says Monsieur Tissot; and when *you* tell me you write under the influence of *five weeks' disorder*, and yet send me a letter full of wit, sentiment, and imagination, I really know not whether to believe you or Monsieur Tissot; he has proved the sympathy of the soul and body in theory, but you *practically* prove there exists no *inseparable* connexion between them, and that the debility of the *frame* has no influence over the "strength of spirit." The fact is, I am tempted to wonder (like an old general on the eve of a great battle to a military invalid), how you *dare* be sick? Had I your mind and imagination I should set the whole College of Physicians at defiance. And, as it is, though gifted with a very small portion of the *vivida vis anima!* (smile at my Latin), I am pretty well enabled to keep the reins of health in my own hands. In the first place I have got possession of the "*citadel the heart,*" and command its *pulsations*, fibres, nerves, &c., with the unlimited power of a field-marshal. Thus, having subjugated my *constitutional forces*, I play them off as I please. When my pulse grows languid, and the heaviness of approaching sickness seizes on me, I immediately set fancy to work, seize the pen, and mock the spirit of poetry; then the eye rolls, the pulses throb, the blood circulates freely in every vein—my poem is finished—I am well. Or should a fever seize my absorbing spirits—memory and hope thrill every nerve—call up the forms of joys elapsed, or paint the welcome semblance of joys anticipated; then the heart beats cheerily, and recruits every artery with new tides of health. Well! *Vive le galimatias!* for when it dies, my epistolary talent dies with it, and common sense may sing a *jubilate* as a requiem. *Seriously* though. Do you know I never was *seriously ill*. But the day I dined with you I was struggling hard with a cold—an influenza—and you might have perceived a fever burning in my cheek, that seized me beyond the power of FANCY to dispel it on my return home. I must have appeared, therefore, to you very different from the thing I am,—"sober, demure, and steadfast." I suppose I looked the personification of authorship or *jeune savante*, when, had I been myself, I should have *romped* with your boys, coquetted with your husband, and, probably, procured my *lettre de cachet* from yourself as a nuisance to all decorous society. Am I indeed of the age and mind to admire the splendid rather than the awful virtues? I am, at all events, glad to find you believe I do *admire* virtue of whatever species or description, for I have been so long attempting to make the "worse appear the better reason," and pleading so strenuously for the errors of superior talent, that I began to fear you put me down as the *decided apologist* of the vices of genius; but I know, had I taken up the right side of the question, there would have been an end of the argument, and I should have lost some of the most delightful passages in your delightful letters. However, the best reason I know of the *great soul* being more liable to *err* than the *little* one, is that given by Mr. Addison. "We may generally discover," says he, "a pretty nice proportion between the strength, and reason, and passion in the greatest geniuses, they having the strongest affections; as on the other hand, the weaker understandings have the weaker passions." So poor *genius* mounted on his high-mettled racer, with no more power to check his pranks and curvettings, than is given to the leaden-headed dulness to guide *his* sorry jade (who sets off at a tangent), suffers thrice the concussion, if the zigzag caprices of his courser do not even force him to lose his equilibrium.

I entirely agree with you that *some women*, in attaining that intellectual acquisition which excite admiration and even reverence, forfeit their (oh! how much more valuable) claims on the affections of the *heart*, the *dearest, proudest* immunity nature has endowed her daughter with—the precious immunity which gives them *empire over empire*, and renders them sovereigns over the world's *lords*. I must tell you, my dear madam, I am *ambitious*, far, far beyond the line of laudable *emulations*, perhaps beyond the power of being happy. Yet the strongest point of my ambition is to be *every inch a woman*. Delighted with the pages of *La Voisine*, I dropped the study of chemistry, though urged to it by a favourite friend and preceptor, lest I should be less the *woman*. Seduced by taste, and a thousand arguments, to Greek and Latin, I resisted, lest I should not be a *very woman*. And I have studied music rather as a sentiment than a science, and *drawing* as an amusement rather than an *art*, lest I should have become a musical *pedant* or a *masculine artist*. And let me assure you, that if I admire you for any one thing more than another, it is that, with all your talent and information you are "a woman still." I have said thus much to convince you that I agree, *perfectly* agree with you, in all you have said on the subject, and that when Rousseau insists on *le cœur aimant* of Julie, he endows her with the best and most endearing attribute woman can possess. Am I to thank you or your *Tom* for the trouble he has had with my commission? *Castle Hyde* I am not a little anxious about, since I have taken the liberty of dedicating it to you, as I dedicated *Ned of the Hills* to Lady Cloubrock—

the two friends whose tastes I most admire and revere. It is but just *Castle Hyde* should be all your own, since your approbation gave it a new value in my opinion, and tempted me to its publication. Have you, indeed, read *St. Clair* a *third* time? You have touched me where I am most vulnerable. I cannot conceive how you can think my hero and heroine dangerous; to have rendered them such I must have been myself not a little so; yet you know long since I am the most harmless of all human beings. There is a young man of some talent here, who has done a hundred profiles of me; one of them was so strong a likeness, *I am strongly* tempted to enclose it you. *L'amour propre aime les portraits.* The vanity of my intentions struck me so forcibly that I determined to expiate my crime by confessing it *to her* against whom it was meditated, and I sent the profile to a poor partial friend who will think more of it than the original itself deserves; but friendship can be *un peu aveugle* as well as *love*.

My sister begs leave to return her acknowledgements for your polite inquiries, and the sympathy you expressed as to the nature of her disorder. She is now perfectly recovered, and very busy tuning the *pianoforte* by my side.

My father is so proud of the recollections you sometimes honour him with in your letters, that though they were not made, I should invent them for the sake of affording him ideal satisfaction. If I had given him leave, he would himself have assured you of his gratitude. S. O.

My dear Madam,

I took the liberty of tormenting you with a long and nonsensical letter some time back, which I was in hopes would have procured me the favour of an answer; for it is so long since I had the pleasure of hearing from you, that I began to fear I had either unconsciously forfeited your friendship, or that you found me a troublesome correspondent. I hope that has not been the cause of your silence, for I really know not whether I should feel most at losing your friendship, or your losing your health—a most unpleasant alternative. But one line from you will be sufficient to obviate my suspicions, or subdue my fears. As I found that these good folks were determined on going for *life* to *Castle-tumble-Down*, and as I never had a very strong propensity for the society of *crows*, who have established a very flourishing colony in the battlements and woods in Court Jordan, I gave in my resignation last week. But, seriously, I do not think I ever was more agitated in my life. They made me every offer it was possible could tempt me to remain with them, even till November, when Mrs. Crawford would take me herself to town; and when they found me irrevocable in my decree, they paid me the compliment of saying, they would not entrust their children to any but one whom I approved. So that the choice of my successor depends entirely on myself. I shall be in Dublin about the 27th, I believe; will it be taking too great an advantage of your already experienced kindness to renew my claim on the little hole *in the wall?* If not, or at any rate, will you have the goodness to let me know, *by return*, whether it will be perfectly convenient to you to accede to my request, that I may make some other provision. I shall stay but a day or two in town, as I am extremely anxious to get home; my father has taken a nice little place about two miles from the town of Strabane, and delightfully situated. Olivia is well and happy, and desires to be most affectionately remembered to my dear little friends, whenever I wrote to them.

Adieu, dear madam; assure Mr. F— of my best wishes and respects, and all the dear young folk of my affection, and believe me

Ever yours, most sincerely,

S. OWENSON.

Mrs. Lefanu to Miss Owenson.

DUBLIN,
April 22nd, 1803.

MY DEAR MADAM,

Illness has prevented my answering your letter; an epidemic cold attended with fever has borne very hard upon my family. My eldest son has been very near death, and I have been myself confined to my bed, and am still obliged to keep the house, with the usual consolatory reflections that I am no worse off than other people, &c., &c. If the miseries of others were to render us satisfied with our own lot, no one would have a right to complain. You remember La

Fontaine says, "Et le malheur des consolations sur croit d'afflictions." In real illness and sorrow one has often occasion to think of that

I shall be very glad to see you when you are in Dublin. Two gentlemen of my acquaintance have added to my wish to know you, and yet they certainly saw you in society unsuited to you, and which I am sure chance alone could have thrown you into. My daughter has been taught music and still continues to learn, but has not, I think, any decided taste or talent for it—both my sons have; the eldest son is a student in Trinity College, plays the harp finely and is also an excellent performer on the pianoforte; for him I shall thank you for the Irish air you mention. No music more than the Irish bears the stamp of originality; none speak more to the affections; I think it possesses more variety than the Scotch, and expresses more forcibly the gay and the tender. Poor Charlotte Brooks, my friend and my relation, assisted in making me in love with the Irish bards. I am sure you know her beautiful translations of some of them. Carolan's monody on the death of his wife, is truly pathetic.

Allow me to say I do not conceive your extreme modesty; why should you not have supposed your charming little work worth dedicating to *any one*. I think it would be a high compliment to the taste of whoever could understand and appreciate it. Adieu, dear madam, I am sick and sad, but hope to be neither by the time I have the pleasure of seeing you.

     I am, very much
      Yours,
       ALICIA LEFANU.

Miss Owenson to Miss M. Featherstone.

STRABANE,
June 15*th*, 1803.

I was on the point of sitting down to write to you, my dear little friend, when I received your welcome letter. The cause of my silence was this: anxious to discharge as much of my debt of obligation as was *dischargeable*, I waited for a Mr. Steward who was going to Dublin, and by whom I meant to send a letter to you, a drawing (which I did since I came here) to mamma, and the money to papa he was kind enough to pay for me; however, to my own little disappointment, my *commissary* is still *philandering* in the streets of Strabane. So I am all this time lying under the imputation of ingratitude and neglect. I hope, however, papa and mamma will add to *all* I already owe, by believing that the kindness and friendly attention I have received from them on every occasion when my interest or welfare has been concerned, is deeply felt and must always be gratefully acknowledged. My father, thank Heaven! is quite recovered; but my poor Olivia had a relapse, and by going too lightly clad at a party at a *Dr.* ———'*s*, has brought on a delicacy that has terrified us with an apprehension of a consumptive habit,—she is but a shadow of herself. The doctors have ordered perpetual exercise and goat's whey. We have got a *gig*, and mean next week to go and visit the city of county Londonderry, so famous in Irish history; we shall spend a few days there; and on our return stop for a day at the races of St. Johnston's. A thousand times have I wished to have you and —— here; amidst your level lawns and young plantations you have no idea of the rude sublimity of our northern scenery. We have no farmers, so, consequently, no tillage; all is bold, savage and romantic; the manners, dialect, customs and religion of the people are all as purely Scotch as they could be in the Highlands, even the better order of people are with difficulty understood, and the manners of the inferior class are ferocious; there is, however, a great spirit of independence among them; "every rood of ground maintains its man," and there are none of those wretched cabins which you perpetually see in the other provinces. They call all strangers *foreigners* or *Irish people*, and have not many ideas beyond their *wheels* and *looms*. A market day presents a curious scene. The young women are all dressed in white, with their hair fastened up fancifully enough and seldom covered. At the entrance of the town they bathe their feet and put on shoes and stockings which are constantly taken off when they are leaving it. I have frequently seen them with flowers and feathers in their heads and their stockings tied up in a handkerchief. In a social sense they are most unpleasant, and, upon the whole, they are the last people in the world that an educated person would wish to spend their life with. We have been pretty fortunate; the rector's family of Raphoe (a little village near us) have paid us every friendly attention, and we are frequently together; this, with a few of the military, make our little circle pleasant enough. We have music every evening. I bought a very fine Spanish guitar from the master of the band here. I have a great deal of music for it, and can accompany myself on it almost as well as on the piano; at which I practice a good deal. There is an excellent drawing-master here, from whom I have got some beautiful drawings, so that I am in a fair way of improvement. I am sure you will be glad to hear that I have got a price far beyond my most sanguine wishes for *St. Clair.* Mr. Harding, of Pall Mall, says, it will be done in a very superior style, and will be certainly at Archer's in three weeks. Mrs. Colbert wrote to me about *Nina*, but her terms were too low. The *Minstrel* goes on famously, I think you will like it best of all,—it is full of incidents. I was very much flattered by the Doctor's (the Knight's I mean,) intention; I do not know which of *St Clair's* poems would answer for composition. I continue to receive the most elegant letters in the world from Mrs. Lefanu; her three children, herself and niece, have been for seven weeks confined with a spotted fever. The Crawfords are in great trouble about a governess—they cannot get one to please them; they write to me in a manner that seems to indicate their wish for my return,—but that is out of the question. I intend to lie *fallow* in the A, B, C, D-way for some time. I am glad to hear that all your friends are well; pray present my respectful compliments at Grange and Riverdale. Poor Fanny, I am truly sorry for her! I wish she was with Mr. B. Tell C. that as she has no opportunity of practising *French*, I will write constantly in *French* to her (provided she will answer me in the same language) it will help her more than she can imagine. I shall be delighted to have it in my power to be in any means instrumental to her improvement. Say everything that is kind for me to papa and mamma; assure the dear boys that I participate in their regret in our not meeting. Adieu, my dearest little friend, continue to write to me, and believe that I am among the warmest of your well-wishers and sincere friends,

SYDNEY O——.

Olivia returns a thousand thanks to her dear little friend for her kind remembrance, although it was with difficulty she got Syd to leave the room to tell her so. They wish to persuade her she is ill, but she feels no kind of indisposition but what is extremely becoming; she is sorry to add that her sister, from a too great sensibility, lets the marriage of a certain little *attorney* prey on her damask cheek, adding paleness to what was already pale. O.'s compliments to mamma.

To Mrs. Lefanu.

STRABANE,
December 9th, 1803.

I read your little secret memoir with much the same species of emotion as Uncle Toby listened to

Trim's account of Le Fevre, for more than once I wished I was asleep.

You allude to the "imprudence of Ellen Maria Williams. Although I am perfectly acquainted with her works, I know not anything of her history. May I hope in your next for a little biographical sketch. Imprudence of conduct so frequently connected with superiority of talent in woman, is, indeed, a solecism. Dare we say with Burns, that "the light which leads astray, is the light from Heaven?" Salvator says, "the primary matter of which woman is constituted is more flexible, irritable and elastic than that of man;" added to this, their delicacy, the ardour of their subtilized feelings, the warmth, the animated tenderness of their affections; then, for a moment, conceive the influence of genius and talent over this dangerous organization; conceive a flowing but dejected heart, refined but desponding mind, escaping from the solitary state of isolation its own superiority has plunged it in,—deceived by a gleam of sympathy, and led "by passion's meteor beam," beyond the barrier virtue has erected and which prudence never transgresses. Then, though we lament, while we condemn, we almost cease to wonder. I had yesterday a letter (four pages long) from Lady Clonbrock, with an account of *St. Clair's* reception at Bath and Bristol. It is just such as I knew you would wish for the bantling, who first sought protection and countenance from yourself. I know you will smile at the vanity of this account; but it set every particle of authorship afloat which had been for some time gradually subsiding Can you forgive me sending such a letter of "shreds and patches," to you as this? the truth is it has been written by snatches,—sometimes with the "buzz and murmur of those unfinished things one knows not what to call," (who come in *droves* to us every day) still sounding in my ears and dissipating every propensity to common rationality; and sometimes by the side of an invalid sister, who is paying the tribute of a rheumatic complaint for having too closely adhered to the fashionable costume of the day; added to this, I begun my epistle in full dress, going to a party, that I continued it in *deshabillé*, and literally concluded *en bonnet de nuit;* and then, if you consider (according to Buffon) that dress enters into the character, and becomes part of the *individual* "man" (or woman), it will account for the *nuances de style* of this letter, which by fits is sad, and by starts is wild! Adieu, my dear madam, have the goodness *de faire mes amitiés* to your fireside circle. My father desires to be respectfully remembered, and I request you to believe, I am yours most sincerely,

SYDNEY OWENSON.

The commissions I troubled you with—were to inquire at Archer's if the London edition of *St. Clair* was come over, and at Power's music-shop, Westmorland Street, if "Castle Hyde"* was published. I shall watch the post,—so have mercy on me!

* An old Irish melody, the words by Robert Owenson.

CHAPTER XXI.

AFTER LEAVING FORT WILLIAM.

WHEN Miss Owenson quitted Fort William, she joined her father and sister at Inniskillen, and there finished her novel of the *Novice of St. Dominic*. It was written in six volumes, for, as she said herself, "in those days one volume or six volumes was alike to me."

Whilst engaged on this novel she paid a visit to a neighbouring family named Crossley, in which there were several young people. It was a visit which materially changed the destiny of one of the family, Francis Crossley furnishing Sydney Owenson with a diligent and patient slave, who did her the good service of copying into a beautifully distinct and legible hand, the *pattes de mouche* of her own writing.

The letters of Francis Crossley have not much literary merit, but they have such an honest simplicity, and speak of so loyal and genuine an attachment, that they interest the reader, as well as throw a pleasant light on the character of Sydney Owenson.

His letters are thus endorsed in her own hand:

"Francis Crossley, aged eighteen, chose to fall in love with me, Sydney Owenson, aged eighteen. He was then intended for a merchant, but the *Novice of St. Dominic* (which he copied out as regularly as written, in six huge volumes), and its author turned his head. He fled from his counting-house, went to *India* and became a great man."

Lady Morgan, when she endorsed these papers, had of course forgotten her own age. It is so sweet to be "eighteen." Of honest zeal on the part of Crossley, there was plenty—of passion on the part of Sydney, none. Among her memoranda of 1822 and 1824, are two or three entries on the subject of Captain Crossley, which may be given in this place:—

"Francis Crossley, my fast friend of the other sex, met me at my sister's house, at dinner, after an absence of eighteen years. It was a singular interview; what was most singular in it is that he remains unchanged. He insists upon it *that in person* so am I.

"*August*, 1824.—Received this day a letter from Captain Crossley, acquainting me with his intention of marrying. I have written him an answer *à mourir de rire*, and so ends our romance of so many years.

"*August*, 26.—Captain and Mrs. Crossley dined this day here, and I never saw such a *triste* looking couple. My poor Francis silent and sad!"

We may now go back to the beginning of this little romance.

Francis Crossley to Sydney Owenson.

Monday Evening 7 o'clock.
3rd April, 1804.

I am just sat down to tell you that I have been thinking of you this hour past, according to my promise. Can you say you have fulfilled yours as well? But why say *this* hour? There is not one in the day that is not full of your idea, and devoted almost entirely to the recollection of the happy hours I have spent in your society, and which are now fled, perhaps, for ever, as you are no longer here who made Lisburn at all tolerable. We no longer hear your voice, " pleasant as the gale of spring that sighs on the hunter's ear," in our little circle, which was so often delighted and enlightened by your bewitching prattle; and I now, for the first time since my return from Belfast, begin to feel Lisburn insupportable. I almost regret having ever known or formed a friendship for you; but I lie; it is impossible any one could ever wish he had not known you, whom you honoured with your esteem. What have you to answer for to me? By over-refining my taste you have made the girls of this town insupportable: after having been blessed with your society it is impossible to be ever on friendly terms with them; and I am convinced I can never experience so sincere a friendship for one of my own sex. I don't know the reason, perhaps you can tell me; but I think those subsisting in general between men are fickle and

very insincere (at least I have found it so); between
man and woman, tender and more lasting. The first
arises from a similarity of pursuits, tastes, and pleasures; the latter from reciprocal esteem, and a stronger
mutual desire to please than can be found in the friendships of our sex; added to, on their side, by a certain
tenderness and refinement almost impossible to define,
which men cannot experience in theirs. I am sure I
feel it so; in that I hope you will permit *me* to bear
to you.

I believe I promised to tell you how we spent
the day, on the morning of which you left us, and
you shall have it as well as I recollect. You left us
a little before eight o'clock; we followed your carriage out of town and watched it till the last winding
of the road concealed it from our view; we then returned across the fields with no very enviable sensations, and climbed every ditch we met with to endeavour to catch another glimpse of you—we got just
one, as you passed a grove on your left, nearly a mile
from town, and then lost you in the distance. I am
almost ashamed to tell you I could hardly suppress a
tear at thinking it *might* probably be the last time I
should ever see those with whom I had passed away
so many pleasant hours: but to quit such nonsense
and finish my journal:—George was with us after
breakfast, and told us he could very willingly sit down
and cry (you may guess the reason), but it would not
be like *a man*. We were talking of you all day, and
cursing the chaise-boy for coming home so soon. Did
you ever hear of such a set of selfish rascals? In the

evening we strolled out of town about two miles, on the same road by which you left us. I cannot describe to you the sensations I felt in looking at the different trees on the road, which a few hours before your eyes had probably rested on, nor can I tell whether the thought was unpleasant; yet surely it cannot be pleasant that brings the departure of our friends so keenly to our mind.

Did you think your friends would have disgraced your remembrance so much as to tell a devil of a lie the very day you left them?

You told me you did not think George possessed of much feeling, but, faith, he has more than you think. He told me on Friday morning he absolutely could not refrain from crying the night before, when alone. Wasn't it good and friendly of him? And though unlike *a man*, d——e but I like him the better for it. "*Certainly, Miss Owenson,*" I think him one of the best, good-natured lads I was ever acquainted with—one of GEORGE's speeches!!

I was employed most of Friday in putting a little cabinet in order, and have it now filled with your wee notes and other dear little remembrances of you. I keep nothing else in it but *Ossian*, *Werter*, and your poems, as the only company worthy of them; and I hope you will soon add another to the number. I have brought into my room the chimney-board that was in Boyce's house the night of our little hop. I would not suffer them to destroy the laurel that encircled it, but have it put up just as it was when you saw it.

I have been reading *Werter;* don't you think the sixty-eighth and the latter part of the seventy-first chapter very beautiful? As yet you have not marked it, and I will turn over to that which the hand of taste and judgment has approved. How kind in doing so! It gives me another remembrance of you in addition to all your dear little relics.

And yet I know not whether I should thank you for so particular a mark as you have left on this page; it seems to imply SOMETHING I am not over-pleased at your thinking, if you *can* think so. You have marked this sentence strongly, "And yet if I was now to go, if I was to quit this circle, would they feel, how long would they feel that void in their life which the loss of me would leave? How long—yes. Such is the frailty of man that then where he most feels his own existence, where his presence makes a real and strong impression—even in the memory of those who are dear to him—there also he must perish and vanish away, and that so quickly." Ah, don't think it will be so with us; you do not, you CANNOT think so. The loss of you has left on us "a real and strong impression" indeed; but if you *will* think you will be forgot by us, you may at least allow that *you* will *first* drink of the waters of *Lethe.*

I have begun, and read the first book of Robertson's *Charles the Fifth,* and it does justice to your recommendation. I have made a good many extracts out of it, and hope I shall be improved by them. It is you I have to thank for this mode of imbibing instruction; as, but for you, I should never have thought of it, perhaps; in fact, what am I not indebted to you for? To you I owe almost every sentiment I at present harbour or am capable of feeling, and I hope they do not dishonour your inspiration.

F. A. C.

A very little of Francis Crossley will suffice. The reader will be glad to know that he went to India in due time, and was not heard of again for twenty years.

The following letter will explain itself:

Mrs. Lefanu to Miss Owenson.

GLASNEVIN,
Wednesday, Oct. 31st, 1804.

MY DEAR MADAM,

Your charming letter, of no date, found me last Saturday very much indisposed with a severe headache, attended with feverishness, to which I am subject. My head is something better, but I am not well in other respects, and in the midst of hurry and preparation for town, where we go the day after to-morrow, to remain for the winter. I leave this quiet spot, liberty and fresh air with regret. In town I am plagued with the bustle of the city without being able to join in its amusements. The theatre I have long ceased to attend: when there is any performance worth seeing I dare not encounter the crowd, and what is mis-named private society, is become almost as formidable on a similar account; and my own immediate little circle that I used to draw about me, time and the chances in life have committed such depredations upon, that, like

Ossian, "I sit alone in my halls." Exclusive, I should
say, of my own family, whose society becomes every
day more pleasing to me, as "knowledge to their eyes
her ample page rich with the spoils of time" gradually
unrolls, I shall be happy to see you in town, and
wish my house admitted of offering you an apartment
in it; but we are already crowded like bees in a hive
and inconvenienced for want of room, in a way that
would try the patience of a female Job. Mind, I do
not tell you that I am one. But though I have no
bed to give you, every other attention I can show I
shall be delighted to do it; and the more I see of you
(without encroaching on your time and the claims of
other friends), the better I shall be pleased.

I make no doubt that your work will succeed:
going yourself to London is certainly the best security
for justice being done you. The Bishop of Dromore's
advice is the best you can possibly be guided by, and
his high literary reputation will give every weight to
his recommendations and approbation of you.

Above twenty years absence from London (to which
place I was never permitted to return), has broken or
relaxed every tie I had there. To some my place has
been supplied, others have pretended to suppose themselves neglected by me, to excuse their own neglect of
me. And there are a few who, with more apparent
reason, have thought themselves forgotten by me because I was not at liberty to explain *why* I did not pay
them all the attention I wished.

When we meet we will converse fully on the subject
of your book, in the meantime rest assured that all I
can do I will, for I have a real wish to serve you;

admiration for your talent and love for your person. All here join with me in kindest wishes for you and yours. Believe me,

Your affectionate,
ALICIA LEFANU.

Miss Owenson, encouraged by this advice given to her by Mrs. Lefanu, as to her literary enterprises, wrote her first letter to a London publisher, Sir Richard Phillips. His answer is among her papers. A note upon it, in Lady Morgan's later handwriting says:—

"Without *one* friend to recommend, when I wished to publish *The Novice*, I took in a newspaper for a bookseller's name—I saw R. Phillips, and wrote to him. This was his answer:"—

BRIDGE STREET,
April 6, 1805.

MADAM,

I have read with peculiar pleasure your ingenious and ingenuous letter. It exactly portrays the ardour of mind and the frankness which always accompany true genius.

It *concerns* me that I am forced to reduce to pounds, shillings, and pence, every proposition like yours—that all the speculations of genius, when they lie in my counting house, become the subject of arithmetical calculation—that if, when tried by this unaccommodating standard, they do not promise to yield a certain rate per cent. profit, I am led to treat them with coldness and neglect, and am finally induced to reject them altogether as *useless* or visionary!

And still I am often (UNDESERVEDLY) complimented as the most liberal of my trade! as the most enterprizing of all the midwives of the muses!

I am ashamed to say, that the cold-hearted calculations which constantly absorb all my faculties in my own interested concerns, have prevented me from seeing or reading the little work of yours, of whose merit I entertain no doubt, since it is demonstrated arithmetically by the number that has been sold.

I am, therefore, unable to write with precision, being in the practice, in all these matters, of *judging for myself;* and although I repeat that I have been charmed with the ingenuousness of your letter, yet my prudence gets the better of my politeness, and commands me to see and read before I engage for your new work, unless I had previously been concerned in the sale of the old one, and was well acquainted with its merit and character.

The Reviews I never read, nor would any person, were they acquainted with the corrupt views with which almost every one of them is conducted. If your work has received their *praise* without its being paid for, your merit must be great indeed, and I shall have reason to be proud of this intercourse.

You can send the MS. through any friendly medium, addressed to me, to the care of Mr. Archer, Dublin, and you can desire him to forward it to me, or bring it with him in his projected journey to London.

I assure you I am not used to write such long letters, but this has been extorted from me by the respect with which I feel myself your obliged,

Humble servant,

R. PHILLIPS.

When the *Novice* was fairly copied out by Crossley, her young and patient adorer, Sydney Owenson determined to take it up to London herself.

In those days the journey was long, and somewhat hazardous for a young girl. There was the sea voyage, and the long coach journey afterwards, from Holyhead to London. She had to travel alone, and she had very little money to help her on her way.

She used to say to her nieces, in after life, that they —carefully-nurtured girls as they were—little knew the struggles and difficulties she had to encounter in her early days.

Her first journey to London was in curious contrast to the brilliant visits she subsequently made. When the coach drove into the yard of the "Swan with Two Necks," in Lad Lane, she had not a notion where to go or what to do next, and sat down upon her small trunk in the yard to wait until the bustle of arrival should have a little subsided. Overcome with fatigue and anxiety, she fell fast asleep. For some time no one remarked her—at last, a gentleman who had been her fellow-passenger in the coach, saw her sitting there, and he had the humanity to commend her himself to the care of the heads of the establishment, begging that they would take care of her, and see that she was properly attended to.

The friend who thus unexpectedly interposed on her behalf, was the late Mr. Quentin Dick. It was the beginning of her acquaintance with him.

After a night's rest, Sydney Owenson arose with unabated spirit, and proceeded to seek her publisher, taking her MS. with her.

Phillips seems to have been charmed with her, and to have been fascinated into a liberality almost beyond his judgment, though, it is only due to him to say, that he struggled hard against giving such a proof of his devotion.

He insisted on having the *Novice* cut down from six volumes to four; and she used to say, that she was convinced nothing but regard for her feelings prevented him from reducing it to three.

He was extremely kind to her whilst she remained in town—introduced her to his wife, and placed her in respectable lodgings. He paid her at once for her book; as soon as she received the money, she was anxious to take it herself to her father; but Phillips persuaded her to have the greatest portion properly remitted, as he had no faith in her power of taking care of it.

This first fruits of her success could do but little towards rescuing Robert Owenson from his embarrassments; but the fact that she could earn money by her pen, was more than relief to both father and daughter—it was hope and fortune.

The first purchase she made for herself out of her literary earnings were an Irish harp, from Egan, and a black mode cloak! The harp was her companion wherever she went.

The following letter, from Mrs. Inchbald, addressed to Miss Owenson, at 30, Upper Eaton Street Pimlico, is the only record of any incident during this first visit to London:—

TURNHAM GREEN, *May* 14, 1805.

Mrs. Inchbald presents her compliments to Miss Owenson. She is highly flattered by the contents of the letter she has received from her, and most sincerely laments that the very same circumstances which a few years ago would have rendered a further acquaintance with Miss Owenson extremely desirable, at the present time precludes her from the possibility of any future introduction. Mrs. Inchbald has the highest esteem for Mr. and Mrs. Hitchcock, and she is grieved to her heart that their remote place of abode should have prevented their knowledge of her resolution, formed after a short acquaintance (something like patronage) with a young authoress, never again to admit the visits of a lady of her own profession.

The young lady to whom she alludes, was a Miss Ann Plumtree, and no one can more accurately describe the loss and inconvenience sustained from her acquaintance than Mr. Phillips.

Miss Owenson, having settled with Sir R. Phillips, and bought her mode cloak and Irish harp, returned to Londonderry; Sir Richard sent after her no end of good advice as to her literary pursuits. The following is amusing.

Sir R. Phillips to Sydney Owenson.

October 16th, 1805.

DEAR MADAM,

Your letter interested me as usual. I thank you for the regard which it expresses for my interests, and for the compliments (most unmerited) which it pays me. I hope to maintain your good opinion, and that we shall be as much in love with each other twenty years hence as we are now.

You are right in your conception relative to the work of Mr. Carr. It cannot interfere with your's. Dr. Beaufort has been so many years beating *about* the subject, and making preparations and promises, that my patience is exhausted. The world is not informed about Ireland, and I am in the situation to command the *light* to shine! I am sorry you have assumed the novel form. A series of letters, addressed to a friend in London, taking for your model the Turkish letters of Lady M. W. Montagu, would have secured you the most extensive reading. A matter-of-fact and didactic novel is neither one thing nor another, and suits no class of readers. Certainly, however, *Paul and Virginia* would suggest a local plan, and it will be possible, by writing three or four times over, in six or eight months, to produce what would *command* attention.

I assure you that you have a power of writing, a fancy, an imagination, and a degree of enthusiasm which will enable you to produce an immortal work, if you will *labour it* sufficiently. Write only one side of your paper and retain a broad margin. Your power of improving your first draught will thus be greatly increased; and a second copy, made in the same way, with the same power of correcting, will enable you to make a third copy, which will be another monument of Irish genius.

I earnestly exhort you to subject yourself to this drudgery. It may be painful to endure for a few weeks, but you will reap a harvest, for years, of renown and fortune.

Every one speaks highly of the *Novice of St. Dominic*, but their praise is always qualified by the remark that it would have few equals in this line, if it were reduced one entire volume in length. Some copies of the novel have been sent for you to Archer, whom you ought to reprimand for not ordering any copies.

  Believe me, dear Madam,
   Your sincere and devoted friend,
     R. PHILLIPS.

PS. A series of letters on the state of Ireland, the manners and characters of its inhabitants, &c., &c., would be well read in the *Monthly Magazine*, would be worth as much to me, and would afterwards sell separately.

Such as it was, the *Novice of St. Dominic* was published—and succeeded. It is certainly a very amusing novel; there is an exuberance of fine words and ardent descriptions of the sensibilities of the heroine,

as well as of her personal charms; but there is also an
idea of something better—an idea of duty and the
preference of principle to inclination. There is the
usual fault of pedantry; the heroine is terribly well
educated by her model lover De Sorville; and they
talk elegant literature together in a style that would
have eclipsed the talk at Mrs. Montagu's parties. It
shows a great improvement upon her first book; and
there is a freedom of hand and a facility of invention
which give promise of entertainment to come. The
Novice of St. Dominic was a favourite with Mr. Pitt,
and he read it over again in his last illness, a piece
of good fortune for a book of which any author might
be proud.

CHAPTER XXII.

A SUCCESSFUL AUTHORESS.

SYDNEY OWENSON was now become a successful writer, with her name in the papers, and her praises in the post-office. She was petted by her publisher and, perhaps, a little spoiled by her public. Private incense, too, was offered to her taste, her beauty, and her genius—offered with the abundance and the fervour of Irish compliment. At times she may have listened to the charmer more than was wise in a young girl; at least, her elders thought and said so. Not that she went wrong, even by implication or in appearance—she had too much sense for that; but she found herself in a circle where every woman paid her compliments, and every man, as the mode in Ireland was, made love to her. She undoubtedly played with the fire; but she was too busy with her literary projects to do more than play—a weaker woman might have been consumed.

The following letter, although it has neither date nor address, was written to Mrs. Lefanu, shortly after

Miss Owenson's return from London. It was probably written from Longford House, as Lady Morgan often referred to the times in which she wrote the *Wild Irish Girl*, and always related that a portion of it was written while on a visit to the Croftons. Miss Crofton sat for the heroine. The cause of the temporary coldness of Sydney's friend, Mrs. Lefanu, was an opinion of the older lady that, in the intervals of business, the young lady had been flirting more than was right. The introduction which Sydney requests is to Mr. Walker, the author of a *History of Irish Music*. She needed some information on the subject for the *Wild Irish Girl*.

Sydney Owenson to Mrs. Lefanu.

January 6th, 1806.

My dear Madam,

I believe the surest mode of reviving your friendship for an object that, God knows, has very unconsciously forfeited it, is to tell you that you can be of some service to her. The foregoing page will tell you how I am at present employed, having engaged with Phillips to have the work* finished by the ensuing month. I left England sooner than I intended, merely to collect those materials and documents which were only to be had in the interior parts of Ireland, especially Connaught, where I have been among my own relations for some time. I have, however, now re-

---

* The *Wild Irish Girl*.

tired hither these two months back, "the world forgetting," though I hope not, "by the world forgot." I see no human being, write eight hours a day, sometimes more, and shall be ready for another venture to London by the first week in February. The favour I have to request of you is this: I am told you know *Mr. Walker*, and that he has written an account of Irish music and Irish bards. In my little work I have treated on both; but after the most diligent research I cannot gain any *certain* information relative to the Irish harp. I have read all that has been written on the subject by historians and antiquaries; but *nothing* on that subject by *a musician*. I know its *construction* and form; but what I want to know and what perhaps Mr. Walker can tell you, is the *musical* system of the instrument; by what rule it was tuned, how the change of keys was produced, and whether it was susceptible of chromatics? This, my dear Madam, is giving you a great deal of trouble, but as it affords you an opportunity of serving another, I am sure it is also giving you some pleasure.

Have you seen my *Novice of St. Dominic?* I long much to hear your opinion of it, that is if you shall think it worth one. Pratt, the author, has written to me, for leave to select the best passages from that and *St. Clair*, and to publish them in a work called *The Morality of English Novels*. This is very flattering, and this you will say, "is all the egotism of authorship," and so it is; but before I check the dear theme, I must tell you that my Irish melodies are doing wonders in London, and that I have published a song at Holden's, Parliament Street, dedicated to Lady Charlotte Homan, which I wish you much to see and hear.

S. OWENSON.

Mrs. Lefanu, who accepted her young friend's *amende* in good part, did what was requested; wrote to Mr. Walker, who expressed himself much gratified by the application, when a friendship began between himself and Miss Owenson, which lasted the remainder of his life. The following letters are interesting for their own sake, as well as supplying a link in Miss Owenson's history and correspondence.

Whilst engaged in writing the *Wild Irish Girl*, Miss Owenson this year published a collection of poems and melodies, most of which had been written at various times. The little book was entitled the *Lay of the Irish Harp*, and was published by Phillips. It had some success at the time it appeared; but Sydney Owenson is one of the many "Sapphos" whose songs have passed away.

J. C. Walker to Sydney Owenson.

ST. VALERI, BRAY,
4th Feb. 1806.

MADAM,

I am just honoured with your obliging favour of 30th ultimo. It would make me truly happy to promote in any way your elegant undertakings. Any assistance I can afford you may freely command.

With Mr. Burton's publication, I am but slightly acquainted. I think, however, with you, that the Preface was contributed by the Bishop of Clonfurt. It was his Lordship who first mentioned the publication to me. He spoke with approbation of the Collection of Airs.

The compass of the Irish harp is certainly confined. It is a very imperfect instrument. The Welsh have improved considerably upon it. Their instrument is much superior to our's. Our harp, however, answered perhaps sufficiently the purpose for which I believe it was usually employed—I mean as an accompaniment to the voice. On many occasions, I presume, the bard did little more than sweep his hand over the strings of his harp while he recited the "Tale of other Times."

I am rejoiced to find that Carolan's harp is preserved.

You are now in a part of the island where many of the Finian tales are familiarly known. You will, of course, collect some of them, and, perhaps, interweave them with the work on which you are at present employed. If you could obtain faithful descriptions of some of the scenes of those tales, you would heighten the interest of your romance by occasionally introducing them. On the summit of Slieve Guillen, lies the scene of *The Chase*, which has been so admirably translated by Miss Brooke. As it does not appear from your letter, that you are acquainted with her *Reliques*, permit me to recommend that inestimable work to your particular attention. Benham, the printer, in Great George's Street, South, is in possession of a few copies. When I shall hear of your arrival in Dublin, my bards shall find their way to you.

With the plan of your work I am unacquainted. Perhaps you have taken for a model, the prose romance of the Irish, which was, I believe, generally interspersed with poetical pieces, like the Spanish romance (see Percy's *Reliques* for an account of the *History of the Civil Wars of Granada*) or, to refer to a modern production, *The Mysteries of Udolpho*.

If I might presume to offer any advice in regard to style, I would beg leave to recommend the *familiar* in the narrative parts. In the impassioned parts, it might rise sometimes to the *lofty*. In real life, the language of the passions is various and always appropriate. This, the writer of fictitious history should always keep in mind. The language of simple narration, where the passions are unconcerned, should be easy, elegant, and familiar. Such, I am sure, madam, is the language you will employ. And I am equally certain, that in the impassioned parts of your work, you will employ the words that *burn*, or *melt*, as the occasion may require. But I am, I fear, taking an unwarrantable liberty with you. My motive must be my apology.

I am happy to find that you still enjoy the protection of your father. He must be a comfort to you, while you are a blessing to him. Be so good as to remember me to him with great kindness; and believe me,

Madam, with much respect,
Your most obedient, humble Servant,
JOSEPH COOPER WALKER.

If Dr. Gamble, of your town, should have a small
packet for me, might I beg of you to take charge of it.

I hope you will be able to draw from the Bard of
the Maygelligans, a complete history of his life. It
would make a very interesting memoir. He is, perhaps, able to supply many anecdotes of the Bards of
the North during the last century.

The next letter, written by Miss Owenson whilst
residing with her father and sister, at Londonderry,
gives a picture of herself and her surroundings which,
as she kept no journal in those days, can only be
seen in these incidental glimpses. For many years
she kept nothing but common-place books full of extracts from the authors she had read.

Sydney Owenson to Mrs. Lefanu.

LONDONDERRY HOTEL,
March 28th.

Your letter is precisely ten minutes in my possession, and while dear papa is playing away, on an old
Cremona, some fine old Irish airs, and a young musician, at the corner of my writing-table, is taking
down the melody, here am I, with my poor whirlgig
brain full of basses, trebles, and accompaniments, and
my warm, impulsive heart, full of the most respected
object of its friendship, scribbling away to her as fast
as I can, and humming "Shelah na Conolan," while
papa plays and little Orpheus writes. Apropos of

these national airs, so tastelessly and so shamefully neglected, I am endeavouring to collect some of the best and least-known, and to put English words of my own to their wild and plaintive strains, and I am taking them down from my father, in preference to any one else, because *he* plays and sings them in the *true attic* style of Conomarra, and I really believe is more *à porté* to the idiomatic delicacies of Irish music than any man living, besides having the best and most original collection of airs. There are three or four (to which I have adapted words) universally known, though never sung in the true strains of Irish musical sentiment, and to which words had been put so vulgar and barbarous as to throw an air of ridicule over the whole. Of these are the "Cooleen," whose date could not be ascertained in the reign of Henry the Eighth, "Savourneen Deelish," "My lodgings on the cold ground;" the words of the latter, however, have a simplicity which I am sure mine will want, though I have endeavoured to imitate them. Have you heard "Shelah na Conolan," an air that breathes the very spirit of pathos; "Kathleen O'Tyrell," playfully arch; "One touch of her finger would do your heart good;" one of the same character "Drimadu," heart-breaking and wild, and "Grace Nugent," whose melody is tinctured with Italian elegance, and is the best of Carolan's love songs; by way of experiment, I put Italian words to "Planxy Power," which is itself truly Italian, and having sung it, *con amore* for one of our rustic amateurs, they acknowledged it at once to be one of Surti's soul-dissolving airs, especially as it was written on the same page with "Lungi." Now, whether it is in my national enthusiasm or my national prejudice, or call it what you will, I really believe this country to have a music more original, more purely its own, more characteristic, and possessing more the soul of melody, than any other country in Europe. The Italians, who now give the key-note to the music of every other country, have, in my opinion, none of their own. Their's is the music of *science*. I have at this moment by me about a hundred and fifty ancient and modern Italian ballads, as sung by the Venetian gondolieri, and by the Roman and Tuscan peasantry, and if the character of national music is anywhere to be found, it must be in those airs, breathed in the "native wood-notes wild" of the natural and unscientific musician. But in these wretched *ariettes* there is only a monotonous recitative strain without *melody*, and incapable of being harmonized before the modern scale of music was given to Europe by the monk Guy Aretin; the sweet airs of my native country were as conformable to the laws of modern compositions, as the *Iliad* of Homer to the rules of criticism before Aristotle drew up his fundamental rules for forming an epic poem; besides that, then and ever, they breathed the sweetest intonations of the passions of the heart, and so now I have beat the Italians out of the field, and my triumph is complete, and there is no more to be said about the matter, only give me your applause! Oh, but there, I intended all this letter should be about a sarsenet mantle and knowing little hoods, which give one that delightful *disin-*

coltura air I love so much; but then papa's violin is ringing in my ears, and then, like other wandering luminaries, I keep moving in my own sphere by the power of harmony (for music is my sphere, and I believe that philosophy is a little obsolete); but no matter, it answers my purpose just now as well as the Copernican or Newtonian systems combined. Pray do you observe, I have given an armistice to my "Il Penseroso" mood, and my good spirits hold an armed neutrality between my real and my fancied sorrow, and that though I am "most musical," I am not "most melancholy," and that, in short, I am restored to my usual *bizarre* random tone of mind. Oh, but *Gresset*, from whom you quote the happiest lines of his happiest poem—I never could get a full feast of that charming writer, but only at intervals snatched a little *bonne bouche* that incited my appetite without satisfying it. I adore those socializing poetic powers that smile in his social and familiar works. His patriotic ode is very fine; his *Merchant* is equal to anything of Molière's, and there is a sentiment in his ode, "Au Roi," which ought to be written in letters of gold. "Le cri d'un peuple heureux est la seule éloquence qui sache parler aux Rois."

As I have not unpacked my books nor music, nor shall do so whilst here, I have been thrown upon the *rational resources* of painting *watch papers*, and rifling the riches of a circulating library. There is a fine romance by a fine scholar of Cambridge, where an Italian lady, in a glowing Italian summer evening, who (after a day's travel in Italian scenery) goes into an Italian inn, and calls for a good fire and a hot supper. This, and a thousand other little incongruities observed in the stuff I have been reading, convinces me of the truth of Walpole's assertions—that even to write a *novel* requires a considerable portion of general information, knowledge, and intelligence, besides talent—not that any of these requisites were necessary to show my poor author that a bower, *al fresco*, would have been more grateful to his fair traveller than the kitchen comforts of an English inn, besides making his heroine talk of a *pounded cow* in the 13th century, and in Florence. Pray ask your learned Domine, Tom, if they *pounded cows* in those days in Italy, or whether it was not introduced in a later age by some tyrant English farmer. The name of this intemperate work is *Isabel*, and you can have a thousand such for sixpence per work, that have gone through three or four editions, which shows that the fools carry it all to nothing in the present day; for my part I know not what the destiny of my bagatelle may be, for like La Chossel, "Je n'ai pas entrepris de plaire à tous les sots." Now tell me, in your next, you are *well*, and then I promise you you shall have no more voluminous farragoes of this kind, for you may perceive I am acting up to Molière's definition of a physician, "Un qui conte des fabrioles dans les chambres des malades," and am I not at this moment in your little boudoir prattling away to you, as I hope soon to do. I envy you the society of *Mrs. Holman*.

S. O.

Miss Owenson had now completed her first national story, the *Wild Irish Girl.* Sir Richard Phillips was charmed with his new author, but he wished to monopolize her talent without paying the price. Miss Owenson, not in the least disposed to meet his views, wrote to Johnson, an opposition publisher, in St. Paul's Churchyard, and the following exceedingly droll correspondence from the rival publishers is the result of this application.

Miss Owenson had received that special blessing prayed for by the quaint Scotch clergyman "a gude conceit o' hersel," and it stood her in good stead all her life.

Sir R. Phillips to Sydney Owenson.

April 3, 1806.

Dear Madam,

I did not suppose that a mother would deprive a father of his child!

She must not, however, be tolerated in an act of extortion, presuming on his affection!

He will do all that can be demanded of parental affection, and he conceives he has *already* deported himself with a liberality dictated by his feelings for both mother and child.

But if she will be headstrong, &c., &c., &c., she must even take her course!

Believe me, dear madam,
Affectionately and sincerely yours, &c.,
R. Phillips.

J. Johnson, to Miss Owenson.

ST. PAUL'S CHURCHYARD,
London, April 5, 1806.

MADAM,

If I had not seen specimens of your powers, an answer to your letter would have been very easy; as it is, I hesitate. You have been offered a very liberal sum; not much more—say a hundred pounds per volume is the most, as far as my knowledge extends—that has been given to the most popular writers, after their characters were established, for works of this nature and size. Admitting this to be your price, the volumes should be large, as they cannot be sold under five shillings, at the least, unbound,—not less than three hundred very honest pages. At my time of life, when, instead of advancing I ought perhaps to withdraw, I may be acting imprudently; but I cannot turn a deaf ear to your superior merit.

In depicting the miseries of the poor, your object, I trust, is not to inflame them, but to excite the attention of the rich to their relief. To whomsoever you send your MS. I recommend your keeping a copy, which should be transcribed page for page, not only to guard against loss, but for the sake of sending remarks should any offer.

I am, Madam, your obedient servant,
J. JOHNSON.

Sir R. Phillips to Sydney Owenson.

April 8, 1806.

DEAR MADAM,

I write because the season, the London season, is now at its height, and this is the moment for a work like yours to appear.

The *Novice* did not meet with due notice at first, owing to the bad season of its appearance.

On sending off the MS. you may draw on me for fifty pounds.

I assure you that I am exceedingly well pleased with the *Novice*, and a second edition will be wanted by the time the new work is launched.

Believe me,
Very sincerely, yours, &c., &c.,
R. PHILLIPS.

J. Johnson, to Sydney Owenson.

LONDON, *April,* 14, 1806.

MADAM,

I am favoured with your letter of the 8th, and as you wish for a more explicit declaration of terms, I hereby agree to give you three hundred pounds, British, for the copyright of your work, entitled the *Wild Irish Girl,* on condition that it make three large volumes in duodecimo. With respect to a further consideration, I would not advise you to look for it — in my own experience I have not had an instance.

when, after giving such a price, even liberality required it. After you are perfectly satisfied with the copy, or, to speak more properly, satisfied that you can make it no better, it will be well to send it, by post if possible to get it franked, as the season is far advanced, to, madam,

    Your very obedient servant,
          J. Johnson.

A dozen copies will be at your service.

Sir R. Phillips to Sydney Owenson.

        April 18, 1806.

Dear Madam,

I write (in the greatest haste) to say, that agreeably to your proposal of my meeting the *overture* of a lady—a young and beautiful lady, one with whom I have been long enraptured—I will give two hundred pounds for the *Wild Irish Girl*, now, and fifty pounds on the publication of the second and the third editions respectively.

The two hundred pounds to be drawn for in three notes, of fifty pounds each, at two, four, and six months, from the 1st of May, and the other fifty pounds at nine months from the day of publication.

The fifty pounds from the new editions to be drawn at six months each.

When I wrote my first of the two letters I thought we had sold but six hundred and fifty copies of the *Novice*, and I then found we had sold seven hundred and ten, my stock-keeper having mistaken.

I gave you leave, therefore, to draw for the premium on the second edition, and also for fifty pounds on account of my own child, which you have hitherto so cruelly detained, but which I was confident you could not persist in witholding from his fond parent!

My terms were those which a *calculation* indicated as just and liberal, and you know I told you at the outset that I was nothing better than a *calculator!*

You will, however, I fear, make something more of me!

I have now advanced fifty steps instead of one, which is more than you desired; you are, therefore, mine, all mine, even by agreement, leaving the *will* out of the question!

God bless you, and believe me always DEVOTEDLY,
Your calculating lover,
R. PHILLIPS.

Sir R. Phillips to Sydney Owenson.

April 26, 1806.

DEAR MADAM,

It provokes me that a foolish spirit of revenge and retaliation in Mr. Johnson, owing to my giving Mr. Carr five hundred pounds for his *Northern Summer*, for which he had offered but one hundred pounds, should have stimulated him to step between you and me, and give so monstrous a price for a work which he has not seen, on a first application; a species of work, too, wholly out of his line of publication.

I am content, however, because such a spirit cannot but meet with its own punishment, and because, though *unlawfully* obtained, you are to benefit by it!

Still I am persuaded that my honest (*legitimate*) two hundred, and fifty pounds per edition, would have produced as much to you, and you would have no qualms of conscience, arising from your having robbed a parent of his own child.

In the first emotions, after receiving your letters, Cherry happening to call at the very instant, I resolved to outbid Johnson, though I might give five hundred pounds; some further consideration of the subject, has however, resolved me not to alter my last offer of two hundred pounds, to be drawn for in any way convenient to yourself, and fifty pounds per future edition after the first of fifteen hundred copies, which will little more than repay the two hundred pounds.

I am sorry you had not faith in me, and that you have been misled and dazzled so as not to feel your true interest. I am ever disposed to give to authors three-fourths of the product of their labours—and I could not live with less than the other fourth.

A little *calculation* (my favourite theme) may satisfy you that I made you a fair offer; and Johnson might as well have given you three thousand pounds as three hundred pounds, stimulated as he is by pique and a spirit of revenge.

The letter of Mr. Cherry must, therefore, be considered as *nothing*. I shall be glad to receive the revised copy of the *Novice of St. Dominic* as soon as possible, because it is likely that *my* little *Irish Girl* may give new vogue to her elder sister.

I am, Madam,
Your very humble servant,
R. PHILLIPS.

Sir R. Phillips to Sydney Owenson.

May 5, 1806.

DEAR MADAM,

I am convinced you will ultimately find that you have been foolish and maliciously advised about the disposal of your new work.

You ought to have done justice to your own feelings and not have been induced to act against your conscience as you have done.

You know well what is due to me in this affair; but you are not to be blamed—you have been led astray by a go-between, whose conduct at my house ought to have excited your lasting contempt.

The history of all literature will do honour to my offers, and I am resolved to stand or fall by the liberality of my conduct towards you. My offer of two hundred pounds and fifty pounds for future editions, is all that *reason* could expect. In asking three hundred pounds, you were advised to be very unreasonable.

I say this in perfect good humour, being stimulated to write by something which has passed to-day from a well-wisher of mine, and friend of yours—Mr. Atkinson. Believe me

    Your friend, &c., &c.,

         R. PHILLIPS.

Sir R. Phillips to Sydney Owenson.

      Bridge Street, May 12, 1806.

DEAR, BEWITCHING, AND DELUDING SYREN,

Not able to part from you, I have promised your noble and magnanimous friend, Atkinson, the three hundred pounds. His appeal was irresistible, and the *Wild Irish Girl* is mine, to do with her as I please!

You were too rapid about the *Novice*. Had her sister gone to Johnson he must have fathered the *Novice*, also, and have answered your drafts in her favour.

Write soon, and endeavour to make it up with me. It will be long before I shall forgive you! at least not till I have got back the three hundred pounds and another three hundred with it.

If you know any poor bard—a real one, no pretender—I will give him a guinea a page for his rhymes in the *Monthly Magazine*. I will also give for prose communications after the rate of six guineas per sheet. Your attention to this will oblige me, and may serve some worthy geniuses.

    Believe me always yours,

      Whether you are mine or not!

         R. PHILLIPS.

CHAPTER XXIII.

THE WILD IRISH GIRL.

INDUSTRY was Miss Owenson's great characteristic. She had no sooner finished and published the *Novice* than she once more set to work—this time it was upon a work by which her reputation was to be made as a novelist.

The *Wild Irish Girl*, or, as it was at first intended to be called, the *Princess of Innismore*, was, in some measure based on a curious circumstance in Miss Owenson's own life.

A young man, Richard Everard, had fallen violently in love with Miss Owenson; his father discovered it and was displeased. This son had no money, no profession, and was a very idle young man. Miss Owenson had no money either, and it looked a very undesirable match. Mr. Everard, the father, called upon Miss Owenson, stated his objections, and begged her to use her influence to make his son Richard take to some employment, and tried to obtain her promise not to marry him. Miss Owenson had not the least inclination to mary him, but nobody likes to be peremptorily desired to refrain even from a course they are "not inclined to." Still, Sydney Owenson spoke so wisely, and conducted herself so pleasantly, that the father actually became desirous of doing himself what he had forbidden his son to think of. Miss Owenson was no more disposed to marry the father than she had been to marry the son. He became, however, a very firm and kind friend to her father, assisting him both with counsel and money. Mr. Everard kept up a long and earnest correspondence with Miss Owenson, confiding to her with singular frankness, all his own concerns and private affairs; and constantly entreating her to use her influence over his son to turn him from his idle courses.

The history of this curious friendship is detailed in the story of the *Wild Irish Girl*, where her father figures as the prince of Innismore, Mr. Everard and his son as Lord M——, and Mortimer; though the beautiful atmosphere of romance which clothes the story in the novel was entirely absent in the matter of fact.

The character of the Princess of Innismore was afterwards identified with Lady Morgan, and until her marriage she was always known in society by the sobriquet of Glorvina.

The great secret of the success of the *Wild Irish Girl* was, that it conveyed in a vivid and romantic story, curious information about the social condition, the manners, customs, literature, and antiquities of Ireland. There was in it a passionate pleading against the wrongs and injustice to which the people and the country were subjected. The work dealt with the false ideas about Ireland which prevailed in England at that period of misconception and misrule. As these pleas were put forth in an interesting form, they were eagerly read. The following letter is from Mr. Everard, the original of Lord M——, the father of the Mortimer of the novel

J. Everard to Sydney Owenson.

Sligo,
November 10*th*, 1807.
Tuesday night.

I have read a letter from Richard,—poor fellow! After dissipating much of *his own time*, and a great deal of *my money*, he has been obliged to enter into a *special pleader's* office (for which I was forced to pay one hundred guineas as his admission fee), in order to become what is called a *black-letter* man—a *mechanical* lawyer. This is no great proof of abilities!

I must *very shortly* leave this for Dublin, perhaps for England, if my health permits. I would like to see you *before* I went. I would gladly spend an hour with you some morning, if I could do it without annoying your family; but, doubtful of my reception, I am somewhat afraid of adventuring. Tell me, if I can go, will I see you *without inconvenience?* Tell me more, in *confidence*. Can I be anything to you? for my hand, my heart, and my purse are freely at your command. You can't confer a greater obligation on me than to suffer me to *minister* to your *convenience.* With cordiality and truth,

I am your attached and faithful friend,

J. EVERARD.

Wednesday morning.

I beg to know where your father is. What is he doing, or what prospects does he entertain? Is there any prospect that his *decline* of life will be *rescued* from that *miserable* state! How, or where is your sister? I am interested for everything that concerns you. *Unjustly* were you dissatisfied at her writing to me; 'tis she who ought to be displeased, not you.

Do you spend the winter at Longford? When do you go to Dublin? I am anxious to see you, and loiter away a little time with you; but, alas! neither you nor I can afford to be idlers, at least indulgence is not for me; but I am trifling, adieu,

J. EVERARD.

PS. Would to God you would write less indistinctly, I am only eternally guessing at your meaning. Perhaps, like the oracles of old, you wish your characters may have *double* meanings.

In July, 1806, Miss Owenson quitted Dublin, apparently on a whim of the moment, and went to visit her mother's relatives in Shrewsbury; who, if surprised, were also highly delighted to see her. She had the faculty of making a holiday wherever she went. Her personal favour kept pace with her public popularity;

her friends' delight in her success, gave it a pleasure and a value not its own. A letter from Shrewsbury gives some pleasant insight into her way of life there.

Sydney Owenson to Olivia Owenson.

SALOP, SWAN HILL COURT,
July 2nd, 1806.

How delightful it is, my dearest darling pet, to address you once more at home, and to know you are comforting my darling papa for my absence; the more I think of his indulgence to all my whims and eccentricities, the more I feel myself unworthy of such a father, and the further I have travelled from home— the more I have lived among strangers—the dearer he and you are to me. If he can forgive me this wild step, I promise never to have a wish or desire independent of him, and never to leave him again whilst he thinks I am worthy of remaining with him.

Every indulgence, every tenderness, even respect that is possible for a human being to receive, is paid to me here. I am carried about as a show, worshipped as a little idol, and my poor aunt says she cannot help crying for joy, when she thinks she has such a niece! Although we have some most respectable folks frequently with us, the chair on her right hand is always kept for me, no matter whether her visitors are married or not.

Whatever I happen to say I like is prepared for breakfast, dinner or supper; and all her fear is that I should look down on everything. As for my uncle, the cold man to his family, I do what I please with him—rattle him about—sit on his knee—and he refuses me nothing; he says I am the wonder of the world, and that there never was such a singer in Shropshire before. The poor man runs about the town to look for judges, as he says, to listen to me, because there are so few capable of understanding me. I am obliged to sing to him every night before he goes to bed.

Last night I had a famous logical and literary combat with a young pedantic Cantab, just fresh from Cambridge, in which I was victorious, and the poor old gentleman was so pleased that he sat up till *one* o'clock, though he usually retires at ten. But kind and good as my uncle and aunt are, they are nothing to my dear little affectionate cousins; the two boys are charming fellows, spirited, clever and polite. Robert, the eldest, is so like me, that people in the street take us for brother and sister. He scarcely lives a moment from me—we draw together and read French—he drives me about in a nice curricle. My uncle's curricle is reckoned the handsomest in Salop, and he keeps four horses. We had the daughters of a Welsh vicar on a visit, beautiful as angels and to the full as insipid. Aunt and uncle are always torturing Robert to pay them attention, but in vain, his reply is always, "I must father give *them* up or my charming little Irish cousin—I have made my election." Mary (my likeness) is my friend, and Bess, who is going to be married to a stupid, goodnatured creature, is all kindness. They think me a first-rate dasher, and my dresses serve as patterns to the whole family. I flatter myself I *have* got something *knowing* in that way! Captain Williams lent me a guitar, which I have tuned like a Spanish one, and spend half the day playing to them all in the garden.

Yesterday we all went to Condover, one of the finest seats in England. The paintings, statuary, study, &c., passed all conception. The Welsh misses walked, and Robert drove "his beautiful cousin" as he calls *me!* Do you know I have had a most extraordinary packet from old Everard; *six* pages! mostly about Dick. He seems afraid his son is going over to marry me; but says he throws himself on my generosity,—and he begs of me to save him from himself, for that without an independence and without industry, a connection of that kind would weigh him down for life. He then recommends him to my care, and begs me to be his preceptress and guardian, that I will guide his actions and direct his study, and to sum up all, he encloses me an order on his banker for twenty guineas for *pocket money!* You know my spirit—the order I returned—and gave him a true and circumstantial account of my acquaintance with his son from beginning to end; assuring him that the expected arrival of his son hurried my *departure* from London; as my obligations to the father precluded every idea of continuing any intercourse with the son, unsanctioned by his approbation. I wrote very proudly and very much to the purpose. He told me you looked well and handsome. (Is he not an angel?) I am not fallen away myself, and enjoy fine health and spirits.

S. O.

Sydney Owenson had so early begun to exercise her own judgment that she was impatient of interference and control. In forming an estimate of her character, it must be borne in mind how peculiarly she had been always circumstanced.

Endowed with faculties for social success—she sang well and played well, both on the piano and the harp—she danced like a fairy (an Irish fairy be it understood), she was very graceful, and if the testimony of the many men who fell in love with her may be believed, she was beautiful. She could tell stories, especially Irish stories, with a spirit and drollery that was irresistible; her gift of narrative was very great; she possessed that rare quality in a woman—humour—and she was as witty as though l'esprit de tous les Mortemart had inspired her. From her most tender years she had been produced in society and encouraged to produce herself; she had the power to amuse everybody; of all personal faculties this gift is perhaps the most seducing and intoxicating to the possessor. Full of Irish fun and Irish spirits she was entirely bewitching. She enjoyed her own gifts, and her own evident delight in her powers was one great secret of her power of pleasing others. From the very nature of her position she was, to a certain degree, an adventuress, for she had nothing, and no one to depend upon, but herself. Her own talents were the means by which alone she could make herself a position in the world.

Sydney Owenson was vain—display was natural to her. She had no mystery, and she never felt the need of either privacy or repose. Her activity both of mind and body was indefatigable. Flattered, followed, admired, she never lost her head, or mistook shadow for substance. She loved flattery—it was a necessary of life to her gay and elastic nature—but she had a wonderfully shrewd appreciation of its actual value. She was conscious of her higher powers and she had higher aspirations than mere social success. Her aspiration was to make her native country better known, and to dissipate the political and religious prejudices that hindered its prosperity. She never used her genius as a vehicle for mere amusement; in her works there was always some principle to be advocated or elucidated. Her social success was the mere overflowing of her life. Neither lovers, friends, nor flatterers, ever turned her attention from the steady, settled aim of her life—and that was to advocate the interest of her country in her writings; and in her own life to set her father free from his embarrassments, and to procure him a provision for his old age.

For this she worked hard. These ideas shaped the purpose of her life, and were to her like a talisman, which she held fast, and they carried her, almost unconsciously to herself, through the changes and difficulties which thickly beset her path.

She was possessed of genius, and there was an indestructible fibre of honesty and reality in her nature that enabled her to resist the attrition of the world. Full of vanity and inconsistencies, she never veiled the one or troubled herself to reconcile the other. She had abundance of good sense, and had firmness enough to abide by its dictates. She had all the selfishness of a woman obliged to fight her own way in the world, and to do the best she could for herself; but she was essentially generous and just. She hated all that was mean or oppressive. She was thoroughly grateful. She made for herself steady friends in her youth, and they continued her friends to their lives' end, and their friendship was kept up by their descendants to the second and third generation. These solid excellences were too often covered by the tide of worldliness and vanity; but they were the solid rock, and were not washed away. Those who knew her best can testify to this. Her love for her father and sister was, in her girlhood, the only sentiment she was capable of feeling; it lay beneath all her vanity and all her acts of display. Her success in society derived its charm from their sympathy; she knew that they rejoiced with her, and were proud of her; her heart always turned to them, and this genuine *home* affection kept her natural in the midst of all that was most artificial in society.

In the course of 1806, Miss Owenson completed her *Wild Irish Girl*. It seemed to set the seal on her literary reputation; but it was only its foundation. She loved praise; but she never wasted a moment in stopping to listen to the voice of her own celebrations. She was incapable of fatigue, and set to work again

at once. The reading and research needed for her
Wild Irish Girl, had given distinctness to her bias
towards all that could illustrate the manners, customs,
ancient history, and present capabilities of what was
then her unfortunate country.

In the autumn of 1806, she made a journey into
the West of Ireland, and there gathered the impressions, scenes, and incidents which she worked up into
two volumes entitled, *Patriotic Sketches*. The language is florid and rhetorical, and the sentiment runs
too much "in the Ercles vein"; but there is a truth
and nature throughout the work which makes the
reader feel that he is in the midst of the scenes described, and that they are drawn from the life.

Miss Owenson had a peculiar faculty for seizing upon
the political significance of the events and circumstances
which passed before her eyes. In the *Patriotic Sketches*
she deals with the political problems which at that
period, and for long afterwards, were thorny subjects
of debate and legislation. She deals with those vexed
questions with a vigour and clearness of insight which
proves her to have been both an earnest and an understanding advocate.

This national sympathy and political sagacity gave
to her national novels a weight and interest, at the
period they were written, far beyond what they would
have obtained as mere works of fiction and amusement; they were read, especially in England, by those
who would have shunned graver works,

"A verse may catch him whom a sermon fails."

She was not a blind, unreasoning partizan. She saw

the faults of her countrymen as clearly as their opponents. She had good sense, and had not only a love of justice, but a knowledge of what justice was—a qualification sometimes lacking in popular advocates. She had generosity, also, which made her eloquent; and she had the gift of putting her views vividly and distinctly before her readers; the romantic accessories never confused or veiled the main point in question.

The topics she discussed in these early works, have long been set at rest. Ireland has had her full meed of justice, and she has now, for a long time, enjoyed both a fair field and plenty of favour. The Ireland of Lady Morgan's days has given place to an Ireland which is fast becoming all that Heaven made it capable of being; it is realising all the gifts and possibilities with which the island is so richly endowed. Lady Morgan's labours to advance this object were in the burden and heat of the day; when, to be liberal, just, and moderate in politics (Irish politics especially) was to be exposed to every species of unscrupulous party abuse and virulence—to be branded as an atheist, and, if a woman, to be taunted with profligacy, and to be considered incapable of any morality. In all she wrote, Lady Morgan was ever conscientious and fearless. She respected her own genius, and always used it to illustrate the opinions which she believed to have grown out of great principles; and no personal consideration of profit or popularity ever turned her aside.

It was during this Autumn journey of 1806, that

the family of Sir Maltby Crofton, Bart., received Miss
Owenson, she used to say, "as a poor relation, in
consideration of the credit she had become to the
family!" She remained many months with them, and
she always spoke of the kindness they showed her.

It must have been with a curious mixture of pride
and amusement that she found herself amid the "old
grandeurs" from which Clasagh na Valla had eloped
with her peasant lover, and which she had never
ceased to regret.

Miss Owenson's steady old friend, Mr. Atkinson,
of the Ordnance Office, kept up a kind and paternal
supervision of her interests. This gentleman had been
as kind and affectionate when she was almost friend-
less as he was in the sunshine of her prosperity. The
following is one of his many letters. It bears witness to the affectionate interest she inspired and kept
up. Lady Morgan never forgot "ancient kindness,"
nor neglected old friends for new ones:—

J. Atkinson to Sydney Owenson.

MELFIELD, DUBLIN,
Sunday, 24th August, 1806.

MY DEAR IMOGEN!

"A rose called by any other name would smell as
sweet." So, in short *Imogen* or *Glorvina*, you are
equally the same. We called, Saturday, at Sir William Homan's, and talked about you. Lady Charlotte
said my tributary verses to you ought to be prefixed
to the *Wild Irish Girl*. Sir William said he was

jealous of me, for he was your *slave;* but I replied I was your *slave* and *blackamoor*, and all this in the presence of Mrs. A——, and Lady Lonsdale, their aunt J—— with them.

I send you a note from *Cooper Walker*, who is in raptures at your novel. You'll see by the papers that *Moore* has very modestly and candidly told the public the nature of the affair between him and *Jeffrey*, who has made him a satisfactory and handsome *amende honorable*, and all is peace again. But he deserves to have his fancy chequered like your ladyship's, which sometimes runs too frisky and floats wildly in the regions of fictitious, indiscreet expression; and, believe me, I am too much the friend of both not to curb your foaming and prancing Pegasus whenever it becomes unruly.

Now, as to your Opera, as I before told you, I like it much; but really it is a pity to smuggle it into an after-piece. I send it, therefore, to you to add to it; you'll perceive some pencilled remarks of mine. There is great opportunity for spectacle and decoration, and the characters, so far, are very well, and the dialogue and songs very appropriate.

I tell you again, it is better to endeavour at a representation on the London stage, both for gain and profit, than here; lose no time, therefore, in adding to it by your fancy and invention. Take care of the rest for your interest. At any rate, in its present incomplete and ill-written state, and without a title, it is not fit to be laid before any manager. You must, therefore, after you have made your alterations, in any way you

choose, get it copied out fairly for a proper book with
a cover. Mind, it is better to write the name of the person speaking above the dialogue than in the margin;
and the songs to be inserted more in the centre, and
distinct from the other writing.

I don't know what name you should give your offspring. Tell me of some, and I'll give you my opinion.

I have at last got your collection of Irish melodies:
it is admirably printed, and I think the words excellent; of course the music is familiar to us. Have you
got a set? If not, if you order one through me I'll
get it forwarded to you.

Had not Z. X. been put to the verses enclosed I
should have sworn them to be yours. Pray keep them
safe for me, I beseech you, for I consider them excellent, and breathe your patriotic tuneful spirit.

With best regards, you'll believe me, my dear Miss
Owenson,

Yours affectionately,
J. A.

PS. Did I send you my verses written at Donning-
ton in 1802, at Lord Moira's, which have just stole
into print?

The following offer from Phillips, for an *unseen*
volume of poems, and the remonstrance coupled with
it are whimsical, and belong to a golden age of successful authorship. Whilst all Lady Morgan's novels are
extant at the present day—having most of them been
reprinted in a popular form within the last few years

—her poetry, with the exception of the sparkling ballad of "Kate Kearney," has passed away and left no trace.

Sir R. Phillips to Sydney Owenson.

BRIDGE STREET, LONDON,
September 29*th*, 1806.

DEAR MADAM,

When you compare me to a Jesuit and a Jew, you must be acting under the conviction of the slavery in which I am held by your fascinations! I would resent such treatment if experience in such matters had not taught me that in struggling against female caprice and despotism, the invariable effect is to draw one's chains the tighter and to make them still more galling and potent.

If I buy the poetry without seeing it, it is obvious that affection gets the better of prudence, and that *you* and not the *poems*, are the chief object of my purchase. On such an occasion, I can only lament that my means are not equal to my inclination. Without meaning to play the Jesuit, I declare that you should draw on me for a thousand pounds, if my other engagements and the profits of my business enabled me to honour such a draft. My personal regard would assign no bounds, if I were not restrained by "Jewish" calculations and "Jesuitical" doubts!

In one word, then, I will give one hundred pounds for the poems, to be drawn for at six and eight months, from the 25th of October; and I will give other twenty-five pounds on the publication of second and third editions respectively. It is my *hope* that this will satisfy you—not from any profit I may derive from the publication, but because I desire to possess a niche in your affections!

The *Wild Irish Girl* begins to move as it ought and as I could wish. Another month's sale equal to this last will occasion me to begin to think of a new edition. Charles Watson read the proofs, and he has great skill in your topics. Send me your corrections directly and I will use them.

The beauties of her younger sisters have brought the *Novice* into vogue, and for every twenty-four admirers of the former half-a-dozen start in favour of the latter.

But really you are too sanguine, even more so than I am; I, who half ruin myself by the *warmth* with which I espouse the interests of those with whom I am connected. You are in the high road to fame and reputation if you will not run out of the course.

Mr. Pratt is still at Woodstock; Dr. Wolcot dines with me every Sunday, at Hampstead, with some others of your admirers. I would not for the whole world tell them of our bickerings and of your hard dealings. Most of them, however (and what men have not), have suffered from the cruelty of your sex.

God speed and mend you, and, believe me, always
Yours, &c., &c.,
R. PHILLIPS.

A letter from the father of Miss Edgeworth has an

interest that dates from "dear long ago," to most readers.

R. L. Edgeworth to Sydney Owenson.

EDGEWORTH HOUSE,
December 23rd, 1806.

MADAM,

I have just read your *Wild Irish Girl*, a title which will attract by its novelty, but which does not well suit the charming character of Glorvina.

As a sincere and warm friend to Ireland, I return you my thanks for the just character which you have given to the lower Irish, and for the sound and judicious observations which you have attributed to the priest. The notices of Irish history are ingeniously introduced, and are related in such a manner as to induce belief amongst infidels.

It is with much self-complacency that I recollect our meeting, and my having in a few minutes' conversation at a literary dinner in London, discovered that I was talking to a young lady of uncommon genius and talents.

I believe that some of the harpers you mention were at the Harpers' Prize Ball at Granard, near this place, in 1782 or 1783. One female harper, of the name of Bridget, obtained the second prize; Fallon carried off the first. I think I have heard the double-headed man. My daughter published an essay on the subject of that prize in an obscure newspaper, of which we have no copy. I shall try at the printer's to obtain a copy, that I may publish it in one of the respectable monthly magazines, with a view to speak my sentiments of your work to the English.

I think it is a duty, and I am sure it is a pleasure, to contribute as far as it is in my power, to the fame of a writer who has done so much, and so well, for her country.

Maria, who reads (it is said), as well as she writes, has entertained us with several passages from the *Wild Irish Girl*, which I thought superior to any parts of the book which I had read. Upon looking over her shoulder, I found she had omitted some superfluous epithets. Dare she have done this if you had been by? I think she would have dared; because your good taste and good sense would have been instantly her defenders.

I am, dear Madam,
Your obedient servant,
RICHARD LOVELL EDGEWORTH.

CHAPTER XXIV.

OLD IRISH HOSPITALITY.

During her stay at Longford House, a real old Irish country-house, Miss Owenson saw a great deal of the primitive manners of the old country gentry. She used to give amusing descriptions of the stately grandeur of these remote "ancestral halls" with the mixture of sordid discomfort. The footmen in splendid liveries somewhat tarnished, with "gold lace galore," coming up to the drawing-room *bare-footed*—unless it happened to be some high festival. The rollicking plenty streaked with meanness of the old Irish housekeeping, and the mincing delicacy of pronunciation in which some of the superfine ladies tried to disguise their brogue were all dwelt on; Lady Morgan used up her reminiscences in a description of a country festivity, a "Jug Day," so called from all the county being invited to drink a cask of claret, sent as a present "from a cousin in Bordeaux." The whole scene is so racy and so evidently a recollection from the life, that the reader who has not read the *O'Briens and O'Flahertics* will be glad to have it in the present chapter, to which in point of time and place it properly belongs:—

THE MISS MAC TAAFS.

THE LADIES OF BOG MOY.

With views as narrow as their sphere of action, and with a sharpness of temperament, concentrated in their own little interests, their eternal expression of their petty grievances and fancied injuries, was humorously contrasted with the remote obscurity of their lives and position. Impressed with the highest sense of their own consequence, full of contempt for all that was not of their own caste, class and sphere, they were yet jealous of the fancied neglect, even of those on whom they looked down, and perpetually at variance with each other. Such as they were, the *Ban Tiernas*, or fair chieftains of Bog Moy, were strong, but not rare illustrations, of the fallacy of those theories which give to the *world* every vice, and to *solitude* every *virtue*. The distance of their residences was considerable, the ways impassable; nothing, therefore, less than some great family festival, like the "Jug day" sufficed to draw together the representatives of the ancient chiefs of Connemara and Tar Connaught, from their nooks in the mountains, or the courts and castles "on the other side of Galway town."

By the great Protestant authorities, the Hawkses and the Proudfoots (and their dependents), these ladies were looked upon like other very old Protestant families, as half Papists and whole Jacobites (a race in those remote regions even then not quite extinct).

The last of the old pack of cards had now been sent out by "Paddy the Post," and distributed through the country. No vague apprehension of who would or would not accept the invitations, disturbed the habitual stateliness of the Miss Mac Taafs. The long contemplated "Jug day" arrived. Each of the sisters sailing about with her hands dropped into the depths of her capacious pockets, gave orders for certain "cuttings and cosherings" on the county, which were always exacted upon occasions.

Tributary poultry and tributary fish came teeming in from tenants on sea and land, in kreels and kishes, with guiggard trout from Lough Corrib, butchers' meat from St. Grellan, and whiskey from every still in the barony. Linen was drawn forth from chests and coffers, which for colour and antiquity resembled the "Singe du Sorbonne;" and mould candles were prepared by the indefatigable Grannie-my-Joyce, which might have come within the meaning of the bye-laws of the town, directed against "candelles that give ne light ne sight."

Cadgers came crowding to the back way, and beggars to the bawn. Pipers and harpers assembled from all parts; and the pipe of claret (*in honour of which the feast was given*) and which occupied the withdrawing-room, that had long served the purposes of a cellar, was crowned with branches, and raised on a lofty bier within view of the guests. As the "Jug day" intimated an invitation of twenty-four hours at least, no particular time was fixed for the dinner. The guests, well aware that they could not come too early nor remain too late, poured in, as their own convenience, distance of residence, &c., dictated. Some came by the coast road, the "tide being out," and others on the coast dependant on high water, sailed at an earlier hour into the creek of Bog Moy; but the greater number, male and female, rode single or double over moor and mountain, "the bog being dry," (an event frequently announced in the invitation), a spigot was given to the holy keeping of Father Festus, for tapping the pipe and filling the first jug.

The gradual "*coming in*" of the "*mere Irish*" as they descended from brake or hill, on saddle or pillion, or on *low-backed cars*, which upon such occasions as the present had a feather-bed and counterpane spread over it, for the double purpose of state and ease, such a vehicle has often transported as much *beauty* and even *diamonds* to the seat of rural festivity, as might grace the dinners of the British metropolis.

The women on horseback were nearly all clothed in the same costume, enormous full-plaited cloth shirts, capotes and calashes.

As the fallen roof of "th' ould withdrawing-room" had not been restored, and the floor of the new one (now the cellar) had never been laid down,—as the dining-room was strictly appropriated on the "Jug day" to its purpose,—the best bed-room, which opened into the dining-room, was constituted into a *salon de réception* for the time being. The room being rarely inhabited, required a fire to render it endurable, and the swallows of Bog Moy, not contented with the chimneys of the Brigadier's tower, had made a considerable lodgment in this room; and on opening the door a sudden gush of smoke rushed down into the chamber, and scattered the ashes in such dark thick clouds, that nothing could be distinctly seen but that the room was crowded to suffocation. "Weary on the smoke," said Miss Mac Tauf. One "dissonant consonant" name followed another, with genealogical illustrations, as unpronounceable as those of the Hebrews; cousinships, twenty times removed, were claimed and acknowledged (a ceremony which seemed to have no end). Several ladies were seated chatting and laughing upon "the best bed," every seat in the room being occupied by the fair portion of the guests, while the men stood in groups in the centre and near the door, all talked gaily and unreservedly—no rustic bashfulness, no awkward reserve. Good stories, *bons mots* and sallies of humour, were plentifully poured forth to enliven the details of country and local topics. As the smoke passed off, it was discoverable that the slough of overall cloth petticoats and capotes had been cast off, like columbine's, and a display of French silks and point lace, of fashions from Bordeaux, and flowers from Oporto, was exhibited, which might have put the *petites-maîtresses* of the capital to the blush, and which proved that the intercourse kept up between the Connaught gentry and their exiled kindred, and commercial correspondents on the continent, was still in considerable activity. Every eye beamed life, and every countenance was full of intelligence, and though the brogue of many was sufficiently obvious, and the prettiest lips made *weavers* rhyme to *savours*, *meat* to *fate*, and *mean* to *gain*, (as Swift did long after he had associated with the Harleys and the Bolingbrokes) yet to voices as soft as the smiles that accompanied them, much might be forgiven on the score of mere pronunciation. At last, *James Kelly, maître d'hotel* and major domo of the establishment, in a most stentorian voice announced, that "the dinner was dished," and the gentlemen, according to order, were bid to "Lade out Lady O'Flaherty, of Limon Field, who, I believe, now that the Moycullens are not to the fore, is the greatest lady in the county; for it's a rule at Bog Moy, that the Milesians ever take the wall of the Strongbownians, and no disrespect meant, neither to the English by descent nor to the thirteen tribes, no, nor the half tribes, since all here are gentry bred and born, and not a Cromwellian nor a Williamite in the whole party, I'll engage."

This exordium being pronounced and followed by a general applause, the lady, the venerable subject of many of Carolan's inspirations, moved slowly on, followed by the O'Maillies (of Achille), the Joyces (of Joyce's country), and others of the great aboriginal families of Counemara and Mayo. Then came the Darcys, the Dalys, the Skirrets, and the Ffrenches, with the Burkes, Blakes, Bells, and Bodkins, and all that filled up the list of tribes and half tribes of Galway, of those who could, and those who could not, claim cousinship. The Protestant clergyman of the parish of Bog Moy (a parish without a congregation), bowed out Father Festus (the priest of a congregation without a church), and the Provost of St. Grellan gave the *pas* to the Mayor of Galway. Sixty persons to be seated! The horse-shoe table, the side-board, side-tables, and window-stools, which, with "a plate on the knee," and "a bit in the corner," at last providing for all. Grace being said, Miss Mac Tnaf stood up, and, with a cordial welcome in her "ye," said aloud, "Much good may it do ye all;" to which all bowed their heads. The striking up of the pipes and harps (outside of the door) announced that the "hour of attack" had arrived. Rounds of beef, which none resisted, haunches of venison and legs of mutton were *entrées* and *entremets*, that required no substitution, and a *dormant* of a creel of potatoes and a bowl of fresh butter, left no wish for more brilliant or less substantial fare, while a vacant place was left for the *soup*, which was always served last. Jorums of punch were stationed round the capacious hearth, port and sherry were ranged along the tables, and the door opening into the withdrawing room, disclosed to view the cask of claret. The idol to which such sacrifices were to be made, on altars so well attended and so devoutly served—and before the palate was blunted by the coarser contact of port or sherry, the new tap was tasted, and it required no skill in augury to divine that the claret would be out before the company.

"Jeemes, is it on the Persia carpet ye lave them dishes; what are the cheers for man?"

James Kelly in vain sought a vacant chair for the dish he was replacing with a tureen of soup.

Before the cloth was removed, one of the party was asked by Miss Mac Tauf (who was passionately fond of music) "Might we take the liberty of troubling you, Meejor, for a song; may be you'd feavor us with 'Molly Astore?'"

The "Meejor," with looks of conscious merit and anticipated success, cleared his voice, and took another glass of claret, pulled up his stock, and fluttered out his hair, and running through a few modulations at last began,

"Had I a heart for falsehood framed," &c., &c., &c.

Applause, loud and long, followed this beautiful air, which, being sung with true Irish pathos and the finest possible voice, produced an enthusiastic effect upon organs the best adapted to respond to such an influence.

"Cousin O'Mailly, I'll take a glass of wine with you, and to your health and song."

"With the greatest of pleasures, madam."

The cloth being removed, James Kelly announced to Miss Mac Tauf, that "the tay was wet, and the griddle cake and Sally Lun buttered an sarved." She arose and gave "The King," after which, the ladies they withdrew to the "best bedrome," amidst many prayers and supplications to remain—always expected as a matter of form from the gentlemen. On the ladies retiring, the claret jugs were again replenished, the punch was placed by Father Festus on the table, and the company continued their joyous orgies till midnight, when the hall was cleared out for the ball.

As many as had preserved their centre of gravity were now busied in looking for partners for jigs and country dances.

Miss Mac Taaf consented to move a minuet with Mr. Joyce (a custom of theirs for the last thirty years on similar occasions). Jigs, danced with a grace and spirit that gave the lovely, animated performers, another "renown" than that acquired by simply "*tiring each other down.*" A supper, plenteous as the dinner, was served up as the morning sun shone upon the unwearied votaries of pleasure celebrating the last rites of the "Jug Day" over a "raking pot of tay," which assembled as many of the party who had not found it absolutely necessary to avail themselves of Miss Mac Taaf's barrack beds and shake-downs. Horses, carriages, cars, &c., then filled the bawn, while sails were hoisted in the creek; and of the merits of the claret there could be no doubt, for not a drop was left in the cask.

Miss Owenson's letters to Mrs. Lefanu, always tell more of her own personal feelings than those to any of her other friends.

Sydney Owenson to Mrs. Lefanu.

LONGFORD HOUSE, SLIGO, 1807.

"Here in cool grot and mossy cell
We rural fauns and fairies dwell."

It is really supremely ridiculous to think by what shabby circumstances and paltry concerns the best

intentions of our friends, and the dearest feelings of
our hearts, are opposed and circumvented in this time-
serving world! For three months back my heart has
incessantly addressed itself to you, without your ever
knowing a syllable of the matter (except instinct or
sympathy favoured the intercourse), and all this for
want of knowing how to free a letter or serve your
purse the deduction of a seven pence! The mere
speculation has so harassed me, that my dear Lady
Crofton's fresh eggs and crammed turkeys have been
nearly counteracted in their nutritive effects; and
though I do look something more substantial than
when I left town, it is like Father Paul, "not *feast-
ing* but *mortification* that *has blown me up.*" Thus
impelled by my *morale* and *physique* (though you paid
the forfeit of a *tenpenny* bit), I must write to you and
prate of *your whereabouts.*

Well, and how are you, and where are you, *belle et
bonne maman?* Are your great stag-eyes as bright
and your arms as white as ever? and do you rise superior to the ridiculous rheumatism, and other contemptible proofs that you are not quite immortal? and
are you sitting in your little boudoir in Cuff Street,
or in your *Cabinet des Fées* at Glasnevin, with the
little stool near your feet that I have so often usurped?
and the little man beside you, I have so often endeavoured to seduce? Wherever you are, from my soul
I wish myself there too, though it were only to talk once
more over Miss Carter's poetical homilies (all of which
should end with an Amen), and to be treated, as I
always am, without any manner of deference to the

red *nightcap* of authorship, or the *bas bleu* of literature; for all you seem indeed to care about it, I might as well never have written a book—been cut up in the reviews, and cut down in the papers; but there is no answering for a want of taste! Since we parted, I have run the risk of being taken up on the Vagrant Act, and have been actually beadled about from house to house like a parish pauper. General Brownrigg's curricle beadled me to Sterling, Mrs. B——'s barouche beadled me to Bracklin, Mrs. Featherstone's carriage to South Hill, Mrs. Tighe's part of my way to Frybrook, Mrs. Fry's to Holybrook, whence I was beadled to Longford House, where, like other vagabonds, I am expiating my past heinous offences by hard labour, though not *spare diet*—in a word, notwithstanding the fatal effects to be expected from the villanies of last winter, "all my original brightness" is not lost, and my "glory, though half obscured," still sends forth some transient scintillations. I write, and read, and think, seven miles a day, and have only to lament that Helvetius on the Mind, Montesquieu on the Laws, or Smith on the Wealth of Nations, have left me nothing to say on the only subject worthy my talent or attention, so, as a *pis-aller*, I have begun a very charming novel, with which I mean to delight the world, if the world will not persist in *delighting me*. What a pity we are never destined mutually to delight each other at the same moment, and that we are still fated to play the respectable parts of two buckets in a well! By-the-bye, a little work of mine will shortly make its appearance

in this world; it is another sketch of Ireland, and
might serve as a—what do you call it?—to the *Wild
Irish Girl.* However, since I sent it two months back,
no tidings have ever been heard of it. So *Vive la
Philosophie,* for I lose only two hundred pounds, and,
heaven knows, how much fame! Now write by return.
I shall calculate the day and hour your letter
should come—so no delay; and when you write, tell
me *how* you are, with all the exactitude you would
to your family physician (to whom, dear, good, kind
saint, my most affectionate regards), and tell me if
my dear, long-suffering Bess is quite well, and gay,
and wicked as ever; and if the infallible Tom is the
same ridiculously-perfect, and provokingly-insensible
Sir Chas. Grandison I left him; and if Mr. Lefanu
cherishes the same unhappy passion as first assailed him
under the shade of a *new straw hat;* and if Mishter
Moses commits the same extortions on people's approbation,
as when he played off his Israelitish tricks
upon an unsuspecting crowd; but before you tell me
a syllable, present my best love and kisses to the whole
dear party without exception; and do you ever see
Mr. W. Lefanu, and does he still waste his sweetness
on a desert air? By-the-bye, that man has committed
a flagrant breach of trust against the confidence of Nature,
who never intended him to

Give up to party what was meant for mankind.

I wish Mr. and Mrs. Le Bas were comfortably
seated in a sledge, driving a pair of rein-deer over the
snows of Lapland Hill, like the couple in the magic

lantern; and that their "*superior friend*" would give a little of those talents to the world which are so much confined to her fireside. I don't know how it is, but I feel I am writing myself into a passion! so, before the paroxysm gets strong, adieu, dearest, kindest and best of friends.

S. O.

It is pleasant to find her keeping up her correspondence with her old pupils at Bracklin Castle; for some cause or other, her connection with the family of her second set of pupils at Fort William, had not ripened into a permanent friendship. The Featherstones had never lost the affectionate admiration with which they had from the first regarded her.

Miss Owenson to Miss Featherstone.

LONGFORD HOUSE,
October 13*th*, 1807.

I was so surprised, and, indeed, mortified by your silence, that at a hazard I wrote to South Hill. I had, however, some presentiment that poor, dear mamma's health was far from being what her friends could have wished. The account you gave me of her danger shocked me very much, for I believe there are not many after her own immediate family that feel a deeper interest in her; indeed, it would be extraordinary and ungrateful were it otherwise, for our knowledge of each other is not a matter of yesterday. Pray present her my most sincere congratulations on her recovery, and assure her I look forward with great pleasure to seeing her well and gay as ever next November; indeed, more so, for this severe attack has, most probably, cleared her constitution of all her old lingering delicacies.

Here I am writing and reading every day until I am black in the face; and eating, and drinking, and sleeping till I resemble nothing on earth but a full-blown peony. I have, not ten minutes back, broken down poor Sir Malby's garden chair with my ponderous weight; little Malby insisted on yoking an old ass and a little mule to it, and then insisted on my gracing it with my presence; so, in I got, he mounted the ass, and away we drove towards the mountains, followed by a flock of ragged children; when, lo! in the midst of a pool of water down came my vehicle, the mule broke his traces, and plump I came into the mountain stream, to the great horror and delight of the surrounding multitude. I am now just enjoying the comfort of *dry clothes;* and while Lady Crofton's maid is actually in the act of curling my unfortunate hair, I am scribbling to you. So much for my morning's adventure.

After an *age* of solitude, during which period a new *face* would have been a matter of astonishment, we have our house at present pretty full; we have, among others, Mrs. and Miss Dowdell (the latter a very accomplished nice little girl), who seem to know your papa and Uncle John, with Sir Thomas and Captain

Featherstone; I believe, they are intimate; we are now, therefore, jigging away, every night, at an amazing rate; notwithstanding, I long for my old solitude again. I like to live either completely *in* or *out* of the world, but a *second-hand* business, a *Birmingham* gaiety, is *woeful!*

I am getting on famously with my new work; there is but one defect in it, namely, I cannot read a line of what I have written,—I wrote in such a furore of authorship! I am sure you will condole with me on the probable loss of my *MSS.* and *bills*, for I never have heard a word about them since I saw you. Lady Cunningham's approbation is *worth* having, I know her character; she is esteemed a woman of superior taste, and 'tis said, contrived to convince the Emperor *Napoleon* his heart was not so adamantine but a woman could melt it. I triumph in Mr. *Goode's* approbation; as much news of that kind as you will, I can take flattery in any way; lay it on with a *shovel* or administer it out of a gallon, I can open my mouth and *gulp* it down—all! I sincerely want to see you all some time in November; but I cannot get dear Lady Crofton to say when she will let me go. Yesterday she said early in November — to-day she talks of *Christmas!* And I am wholly dependent on her, as she takes me herself to *Holy-brook*, 120 miles—*Connaught miles.* I find I shall not be in to *Mullingar* till eight in the evening; now I greatly fear it will be inconvenient for papa to send any kind of a vehicle for me; pray use no ceremony, I can easily get a chaise there; at all events, I think I had better sleep that night at

Mullingar—*advise me*. Well now, bye, bye, dear little gentle Margaret, my love a thousand times to all your *fireside*, and best compliments and wishes; as well as I can judge, I shall kiss your fair hand about the middle of November, as I am anxious to go to *town* before the 1st of December; till then and ever

Most affectionately
Yours,
S. O.

CHAPTER XXV.

A NEW FRIEND AND A BROTHER-IN-LAW.

THE following letter marks the commencement of a friendship which lasted unbroken and unclouded till death set the final seal upon its permanence. Lady Charleville loved and esteemed Lady Morgan; she had a great respect for her as a woman, and a profound admiration of her genius. That Miss Owenson won such a friend for herself in the height of her first flush of worldly success, that she was able to retain her as a friend for life, speaks with emphasis for the sterling quality of her character. Lady Charleville was herself a very remarkable woman, remarkable for her own strength of character and soundness of judgment; a woman not to be led away either by affection or vanity. If Miss Owenson had not deserved Lady Charleville's friendship it would not have been bestowed upon her.

"So many deaths we suffer ere we die,"

that it is a singular felicity when an early friend continues a friend to one life's end.

Lady Charleville was the daughter and sole heiress of Thomas Townley Dawson, Esq.; she married first, James Tisdall, Esq., and after his death, she married, in 1798, Lord Tullamore, who was created Earl of Charleville in 1806.

The letter which will introduce this clever and charming woman to the reader, is endorsed by Lady Morgan, "Lady C.'s first letter to me."

The Countess of Charleville to Sydney Owenson.

CHARLEVILLE FOREST,
June 11*th*, 1807.

MADAM,

I return you a thousand thanks for the honour of your letter, and I can only say in reply to those too flattering illusions, which you teach me to believe at present exist in my favour, that, what though a very few hours intercourse must put them all to flight,— you shall not find me deficient in taste to acknowledge your merit, or zeal to prove it by every attention in my power.

Lady Asgill certainly intended me the pleasure of presenting Miss Owenson, and has a genuine wish to make known a person whom she esteems and admires; but crowds and local matters defeat half the time our most rational objects; however, as neither my health nor taste permits me to lead a life of hurry anywhere, I shall request your company in Dublin the first time I am there, with the select few who are willing to enjoy a little society, and if anything should bring you to this country, I should rejoice in the honour of seeing you at Charleville Forest.

I am, madam, with perfect esteem of your character and sincere admiration of your very elegant talents,

   Your very faithful, humble servant,
    CATH. MARIA CHARLEVILLE.

It is only by the incidental mention of them in letters that we can gather any particulars of Miss Owenson's life at this period. She kept up a constant correspondence with Mr. Walker, who was not only her friend, but her book of reference and her encyclopædia of all things connected with Irish history or antiquities.

Mr. Walker to Sydney Owenson.

    ST. VALERI, BRAY,
     18*th February*, 1807.
      (*In great haste*).

MY DEAR MADAM,

You are perfectly right in enjoying the gay season of life. When time advances, we must be content to look on the world through "the loopholes of retirement," as Cowper says. The delicate state of my health has, in a great degree, banished me from society; but I am not the less sensible to its charms, and do not yet despair, if it should please God, of enjoying them again.

Lady Worthington is an old friend, for whom I have

the highest regard. I beg you may remember me to
her in the kindest manner. She is not only lovely in
her person, but has a most amiable disposition, and an
elegant mind. Cherish her as a friend.

Poor Mrs. Tighe! Still, however, I am not without
hopes of her perfect recovery. Of Lady Moira's
illness I heard last Wednesday, with the deepest concern. I have since heard, with infinite pleasure, that
she is recovering. Heaven, I trust, will yet spare her
many years to her friends. I have no friend whose dis-
solution I should more deeply deplore.

I am rejoiced to find that you have another work in
contemplation. From you more than *common success*
will be expected. Your name (to use, perhaps, a
vulgarism), is *up*; and I have no doubt that your
future productions will raise it still higher. As you
visited a part of the country where society is, in some
degree, in a primitive state, you will, of course, be
minute with regard to customs and manners. You
should also give all the traditions that prevail, particularly those relating to the heroes and heroines of the
metrical tales of the Irish, some of whom, it is said,
may be traced to oriental tales. It is not improbable
but you may have heard stories similar to some of
those which you have read in the *Arabian Nights En-
tertainments*. Keep these hints in your mind when
you are reflecting upon the days you spent on the
shores of the "Steep Atlantic." Allow me further to
observe, that you should look over the Irish historians
(Keating, O'Halloran, Leland, &c.), for such remarkable events as may have occurred in any of the scenes

which you mean to describe. By relating, or referring to such events, you will give a stronger interest to your work. But, above all, do not neglect to describe particularly, all the ancient buildings (either houses or castles), and the gardens. You will thus render your work historic in regard to the early state of architecture and gardening in Ireland. You will, I am sure, excuse the liberty I am taking with you, as I write *en ami*.

I shall embrace an early opportunity of sending you the romances. In the meantime I would beg leave to recommend it to you. Borrow and read Mr. Ellis's *Specimens of Early English Romances*, particularly the first volume. Mr. Ellis read your *Wild Irish Girl*, and was much pleased with it.

I have not seen any of the criticisms on your publication in the *Freeman's Journal*. Permit me, as a friend, to recommend it to you not to disregard the critics. If they should point out any faults (for no human work is perfect), silently correct them in a second edition. Adieu, dear madam. Make my best compliments to your father, and believe (in haste),

Your obliged and obedient servant,

J. C. W.

I think you should look over the antiquity papers on the Transactions of the Royal Irish Academy. Any of the members could get you access to the library, where you might pass two or three hours with pleasure and advantage.

It is not, I am sure, necessary to recommend it to you to avoid all political reflections in your tour.

Miss Owenson had been a *collaborateur* in writing a musical operetta, called "The Whim of the Moment." She wrote the words, and Mr. Cooke, a popular composer of the day, wrote the music, or adapted old national airs. The operetta itself has long since disappeared, but an occasional copy of the songs and music may still be found at old book-stalls. It is quite impossible to guess from them the story of the drama. The scene was laid in Spain. Spanish ladies and Irish lovers, who seem to have escaped from shipwreck, sing pleasantly together. The old-fashioned music lesson for young beginners, which used to be strummed in all school-rooms, under the inscrutable title of "Tink a Tink," occurs in this operetta; it forms the *refrain* of a Spanish girl's song to her guitar:

"Tinkle, tinkle; tink a tink!"

Miss Owenson's songs are lively and spirited, and seem to sing of themselves. There was one charming, rollicking, Irish song, written with a view to her father, all about kissing and fighting. The "shilelah" figures as "This Twig in my Hand," and serves both to swear by and to fight with. Mr. Atkinson wrote the prologue. The operetta was produced in Dublin, before a crowded audience. The Lord-Lieutenant went in state to the first night. It was completely successful; and it was the last play in which Mr. Owenson sustained a character. He had not acted in Dublin for many years previously; and the year following the production of the "Whim of the Moment," he quitted the stage entirely.

One of the few letters existing from Mr. Owenson to his daughter relates to this operetta, and is very touching: it shows how completely Sydney Owenson had become the stay of her family.

Robert Owenson to Miss Owenson.

[*No date.*]

I am afraid my dear *Syd* your little head will be quite turned giddy with pleasure and applause. Your dear sister, my darling Livy, will leave me on Monday, and I should be willing my life should leave me at the same time; for parting with her, and you away, is separating soul and body; remember, however, what I say, *as if they were my last words to you,* that the very first time she finds the least thing disagreeable, that you take her away and send her back to me. She is, I am afraid, in a poor state of health. I have made her take four glasses of wine every day for ten days back, and it has done her, I think, much good. Be kind to her, and keep her two or three days with you before she goes. I got her three gowns, and some other clothes, as well as I knew how. Be sure you meet her at the coach-office on Tuesday evening, and have a coach ready. Bring some *male* friend with you, that she may not be imposed upon. She will leave me in *very, very* low spirits; and God only knows what I hourly feel for her, and what I am still to feel when she leaves me. She goes in the same coach you did.

I think the terms you mention for your farce, hard.

If Cooke is concerned, of course he will exert himself for the benefit.

Paying the full expenses, which I hear will be a hundred pounds, is out of all reason. I would stipulate for sixty pounds, or guineas, at most.

Bargain I shall go up to play for you, and which I think he will not refuse, and it would be a great deal in your way. Phillips, like all the rest, is a thief. Write fully by Saturday night's mail.

God bless you,
ROBERT OWENSON.

The foregoing letter refers to the separation between Mr. Owenson and his youngest daughter Olivia. His circumstances had become more embarrassed, his health was breaking, and he was not able to keep together such a home as was desirable for a young and very beautiful girl. Nothing but the sense of what was for her welfare would have induced him to allow her to leave him. He was proud of Sydney, who was his friend as well as his daughter; but for Olivia he had a peculiar tenderness. Amongst the many friends and acquaintances which Sydney had made for herself, was Mrs. Brownrigg, whose husband, General Brownrigg, held a high military position in Dublin at that time. They had two little girls and they proposed to receive Olivia as governess. Olivia's health was delicate; and she needed care and comforts which her father could not supply. The Brownriggs were most kind and considerate, and treated her as though she had been their own child. The separation that was so grievous to Mr. Owenson, proved to be a most fortunate event. Olivia had been but a short time in the family, when Dr. Clarke, physician to the navy, and a man of high reputation in his profession, saw her and became attached to her. Arthur Clarke was in those days one of the celebrities of Dublin. Small in height, careful in dress, a wit, a musician, a man of science, a lover of quips and anecdotes, a maker of pleasant verses, an excellent table talker, a lion and a lion-hunter, an adorer of learning, and genius, and success; such was the tiny, seductive, and most respectable gentleman, who proposed to the charming sister of Sydney Owenson. Arthur Clarke belonged to the same Irish set as Tom Moore; and the brilliant little men had a good deal in common, especially in wit and song, though Moore had both in far more affluence than his friend. Clarke, however, had more good sense and solidity of character. Soon after his acquaintance with Olivia Owenson began, he made her an offer of marriage eligible in every way; for he was not only a most excellent and intelligent man, but he had a good house in Great George Street, and he kept a carriage, an advantage which a woman must have lived in Dublin thoroughly to understand. He possessed the means of raising his wife above all the harassing anxieties of which she had seen so much. Mr. Clarke offered a home for her father and for old Molly, their faithful servant for so many years. These advantages were too substantial not to be thankfully considered by the beautiful Olivia. Pleasant in countenance and agreeable in manner, as Dr. Clarke was, he was not exactly the man to captivate the fancy of a young girl; but the prospect of a home for her father was an attraction stronger than personal romance, and Olivia Owenson engaged herself to become, in due season, Mrs. Clarke.

CHAPTER XXVI.

IDA OF ATHENS.

Miss Owenson, on her return to Dublin, after her visit to Longford House, had established herself in handsome lodgings, in Dublin, with her faithful Molly Cane for her guardian angel.

She was now very much the fashion; all that was best and pleasantest in Dublin society was at her disposal; she went everywhere, and knew everybody best worth knowing. But what was far more valuable than social success, was the increased number of those who became her true and sterling friends. In addition to Mrs. Lefanu, and her family, Dr. and Mrs. Pellegrini, the Atkinsons—who had all proved themselves friends when she most needed them—the circle now included the Countess of Charleville, the Dowager Lady Stanley (of Penrhôs), with whom she had become acquainted through the interest of the *Wild Irish Girl*, and many others. She had the gift of making friends, and the still more valuable gift of retaining them. No one ever better understood the difference that exists between true friends and pleasant flatterers; and she estimated both at their real worth.

In the midst of the first flush of celebrity, flattery, the homage of society, and the pleasant things of all kinds that at this period came to her, with the consciousness that she owed everything to herself, and had earned her own position, she never relaxed her labour, but held fast to industry as her sheet anchor; she took all the rest at its true value—a tide that might ebb, and not a stream that would flow for ever. She had an intuitive sagacity to discern between what was really valuable, and what possessed mere glitter; but she was none the less delighted at having effected her entrance into high society; it marked the measure of the distance she had placed between Miss Owenson, the distinguished authoress, with a success as brilliant as a blaze of fireworks, and the two forlorn little girls left in lodgings, under Molly's care, with no money to meet their expenses. To the end of her days she always thought of her position in life as a conquest—the titles and equipages of her great acquaintance were to her what scalps are to an Indian "brave," outward and visible signs of conquest, not inheritance. Mrs. Tighe, the authoress of *Psyche*, was one of her intimate friends. Here is one of her graceful notes:—

Mrs. Tighe to Sydney Owenson.

MY DEAR MISS OWENSON,

I have very often thought of you, and the pleasure you kindly promised me since I had last the pleasure of seeing you; but the weather has been so unfavourable for walking, that I could hardly wish you to come so far unless you dined in the neighbourhood, and could steal an hour for me, as you did before; if it should happen that you could dine with us *at five*, on Thursday, it would make us very happy; but I am so uncertain about Mr. T——, that at present I cannot name any other day. You know you promised to try and prevail on your sister to accompany you; but indeed, I am ashamed to ask, to a sick room, two so much fitter for a ball room. If this does not find you at home, do not trouble yourself to send an answer till my messenger can call again Tuesday.

I am, very truly,
M. Tighe.

Miss Owenson paid another visit to England in 1808, in all respects a complete contrast to her journey thither, two years previously. In the *Book of the Boudoir* she describes her first party at Lady Cork's; but now Miss Owenson took her place in society as a guest, not as a curiosity.

The object of her journey was to arrange with Sir Richard Phillips for the publication of a new novel. "Violent delights have violent endings," and the gallantry of the man of the Million Facts was destined to give way over this novel to the trickery of a publisher's dispute.

On her way to London, Miss Owenson paid a visit to Lady Stanley, at Penrhôs; and a letter addressed whilst there to Sir Charles Ormsby, lets us into the secret of a romantic flirtation which occupied much of her time at this period of her life.

Charles Montague Ormsby, was a barrister at law, a King's counsel, baronet, and a member of parliament. He was of Irish blood and of Irish temperament, being a grandson to Charles M. Ormsby, of Cloghan's Castle, County Mayo, Ireland. He was older than Sydney, had buried a first wife, who had left him with a family of sons; was the ugliest fellow and the most accomplished gentleman in Dublin. Sydney Owenson's graces and successes had charmed the brilliant man of fashion and society; intimacy between them ripened into friendship and affection. How far either of these sparkling players in this comedy was in earnest, who shall say? Let the sagacious reader judge.

This letter shows the acquaintance of Sydney Owenson and Sir Charles Ormsby to have stood on the debateable and dangerous ground between love and friendship.

Sydney Owenson to Sir C. Ormsby.

ANGLESEY,
May 8th, 1808, Saturday morning.

I am still here, delighted with everything around me—let me add (and not in the mere vanity of my heart) not undelighting. All here is stamped with a character new and impressive to my fancy. The fine old Welsh mansion, ponderous furniture, and, above all, the inhabitants! The figure and person of Lady Stanley is inimitable. Vandyke would have estimated her at millions. Though old, her manners, her mind, and conversation are all of the best school. She is a wonderful woman! The daughter advanced *et un peu passée*, has a character all her own. Sir John Stanley (the eldest son, and just come into possession of his property) is a man "*comme il y en a peu.*" Something, at first, of English reserve; but when worn off I never met a mind more daring, more independent in its reflections, more profound or more refined in his ideas. He said a thousand things like you; I am convinced he has loved as you love. We sat up till two this morning talking of Corinne. Oswald, Ormsby, and Stanley, seemed to speak and feel with one heart and one voice.

I have found a harp and piano here, and Sir John has given me a splendid little edition of Burns for singing one of his songs. They have loaded my dressing-box with perfumes and such simple things as you know I like. All this brings you to my recollection—oh, what does not? In all my joys and sorrows you have a part. The flattery, the kindness addressed to me here! I think it is all to you it is offered, and it is most gratifying. I have been obliged to sing "Deep in love" so often for my handsome host, and every time it is *as for you* I sing it—people of true taste have but one opinion.

Adieu; write directly to London. I leave this to-morrow.

Aimons toujours comme à l'ordinaire.

S. O.

PS. I forgot to mention in my last, *Parkhurst* was

not on board. I never thought of him—of whom did I think? Ingrate!

A great number of letters from Sir Charles to Miss Owenson remains among her papers; they are certainly the letters of a lover. Miss Owenson encouraged his addresses, and even gave him the pledge of a ring. But they had begun to quarrel long before she left Dublin, and her present visit to England was destined to be the occasion of a violent quarrel, from which their intimacy never thoroughly recovered. It is evident from the letters written by him, that he was very much attached to her and she to him. It seemed probable that they would marry each other; but there was no engagement between them. The intimacy continued on and off for several years, and they were generally quarrelling. He was *criblé de dettes*, and involved in difficulties and embarrassments of various kinds which excited her impatience, and she was a great coquette, surrounded by a crowd of admirers, who excited his jealousy. Ormsby was unable to extricate himself from his entanglements so as to be free to marry again. Miss Owenson, at length, definitely broke with him; but he always continued to evince a friendly interest in her career. Lady Morgan left behind a packet of his letters endorsed in her own hand, "Sir Charles Montague Ormsby, Bart., one of the most brilliant wits, determined *roués*, agreeable persons, and ugliest men of his day!" It was not until after his death that she received back her letters to him and the ring she had given him.

A visit to her relations at Shrewsbury came into this journey to England; but although they were the same, she was not, and she found the place much less enchanting than on her first visit, but she always continued on the most friendly terms with them.

The Lady Stanley, with whom she stayed at Penrhôs, on her way into England, and to whom the next letter from Sydney Owenson is addressed, was Margaret, daughter and heiress of Hugh Owen, Esq., of Penrhôs, in Anglesea. She married, in 1763, Sir John Thomas Stanley, Bart. Lady Stanley died February 1, 1816. They had two sons and three daughters. The letter will explain itself.

Miss Owenson to the Dowager Lady Stanley.

Salop,
Friday, July 28th, 1808.

It is so natural to anticipate the return of hours that were dear to us, and take the enjoyment we can estimate by experience, that you cannot be surprised, my dear madam, if the *Wild Irish Girl* again seeks that welcome at Penrhôs which has been already so kindly lavished upon her. In the midst of the inebriety of London pleasures—of gay connexions and kind and flattering attentions equally beyond the hopes or merits of their object; Penrhôs, its perfumes, drawing-rooms, its gardens, the *strawberry plants*, and above all, the endearing and accomplished circle of its cheerful fire-side, have never been forgotten. Oh! no, the mind and the heart had too many sweet subjects of recollection afforded them to become so far insensible, or not to court their return with pleasure and anxiety.

I shall leave Salop on Wednesday next (2nd of August); I shall stay Thursday at Llangollen, with the Ladies of the Vale; on Friday, I suppose I sleep at *Capel-Cerni;* and on Saturday evening I shall be at Holyhead. Such are my arrangements, if I am not disappointed in a place in the Shrewsbury coach, for I shall not go by mail.

If, therefore, dear madam, you do not repent your kind and flattering invitations, I shall be delighted to pass a day with you in going back to Ireland; but I hope your Ladyship will be entirely governed by your convenience, without taking my wishes or inclinations into the account.

I have brought with me a little plant from London as a companion for the strawberry plant. I do not know that it is very rare; but it is very curious and VERY SENTIMENTAL; I like it selfishly for its resemblance to her whom your kindness touched so deeply. It is a little twining, clinging thing, that fastens gratefully on whatever is held out to its support; it is humble and unattractive, but perennial! You shall, if you please, call it the *Wild Irish Girl*, for I really believe it has no name; and so observe, I imagine it forms a little class by itself. Adieu, dear madam; I request my affectionate *souvenir* to Miss Stanley, and as tender respects to Captain Skinner as you may think prudent to deliver.

I am with every grateful sentiment,
Your ladyship's obliged friend,
SYDNEY OWENSON.

PS. St. Pierre says, a woman always keeps the part of her letter in which she is most interested for the postscript—dare I then add my respects to Sir J. Stanley, whose little *premium* for singing the Scotch songs is now before me.

I send this by hand to Holyhead.

Lady Stanley received her youthful and lively guest. A note, dated Penrhôs, tells Mrs. Lefanu of her doings in London:—

Sydney Owenson to Mrs. Lefanu.

PENRHOS, ANGLESEY, HOLYHEAD.
August 12, 1808.

Since I left London (until within this week back) my life has been so unvaried, so wholly devoted to the irksome labours of my *trade*, that I have not written to you, because I wished to spare you the *ennui* of reading the effects of my stupidity, or being teased with unavailing complaints at the distress of a life no longer in consonance with my habits and my feelings; while that anxiety which never slumbers for YOU—dearest of dear friends—and all that concerns you, depended upon Olivia for information, who always mentioned you in her weekly letter, either *par rapport*, or from what she herself had ascertained. It is from a letter I received from her yesterday, that I learn that that miserable and treacherous constitution, which can keep no pace with your mind and spirit, is again betraying its weakness, in spite of change of air and place. Think of me as you will (and my frequent negligences and inadvertencies must inevitably lessen me in your opinion). I feel towards you the mingled tenderness of a child and friend, and whenever I hear of your ill-health, I suffer not only for you but for myself. I never expect to meet one who shall exactly resemble you; perhaps I may find some one who excels you in one way, and some in another, but it is you I *should want*.

My affection for you is connected and associated with some of the most interesting moments of my early life; it does and must influence, in some degree, the present and future events of my existence—your tender little councils, your affectionate solicitudes, your smiling reproofs, your kind indulgences, dear friend, *they are all present to me*. You are sometimes neglected, and I am a wretch; but never has my heart ceased to love or to remember you—and when I hear you are not all your friends could wish you in health and spirits, my tenderness to you increases with *reprobation* towards myself.

I suppose Livy told you how gaily I closed my campaign in London. Mrs. Sheridan continued her attentions to the last. I spent two dear mornings with lovely Mrs. Tom Sheridan; he was at Lord Craven's lodge, fishing. My six weeks in Shropshire were industrious, but stupid—*à mourir*, I passed two singular and charming days with Lady Eleanor Butler and Miss P——, in Langollen, of which you shall hear an account when we meet, and have been now near a fortnight the guest of one of the most superior women in the world—Lady Stanley. Oh! how you would like each other. She wishes much for the happiness of being known to you; we talked you over this day. She is a woman who has seen much of the world, lived a great deal abroad, and carried away many foreign graces which she has blended with the strongest and most original mind I ever met. She is old, "*mais il y a des graces dans ses rides.*" She has a princely fortune, and though she has one of the finest houses in London, she lives most in elegant retirement on her own estate in Anglesea. I know not when I shall be able to get away from her, but I long much to see you all, and think it will *not be long* till I do. Till then and ever, best and dearest friend,

Most truly yours,
SYDNEY O.

A thousand loves and kisses to Mr. Le F——, to the *Tom*, Bess, and Joes; respects to Silky.

The book goes on *swimmingly*.

A few days later she crossed the Irish Channel, when she was seized upon by all the heroine seekers in the Irish metropolis. A series of visits to the Asgills, Alboroughs, and Arrans, broke upon her time, but scarcely interrupted her new story. At length, she got down to the house of her old friend, Mr. Atkinson, Black Rock, near Dublin. From this kindly home she wrote the following letters, which contain notifications of her works and days.

*Miss Owenson to the Dowager Lady Stanley,
Penrhôs, Holyhead.*

MELFIELD, BLACK ROCK,
Sept. 15, 1808.

Am I never to hear from you, my dear madam? am I to admire and to love you, and to have received a thousand kindnesses from you, and is it all to end thus?

The day after my arrival, I wrote to you and sent you the songs you flattered me by approving. I sent them by hand, under cover to Mrs. Spencer. Of course, you have received them, and I am reduced to the pleasant alternative of believing that you are ill, or I am forgotten. Write me but a single line merely to say, "I am well, and you are remembered," and I will try and be contented.

Since I have left you, I have been in one continued round of dissipation. They have actually seized me and carried me off to this little Versailles by force of arms. I have been on a visit to Judge Crookshank's. I am now with the dear Atkinsons, and I have been a day or two with the Asgills, Alboroughs, and Arrans, and am now going off to the other side of

the country. Poor Lady Arran! what a loss, and
what an unexpected loss is hers. My heart bleeds
for her. I am just returned from visiting her—she
was not visible; but her woman told me she is still
poorly. Lady Cecilia is quite inconsolable.

I write with Mr. Atkinson at my elbow, waiting to
take this into town, and with General Graham and his
lady, and twenty more in the room.

A thousand loves to dear Miss Stanley; if you won't
write, perhaps she will. I shall be delighted to hear
from either.

Miss Owenson to Lady Stanley, Dowager.

September 28*th*, 1808.

I have this moment reached town (for I live at the
Black Rock), and am seated at dinner with Olivia, and
dinner and Livy are all thrown by till I tell my own
dear kind mamma of Penrhôs how much her charming
and affectionate billet delighted me. Mr. Atkinson is
not the only one who longs to know and see you. A
dear family, Judge Crookshank's, are languishing to
have you at their beautiful seat, and many others
worthy of being known to you, long to have you
amongst them. Do, do come; it is Sydney (and
never call me odious Miss O.) who requests it.

Why not come and live amongst us? We are full of
heart—we have some talent, and we should idolize you.

I go off the 8th to the Bishop of Ossory's, and shall

remain till the plays at Kilkenny are over (three weeks).
Then I go to Cork, to General Graham's, who commands there, and proceed with him and Mrs. Graham to
Killarney; so that I shall not return to town till December. Oh, if you would meet me there, I should
have such a nice house ready for you, and on such
reasonable terms! *Do, do* think of it, it would be
worth coming to a *"creature who knows how to love so
well."*

I am just sending my maid over with this to Daddy
Atkinson and to Lady Asgills, with whom I return to
meet the commander-in-chief at dinner to-morrow,
meantime the poor book lies by—heart still taking the
lead of the head in the old way,

Ever yours,
S. OWENSON.

Miss Owenson, notwithstanding that she had her
literary credit at stake, and a half-written novel on
hand, accepted an invitation to join in all the "gaieties
of the season," at the Bishop of Ossory's. How *Ida
of Athens* was ever written at all is wonderful. At
that period she had an inexhaustible fertility of resource, and writing a novel was as natural as breathing, and not more fatiguing. She obtained, through
the kindness of one of her friends, a plan of the City
of Athens, with the different sites marked upon it to
which her story refers. It did not render the story
less romantic and unlike real life, but it showed a commendable desire to obtain all the information in her

power, illustrative of manners and customs, scenes and
places. The next letter to Lady Stanley is from
Kilkenny.

Miss Owenson to Lady Stanley.

KILKENNY CASTLE,
October 13*th*, 1808.

Your kind letter and highly estimated present
reached me two days before I left town, and I thought
the best way to express my gratitude for both, was to
wait until I could address you from a scene of splendid
gaiety, that might enhance the value of my otherwise
valueless letter.

A sentiment of affection and friendship must have
deeply penetrated a heart, which, when united to a
young, a gay, and giddy spirit, turns from pleasure
and amusement, and pauses in the midst of its little
triumphs, to think of the friend that is far away, and
almost to regret the solitude which that dear friend
rendered so gracious to every better feeling.

This, dear madam, I assure you, is frequently my
case, and in the midst of ovntions decreed me, I think
of the sweet walks and quiet crags of Penrhôs; I think
of the mass of black rocks I have so often scrambled
over with Miss "Munchee," of Mam'selle Gavotte,
and the bathing-house; and, above all, I think of HER
who gave the spell, the charm to the whole. I write
to you from a fine old Gothic episcopal palace, and
one of the oldest of our Irish families, and I certainly

write to you from one of the gayest scenes in Ireland. All Dublin has removed to Kilkenny, and seems wonderfully improved by the journey. The Atkinsons, and many of the friends you have heard me gossip over are here. We have crowded and sumptuous dinners every day, at night the theatre (open three times a week), after which *petits* or rather *grands soupers*—and on the other nights balls and concerts. All day we drive about the town and gossip, and in the shops; and we are wearing ourselves to death that we may enjoy life. You would tremble for *Ida*, but I have sent off three volumes to London, the other I have brought to finish here (! ! ! ! ! !), and these are the only notes of admiration that ever will be made on it.

This is my first appearance in this part of my native country, and the attention I receive produces the desired effect; but the little heart is still worthy of you, so don't fear for me. Your gown is quite beautiful, and has been a great ally, for never wardrobe was so called on. Dressing three times a day, without interval or cessation, for dinner and the theatre leaves one's dress quite unfit for the ball afterwards. Now do, dearest madam, if you will not come, write to me. Your kind and affectionate letters, your friendship and esteem, are infinitely more necessary to me than balls and concerts. I hourly feel the strong line of demarcation that exists between pleasure and amusement, and that it is to the heart we must all return. I am indignant against Miss Munchee, and send her no *souvenir*. She is a recluse, and might spare a moment from lilies and roses to ask me how I do. I do not believe a word of the *baise-mains* you send me on her part, but I believe her to be a very ungrateful young woman. Adieu, dearest madam. If you love me, you will write and tell me so,

Your devoted,
S. O.

A note from John Wilson Croker is curious in its voluntary politeness, as contrasted with the subsequent rancour of that critic towards Lady Morgan and her works.

Croker was one of the Irish crowd of Miss Owenson's adorers, and his vanity led him to believe that his person and address were invincible. Miss Owenson, courted by the most wealthy and accomplished men of Irish society, had no eyes for the briefless barrister; not much patience with his audacities and personalities. Croker's talents had begun to make the disreputable noise in Dublin which talents like his always do make in a society loving scandal and sarcasm more than truth, for he had not only published— anonymously, of course—his *Familiar Epistles to J. F. Jones*, and his *Intercepted Letter from China* (papers which no man of good feeling could have written) but the more important essay on *The State of Ireland*. This work had brought him into notice, and was soon after to bring him into Parliament for Downpatrick, when he rose into favour and office by his vigorous subserviency to the Duke of York, then on trial at the bar of public opinion for the sale of army commissions. A man of such attainments and such principles was not likely to find grace in the eyes of Sydney Owenson. But she was civil to him, and he approached her, as will be seen, with what diplomatists call " the expression of his high consideration."

October 19th.

Mr. Croker takes the opportunity of this frank to request that Miss Owenson will present his best respects to the Bishop of Ossory and Mrs. Kearney, and to inform them that he would have written specially to them, but that on his return, he found his brother so dangerously ill that it occupied all his time and thoughts; and that a sea voyage having been advised to his brother, Mr. Croker sails this very day to accompany him to Cork, on his way to Spain and Madeira.

Mr. Croker requests Miss Owenson's pardon for taking the liberty of requesting her to deliver this message to his friends at the palace.

The bitter fruit of Croker's disappointment will be seen by and bye. Meanwhile, there are pleasanter things in our way. Another letter from Lady Charleville. One secret of the preservation of this friendship between the noble lady and the working authoress, was the punctilious politeness and high breeding evinced—there was never the abrasion of familiarity. Lady Charleville placed some valuable prints and views of Greece at the disposal of Miss Owenson, for her assistance whilst engaged upon *Ida;* and it was probably through Lady Charleville's means that Miss Owenson obtained her plan of Athens.

The Countess of Charleville to Miss Owenson.

Worcester,
November 2nd, 1808.

My dear Madam,

I received your letter at Shrewsbury, where I have staid five weeks under the care of Dr. Darwin; from some part of his prescription I have benefitted, and my case seemed to me of that nature which warranted applying to an eccentric practitioner. Life is certainly valueless under torments; and I think it right to struggle with physical calamity, and yet endeavour to be ultimately resigned to the will of the Supreme Disposer of all events.

I thank you very much for wishing for my return to Ireland, inevitably postponed, now, until next summer; I hope in God to be then able to reside where only I feel myself useful, and consequently happy. I am delighted that your last effort promises a fair superiority over your former productions. You should think so, that it may in fact attain it; nor am I slow to believe that every work you shall write the next thirty years will still deserve a higher degree of estimation. A person gifted as you are with fancy, taste and feeling, requires only a correct attention to the language and the ripening hand of time (to prune away juvenile exuberance and consolidate the judgment,) to write well. A woman's writings, too, should ultimately forward the cause of morality and virtue; and, I believe, the novel writer can do more in that way than rigid spirits allow; for we are apt to acknowledge the principles are right that a very lovely object professes, who is skilfully presented to amuse and not to *preach* to us! Therefore, my dear Miss Owenson, much, very much, is in *your* power, who have all the talents to attract your reader, without, thank Heaven! like Madame Genlis, a possibility of the truths you shall *sing* losing their due estimate from the suspicion of hypocritical assertion in the authoress. Quintillian tells us very often that none but a man morally good can ever become a great orator, can affect truly his auditors, or exercise the rights of genius with due effect.

Now I do think, though you may smile at my notion, that you had written with more simplicity and verve, and had less chance of your talent being tainted and sullied, under the humble roof of Mr. Hill, than in the circle you describe to me. Virtuous, laborious life offers no sophisticated views, though sometimes, perhaps, coarse ones; but, from those refined and alive to refinement as you are, you had nothing to fear; whilst empty circles and ignorant fine ladies will taint your nicer judgment, by not offending your lighter tastes, they will corrupt your talents and and reduce you to the vacuum of their conversation, which you must (to mix with them) of course, form yours upon, and they shall (like cards) soon level all distinctions, which talent and genius marked originally out for you, and lead you imperceptibly on to the standard they, as fine ladies, have a right to unfurl with *éclat*, and that is *at best* idle, lively mediocrity!

What did poor Versailles ever do, you should in your wrath compare it with Dublin? . . . . The ghosts of Maintenon, Sevigné, Coulanges, nay, even Fontany, La Valière and Montespan rise against you. Some of them had hearts—and most of them talents; they were at least elegant and refined in the manners of the politest court in Europe. In our days that court showed us, in the Duchess of Coigny, most extraordinary talent; and even in Diana de Polignac, a woman who could write as a gentlewoman and act as a friend. But what can *your* Versailles say or do, that shall tempt the heart of feeling to sympathy, or the eye of genius to rest with complacency upon them? Nature seemed to have intended Lady Aldborough for an exception to this sentence, the world, even their own world, has long since pronounced upon them! And I have felt deeply shocked for what she must have lately suffered.

But, wherever you are, accept my best wishes, burn my nonsense, and only consider it as a proof of the pleasure I find in corresponding with you that I have written so long a letter. And that I am, dear madam,

Your very faithful servant,

CATH. MARIA CHARLEVILLE.

I am on the road to Bath.

The year ended pleasantly with the marriage of Olivia Owenson to Dr. Clarke. She was married to him from the house of General Browurigg in December, 1808, and became a happy and attached wife. Mr. Owenson went to live with them in Great George Street, and if Dr. Clarke had been his son, he could not have shown more tender and constant filial duty to the wearied comedian and musician.

For the remaining years of his life, Mr. Owenson was freed from the anxieties he had suffered for so many years; his declining age was made happy in the society and care of one of his daughters, and in witnessing the increasing fame and prosperity of the other. He had been an exemplary father to the utmost of his power, and he had his reward. The Doctor was knighted by the Lord Lieutenant for his public services, and the son of Clasagh na Valla had the pleasure of hearing his younger daughter addressed as Lady Clarke. Sir Arthur and Lady Clarke wished Miss Owenson also to reside with them, but her love of being independent in all her movements and her many engagements in society prevented her acceding to this; she continued in her own lodgings with Molly for her maid; but Sir Arthur's carriage and house were as much at her disposal as though they had been her own.

CHAPTER XXVII.

FIRST TASTE OF CRITICISM.

Miss Owenson, in spite of episcopal gaieties and dissipation, had finished her novel, *Ida of Athens;* but Sir Richard Phillips, her "prince of publishers," was showing himself tenacious of his "right divine to govern wrong." The exact cause of their quarrel is not recorded, beyond Miss Owenson's declaration, "that he had used her barbarously." She possibly asked too much money for her work,—or Sir Richard had not the same faith in its value, seeing the haste and distractions under which it had been written; he threw up the work after the first volume had gone to press, and Miss Owenson had to look elsewhere for a publisher. The novel was accepted by Messrs. Longmans. There was a good deal of "perilous stuff" in the work, and the letter to her publishers, shows her to be quite conscious of it, and yet capable of taking her own part. Previous in date, however, comes a fragment of a kind letter from Lady Stanley, with a motherly present of a piece of velvet for a dress. Her

knot of true friends kept her from much of the evil
incident to her present position in the world; they
preserved her from the intoxication of over praise and
the ardent sunshine of worldly success; they also
deadened the influence of the envy, malice and un-
charitableness which followed her as dark shadows
upon bright lights; she often used to say that no one
but herself knew what she owed to her friends.

Lady Stanley to Miss Owenson.

PENRHÔS,
January 21st, 1809.

Yes, my dear Sydney, I would we were placed vis-
à-vis in some chimney corner; that I should understand you well, I have no doubt, nor should I laugh,
or rally at your romance, as you call it; for I have
not forgotten the aspirations of a youthful heart, and
I have *some* sense of the fastidiousness of a refined
spirit; and I do think, that somehow, I might be able
to insinuate some little drop of cordial towards the se-
renity of your's. May we some day meet and discourse in peace! but, alack! here am I now in all the
agitation of an impending journey, methinks, a sort
of dreary and perilous pilgrimage, and my thoughts are
all distracted; I dispatch to you, therefore, but these
few hurried lines, just to say I love you well, and to
bid you cheer your spirit; believe me, its droop is but
a passing cloud. Often shall I think of you, and wish
for you, when in that tumultuous yet vague city of

London; think you of me sometimes, and as a being who can feel, yes, and fellow feel; and when you have leisure, and are not in tune for the pleasures of the world, write to me; and farewell, my precious Glorvina.

Ever truly yours, &c., &c.,
M. Stanley.

I am tempted to send you a bit of black velvet for a warm winter garment; 'tis only English velvet, as you will see, but it looks nearly as well as the best by candlelight, and is much wore, and will, I think, be a convenient gown for many occasions, especially at this freezing season.

It has been said that there was perilous stuff in *Ida*. The Messrs. Longman remonstrated against some parts of it; and put Miss Owenson on her defence.

Letter to Longman on his disapprobation of some parts of *Ida*, which he published in 1809:—

Miss Owenson to Messrs. Longman, Hurst, &c., &c.

Great George Street,
December 10*th*, 1809.

Sir,

I am honoured by the attention with which you have perused my work, and obliged for the hints you have suggested for its improvement. I am at all times open to conviction, but particularly so, when I observe great nicety of judgment united to great kindness of intention, as in the present instance; as far as is consonant with my feelings, my principles, and the *true* and LASTING interest of the little work in question, I shall gratefully submit, sir, to your criticisms and alterations. While I regret that my approbation of your judgment in a *general* sense is not accompanied by a perfect coincidence in our opinions in a *partial* one.

Your apprehension that some of my readers will suspect the work of being tainted with the philosophy of the new school of French moralists, and of promulgating Deistical principles, give me leave to say, I think unfounded. I solemnly assure you I am wholly unacquainted with the works of the persons alluded to (except a very partial perusal of Helvetius and the travels of M. Volney come under that head); the habits of my life and situation have all thrown me dependent on my own mind, and have been as favourable to the study of Nature in her moral operations and an admiration of her works in their spirit and their forms, as they have been inimical to that description of information and system which books are calculated to bestow.

Whatever, therefore, are my errors, they are exclusively my own; are, consequently, free from the *criticisms* of common-place imitation, and in an age when human intellect has nearly reached its goal of attainment, the writer who has (in the least degree) the power to be *original*, inevitably possesses the spell to be *attractive*. Were I writing for *certain sects*, or for a *certain class* in society only, some part of your apprehensions, sir, might be justified; but I trust I am writing for society at large. I do not assert it in the egotism of authorship or the vanity of youth, but in the confidence of a mind whose principles are drawn from Nature; and who, FEELING what it believes to be the *truth*, has no hesitation to declare it; but, though sir, your private opinions may harmonize with mine, you will observe that the interest of the persons who publish the work is also to be considered, and in *this* I perfectly agree with you; but it would argue great want of knowledge of human nature in general, and of literary experience in particular, to suppose that a work original in its sentiments, or remotely inimical to an established system of opinion, will, by the boldness of such an effort, be injured in its circulation. On the contrary, the fermentations in public opinion, which it gives rise to, awakens a public interest, and rouses a species of fanaticism in its readers (whether for or against the leading tenets of the work,) which eventually promotes its sale and circulation, and, consequently, the interests of its *publisher*. God forbid, however, that I should attempt to procure emolument to them, or a transient fame for myself, by any other means than by the honest exertion of my little talent, contributing its mite to the well being and happiness of society; and so *invariably true* have I ever found myself to its moral and religious interests, that though I knew it was almost impossible to limit the inference of prejudice and bigotry, yet I did not suppose the utmost stretch of sectarian zeal could have tortured out an immoral or irreligious sentiment from anything

I have ever written, until your letter, sir, suggested the possibility. If, therefore, any correction is made in the conversations between the *Diako* and his pupils (which I submit to *with the very greatest reluctance*) I request it may be with very great delicacy; as there is not a word in them which (in a moral point of view) I should wish to erase even on my death bed, or which I think would be received with *the shadow* of disapprobation by an enlightened, a tolerant, or philanthropic reader.

If I have, in the hurry of composition, asserted that the union of social and selfish love constitute the perfection of human Nature, I have written nonsense, for the union might exist upon very unequal terms, and the SELFISH preponderate very much over the social. I meant to assert that the subjection of the selfish passions to the social or general good of mankind constituted the perfection of human Virtue; but of *human virtue*, I do not believe that any peculiar mode of faith is to be considered, as it must be admitted that a Brahmin or Mussulman, a Catholic or Protestant, may all be perfectly virtuous men, though they differ in points of faith, and that a man who promotes the happiness of his fellow creature is a virtuous man, even though he is a Jew, which is but his misfortune, and it might have been yours sir, or mine, had we been born of parents of that persuasion; for, after all, we must confess, that our religion is more frequently our inheritance than our *conviction;* though it may be both—and certainly, when Mr. Pope asserted, that "his faith can't be wrong whose life is in the right," he broached a much more heretical tenet than I ever wrote, or, indeed, thought, either true or justifiable. I believe, therefore, if you substitute VIRTUE for NATURE, I believe you will find the passage perfectly innocent. As to the allusion to Mr. Addison, you may do with it as you please; I always thought highly of him as a writer for the age he lived in, and weakly of him as a man for any age. His ostentatious speech was false in its tendency, both as to experience of human nature and to the humility of religion. Multitudes of infidels, or even of criminals, have died with equal fortitude and calmness.

SYDNEY OWENSON.

This letter to Lady Stanley shows the natural reaction, after the life of over-work and social dissipation she had been leading for so many months. She was always subject to fits of depressed spirits, though she carefully kept them to herself. In the present case, her relations towards Sir Charles Ormsby had, no doubt, a good deal of influence in producing this discouragement; they had assumed a very uncomfortable aspect.

Miss Owenson to Lady Stanley.

[*No date.*]

I have not answered your letter immediately, dear lady, first, because you advise me not to be in too great a hurry, and next, because I did not find myself worthy to answer it; but, nevertheless, it has been a precious letter to *me*, it is full of the *heart* that I love and the spirit I admire; it raises me in my own estimation, and I turn to it as my resource against that *internal oppression* which at intervals preys on me so heavily; it is but *too* true, dearest friend, I feel that, young as I am, I have lived long enough; my existence (made up of epochs) has given a high and false tone to my feelings, which calls for that *excitation* no longer to be obtained. I live in a state of torpor—nothing touches me—and I resemble some unfortunate animal whom experimental philosophy has placed in an *exhauster*, with this difference, that it is still susceptible of vital powers, but that I am beyond the possibility of renovation. This will all seem romance to you, and you will laugh; but were I sitting with you over the fire, I could make you understand me, though I know it would not be easy to make you *feel* with me; you, who bear about you the animation of the greenest youth! My general apathy enters into my feeling for *Ida*. I know she is published, *et voilà tout!* I dined yesterday at my Lord Arran's, Mrs. Mason was of the party, and I was delighted to be with persons who had seen and know something of you. Just as I had received your last letter, Lady Charlemont came to sit with me, and brought her little boy, Viscount Caulfield with her; it was in vain I sought for your letter, and it was many days before I found it, as my sister's maid had carried it away with some papers. I, however, repeated verbatim to her Ladyship, the flattering things you said of her; so deserved by her, and so happily expressed by you. Dublin is *atrabilaire*, and though I am asked to whatever is going on, I scarcely appear anywhere, except at *les petites soirées* of the dear l'syche.

S. O.

Ida of Athens encountered more criticism than any of its predecessors. It had been written under distractions, of which it bears the traces. It possesses, however, the merit of being very interesting, and extremely romantic. The descriptions both of the personal charms of the heroine, and the declarations of love to which they give rise, are ardent and eloquent, and of an intrepidity which, in these days, would be highly astonishing. Ida is not only a heroine—a houri and a woman of genius—but she is also "a woman of the strictest principle," and never goes even "a kennin wrang;" indeed, we never recollect to have heard or read such logical arguments as Ida sets forth on behalf of female rectitude, nor to have seen such a signal instance of female virtue and feminine imprudence. Her maxims are her guardian angels, and, strange to say, they are strong enough to save her in situations of peril. Although she is pleased to dress in "a tissue of woven air" for a best gown, it is as effectual a protection as the tenfold shield of heavy petticoats in which Knickerbocker's Dutch heroines attired themselves. Ida discourses like a very Corinna about Greek art, literature, morals, and politics, in a manner eloquent, pedantic, enthusiastic, and absurd. The real interest of the book lies in the unexpressed but ever-present parallel between the condition of the Greeks, their aspirations after liberty, their recollection of old glories, and the condition of Ireland at that time. This gives a touch of earnestness and real feeling to what would be otherwise high-flown nonsense. The story is hampered and overlaid with the classical and topographical illustrations, which Miss Owenson had got up with so much diligence.

This novel procured for her the thorny honour of a review in the *Quarterly*—a foretaste of what was to be her lot hereafter! The bitter ill-nature of the article is more remarkable than its brilliancy or its justice; and the ill-nature defeated its object. It would be difficult to find a novel offering fairer mark for ridicule than *Ida*, and the *Quarterly*, in its heavy cannonade, entirely missed it. Lady Morgan was always rather ashamed of *Ida*, and spoke of it as "a bad book;" but she wrote out in it many thoughts and feelings which were fermenting in her own mind, and the novel carried them safely off.

CHAPTER XXVIII.

THE CONDEMNED FELON.

In the month of February, 1809, the incident of the condemned felon occurred. The letters now to be published tell their own tale. It is difficult to realise, in the present day, the disproportion betwixt crime and punishment which then existed, and which, as a rule, neither shocked nor startled even humane and thinking people. Among Lady Morgan's papers is this memorandum:—

"A person condemned to death, after sentence was passed, wrote to me from his dungeon in the confidence that I could save him. I received his letter on the Saturday—he was to be hanged the Tuesday following. I hurriedly addressed, by letter, the Judge, the foreman of the jury, and the Lord-Lieutenant. I procured a reprieve of a month in the first instance, and finally saved his life. The man's name was Barnaby Fitzpatrick, and he had been tried and condemned to death by Baron Smith. The correspondence tells the rest."

S. O.

Miss Owenson to Baron Smith.

February 22, 1809.

Sir,

An unfortunate man, who was yesterday found guilty before you for the embezzlement of a bank post-bill out of a letter, was induced to cherish a faint hope of salvation from your eloquent and humane charge to the jury. To this hope he still clings, not from the consciousness of an innocence he cannot plead, but from the belief that you, sir, who seemed to think one solitary instance of error in the life of a human being was scarcely sufficient in the eye of morality or of mercy to extinguish that life; and that as one whom a transient weakness seduced, or a temporary distress impelled—as a father and a husband, he might awaken your interest in his unhappy destiny, and by benevolently recommending him to the mercy of the Lord-Lieutenant, restore him to a life of future honesty and exertion—to a young and helpless family who depend solely upon his exertions for subsistence and support.

For myself, sir, I am at a loss almost to account, still more to excuse, the liberty I take in thus presuming to address you; but your character has been long known to me.

SYDNEY OWENSON.

Miss Owenson to Sir Charles M. Ormsby.

A circumstance of *life and death* induces me to write to you. An unfortunate man—a husband and a father—was found guilty, two days back, of embezzling a bank note out of a letter. There were many extenuating circumstances in his favour; his judge felt them, and recommended him to the mercy of the jury; but in vain. The wretched man sent to me (why I know not) to request I would use my interest with Baron Smith, who spoke so eloquently in his favour—this was late yesterday. I sent instantly to him; but he had gone to the country. I wrote a petitionary letter which he did not get till this morning in Court; I have yet received no answer. I have been all day driving about to try my interest; but all my legal friends were engaged on business. Pray let me know, by a line, *any time to-morrow before two o'clock*, to whom I ought to apply, or what can be done? If Smith recommends him to the Duke's mercy, or if I get a memorial presented to the Duchess, will it be of avail? The interest I take in a wretch who thus throws himself on me is beyond all expression.

Pray forgive this liberty, this trouble; it is my *dernier ressort*. I should not like to commit myself unavailingly by getting a memorial presented to their Graces. You, perhaps, know to what purpose I should do it. I fear you cannot read this; I write it in a carriage at Lord Arran's door.   S. O.

Baron Smith to Miss Owenson.

COMMISSION COURT,
February 24th, 1809.

MADAM,

I am just favoured with your letter of the 22nd. Your benevolent interference on behalf of the unhappy man whom it regards, required no apology; and as I concur in the sentiments and opinions which you express, it is with deep and unfeigned concern I communicate my apprehensions that I shall not be able to second your humane wishes in the degree in which it would be my inclination to co-operate with them. I fear that under the circumstances of this case, a recommendation, *coming from the judge*, of this poor man to mercy, might neither be considered as justifiable, nor produce the desired effect.

I agree entirely with you, madam, in thinking that the principles of moral justice would not be infringed by an occasional extension of mercy, under special circumstances, to the case of offences, which, like the present, are not of great enormity in the criminal scale. But taking into consideration the pernicious consequence, in the present state of society, of such transgressions, not only the Legislature has annexed to them the punishment of death, but Government, I am afraid, is accustomed upon these occasions, to act with a severity bordering upon rigour.

I, however, have to add, that any co-operation with your compassionate wishes, compatible with a due regard to the (sometimes painful) duties of my situation, which you can suggest, you also may command. In the mean time, your good sense and your humanity will demonstrate to you the necessity for discouraging those expectations of mercy, which are but too likely to be disappointed; and, in short, for preparing this poor man and his friends for the worst.

Applications to Government in his behalf might, perhaps, especially in the first instance, come from another quarter; at once more correctly and more efficaciously than from me. For the making of such applications I will give you a reasonable time; and, as I have already mentioned, shall be happy to receive from you the suggestion of any step which, consistently with my duties, I can take towards saving the life of this unhappy young man.

With many thanks for the obliging terms in which you have been pleased to express yourself with respect to me,

I have the honour to be,
Madam,
Your most obedient
and very humble servant,
WILLIAM C. SMITH.

Miss Owenson wrote again, begging an interview with the judge. To this letter Baron Smith replied:—

Baron Smith to Miss Owenson.

DEAR MADAM, *February 27th*, 1809.

I am just favoured with your letter, and assure you that the compassionate anxiety which you feel, and the consequent exertions which you make, and which I think are highly honourable to you, I am very far from considering as importunate.

I cannot see the slightest objection (quite the contrary) in point either of prudence or propriety to the step which you suggest. I will do everything in my power towards having the honour of paying you my respects between one and two o'clock to-morrow.

I have the honour to be, my dear Madam,
Your obliged and humble servant,
WILLIAM SMITH.

The first consequence of this intercession was a respite of execution for a month. Baron Smith communicated this result to Miss Owenson.

Baron Smith to Miss Owenson.

February 28th, 1809.

MADAM,

In order to afford time for any interference which may take place on behalf of the unfortunate person in whose fate you take an interest, and, on the other hand, to avoid exciting hopes which it might be cruelty to encourage, I have appointed Saturday, the 25th of March, for the execution. I think it right to apprize you of this fact without delay, and

Have the honour to be, Madam,
Your most obedient and very humble servant,
WILLIAM SMITH.

She also wrote an eloquent appeal to the Duchess of the Lord Lieutenant. This appeal she entrusted to Sir Charles Ormsby, whose friendship for her had survived their old and unforgotten flirtation. There is an air of coquetry in the letter which enclosed the note addressed to her Grace.

Miss Owenson to Sir Charles M. Ormsby.

I enclose you the letter for her Grace. St. Augustine be your speed (who was the patron of all pretty women, and of course *your* titular saint as well as mine).

I should wish that if you did not dine at the Park to-morrow, or the day after, you would enclose my letter directly to the Duchess, as I wish her to have it whilst she reigns lady paramount, and before the Duchess of Richmond comes over. This is the season for urging requests—so let us make hay, &c., &c. Seriously and without sentiment, my dear friend, rally your *deceased feelings* in my favour. I depend on you for ONCE—*forget yourself* and remember *me*.

S. O.

Lady Morgan, who kept copies of all the correspondence about Barnaby Fitzpatrick, must have read this note in afterlife; perhaps have felt that, as manners had changed since 1809, it was open to misconstruction. She has carefully endorsed it: "This application was relative to a poor man condemned to death." The next letters are from the judge, and show that her humane design succeeded.

Baron Smith to Miss Owenson.

March 3rd, 1809.

DEAR MISS OWENSON,

I return you many thanks for your Athenian air, and the *bon voyage* by which it is accompanied. I this day received and answered a letter from Sir Charles Saxton, and sincerely wish that what my duty permitted me to say, may tend to the accomplishment of your humane wishes. I have not yet received any memorial from the jury. If, and when I do—it shall be transmitted without delay.

I shall proceed upon my journey at an early hour to-morrow. But the memorial can be sent after me; and if it form a bulky packet, Mr. Taylor will give an official frank.

With best wishes for the speedy and complete re-establishment of your father,

I remain, dear Madam,
Your obliged and humble servant,
WILLIAM C. SMITH.

PS.—Since writing my acknowledgments of Miss Owenson's note, I am favoured with her second, enclosed along with the memorial. This latter shall be forwarded to Government at an early hour to-morrow.
Friday evening.

Baron Smith to Miss Owenson.

DERRY,
March 24th, 1809.

MADAM,

I had at Lifford the honour of receiving your letter relative to the case of Barnaby Fitzpatrick.

Upon a reference to me, by his Grace the Lord-Lieutenant, I had, before my leaving Dublin, delivered my opinion that the ends of justice and mercy would be reconciled by extending a pardon to this convict, on the terms of transportation.

As I apprehend it to be usual, when Government calls for the opinion of a judge, to abide by his recommendation, perhaps some hopes may be founded on the usage in this respect. But whatever hopes you, madam, may indulge, I must strongly dissuade you from encouraging the unfortunate man in whose fate you take an interest, from entertaining any; both because the prerogative of mercy is not in my hands, and that from the Government (whose wisdom and clemency are to decide upon this case,) I have not been favoured with any communication of their intentions; and, consequently, am ignorant whether they mean to neglect or attend to my recommendation. I have further to apprize you, that the day after to-morrow is appointed for the execution.

I have the honour to be,
Madam,
Your most obedient
and very humble servant,
WILLIAM C. SMITH.

Baron Smith to Miss Owenson.

NEWTOWN FARM,
April 7th, 1809.

DEAR MADAM,

I am this moment favoured with your very obliging letter of the 5th; and have sincere pleasure in felicitating you on the success of your interference on behalf of poor Fitzpatrick. To me he is not under the slightest obligation. I have done no more than, my duties as a judge permitting, my duties as a man required.

To the clemency of Government, indeed, I feel that he is much indebted; and it must afford you great satisfaction to reflect—that your compassionate exertions have essentially contributed to procure for him the mercy which he has obtained.

With every respect for the humane feelings which led to those exertions,

I have the honour to be,
Dear Madam,
Your sincere and obliged humble servant,
WILLIAM C. SMITH.

CHAPTER XXIX.

1809—FRIENDS AND COUNTRYMEN.

This girl's letter from Miss Stanley is amusing for its details of fashions long since changed.

Miss Stanley to Miss Owenson.

23, NEW NORFOLK STREET,
March 20th, 1809.

With the greatest pleasure and ease have I executed your little commission, and only hope it will meet with your approbation. I should have been something happier had you given me a hint of about what breadth you would have liked it, but what I have sent is between broad and narrow; and should you like more of that kind, or any other, pray send me a line, and I can procure it with the greatest ease. You particularly mentioned *mitred* lace, but I think the present fashion rather runs on the scolloped edge.

I shall be very glad of a few lines from you, announcing the arrival and your opinion of the lace, but let the money remain in your possession till a better opportunity. I had almost forgot to tell you the price. I, myself, did not think it dear; it was nine shillings a yard. And now, as I am writing from London, you will perhaps expect some account of the fashions; I am afraid I can give you but a very imperfect account, for I go out but very little, and have not been at any smart parties; but the greatest novelty is gold lace, which in a morning appears on hats and pelisses, and in the evening on the head and on gowns; and you may wear a broad gold girdle and clasp with any gown you like. They now wear the girdles rather broad, and it is by no means necessary they should be a piece of the gown, as formerly. Very few white muslins are to be seen; either velvet, cloth, gauze, crape or coloured muslins. Waists are making a bold attempt to get long, but I do think a very long waist gets stared at. Young ladies are certainly very economical in the quantity of materials they put in a gown, for I saw a few the other night who looked as if they were sewed up in bags. Spanish hats, turned up in front, with feathers, are a good deal worn; but the account I now give you is but the winter one, and in about a month the spring fashions may have more novelty; but I dare say I have told you of nothing but what you already know, for fashions must pass with great rapidity from London to Dublin. I imagine you at present in the height of gaiety. London is said to be very dull at present. I go out so very little that I know not what is going on. Alas! one pleasure is greatly curtailed: only think of the two great theatres burnt to the ground within five months. I have not yet been to the opera, but I hear the singing is very bad, but the dancing tolerable. I think our stay in London will not be much longer.

Good bye, then, dear Miss Owenson, and believe me to remain ever,

Yours sincerely, &c.,
EMMA STANLEY.

I have just heard that the Duke of York has resigned.

Few letters are better worth reading than Lady Charleville's, and her criticism on *Ida* is in curious contrast to what such a novel would suggest in these days. Although "social evils" and "pretty horse-breakers" are discussed with composure, as familiar themes, so much rhetorical female virtue in such hazardous situations as abound in this Greek novel, would drive the whole class of readers from their propriety.

The Countess of Charleville to Miss Owenson.

41, GROSVENOR STREET,
May 1st, 1809.

DEAR MADAM,

I hasten to do away any painful impression you could feel at my silence. I never received any letter from you since I left Weymouth, which I answered from Shrewsbury. Your politeness and kind inquiries for my health, after my having the pleasure of being known to you in London, were quite flattering, nor could I imagine, so well employed as your pen may always be, that it was to be trifled with often in casual correspondence. The expression of solicitude for me now, I beg to offer you ten thousand thanks for; and though I have nothing comfortable to say of my miserable confirmed state of suffering, yet it is certainly a sort of alleviation to think I have obtained sympathy more than common, from so amiable a mind as yours.

I read *Ida* before it was all issued from the press, a volume being sent me as soon as sewed: and I read it with the same conviction of the existence of excellent talent, great descriptive powers; and in this work I find particular ingenuity, in the novel attempt to interest us for a woman who loved *two;* and for each of the lovers, the episode was happily contrived in this plan and executed with great taste and spirit.

I could have wished the situations had been less critical in point of delicacy, as the English gentleman has incurred great blame from all sides for having suffered her to escape; and the poor Turk too. The politics of Athens are ingenious; but, alas! our poor Emmet hanging so recently in our streets, does not suffer us to enjoy our miseries in any fiction for some years to come.

I have not read the *Monthly Review*, where it is criticised. I choose to be pleased with what you write now; though I do heartily reprobate your putting off the period of polishing and purifying your language for pique to those censors, who, after all, may be the best of friends, if they point out a path so attainable to fame. Assuredly to those whom God has given fancy, and a touch of the ethereal spark, it is doubly a duty to write pure language, under the penalty of else rendering the very best gift of heaven valueless. Where little is to be done, it is inexcusable to neglect that; and assuredly you promised me that *Ida* should be more correct than your former publications, even, as you imagined, at the expense of fancy . . . . . Now we found as much imagination as ever, and not more of the square and compass than hitherto.

Now I hope I have fulfilled your notions of goodwill by this essay on the fair Greek, and at all events effaced every idea you could have conjured up to scare away the recollections of politeness and sympathy for my sad state which you have often so prettily and kindly expressed.

C. M. CHARLEVILLE.

This amusing letter of criticism and compliment, very Irish and jolly, from Sir Jonah Barrington, whose Memoirs, when subsequently published, made such a noise, reached Miss Owenson at the Marquis of Abercorn's.

Sir J. Barrington to Miss Owenson.

Friday, 5th July.

MY DEAR MISS OWENSON,

I hasten to acknowledge the receipt of your letter, not because it is friendly, nor yet because it is flattering, but simply because it was yours. Fate, alas! my grand climacteric is in view—my years are beginning to outnumber my enjoyments, and abominable fifty tells

me I must now present to Glorvina and to Ida that
incense which in my early days would have burned at
the shrine of their mistress; I therefore cannot afford
to lose a single pleasure, and your letter was a substantial one.

When your note arrived I was merged in politics—
my circulation was moving historically slow—the head
was in full operation—the heart a-slumbering—of
course my state was drooping, and the theory of patriotism was sinking under the pressure of application.
You changed the scene. Refreshing ideas crowded on
my fancy, and gave birth to some of the best sentences
I ever wrote in my life.

What an advantage you writers of *fiction* have. If
Homer and Virgil had been confined to fact they
would have been wretched poets. Milton triumphs
over Hume because he treats of impossibilities; and
Ovid eclipses Sir Richard Musgrave because he is
somewhat more incredible. Fiction is liberty—fact,
incarceration. Our correspondence is unequal—you
write to a slave, I to a free woman; and I plainly see
I must either curb my volatility or give up my reputation. In truth, I hate bagatelle—I wish it was high-
treason. It has been my bane all my life, and you see
I am trying to get rid of it. Be assured that in these
days a good steady impostor, who cuts out his risible
muscles, and ties his tongue fast to his eye-teeth, is the
only person sure of succeeding, or, indeed, countenanced in rational circles; and as I have undergone
neither of these operations I intend to die in obscurity.

But come, I had better stop this sort of farago in

time, or Heaven only can tell where it might end. I have heard of a tragic poet who went on very well until he wound himself up to the enthusiasm of composition, and gave a loose rein to the flames of sublimity; but having at length written:

"When gods meet gods and jostle in the dark,"

the idea expelled his reason, and he went stark mad.

Of all your characters I love Glorvina most. I hate to doubt of her existence—like a she Prometheus (as you are), I believe you stole a spark from Heaven to give animation to your idol. I say all this because I think the society in which one writes has a great influence over their characters. You wrote the *Novice* in retirement—you wrote *Glorvina* in your closet—but you wrote *Ida* in Dublin; and depend upon it, if you are writing now, you will have your scenes and character in high life—Lady B—— to the Duke of Q——, and Lady Betty F—— to the Countess of Z——. I really think luxury is an enemy to the refinement of ideas. I cannot conceive why the brain should not get fat and unwieldy as well as any other part of the human frame. Some of our best poets have written in paroxysms of hunger. I really believe even Addison would have had more point if he had less victuals. I dined a few days ago with the Secretary, and never could write a word since, save as before mentioned: and in the midst of magnificence and splendour, where you now are, if you do not restrict yourself to a sheep's trotter and spruce beer you will lose your simplicity, and your pen will betray your luxury. I hope in a few days to get the better of the Secretary's dinner, and resume my labours for your amusement and that of Lord Blaney, to whom I beg my best regards.

Upon reading over this letter it is easy to perceive my head is not perfectly settled. Have you any recipe to cure a wandering fancy? If you have, do let me have it, and you will, if possible, increase the esteem with which I am.

Very faithfully yours,
JONAH BARRINGTON.

One of her friends at this time, whose notice she considered a distinction, was Richard Kirwan, of Cregg Castle, in the county of Galway, one of the most ancient and respectable families of Connaught, a province where few families condescended to date from a more modern epoch than the *flood*.

The Kirwans are the only aboriginal family who were admitted into the thirteen tribes of Galway. "As proud as a Kirwan," is a Galway proverb.

Richard Kirwan was a distinguished chemist; and there is an account of him in the *Book of the Boudoir*.

Mr. Kirwan induced Miss Owenson to write a *History of Fictitious Literature*, which was published many years after as a magazine contribution. Miss Owenson gathered her materials diligently; but they always retained their alluvial character; they were brought together by the reading of the moment, and likely to be carried away by the next current that set in. Nothing she read ever seemed to become assimilated by the action of her own mind—everything retained

its form as imported from books. Her mind was too
active and incessantly in action; she lived too much
on the surface, and amid the turmoil of passing events,
to leave her time or inclination for meditation. She
allowed neither facts nor sentiments to sink deeply.
Whatever information she obtained (and she was always reading and picking up facts and opinions) was
reproduced immediately, either to illustrate the subject
upon which she might be writing, or to decorate her
conversation as a quotation or allusion. A vivid imagination, and a lively fancy threw off bright, glancing
lights, and made her allusions to facts in history or
philosophy, as brilliant as pebbles under a flowing
brook in the sunshine; but they did not indicate any
deep vein of quiet thought. She had vivid instincts
and a quick insight into things; but she hated to dwell
upon any subject.

CHAPTER XXX.

DR. MORGAN AND DR. JENNER.

As yet, Miss Owenson had not met the man who was to win her from the vanities of her own fancy. At this date of 1809, Thomas Charles Morgan, doctor of medicine, was mourning over a dead wife, tenderly nursing a little girl, the child of his lost love, helping Dr. Jenner to make people believe in vaccination, struggling into London practice, and proceeding to his degree of doctor in medicine. Morgan had been born in London, in 1783, being the son of John Morgan, of that city, and his early life had been spent in the neighbourhood of Smithfield. He was several years younger than Miss Owenson; in later life Lady Morgan confessed to having two years of disadvantage over Sir Charles: but the unromantic truth may be set down without exaggeration at three or four. From the Charter House, he was sent to Cambridge, where, in 1801, he graduated at St. Peter's, and, in 1804, took his degree of M.B.; thence he removed to London, set up in his profession, became a member of the College of Physicians, and entered heart and soul into the controversies about cow-pox and small-pox. Handsome, witty, prosperous, with a private income of about £300 a-year, and the prospect of a great name in his profession; he was not long left to the miseries of a bachelor's life. Miss Hammond, daughter of Anthony Hammond, of Queen's Square, then a fashionable part of town, the residence of judges, privy councillors, and bankers, became his wife, but died in about a year, in giving birth to her child. Little Nannie was left the Doctor's chief playmate; while his serious study was bestowed on his profession, little dreaming of the brilliant distraction then preparing for him in Dublin.

Jenner's letters to him are well worth reading; and there will be no need for any apology in introducing some of them, episodically, at this early stage. They show the difference between the condition of a hero, after he has been accepted by posterity, placed in his niche, and his reputation rounded into "one entire and perfect chrysolite," in which nobody sees any flaw, and the same man when he was alive—his views misunderstood, he himself painfully struggling against ignorance and calumny, and his heart nearly broken by petty vexations and hindrances. Jenner is now an acknowledged benefactor to the human race, he has a statue in London; but it was scant reverence that "hedged him," and small justice he obtained in the days of his life. Dr. Morgan was the friend and supporter of Jenner in the time of contradiction, and it is pleasant in the correspondence which passed be-

tween them to remark the tone of cordial respect in
which Jenner addresses him.

Dr. Jenner to Dr. Morgan.

BERKELEY,
December 20, 1808.

MY DEAR DOCTOR,

There is nothing enlivens a cottage fire-side, remote
from the capital, so much as a newspaper. The *Pilot*
of last night was particularly cheering, as it told me
you had finished your academic labours and received
your honours. Allow me to congratulate you, and to
assure you how happy I shall ever be in hearing of
anything that adds to your fame, your fortune, or
to your general comforts.

The horrid fever my eldest son has undergone, has
left him quite a wreck; but I don't despair of seeing
him restored. I should be quite at ease on the subject, if a little cough did not still hang upon him, and
too quick a pulse.

The Regius Professor of Physic in the University of
Cambridge, corresponding with the contemptible editors of that miserable catch-penny Journal, the *Medical Observer !!!* What phenomenon, I wonder, will
vaccination next present to us? Atrocious and absurd as this man's conduct has been, there will be a
difficulty in punishing him, as he seems insensible to
everything but his own conceit. However, he is in
able hands, and my excellent friend Thackeray (to

whom I beg you to remember me most kindly) I know will not spare him.

Sir Isaac has certainly out-blockheaded all his predecessors. Pray tell me what is going forward. Alas! poor thing! He has been too daring, and I tremble for his fate. The scourge is out, and I don't see that he erased a single line that was pointed out to him as dangerous. This venomous sting will produce a most troublesome reaction, and injure the cause it was meant to support. You know the pains I took to suppress it; but all would not do.

I have not heard anything of the new Vaccine Institution since my arrival here, except a word or two from Lord Egremont, who says the Ministry are so incessantly occupied with the affairs of Spain, that matters of a minor consideration cannot at present be attended to. I shall thank my friend in Russell Square, for the communications which, through you, he was good enough to make to me, but am of opinion that the proper time to object will be when anything objectionable rises up. Whatever is going forward either in the College or out of it, is at present carefully concealed from me. The proposition hinted at by Dr. S———, respecting an equal number from both Colleges to form the Board, I mentioned to Sir Lucas as the certain means of keeping off those jealousies which otherwise I thought would show themselves.

It affords me great pleasure to assure you that your pamphlet is *much* liked by all who have read it in this part of the world, and by no one more than by myself. A few trifling alterations will be necessary for the *next edition*. I think you may be more copious in your extracts from some of those letters of which Murray availed himself. By the bye, it might not be amiss, perhaps, if, by way of firing a shot at the head of your knight, the extract from Sacco's letter (see Murray's Appendix) and that from Dr. Keir, at Bombay, were to appear in the Cambridge newspaper.

With the best wishes of myself and family, believe me, dear Doctor,

Most faithfully yours,
EDW. JENNER.

Mr. Jenner to Charles Morgan.

BERKELEY,
March 1st, 1809.

MY DEAR SIR,

I ought to make a thousand apologies to you for suffering your last obliging letter to remain so long unanswered. Did my friends whom I serve in this manner but know the worrying kind of life I lead, they would soon seal my pardon. However, I feel myself now more at ease than for some time past, having crept from under the *thick*, *heavy* Board, which so unexpectedly fell upon me and crushed me so sorely. To speak more plainly, I have informed the gentlemen in Leicester Square, that I cannot accept of the office to which they nominated me. Should the business come before the public, as I suppose it will, I am not afraid of an honourable acquittal. Never was anything so clumsily managed. If Sir Isaac himself, instead of Sir Lucas, had taken the lead, it could not have been worse, as I shall convince you when we come to talk the matter over. By the way, what is become of this right valiant knight? Thackeray, I hope, has not done exchanging lances with him, unless he is ashamed of the contest. I was glad to see your pamphlet advertised on the *yellow cover*. Give it as much publicity as you please, and remember, you are to draw on me for all costs. Does it go off, or sleep with the pages of Moseley? Opposition to vaccination seems dead—at least in this part of the world we hear nothing of it. Through a vast district around me, I don't know a man who now ever unsheaths that most venomous of all weapons—the variolus lancet; and the small-pox, if it now and then seizes upon some deluded infidel, soon dies away for want of more prey.

I have not written to my friend Dr. Saunders a long time, but if you see him, assure him he shall hear soon from me. If he considers the business between me and the Board, and looks steadfastly on all its bearings, I am confident he will not condemn my conduct. If it should be thought of consequence enough for an inquiry, I shall meet it with pleasure; but, though I say "with pleasure," I had much rather they would let me alone, and suffer me to smoke my cigar in peace and quietness in my cottage.

My boys are better. How is your little cherub?
   Adieu, my dear Sir,
     Most truly yours,
       EDW. JENNER.

Mr. Jenner to Charles Morgan.

BERKELEY,
11th July, 1809.

MY DEAR SIR,

You have some heavy accusations I know to bring against me on the subject of my long silence. I have no other excuse to offer you than that of pecuniary bankrupts, who have so many debts, that they discharge none. However deficient I may have been in writing, I have not been so in thinking of you and your kind attentions. If you have seen your neighbour Blair lately, he must have told you so.

You supposed me at Cheltenham when you wrote last. Unfortunately, I have not yet been able to quit this place, and have been detained by a sad business, the still existing illness of my eldest son, the young man who was so ill when I was in town. His appearance for some time past, flattered me with a hope that he was convalescent, but to my great affliction he was seized on Saturday last with hæmorrhage from the lungs, which returned yesterday and to-day exactly at the same hour, and almost at the same minute—seven in the morning. This is a melancholy prospect for me, and I scarcely know how to bear it. The decrees of Heaven, however harsh they may seem, must be correct, and the grand lesson we have to learn is humility.

I wrote two long argumentative letters to Dr. Saunders soon after I received your hint, on the subject of the new institution; but from that time he has dropped his correspondence with me. When next you fall in with the doctor, pray sound him on this subject. Have you seen the last number of that infamous publication, the *Medical Observer?* There is the most impudent letter in it from the editor to me that ever was penned. I think our friend *Harry* would at once pronounce it grossly libellous. The thing I am abused for, the effects of an epidemic small-pox at Cheltenham, is as triumphant as any that has occurred in the annals of vaccination. A child that had irregular pustules, and was on that account ordered by me to be re-vaccinated, which order was never obeyed, caught the small-pox. This is the whole of the matter, and on this foundation Moseley, Birch and Co., have heaped up a mountain of scurrility. Between 3,000 and 4,000 persons have been vaccinated there and in the circumjacent villages, *who remained in the midst of the epidemic* untouched. This *trifling* circumstance, these worthy gentlemen did not think it worth their while to mention. Adieu, my dear Sir, I hope you are very well and very happy.

Most truly yours,

E. JENNER.

Mr. Jenner to Charles Morgan.

BERKELEY,
9th October, 1809.

MY DEAR SIR,

You may easily guess what a state of mind I am in, by my neglecting my friends. This I was not wont to do. I am grown as moping as the owl, and all the day long sit brooding over melancholy. My poor boy still exists, but is wasting inch by inch. The ray of hope is denied only to a medical man when he sees his child dying of pulmonary consumption; all other mortals enjoy its flattering light. You say nothing of your little girl in your letter from Ramsgate. I hope she is well and will prove a lasting comfort to you.

If Dr. Saunders is displeased, his displeasure can have no other grounds than caprice. I never did anything in my life that should have called it up. I wrote twice to him in the spring, and since that time he has not written to me. Why, I am utterly at a loss to know. In one of these letters I went fully into an explanation of my conduct with regard to the National Vaccination establishment. Depend upon it neither Mr. B. nor Sir Lucas will ever make it the subject of public inquiry. They know better. I have always treated the College with due respect. They made an admirable report to Parliament of vaccination; but in doing this they showed me no favour. It was founded on the general evidence sent in from every part of the empire. I love to feel sensible of an obligation, where it is due, and to show my gratitude. If the College had published the evidence, which they *promised* to do, then I should have been greatly obliged to them. Why this was not done, I never could learn, but shall ever lament that such valuable facts should lie mouldering on their shelves, as they must from their weight have lain too heavy on the tongue of clamour for it ever to have moved again. I wish you had been there, and that I had first made my acquaintance with you. Our strenuous friend in Warwick Lane would have effected everything by filling up this lamentable chasm. I enjoyed your dialogue. *Poor* Sir Isaac! Your pamphlet is highly spoken of, wherever it is read. After this *spice* of your talents in lashing the anti-vaccinists, I hope you don't mean to lay down the rod. Moseley, as far as I have seen has not taken the least notice of it. A proof of his tremors; for he has not been sparing of his other opponents. And now my good friend let me request you, without delay, to let me know the expenses of printing, advertisements, &c., &c. I don't exactly know where this may find you, but shall get a cover for Ramsgate. If you are not there it will pursue you. Dr. Saunders's throwing me off, I assure you, vexes me; but I have the consolation of knowing that it was unmerited. Remember me kindly to our friend *Harry*. He will soon climb the hill, I think. He may be assured of not reaching the top a day sooner than I wish him. Will you have the goodness when in town to order Harward to send the *Annual Medical Register* with my next parcel of books? I have not seen it, but shall, of course, turn to the article "Cow-pox" with peculiar pleasure. Do you recollect my exhibiting some curious pebbles which I had collected during my stay in town, to some friends of yours in your apartment? By some mishap they were left behind me. They were good specimens of wood and bone converted into silex. I don't think there is a corpuscle of the globe we inhabit that has not breathed in the form of an animal or a vegetable. Adieu!

    Believe me, with best wishes,
      Most truly yours,
        EDWD. JENNER.

We must leave the two doctors to their controversies and incriminations. The story of the introduction of vaccination into this country is one of deep interest, and especially to female readers; but that story is not the property of Lady Morgan's biographer. We shall not see Mr. Morgan again for a year or more.

CHAPTER XXXI.

OLD FRIENDS AND NEW.

MISS OWENSON'S visit to Lady Abercorn has been mentioned. It was in her hospitable house that Miss Owenson received the riotous letter from Barrington. Lady Charleville refers to this visit, congratulating her young friend on "acquiring" the favour of Lord and Lady Abercorn's protection. Lady Charleville's good sense and strong affection for Miss Owenson, and her total freedom from the jealousy that old friends too often feel privileged to indulge, is very pleasant.

The Countess of Charleville to Miss Owenson.

CHARLEVILLE FOREST,
December 12*th,* 1809.

DEAR MISS OWENSON,

I am extremely sensible of the politeness of your inquiry for my health, which remains nearly stationary, or if any ways changed, certainly not for the better. It is such as to preclude any idea of town amusements mixing with my scheme of enjoyment; but, indeed, at all times I greatly prefer Charleville Forest to residence in any city.

I congratulate you very sincerely on your acquiring the favour of Lord and Lady Abercorn's protection. It is not always that both parties accord to approve of the same person's character and abilities, or indeed, to make due allowances for them. As I believe the noble lord to be, like many others, omnipotent in his own family, I am to suppose HE acknowledges the existence of those charming talents, which certainly must be improved by the intercourse of highly educated people; and once more I congratulate you on the enjoyment you must find in such society.

I am glad you write for every reason of emolument and amusement; and I do hope your next publication may have as beautiful fancies interspersed, and give less room to the gentlemen to criticise Englishmen's *sang-froid* than the last has done! ! ! !

I believe you will find Lady Costre settled in London, and very happy to do you service in her way.

I am grieved to find Mrs. Henry Tighe is very ill; I know how good she has been to you; and I think her taste should bias every creature who has a heart to feel for her, or soul to acknowledge her, as the first genius of her day . . . . .

I am, Dear Madam,
Your very faithful servant,
CATH. MARIA CHARLEVILLE

Sir Jonah Barrington to Miss Owenson.

MERRION SQUARE, *Thursday.*

DEAR MISS OWENSON,

I hasten to acknowledge what I value—a note from you. But why remind me of my advancing years by supposing me capable of *forgetting* a promise to Miss Owenson, which, at the period of my second climacteric, would have been a suspicion of my honour and an insult to my gallantry. Think you, that because I approach my year of *jubilee*,—because the freezing hand of Time has checked the rapid course of my circulation, and seized in his cold grasp a heart whose ardour would once have bid defiance to his icicles,—that, therefore, my memory and truth must have taken flight with my passions and left your unfortunate correspondent a mere *caput mortuum*—if you think so, you err, for my *vanity* has survived and could not be more highly gratified than by your acceptance of my labours.

The book, such as it is, is the true and unadulterated offspring of Irish feelings, and as such too congenial to your own, not to excite your attention and demand your indulgence. Our works differ, however, in a point the widest in the world—yours much the most difficult—all the talent of *inventive* genius must be cultivated by you —anything in the nature of invention would destroy my reputation. You must invent incident, I need only tell it; you must combine events. My events are already combined, and I have only to recite them. You must describe passions which you never felt; I felt all the passion I have to describe. You write to *please*; I write to reprobate; and in *that* alone *you* will find the less difficulty.

However, my vanity is not like other people's, for it is perfectly *candid*, and desires me to tell you that I think you will like the book—at least, I like it myself, and that is all that can be expected by any author.

The second part will rise from the dead, I trust, in January next; and a most flattering letter received from the Prince of Wales, at once feeds my ambition and promotes my courage—so on I go—and heaven send me a good deliverance; there will be ten parts, one hundred portraits, thirty vignettes, all comprised in two volumes—eleven engravings, *very superior*, to those you see, will honour the next number; but I do not think anything can much exceed Bush and Curran in the last, except Durginan and Napper Tandy in the next part. You see, gentlemen must keep bad company on these occasions.

You greatly mistake if you suppose the *ravenous appetite* you mention can be at all sated by my morsel—it will only be a mere lunch; I hope, however, it may increase your appetite, and give you relish for the second course which I am cooking for your table.

I wish you a happy Christmas, as I entertain no doubt you will have a merry one; and if the good wishes of Lady B—— &c., can add to your pleasures, be sure you possess them.

   I am, with real sincerity,
    Your affectionate brother author,
Vive Irlandois.   JONAH BARRINGTON.

The following letter is from "a sound divine," and a dignitary of the Church, who was one of what her sister used to call "Sydney's Army of Martyrs;" at that period a tolerably numerous train! It would be curious to speculate on the effect it might have produced on the orthodoxy of this ardent admirer, had his prayer been granted and Sydney Owenson had become an Archdeacon's wife instead of Lady Morgan!

Archdeacon King, to Miss Owenson.

Dear Miss Owenson,   1810.

Enclosed is the elegant trifle* you were desirous to obtain. I have lost no time in executing the little commission with which you have honoured me. Oh that I were destined to contribute to your felicity in the serious and important circumstance which was the subject of this evening's conversation!—to contribute to your felicity and to complete my happiness. But the unfortunate Rector of Mourne Abbey cherishes the hope, that if he cannot be blest with the *hand*, he will be *immortalized* by the pen, of the elegant and interesting Glorvina.

Rupert King.

Mr. F—— is not permitted to give a copy of the song; you must prevaricate, and pretend that you retained it in memory after having heard it repeated.   R. K.

The "white lies" recommended in this postscript are surprising in a divine; possibly, Sydney Owenson,

---

* A copy of some song, by P. Fitzgerald, Esq.

like Sweet Kitty Clover, had "bothered him so," that the poor archdeacon was bewildered. It is not surprising that Miss Owenson should have refused to become his wife.

Miss Owenson had begun to collect materials for another novel, upon an Indian subject. Her old friend—not now her lover, though some folks thought so—Sir Charles Ormsby, lent her a number of very valuable works of reference from which, as her custom was, she made extensive notes.

The following letter refers to them; the date is omitted, as generally happens in her letters.

Miss Owenson to Sir C. Ormsby.

I have, at last, waded through your *Oriental Library*, and it is impossible *you* can ever feel the weight of the obligation I owe you, except you turn author, and some *kind* friend supplies you with rare books that give the sanction of authority to your own wild and improbable visions.

Your Indian histories place me upon the fairy ground *you* know I love to tread, "where nothing is but what is not," and you have contributed so largely and so efficiently to my Indian venture, that you have a right to a share in the profits, and a claim to be considered a silent partner in the firm. I have to request you will send for your books, as I fear to trust them to a porter.

Yours always,
S. OWENSON.

CHAPTER XXXII.

BARON'S COURT.

LADY CHARLEVILLE, in her last letter, congratulated her young friend on having obtained the favour and protection of Lord and Lady Abercorn. These Abercorns were very great people. John James Hamilton, ninth earl and first marquis of his line, was of kin to the ducal Hamiltons, with their triple titles in Scotland, France, and England. He enjoyed in his own person the honour of four baronies,—Paisley, Abercorn, Hamilton, and Strabane; of two viscounties,—Hamilton and Strabane; as well as an earldom and a marquisate. In one respect he could boast of an advantage in rank above his cousin, the Duke of Hamilton, Brandon, and Chatelherault,—he was a peer in each of the three kingdoms, and could take his seat in the parliaments of London, Dublin, and Edinburgh. Only two other peers, Lord Moira and Viscount Grimstone, shared with him this great distinction. His Lordship had been married three times, had been the hero of a wretched and romantic divorce, and was now living at

Stanmore Priory, with a third wife and a grown up family of children. This third wife, Anne-Jane, was a daughter of Lord Arran, and the widow of Mr. Hatton. Lord and Lady Abercorn had read the *Wild Irish Girl* and *The Novice of St. Dominic*, and been pleased with them; they had seen the authoress herself, and been equally pleased with her, and they thought they would like to take the young woman of genius to live with them and amuse them in their own house.

Lady Abercorn proposed to Miss Owenson, in a very kind and flattering manner, the wish of herself and the Marquis, that she should pass the chief part of every year with them, either at Baron's Court, in Ireland, or at Stanmore Priory, their seat near London; in short, that she should belong to them altogether, and only leave them occasionally to see her other friends.

Miss Owenson was, at that time, living in Dublin, more pleasantly situated than she had ever been in her life. She was quite independent, and yet close to her father and sister, enjoying for the first time the comfort of a family position surrounded by friends and pleasant acquaintances. She did not, at first, feel inclined to relinquish all these things for the sake of accepting Lady Abercorn's offer.

The friends who had, for so many years, taken an interest in her welfare, joined in representing the great advantages of the position offered to her, and induced her to consent to go to Baron's Court for a time, without, however, binding herself to remain there. It amounted to a complete banishment from her own circle of society, as the Marquis and Marchioness were far too grand to recognise Dublin society. They were, however, eager to make their proposal pleasant to her in every way, and both before and after her acceptance, nothing could be more kind or highly bred than their conduct towards her on all occasions.

The Marquis was a very fine gentleman, the type of a class now extinct. He was convinced that the people of the lower orders were of a different nature, and made of different stuff to himself.

The groom of the chambers had orders to fumigate the rooms he occupied after liveried servants had been in them; and the chambermaids were not allowed to touch his bed except in white kid gloves. He himself always dressed *en grande tenue*, and never sat down at table except in his blue ribbon with the star and garter.

He was extremely handsome; noble and courtly in his manner; witty, sarcastic; a *roué* as regarded his principles towards women; a Tory in politics; fastidious, luxurious; refined in his habits, fascinating in his address; *blasé* upon pleasure and prosperity, yet capable of being amused by wit, and interested by a new voice and face. Altogether, he was about as dangerous a man for a brilliant young woman to be brought near as could easily be found. Miss Owenson had, however, the virtue for herself which she bestowed upon her heroines; her own sentiments and romance found their outlet and exercise in her novels, and she had, for all practical purposes, the strong, hard, common sense which called things by their right names, and never gave bewildering epithets to matters of plain right and wrong. She had no exaggerated generosity, nor sentiments of delicacy about other people's feelings. The veracity of common sense had become the habit of her mind, and she never tampered with it.

The Marchioness of Abercorn was as genuine a fine lady as the Marquis was a fine gentleman. In after years, Lady Morgan drew her portrait in *O'Donnel* as Lady Llanberris. She was good-natured and *inconséquente*. She took up people warmly and dropped them easily; she was incapable of a permanent attachment except to those belonging to herself.

Her enthusiasm for Miss Owenson was, however, marked by steady kindness for a considerable period; but their intercourse was of quite a different nature to that which existed between Miss Owenson and Lady Charleville, or Lady Stanley, or Mrs. Lefanu.

Miss Owenson's letters tell their own tale of the scenes and impressions of this period of her life.

She used to say, in referring to her life at Baron's Court and Stanmore Priory, where there was a succession of visitors, how little toilette was required in those days. Whilst at the Marquis of Abercorn's, she seldom wore anything except a white muslin dress with a flower in her bosom, until after she married; ornaments she possessed none, and her hair was dressed by the simple appliance of a wet brush to her abundant curls.

Miss Owenson to Mrs. Lefanu.

PRIORY,
January 18*th*, 1810.

Well, I am everything that by this you have said. I am "an idle, addle-pated, good-for-nothing thing," who, at the end of three months' absence, begins to remember there is somebody whose demands upon her grateful and affectionate recollection are undeniable; and who, in fact, she never ceases to love and respect, though she does not regularly tell her so by the week, "in a double letter from Northamptonshire;" and now, I dare say, a very clever letter you will expect. Alas! madam, that which in me "makes fat the ribs but bankrupts out the wits," the *morale*, in its excellence, bears no proportion to the physique, and I am, at this moment, the best lodged, best fed and dullest author in his Majesty's dominions. My memory comes surcharged with titles and pedigrees, and my fancy laden with stars and garters,—my deep study is pointed towards the red book, and my light reading to the French bill of fare which lies under my cover at dinner; but you will say, "hang your fancy, give me *facts*." *Hélas! ma belle*, I have none to relate, that your philosophic mind would not turn up its nose at. What is it to you that I live in one of the largest palaces in England? and that the sound of a commoner's name is refreshment to my organs, wearied out with

the thrilling vibrations of "your Royal Highness,"
"your Grace," and "your Majesty!" Aye, now you
open your big dark eyes, not knowing all the time (as
how should you, poor soul!) that I am surrounded by
ex-lord-lieutenants, unpopular princesses, and "deposed
potentates," (for in the present state of things, we here
are in the wrong box); on either side of me I find
chatting Lords Westmorland and Hardwick (poor
dears!) pop, then comes the Princess of Wales, with
"quips and cranks and wreathed smiles," and "anon
stalks by in royal sadness," the "exiled majesty of
Sweden," who certainly deserves to reign, because he
boldly *affiches* himself as *not* deserving to reign and
says *tout bonnement*, "that his people were the best
judges, and they were of *his opinion*." This is *fact*,
not fancy. The truth is that the *wonderful variety* of
distinguished and extraordinary characters who come
here, make it to me a most delicious *séjour*,—and
though I am now going on my *fourth month* it seems
as if I was beginning my first day. It were in vain
to tell you the names of our numerous and fluctuating
visitors, as they include those of more than half the
nobility of England, and of *the first* class; add to
which, many of the *wits*, authors, and existing minis-
ters (poor dears!) The house is no house at all, for
it looks like a little town, which you will believe when
I tell you that a hundred and twenty people slept
under the roof during the Christmas holidays without
including the under servants; and that Lords Abercorn and Hamilton have between them nine apartments *de plain-pied*, and Lady A. four. The Queen's

chamberlain told me, indeed, that there was nothing
like the whole establishment in England, and, perhaps,
for a subject, in Europe. I have seen a great deal of
the Devonshire family; the daughters are charming,
and I am told, Lady G. Morpeth very like her mother,
whom they all say, actually *died* in consequence of the
shock she received from the novel of *The Winter in
London*. What will please *you* more than anything is
that I have *sold my book*, *The Missionary, famously*.
That I am now correcting the proof sheets, and that I
have sat to the celebrated Sir Thomas Lawrence for
my picture, from which an engraving is done for my
work.

I was presented almost immediately on my arrival
to the Princess of Wales, who received me most gra-
ciously, and with whom I have dined. The Duchess
of Gordon has been particularly kind and attentive
to me, and is here frequently. We have at present
a very celebrated person, *Payne Knight*, and Lord
Aberdeen, who has a farm *at Athens*. He is married
to one of our daughters.

I swore like a trooper to Livy I *would* be back by
the 1st of January, but as that is past, I will be back
before the 1*st of March*, for these folk then move
themselves for Ireland, and it will be then time to
move off myself; so I propose myself to take a family
dinner *with you* the 1st of March *new* style. Poor
Mrs. Wallace! she held out wondrously. The last
day I saw her I did not think she would live a week,
and she lived twelve. I hear he is *inconsolable* (poor
man!!) (do you perceive through all this a vein of

tender pity!) I wish he would get a star or garter that I might smile on him, as it is "*nothing under nobility* approaches Mrs. Kitty.") The majesty of the people!! Oh, how we laugh at such nonsense! My dear Mistress What-do-ye-call'em, can I do anything for you, or the good man, your husband? command me. As to the worthy person, your son, I have nothing interesting to communicate to him, but that we have had the Archbishops of York and Canterbury, and they have exorcised the *evil spirit* out of me, so that I shall go back to him a saint in grain. Have you seen Livy? Love to all in a lump, and pray write to me under cover to the Marquis, St. James's Square, London.

Yours affectionately,
S. O.

The Mr. Wallace, who is referred to in the foregoing banter, was an eminent barrister and Q.C. at the Irish bar. A very warm friendship and esteem of long duration had subsisted betwixt him and Miss Owenson. His wife had been a confirmed invalid, who did not go out into society. It may be inferred by the sagacious reader, that Mr. Wallace had pretensions to the hand which Sir Charles Ormsby and Archdeacon King—not to speak of the minor crowd—had not succeeded in winning. There is a sly undertone of love-making in the following note of good advice:—

J. Wallace to Miss Owenson.

[*No date.*]

I cannot tell you, my sweet friend, how much pleasure your letter has given me! not because you have been panegyrizing me to your great friends,—nor because I have any, the most remote fancy, that those panegyrics can ultimately produce benefits to your friend; but because the unsought, disinterested, spontaneous testimonies of friendship, are with me above all value! Even if they were not *rare* they would be *precious*,—but when one who has seen as much of mankind as myself, and knows, *au fond*, how seldom a heart or a head can be found that is not exclusively occupied with its own cares, or pleasures, or interests; when such a one meets an instance of gratuitous and friendly solicitude about the interests or reputation of an absent connection, he gets a new consciousness of the value of his existence, by finding there is something in his *species* better than he expected. I profess to you to feel a sentiment of that kind from this last instance of your recollection of me; for I am so far a misanthrope, that I should not have been much surprised if a volatile little girl like *yourself*, fond of the pleasure and of the admiration of society, should have forgotten such a thing as *myself*, when immersed in the various enjoyments of such a circle as you are now surrounded by; not that I doubted you had friendship for me,—for of that I would have been certain; but I would have been easily persuaded that *present pleasure* might, for a time, have superseded *memory*, and postponed a recollection of *distant* friends and *past* scenes till a more convenient season. I confess, however, my sweet friend, that I entertained some fear that your zeal may have carried you a little too far in the conversation you mention; for anything in the way of *solicitation* or *canvass* would certainly, my dear Sydney, be to me one of the most mortifying things on earth; it would be at war with all my feelings and outrage all my principles; for there is but one thing in this world of which I can be vain—and it is a source of pleasure which nothing would induce me to forego—a *consciousness* that whatever I am, or whatever little success I may have in life, it is the pure and unmixed result of my own labours, uncherished and unpatronised. *One* instance only occurred in the course of my life, in which any attempt was made to promote my interests by the solicitation of friendship, and that became a source of great vexation to me,—it was that Mr. C. adverted to when he spoke of Ponsonby. Grattan, meaning to do a kind thing for me without my knowledge, applied to T. when he became Chancellor for a silk gown for me, and having got what he considered an explicit promise, he then mentioned the thing publicly, and it was known to half the profession before I heard of it. T. afterwards falsified his promise—by pretending that the promise was not for the *next* creation of king's counsel, but for the next but one. The consequence was the open declaration of war I made upon him—which most probably will for ever prevent me and Chancellors from being very good friends; for those fellows, like other classes of men, have a certain *esprit de corps*, and make common cause. Speak of me, therefore, dear Sydney, *as your friend* as much as you please, praise me in *that* character as far as you can, and you confer an honour on me of which I shall ever be most proud; but beware, my sweet girl, of *patronage* or solicitation. Here has been twenty times too much of myself; but *you* have made the subject valuable by the attention you have paid to it.

What is the meaning of your question, "What are you to do with the rest of your life?" Can it be possible that a mind like yours should prove itself so feeble, that the passing enjoyments of a few months in "splendour and comfort" would disgust you with the ordinary habits of the world? This would be neither reason, nor philosophy, nor good taste; for good taste is good sense directed in a particular way; and good sense has a very *assimilating* quality and always fits us for "*existing circumstances.*" I do hope, notwithstanding the horror with which you seem to look at your *descent* from the pedestal, that you will be capable of enjoying the circumscribed, social, laughing, wise, foolish, playful little suppers which Mrs. * * * has given us, and, I hope, will again. By the way, *when* will you return? Mrs. Lefanu told me, on Saturday, you mentioned to her that you would be here in a fortnight and go back; and yet Mrs. C. knows nothing of it—*nor I*. I cannot help recurring again to your question, *What will you do with the rest of life?* I put the interrogatory to *myself* when I read your letter,—indeed, I have often asked myself the question—and what do you think I am likely to do? Most probably I shall retire to some very remote spot, where a small income will be an independence—and what then? J. W.

Miss Owenson had been slyly asking Mr. Wallace what he meant to do with the rest of his life; and the dull gentleman had not seen her joke. It was the fashion for all the men to adore her; Sir Charles Ormsby, Lord Guildford, Mr. Archdeacon King, Sir Richard Phillips, even the Marquis of Abercorn; and the crowd of lovers who were always flying about her was the standing comedy of Lady Abercorn. Some weeks after the death of his wife, Mr. Wallace received a droll and wicked note from his fair correspondent. Voltaire himself has nothing more droll than the alternative consolation offered to the widower—some being who could think and feel with him—*or* a perusal of the Essay on Manners. The political gossip is no less amusing than the personal.

Miss Owenson to Mr. Wallace on the death of his Wife.

[*No date.*]

I write to you with reluctance, in which my heart has no share; its natural impulses are always true to pity and affection; to solace the afflicted is in me *no virtue*, it is at once my nature and my habit, and if in prosperity and joy my feelings vary their direction and ebb and flow to the influence of peculiar circumstances, in sorrow and in sadness they become fixed and invariable, for, "laugh with those who rejoice," is less natural to me than to "weep with those who weep;" yet respecting your grief (and the grief of a man is to me always awful), not knowing in what mood of mind my letter might find you, I waited till it could be naturally supposed the first strong impressions of scenes of suffering and of melancholy might be softened if not effaced, until nothing but a tender sadness not ungracious to the feelings remained. I know not how to use the common-place language of condolence; death has broken a tie which sometimes *galled* you; but it has also taken from you a *friend*, a sincere, an affectionate and faithful friend; for myself, young as I am, I have tried long enough to know and to feel the inconsequence of *life*. To *act right* according to those moral principles which nature has interwoven with our very constitution, and from which all the moral institutions of man are derived, is, I most *sincerely* and *solemnly* believe, the *sole good*, imperishable and lasting as long as we shall ourselves last, whether here or hereafter; that all the rest is subordinate and frail, I can assert upon my own experience. To-day, glancing my eyes over the *Novice of St. Dominic*, I was struck by the ardour, the enthusiasm, the fertility of invention, in short by all the brilliant illusions of untried youth, which gleamed in every line. I opposed them by the cold, tame nature of my present feelings;—my *disappointed* heart, my *exhausted* imagination, and I had the weakness to drop tears on the page as I read; but *I dried them soon*, and I could not help thinking, that while the pleasures of the senses and the fancy of youth and the world, left behind them but idle and transient regrets, the consciousness of having always *acted right* alone remained to comfort and support, to cheer and solace; it is a triumph purchased, indeed, by many temporary sacrifices; and many an imperious wish, and many a fond desire is trampled on to obtain it. This is a very *triste* style for me, you will say, but it is my prevailing tone at this moment, and, indeed, in spite of those states of vivacity to which I am subject, my susceptible spirits reflect back the trouble of gay and brilliant objects. My natural character is that of one who thinks deeply, and who naturally loves to repose in the tranquillity of meditation, who "sets loose to life," and who is almost wearied out by the harrassing vicissitudes which "flesh is heir to." This you will not believe; for it is among the things I have most to lament, that you have not had *tact* to come at the real character of your friend, nor the confidence to believe her own assertions on the subject; you would be surprised to see me here, stealing away from the dazzling multitude, and passing whole days in my own room, reading some *grave* philosophical work; thinking deeply—and feeling acutely—going to the *source* of some obscure subject—or giving myself up to tender and pensive memories, which have for their object those that are *most dear* and *most distant*. Yet this I do constantly . . . and yet I return to society—not its most undistinguished or least brilliant member.

If I could be of the least use to you, I should not hesitate to fly to you in your afflictions; believe me, when I solemnly assert, *that nothing on this earth should prevent me*, neither the *pleasures* of the world or its OPINIONS; but you are surrounded by friends, and I think you have that confidence in my friendship, that you would *call* on me if *you wanted me*. My return to Ireland is uncertain. I am pretty *weary of the sameness* of things *here*, where there is nothing in the least *to interest the heart*,—they are all extremely anxious I should stay till March, as they then mean to have private theatricals; but I would fly to the end of the world from a species of amusement to me, of all others, the most faded and egotistical; it is, therefore, most probable, I shall abide by my original intention and leave this early in February.

I hear of nothing but politics, and the manner in which things are considered, give me a most thorough contempt for the "*rulers of the earth;*" I am *certain* that the country, its welfare or prosperity, never, for a moment, make a part in their speculation; it is all a *little miserable system of self-interests*, paltry distinctions, of private pique, and personal ambition. I sometimes with difficulty keep in my indignation when I hear them talk of such a person and his *eight* men, and such an one and his *five*, and so on, for there is not one of the noted demagogues you read of, who do not carry with them a certain number of followers, who vote *à tort et à travers*, as their leader bids them; it is thus we are *represented*—the order of the day is as follows, Lord Grey, *Premier*, with the *common consent* of the nation, (except the particular party going out) Lord Erskine, Chancellor; Lord Moira, Commander of the Forces; Lord Lansdown, Lord Lieutenant of Ireland; Lord Manners resigns—they *murmur* something of *Plunket* succeeding him; Lord *Holland nothing*; notwithstanding what the papers say, nothing has been laid out for *Ponsonby*, he is looked on as the captain or ringleader of the House of Commons. Sheridan is held in contempt on *all sides*; but the Prince, who is cold to him, will make him, they say, *Paymaster* to the Navy. Such are the appointments the Prince has made out; but *Lord Abercorn* thinks they will not take place, as the King is mending fast. The anxiety and solicitude in all whom I see here, and who are interested for the issue of the business, *have disgusted me* for ever with those *falsely* called the *great*. Lord Abercorn, who always votes himself a *King's man*, preserves an armed neutrality, and though, according to *my* principles and feelings, he is *decidedly wrong*, yet it is impossible not to respect his independence. All wonder at Erskine's elevation, as he is deemed *literally mad*. Your future viceroy proposed, some time ago, for my sweet new friend, whom I believe I have mentioned to you—*Lady Hamilton* (don't mention this to any one); but was refused by *Papa*. She has become a great tie to me now, and her obvious affection for me is my greatest pride. She is a most superior and charming woman, though cold in her general manner and rigid in her principles. She is, in her person, like Lord Abercorn more than any of his children; but her character is composed of firmer stuff. I hope, one day or other, to present her to you. She met lately, by chance, at Brighton, with the *Grattans*, and is an *enthusiast* in admiration of *them*, as they *must be* of her. She says she envies that middle rank of life, and would give up her own situation willingly for *theirs*.

Farewell; this is a dull epistle, but I am as little in the mood to write gay letters as you are probably to read them. I hope Clarke has made you the offer of his house till your own is made comfortable for your residence. How and where is your dear boy? How is Mr. Handle—and where? It was in a letter from *Old Atkinson* that I first heard of your loss. I was shocked and surprised, for I all along thought that, though perfect recovery was impossible, yet that *years* of life might be still enjoyed, or rather endured. To me death has little terrors. I always look to it as to a wished-for, and necessary repose; they alone know to estimate life who, like me, have known *its great extremes*, and, let me add, they alone *can despise it*.

Once more farewell.

PS. Let me *entreat* that you will take particular care of my letters. Did you receive one from me dated the 12th. I have written *five* letters to the Clarkes since Twelfth-night, and they deny getting a single letter.

Nothing, perhaps, under your present feelings, would so much *distrait* your mind as an interview with some being who would *think* and *feel* with you, for sorrow can know no solace. With the sympathy of intellect and sensibility blended in one, but next to that, you will find most relief from a particular style of reading which *awakens*, without fatiguing, the mind. Let me, therefore, recommend to you a work in which this moment I am deeply engaged, and which is beside me. It might be called " L'Esprit de la Raison," for never was so much delicate wit, such exquisite irony, and such incomparable humour, applied to the development of the most profound subjects that Philosophy ever *called to* the tribunal of human reason. I mean Voltaire's *Essai sur les mœurs et l'esprit des nations et sur les principaux faits de l'histoire depuis Charlemagne jusqu'à Louis XIII.* Read it, if you have not already read it, or if you have!—

Ah! what a woman's postscript!!!

CHAPTER XXXIII.

THE MISSIONARY.

WHILST at Baron's Court, Miss Owenson completed her Indian novel of the *Missionary*, and every day, when there were no visitors, she used to read aloud, after dinner, to the Marquis and Marchioness, what she had written in the morning. She said, when talking of these times in after life, that the Marquis used to quiz her most unmercifully, declaring that the story was "the greatest nonsense he had ever heard in his life," which did not, however, prevent him from listening to it with great amusement. Lady Abercorn yawned over it very dismally. Certainly, a more romantic or a more foolish story could scarcely be imagined.

When the book was completed, she purposed to go over to England to arrange about the publication, and left Baron's Court on her way east for that purpose; but she delayed her journey, loitering in Dublin to see her friends. The Marquis and Marchioness of Abercorn wrote to her whilst she was there.

From their letters, by the way, a few amusing extracts may be culled. The "glorvina," about which her ladyship writes, was a golden bodkin for fastening up the hair, after the pattern of an antique Irish ornament, and was called a "glorvina," in honour of the *Wild Irish Girl*, who, in the novel, wears one of similar fashion. The Marchioness had a passion for ordering anything she heard of, and she invariably disliked it, or grew tired of it, before it could be sent to her—a peculiarity extremely embarrassing to those whom she honoured with her commissions. The reference to *le bien aimé* is to Sir Charles Ormsby, whom Lady Abercorn still regarded as Miss Owenson's adorer.

Marchioness of Abercorn to Miss Owenson.

[*No date.*]

DEAR MISS OWENSON,

You know so well the way we contrive to find no time for anything in this house, that I am sure you will not accuse me of ingratitude in not having thanked you, either on Saturday or Sunday for two delightful letters I have of yours, as well as for the songs and French letters, and the designs for glorvinas, &c., &c.; but Saturday was so delightful, that I was out from breakfast till dinner, and yesterday, I went to church (where, *par parenthèse*, there is the most delightful singing you can imagine), and after church, my usual Sunday walk with *mon époux* filled up the morn. You also know, that after dinner, what with hot wine and hot dishes, I am never in a state to write a *clear* letter; and after this *exposé*, you will not be surprised that I have not sooner taken notice of what I neither admire or like the less for not having said so.

I hope you yourself did not suffer from fatigue and anxiety, and that you are now in as perfect health, beauty, and spirits, as you ought to be.

Now for my glorvinas. Could you not enclose the one you think "*precisely what I should like*," the price three guineas, and I can order the others after I have seen it. I think I should like to have the motto on Lady Hamilton's glorvina "Our hopes rest on thy dear black head." Now do not laugh at my way of expressing what I wish *you* to put in *better language*, and in Irish; but I think we might unite *notre espérance* and the *black head*, which we fixed upon, for this glorvina.

As to the Princess's, I intend only a glorvina, and the motto you mention would be very pretty; but that must be very handsome, and as it will not take long to make, I conclude, it shall be the last.

I should like to see a small ten guinea Irish harp; but it would not be advisable to risk sending it by post.

Before this, you will have seen Miss Butler; I did hope to have heard from her to-day. I trust she did not catch cold on the journey, and that she will find the *festivities* of Dublin repay her for the inconvenience.

Nothing new has occurred since you left us; you, and your harp, we miss in every possible way. It was a pity you did not wait till the *Councillors* returned to town, for perhaps, had you been with us, we might have invited *le bien-aimé*, who will, of course, be at Armagh this week; as it is we shall not.

Have you sent the *Lurima* to England, yet? pray tell me, for though I never wished to hear it read ten pages at a time, I am very impatient to see it all together, and sincerely anxious for its success.

Yours, dear Miss Owenson,
Very sincerely,
A. J. A.

This is a most horrible griffonnage; but if I attempted to write it over again I should never send it, and I dare not even read it for fear I should think, for my own credit, it should be consigned to the flames.

The "Jane" mentioned in Lord Abercorn's note, which follows next, is Anne Jane, his third wife and Marchioness. The "Livy," with whom Lord Abercorn threatened to fall in love, is Lady Clarke, Miss Owenson's beautiful sister.

Lord Abercorn to Miss Owenson.

Wednesday.

This, you know, is audience-day, *dear little Glo.* (what familiarity to a great Princess!), so I have not a minute of morning to myself. But, as to-morrow is audience-day too, and next day Friday, I determine to thank you for your letter, in a hurry, rather than seem ungracious and ungrateful in the first instance; for though I have made my bargain to be allowed dryness and delay in general, I must begin with sweetness and punctuality.

So here I am, with my dinner in my throat, and my coffee in my mouth (having left my arm chair and your "boudoir," to console each other in our absence), just to assure you what you know well enough, that I have not yet forgotten you; and also what I have already assured you through June, that I understood, and (in your own phrase) appreciated your dislike to parting words and looks. I was going on, but will stop for fear of falling into the tender and sentimental, so, once for all, assure yourself that I feel your feelings as they deserve—as our friends the Orientals say, "what can I say more?"

I think, under the various circumstances of the case, I have written as much now as I well can, or you will wish, so, till your next letter and "Livy's" postscript bring me fresh materials, bye! bye! Have you told her that I have some thoughts of falling in love with her, if we ever meet?

Need I say, that I am and ever shall be,

Your affectionate

A.

Lady Abercorn to Miss Owenson.

[*No date.*]

DEAR MISS O.,

I received the Glorvina this morning, which I do not very much admire, and as *I do know* you do not mind trouble, I sent it back to you, and wish you would ask the man what he would do one for me of Irish gold, with the shamrock on the head in small Irish diamonds, which I think would look very well.

My harp will be beautiful, and of course I chose Hawk head, and should also like the threefold honours as ornaments; it is a pity we cannot introduce the crest and the garter, that it might be perfect. I believe, when the Garter was instituted, that the wives of the knights had a right to a bracelet with the motto; if so, I do not know why I should not introduce it on my harp, as it will, I hope, be a specimen of Irish ingenuity long after I am in another and a better world, and may be the cause of considerable curiosity (to some persons unacquainted with the history of the noble house of Hamilton) in future ages, which is an interesting consideration to me. I hope *the groupe* will not be preserved so long, unless you write a novel in which you introduce the modern Solyman and his sultanas, for I confess I should never lament that such a quiz had lived a generation before. Seriously, it is quite a monster; I hope you did not really see him as you drew him. Julia was quite angry that such a thing was intended for *pretty brother*.

Why do you tell me of Mademoiselle Espinasse's letters if you cannot get them for me? perhaps you could get them at Archer's—pray try. *Alfieri* has been long promised to me from England, but has never arrived.

I do congratulate you upon the conquest you have made of the Duchess of Gordon. If she does not *find you in her way*, you will find her pleasant; but beware of that.

You know I never felt much for any mortifications the Miss G—— might receive, so the present does not make me very unhappy. I dare say the Duchess of Gordon will be more kind to them.

We have had Captain Pakenham here some days; he has just gone to Lifford, but is to return on Wednesday. He is a very pleasant young man; I wish he had been here when you were, that your recollection of Baron's Court might have been more lively.

I have got two cantos of the *Lady of the Lake*—as beautiful as possible. You cannot write too much or too often, so make no excuse for doing so; but do pray fold your letters as *I do*, and put a cover over them, as I lose half of your precious words by the way they are put up.

I am very glad your friend Mr. Atkinson will not give your money to the Granards; it would be too foolish to lose one's *all* out of delicacy. When it is well disposed of, let me know, as I shall feel very anxious.

As I cannot, in any other way, copy Glorvina, I am trying to make my handwriting as unintelligible as possible, that at least in something there may be some similitude, and, therefore, scratch and blot at a great rate, and console myself, when I look at a horrid griffonnage, by the conviction that it is a proof of genius!!!

Remember, I am only joking about the garter and crest.

   Yours, dear Miss O., sincerely,

         A. J. A.

Lord Abercorn thinks you very foolish not to send your novel to London immediately, as the season is passing over. So mind you do.

The Missionary was sent over from Dublin; and Phillips, who was her regular publisher, put it to press. But the publisher and author began to quarrel about terms, as they were pretty sure to do; the young Irish girl being quite as sharp as the experienced Welsh tradesman. On which side the wrong lay, and on which the offence, it would be idle to enquire. Most authors quarrel with their publishers, and will probably do so to the end of time. Miss Owenson had the highest sense of her own worth, not only to the public but to the trade. She thought her right to the lion's share of profit on her book clear; a pretension which Phillips would not allow. After printing a volume, the press was stopped. The manuscript had to be recovered, and a new "adventurer in setting forth" found. Stockdale and Miller were the rival powers in the trade; and, with these gentlemen, Lady Abercorn, on her removal to Stanmore Priory, began to negociate for her friend, who still remained in Ireland.

Lady Abercorn to Miss Owenson.

[*No date.*]

MY DEAR MISS O.,

I shall go to town in a few days, and I will call on Miller, and see whether he is worthy of introducing your *Wanderer*. I am sorry you had anything to do with that shabby man—Phillips; I hope, however, you have recovered the manuscript, and that you will learn wisdom from experience, for I think, notwithstanding your talents—which I do not underrate, I assure you— a little worldly wisdom is one you do not possess; so pray set to work and acquire some small share of it, if you can. If you should think coming to England will forward any of your plans, *you know where to come*, and this is a very convenient distance from London, you can get there as often as you like.

My harp, I have no doubt, will be perfect; alas! who is to play it? for Lady Aberdeen is the only one in this family who can, and she is soon going to the sea—the rest of the family will remain here till after Christmas.

You do not say to whom you have consigned my harp, nor do you mention having sent your picture, which I was to have if I liked it better than the one I now possess.

Walter Scott's success exceeds everything; the quarto edition of two thousand did not last a fortnight, and upwards of four thousand of the octavo are gone; it is liked much better than any of the others.

I have seen both Mr. Knight and Mr. Price, here, since my arrival, and many other friends; but none that you know from reputation, except those two. I think Mr. Knight more agreeable than ever. I am sorry to tell you Lord Guildford is to be married next Thursday, so you must think of some one else.

None of your friends forget you, I assure you; Julia often talks of you—she is as *violent* an Irish girl as she ever was. Her brother Charles has been here for a week, which gave her great pleasure. He is a very fine boy—or a little man, I may venture to say.

Pray who are your two new lovers?

I am not a little stupid at present, I can tell you. I want the harmony of the Irish war harp to revive me. I have felt a little *le mal du pays* since I returned here; but you must not tell, mind!

God bless you, my dear Glorvina,

Yours, sincerely,

A. J. A.

Lady Abercorn to Miss Owenson.

Stanmore Priory.

Dear Glorvina,

Your harp is arrived, and *for the honour of Ireland, I must tell you*, it is very much admired and quite beautiful. Lady Aberdeen played on it for an hour, last night, and thought it very good, *almost* as good as a French harp, and perhaps will be quite as good when it has recovered the *fatigues* of the journey; pray tell poor Egan I shall show it off to the best advantage, and I sincerely hope he will have many orders in consequence.

The Baron's Court field flowers were very well received; but as Frances is thanking you herself I have nothing more to say. The harp suffered a little in the journey; but I shall, I hope, be able to get it repaired.

I went to Miller, the day before yesterday, and was as civil as possible to him; paid him many compliments upon his liberality to people of genius; talked of Walter Scott, and proposed his publishing your new novel, saying, you expected five hundred pounds for it; but I do not think he answered as *your proud spirit* would quite like, for he said he would not purchase a *novel* from any one in the *United Kingdom* (nor did he except Walter Scott) without reading it first; and, in short, I did not proceed, for I know how high Glorvina is, and I was satisfied he was not the person who was to introduce her *Missionary*. He is, however, to be in Dublin in three weeks, and I was to give him a letter to you; but I did not, as I am sure he can *find you out* in Dublin.

I shall be very happy, I assure you, to see you when you come to England, nor do I at present see any thing that would make it necessary for me to say, "your hour is not come." I know of nothing that could, except what I trust in God will not occur —the illness of those dear to me. I have seen your friend, Mr. Gell, and heard him speak very *prettily* of you.

If you knew how much I am hurried, and what a pain I have in my shoulder from the rheumatism, you would say, I was *very good* to write to-day; but I had those things I wished to *express* immediately—my failure with Miller, my admiration of the harp, and that I shall have great pleasure in seeing you here whenever you come.

A. J. A.

CHAPTER XXXIV.

VISIT TO LONDON.

When Miss Owenson at length came to London to arrange with the publishers about her *Missionary*, she took up her abode with Captain and Mrs. Patterson, who resided in good style in York Place, Portman Square, a residence more convenient to her than Stanmore Priory. She mixed eagerly and freely with the best people in London, and was particularly at home with the lions and lionesses. At this time she made the acquaintance of Lord Cochrane, then just home from his glorious exploits in the Basque roads. A note to Lady Stanley will also show that she had also become an acquaintance of Nelson's Lady Hamilton—"the famous"—as she calls her, by way of distinction from the Lady Hamilton of Stanmore Priory. The letter is franked by Lord Cochrane.

Miss Owenson to Lady Stanley.

12, York Place, Portman Square, London,
April 20*th*, 1810.

Your letter made me roar. I was in Berkshire when it arrived, and only got it three days back, but as my franker is not in town, I must defer placing the *Missionary* in your hands until the same moment I kiss them, which will be this day week. I leave this the 30th (*the evening of Tuesday next*), so that is pretty plain. My trunk goes directed for your ladyship's *to-morrow*. To-night I expect your enchanting son to sup with me; were it not *a sin to love him*, what a passion I could feel for him! I have asked Lady Hamilton to meet him—*the famous*. I will explain the mistake of the book when we meet—till that, *joyeux revoir*, and ever

Your devoted
GLORVINA.

Will you not send for me to Holyhead?

Lady Morgan used to tell a story about herself in these early days of her first introduction to fashionable society. She had little money, and but a slender wardrobe of smart things. In those days, dress was expensive, and white satin shoes were *spécialités* that every young lady did not command. One evening, at some party, the company were practising the waltz, then very recently introduced into England; Lord Hartington was Miss Owenson's partner; she was dancing with energy, when her foot slipped, and in the effort to recover herself, one of her white slippers, the pride of her heart—her only pair—was split beyond retrieval. She felt so mortified at the accident that she burst into tears. Lord Hartington was distressed, and entreated to know the cause of her sudden affliction.

"My satin shoes are ruined, and I have not another pair!" Lord Hartington did not laugh, but said very kindly, "Don't cry for that, dear Glorvina, you shall have the very prettiest pair of white satin shoes that can be found in all Paris."

He was then on the point of starting for France, and he was good as his promise. The shoes came in the next ambassador's bag, and were sent to her with the following note.

From the Duke of Devonshire, when Lord Hartington, to Miss Owenson.

Tuesday.

MY DEAR MISS OWENSON,

I send you the long-promised shoes, which, however, without your encouragement last night, would not have dared present themselves to you. They are not what I intended, being like all other shoes; but Paris could never produce anything like the vision of a shoe that I had in my mind's eye for you. I depend upon your sending me Luxima, and beg you to believe me, dear Miss Owenson,

Most truly, your obliged servant,

HARTINGTON.

In the reply which she sent to this gallant epistle, Miss Owenson referred to the loss of her liberty—meaning that she had made up her mind to close with Lady Abercorn's offer, and go into her household.

Miss Owenson to the Duke of Devonshire.

Before *The Wild Irish Girl* was *aux abois*, and taken alive in the snare that has been artfully laid for her, she begs to lay at your grace's feet the last offerings of her liberty; and by whatever name your Grace may prefer of the four you bestowed on me—whether *Puck* or Glorvina, Luxima or *Mother* Goose, she invokes your acceptance of the trifle which accompanies this.

She is ignorant whether her *keepers* mean to exhibit her for her intelligence or ferocity, like the learned pig at Exeter Change, or the beautiful hyena at the Tower, which never was tamed. But whatever part she is destined to play in her cage, it is certain that she will often look forth with delight to those days of her freedom, when, untaught and untamed, she contributed to your Grace's amusement, and imbibed those sentiments of respect and esteem for your character, with which she has the honour to subscribe herself your

Obliged and obedient servant,
GLORVINA.

There is some mystery about Miss Owenson's relations to Sir Charles Ormsby at this time, which is not wholly explained in Lady Morgan's papers. Among them is a letter endorsed in her own handwriting:—

"Last farewell letter to Sir C. Ormsby, returned with the rest of my letters and my ring after his death, which took place in 1816."

Miss Owenson to Sir C. Ormsby, Bart.

Tuesday.

I am told you have had the kindness to call more than once since your arrival in town at my door. I should have anticipated the intention and endeavoured to prevent it; but the fact is, I did not wish to intrust a letter to another person's servant, and still less to send my own to your house.

It is with inexpressible regret that I am obliged to decline your visits. I have no hesitation in declaring that I prized your society beyond any enjoyment within my sphere of attainment, and that in relinquishing it for ever, I do a violence to my feelings which raises me in my own estimation, without reconciling me to the sacrifice I have made.

The only intercourse that could subsist between us, proximity has destroyed. I thought your circuit would have lasted five weeks. I thought I should have been in England before your return, and all this would have been spared me. Were I to tell you the motive that detains me in Ireland longer than I wish or expected, you would give me your applause. At least do not withdraw from me your esteem, it is the only sentiment that ever ought to subsist between us. I owe you a thousand kindnesses, a thousand attentions; my heart is full of them. Whilst I exist, the recollection of all I owe you shall form a part of that existence.

Farewell!

Have the goodness to send me my answer to your last letter,—it was written under the influence of a nervous indisposition and exhibits a state of mind I should blush to have indulged in.

The affair between Miss Owenson and the *bien aimé* had cost her a good deal of trouble and anxiety —and it had been for some time on a very unsatisfactory footing. They met in society afterwards, and he always retained a strong and friendly interest in her career.

Miss Owenson went from York Place to the Priory and remained there some little time. During this visit, Lord Castlereagh, who had been favoured with hearing some of the MS. read aloud—which he greatly admired —offered to take Miss Owenson to town in his chariot, and to give a rendezvous to her publisher in his own study; an offer which was, of course, accepted. Stockdale was the publisher with whom she was then in treaty.

He was punctual to his appointment, and was naturally impressed by the environments, which gave him a higher opinion of Miss Owenson's genius than he had felt before. The opportunity to make a good bargain was improved by Miss Owenson, Lord Castlereagh himself standing by whilst the agreement was signed. His lordship was, perhaps, the greatest admirer the *Missionary* ever found; it was not so popular as her other novels. She had read up a great deal for Indian customs, history and antiquities; but India was India to her; and the manners and customs, races and

countries, were all confounded together in the rose-
coloured mist of fine writing and high-flown sentiment. The subject is the attempt of a Spanish priest
to convert a Brahmin priestess; but the flesh gets the
better of the spirit in this trial; they fall in love with
each other's fine eyes, and elope together. The love
scenes are warmly coloured, and the situations of the
Hindoo priestess and her lover are highly critical; but
the reader feels disposed to say as Sheridan said, when
the servant threw down a china plate with a great
crash, without breaking, "You rascal! how dare you
make all that noise for nothing?" Nothing comes
of all the danger, and everything remains much as it
was in the beginning.

Miss Owenson to Lady Stanley, Penrhôs.

PRIORY, STANMORE,
November 20, 1810.

MY DEAR LADY STANLEY,

I ought to have announced my arrival to you before this; but I have been involved, engaged, dazzled,
and you who are a philosopher, and see human nature
just as it is, will account for and excuse this, and say,
she is not ungrateful nor negligent, *she is only human*.
My *entrée* here was attended by every circumstance
that could render it delightful or gracious to my feelings. A coach-and-four was sent to meet me thirty
miles off, and missed me. I remained a day or two in
London with my very kind friends the Pattersons. I
hold my place of *first favourite*, and the favour I for-

merly enjoyed seems rather increased than diminished. No words can give the idea of the *extent* or splendour of this princely palace. Everything is great and magnificent. We have had some of the noble house of Percy with us—very good sort of people—Lord Bathurst, and others; at present we are *en famille*, but expect a reinforcement to-morrow. There is something so singular and brilliant in the place that we are almost independent of society. My journey was uncommonly comfortable and snug, and I was very little fagged, all things considered, and went through the two nights without drooping. We are going to drive into town. Kindest of all kind friends, remember

GLORVINA.

Among the visitors at Stanmore Priory was Sir Thomas Lawrence, who painted the exquisite sketch of Miss Owenson prefixed to this volume; the story of which is told in his graceful epistles:—

Sir Thomas Lawrence to Miss Owenson.

GREEK STREET,
December 7th, 1810.

MY DEAR MADAM,

If you knew how little at this moment I am master of my time, you would readily pardon me for the freedom I take with the Marchioness and yourself, in naming Wednesday next for my waiting on her ladyship, instead of the appointment fixed for to-morrow.

The considerations you have mentioned, do, indeed, make it necessary that the drawing should be finished in the next week, and upon my word of honour to you, if the Marquis and Marchioness permit me to go to the Priory on Wednesday, the drawing *shall* be finished within the week.

You write to me with so much good humour, and so far below your claims on my thankfulness, for allowing me to attempt this gratification to your friends and the public, that I am the more vexed at my ill fortune, in dooming me to begin it with so ill a grace.

The temple you speak of is a pretty, fanciful building, but there is something very cold and chilling in that said "vestibule." If another door opens, let me go in with you!

Believe me, with the greatest respect,
My dear Madam, yours,
T. LAWRENCE.

Sir Thomas Lawrence to Sydney Owenson.

December 21, 1810.

My evil genius does haunt me, my dear madam, but not in your shape—on the contrary, I believe that it takes you for my good one, for it is very studious to prevent my seeing you. To morrow I cannot, Sunday I cannot; but I will make it as early in this ensuing week as my distractions will admit.

"*Doldrums and bother,*" are weak terms for ladies of your invention—at least, they touch not my state of misery. You tell me that any hour will do, because the Duchess of Gordon and Lord Erskine are satisfied with the likeness. It is because they are enemies of my reputation. The former because I once (as she fancies) painted an arm or a finger too long or too short in her relation's[*] picture. The latter, because I neglected to make an animated beauty of a dead wife (but good faith and forgetfulness of this fact, I beg of you); but still I have a great respect for him, and will try to think better of the drawing that he has liked. "*Striking and beautiful,*" is certainly a most liberal translation of "*flagrant and inveterate*"; but Miss Butler's connections are always on the favorable side. If she knew but how to quiz, she would be very captivating.

I have seen Mr. Campbell,[†] who is more anxious than you are for the meeting. But I will tell you of his *admiration, delight, impatience,* &c., &c., &c., when we meet, which I repeat shall be as soon in the next week as possible.

I remain, my dear madam,
Most truly yours,
J. LAWRENCE.

PS. I have written in haste, emulous of the restless rapidity of your hands; but it is Scrub's imitation of Archer—you have a happy insolence of scrawl that I never yet saw equalled.

[*] The Marchioness of Cornwallis.
[†] The poet and author of the *Pleasures of Hope.*

CHAPTER XXXV.

LADY MORGAN PAINTED BY HERSELF AND SIR THOMAS LAWRENCE.

THE following passage is a frank confession of principle and practice from a young, much admired, and unmarried woman. It is from a diary of the year 1811. In Lady Morgan's own writing it is endorsed

"*Self*, 1811."

Inconsiderate and indiscreet, never saved by prudence, but often rescued by pride; often on the very verge of error, but never passing the line. Committing myself in every way—*except in my own esteem,*—without any command over my feelings, my words, or writings,—yet full of self-possession as to action and conduct,—once reaching the boundary of right even with my feet on the threshold of wrong; capable, like a *menage* horse, of stopping short, coolly considering the risk I encounter, and turning sharply back for the post from whence I started, feeling myself quite safe, and, in a word—*quitte pour la peur*.

Early imbued with the high sentiments belonging to good birth, and with the fine feelings which accompany good education. My father was a player and a gentleman. I learned early to feel acutely my situation; my nature was supremely above my circumstances and situation, the first principle or passion that rooted in my breast, was a species of proud indignation, which accompanies me to that premature death, of which it is finally the cause. My first point of society was to behold the conflict between two unequal minds—the one (my mother) strong and rigid—the other weak and yielding; the one strong to arrest dispute—the other accelerating its approach. The details which made up the mass were—seeing a father frequently torn to prison—a mother on the point of beggary with her children, and all those shocks of suffering which human nature can disdain, and which can only occur in a certain sphere of life and a certain state of society. Man, who has his appetites to gratify, which Nature supplies in his social or artificial character, has thousands of wants which suffering poverty may deny; and even their gratification is not always attended with effects proportionate to their cause. So delicately and fatally organised, that objects impalpable to others, were by me accurately perceived, felt and combined; that the faint ray which neither warmed nor brightened, often gave a glow and a lustre to my spirits; that the faintest vapour through its evanescent passage through the atmosphere, threw no shadow on the most reflecting object, darkened my prospects, and gloomed my thoughts. Oh! it was this unhappy physical organisation, this nervous susceptibility to every impression which circulated through my frame and rendered the whole system acute, which formed the basis of that condition of my mind and being, upon which circumstances and events raised the after superstructure. So few have been the days on which I sighed not that night close on them for ever—that I could now distinctly count them—alas! were they not the most dangerous of my days; the smiling and delusive preparations of supreme misery which time never failed to administer.

It may be supposed that life hastens to its close when its views are thus tinged with hues so dark and so terrific? But the hand which now writes this has lost nothing of the contour of health or the symmetry of youth. I am in possession of all the fame I ever hoped or ambitioned. I wear not the appearance of twenty years; I am now, as I generally am, sad and miserable.

SYDNEY OWENSON.

July 12th, 1811, Dublin.

This tendency to depression of spirits—which, the reader should remember, was exhibited before the whole world had learned from Byron to turn down its shirt collar, and express the elegant despair of Childe Harold,—induced her to put away sorrow as an evil thing; her cheerfulness was a reality—a habit of mind which she carefully and systematically cultivated.

Another entry in the next page is of the same tone.

"It is a melancholy conviction that all my starts of happiness are but illusions; that I feel I do but dream even while I am dreaming,—and that in the midst of the inebriety I court, I am haunted by the expectation of being awakened to that state of hopeless melancholy which alone is real—and felt and known to be so. It is in vain that my fancy steeps me in forgetfulness. The happy wreath which the finger of peace wreathed round my head, suddenly drops off, and the soft vapours that encircled it, scathe and dissipate;—all in truth and fact, sad, dreary and miserable—

"'I may submit to occasions, but I cannot stoop to persons.'

"I may not say with Proverbs—'Wisdom dwelleth with Prudence.'"

The position of this young woman of genius in the household of a great family, if brilliant in outward show, was accompanied by a thousand vexations. The elopement of Marchioness Cecil with Lieutenant Copley had not increased Lord Abercorn's native respect for female virtue. The third wife and her husband lived on terms of excessive politeness with each other; and poor Miss Owenson was expected to bear their tempers and attentions; to sit in the cross-fire of their humours, and to find good spirits and sprightly conversation when they were dull. Add to this, that heavy pressure of anxiety about family matters which was laid upon her before her nerves and sinews were braced to meet it, and before she had any worldly knowledge, produced a feeling of exhaustion. In the material prosperity of her life at Baron's Court, the tension relaxed, and the fatigue of past exertion asserted itself.

Her own ambition had never allowed her to rest; she had been wonderfully successful; but, at Baron's Court and Stanmore Priory, all she had obtained looked dwarfed and small when measured by the hereditary power and consequence of the family in which she was for the time an inmate. She did not become discontented; but she was disenchanted (for the time) with all that belonged to herself, and saw her own position on its true comparative scale. Sydney Owenson, from earliest childhood had depended on herself alone for counsel and support. There is no sign that she ever felt those moments of religious aspiration, when a human being, sensible of its own weakness and ignorance, cries for help to Him who made us; there are no ejaculations of prayer, or of thanksgiving; she proudly took up her own burden and bore it as well as she could; finding her own way and shaping her life according to her own idea of what ought to form her being's end and aim. She was a courageous, indomitable spirit, but the constant dependence on herself, the steady concentration of purpose with which she followed out her own career, without letting herself be turned aside, gave a hardness to her nature, which, though it did not destroy her kindness and honesty of heart, petrified the tender grace which makes the charm of goodness. No one can judge Sydney Owenson, because no one can know all the struggles, difficulties, temptations, flatteries and defamation, which she had to encounter, without the shelter or support of a home or the circle of home relatives. She remained an indestructibly honest woman; but every faculty she possessed had undergone a change, which seemed to make her of a different species to other women.

The portrait of Miss Owenson was at length finished by Sir Thomas Lawrence, and the romance of *The Missionary* printed by Stockdale. The portrait was to be prefixed; but Lawrence, for the reasons given, requested that his name might *not* appear.

Sir Thomas Lawrence to Miss Owenson.

GREEK STREET,
January 21st, 1811.

DEAR MADAM,

I must be indebted to your kindness (and I fear it must put you to the trouble of writing) for preventing the insertion of my name in Mr. Stockdale's advertisement.

I have an anxious desire that the readers of *The Missionary* may be gratified with as accurate a resemblance of its author, as can in that size be given, but from the drawing being so much reduced, the engraving must be comparatively defective; and besides this, I have no wish to be seen to interfere with the province of other artists who are professionally employed in making portraits for books.

There are many of them whose talents I very highly respect, and might reasonably be jealous of, did they encroach on *my* province in painting, but our present walk in art is distinct.

I will take the greatest care that the drawing be as well copied as possible; the engraver has just left me.

Let me beg the favour of you in your communication to Mr. Stockdale, to give it simply as your demand (as a condition of the drawing being lent by you for the purpose,) without stating the reason I have advanced, which might by that gentleman be made matter of offence to others.

Believe me, with the truest respect,
Dear Madam,
Most faithfully yours,
THOS. LAWRENCE.

On the publication of the book, Miss Owenson came from the Priory to London, to her old friends, the Pattersons. From York Place she wrote to Lady Stanley.

Miss Owenson to Lady Stanley.

LONDON, 12, YORK PLACE,
PORTMAN SQUARE,
April 12, 1811.

DEAREST, KINDEST OF LADIES,

By this you have received my little packet; it is near a fortnight since I sent it to be franked, and I have been rather anxious as to its fate, but perhaps at this very moment you are seated at your fireside, Poll at your feet, and Pug beside you, and *The Missionary* in your hands; but in a few days I shall cease to envy Poll, Pug, or *Missionary*, for I shall be in your arms. I leave this heaven upon earth on the evening of the 30th, so I suppose I shall be with you about the 2nd of May, and you will, perhaps, meet me at Holyhead. And, now, who do you think I am waiting at home for? only Sir John Stanley—it is all very true! Both your sons openly avow their passion for me; and Lady Stanley is the most generous of rivals! I have been now one blessed fortnight in this region of delight, and were I to describe to you the kind of attention I excite and receive, you would either laugh at, or pity me, and say "her head is turned, poor little animal;" and you would say very true. But I will tell you all when we meet, a period now not far distant. I mean to send my trunks, directed *for you*, to Mr. Spencer's, by one of the *heavy coaches*, so pray have the goodness to mention the circumstance to him, as it will ensure the safety of my poor little property. Your letter was most gracious, and received with infinite pleasure. Dearest and kindest of friends,

God keep you ever,

GLORVINA.

I am on a visit to an East Indian *nabob's*, whose wife and family are all kindness to me.

This "East India nabob and his family," were Captain and Mrs. Patterson; they admired the young authoress, and were glad to have her in their house, and they placed it and their carriage at her disposal. Sometimes Mrs. Patterson was invited to accompany her on her visits, and Miss Owenson received her friends in their house. The Pattersons were not brilliant people; but they were thoroughly kind-hearted; they enjoyed Miss Owenson's success, and also the glimpses of high society which they obtained through the visitors who called on their guest. Lady Morgan used to tell, in a most amusing way, a story of how, one evening, she and Mrs. Patterson being engaged to a grand party, were obliged to go there in—a hackney-coach; some accidental hinderance about the carriage having occurred at the last moment. The thought of this hackney-coach tormented Miss Owenson all the evening, and destroyed both her peace and pleasure; the idea of what people would say, and, still worse, what they would *think*, if they discovered she had come in a hackney-coach!

She persuaded Mrs. Patterson to depart early, in the hope of escaping detection; but Lord George Granville, who was very much her admirer, perceived her exit, and insisted upon "seeing her to her carriage!"

Lady Morgan used to declare, that her agony of false shame was dreadful; but sooner than confess, she allowed the servants "to call her coach, and let her coach be called"; but of course it did not come. She then insisted upon "walking on to find it," and entreated Lord George to leave them to the servant, whom they had brought with them; but he was too gallant, and still insisted on keeping them company "till they should find their carriage."

The hackney coachman, who had been ordered to wait, espied them, and followed to explain that he was there and waiting. Mrs. Patterson took no notice; Miss Owenson took no notice; the footman, who guessed their troubles, took no notice either. The hackney-coachman continued to follow them.

"What *does* that man mean by following us?" asked Lord George.

"I really cannot imagine," said the elder lady.

"I wish he would go away," said the younger one.

"What do you want, fellow?" asked Lord George.

"I want these ladies either to get into my coach or to pay me my fare."

"What *does* he mean—is he drunk?"

"No," said Miss Owenson, at last, laughing at the dilemma; "but the fact is, that we were so ashamed of coming in a hackney-coach, that we wanted nobody to know it."

Mrs. Patterson proceeded to explain all about how it had happened that they were deprived of the use of their own carriage; but her representations were drowned in the peals of laughter with which Miss Owenson and Lord George recognised the absurdity of the situation.

"So you came in a hackney-coach, and would rather have walked home in the mud than have had it known. How *very* Irish!" was his lordship's comment. He put them into their despised coach, and saw them drive away.

The comparative failure of *The Missionary*, together with the troubles she had met with from her publishers, turned Miss Owenson's mind for a moment from the romance towards the drama. She had an hereditary leaning to the stage. Her father had been a manager and a comedian. She herself had written a successful musical piece. The theatre offered her many inducements to try her hand at a play; and she had so far thought of it as to consult Lord Abercorn on the choice of a hero. Lord Abercorn's answer is among her papers.

Lord Abercorn to Miss Owenson.

[*No date.*]

I read your letter to the person you desired, dear, and if I did not write "by RETURN" (O you Irish expression, why cannot I write the proper brogue for such a broguey expression?) you must still impute it to the penny postman's life I am living, for when you ask me a question worth an answer, I will never delay it.

What your genius for melodrama, or any drama may be, I have no other reason for guessing than my suspicion that you have genius enough for anything that you will give proper attention to. I should, however, be sorry that the drama, in any shape, should supersede the intentions of the romance or novel production that you last professed.

Hand-in-hand with it I have no objection; and as you give me my choice of two heroes, I will so far decide that he shall not be Henry the Fourth (Henry the Fourth of France). In the first place he is hackneyed to death and damnation; in the second, between ourselves (and spite of the whole female race whose favourite hero he is) he was no hero at all; he was a brave, good-natured, weak, selfish gentleman, and had he been endowed with higher mind and nature than he was, still his infamous conduct to the Prince de Condé would have blotted him out of my list.

The qualities, virtues, and vices of Francis the First were of a more kingly kind; and though he was hardly a hero, he was a good deal more like one; his time, too, was more chivalric, and the events of it, as well as his own words and actions, having been less hackneyed, may be worked up far more entertainingly and interestingly.

So much for my wisdom with which I shall begin and end.

So bye-bye, sweet Glo.

Lord Abercorn's objection to Henri Quatre as a hero, in spite of all feminine preferences to the contrary, were probably personal. Henri's "infamous conduct" towards Condé, perhaps reminded him of Lieutenant Copley's "infamous conduct" to the Marquis of Abercorn.

During this visit to London, Miss Owenson made the acquaintance, and won the enduring friendship of that woman of unhappy genius, Lady Caroline Lamb. Born in the highest rank, gifted with the rarest powers, at once an artist, a poetess, a writer of romance, a woman of society and the world, Lady Caroline Ponsonby had been the belle of her season, the toast of her set, the star of her firmament. Early loved and early won by a young man, who was at the same time a nobleman and a statesman, every wish of her heart, every aspiration of her mind, would appear to have been gratified by success. As Lady Caroline Lamb, and future Lady Melbourne, she was an adored wife, with a fixed and high position in society, and with everything that wealth, beauty, youth, talent and connexions can command to make life happy. But the woman was not content. Is any woman of genius ever tranquil? Is not genius, whether in man or woman, the seed of what Schiller calls "a sublime discontent?" Lady Caroline had that restless craving after excitement—after the something unattained and unattainable—which pursues all spirits that are "finely touched." Sometimes she sought this in the exercise of her pencil and her pen; sometimes in the more dangerous exercise of her affections and her imagination. She was not wicked. She was not even lax in her opinions. But she was bold and daring in her excursions through the debateable land which divides the territories of friendship from those of love. If she never fell, she was scarcely ever safe from falling. At the date when her correspondence with Miss Owenson began, she was a young wife of five or six years, and the image of Byron, beautiful and deadly as the nightshade, had not thrown its shadow on her life. When the letter, which is now to introduce Lady Caroline to the reader, as one of the most charming figures of this correspondence, was written, Byron had just returned from the East, having his *Hints from Horace* and the early cantos of *Childe Harold* in his pocket. His *English Bards*, which he found in a fourth edition, had made him famous; and his poetry, his travels, his singularity of manners, his extraordinary personal beauty, and his reputation for gallantry, made him one of the chief lions of the London season. Half the women were soon in love with him, more or less platonically; among others, at first very platonically, Lady Caroline Lamb. How far this friendship and flirtation went between the noble poet and the noble lady, has never yet, for want of full materials, or in deference to living persons, been truly told. These reasons for observing silence are no longer binding. Lady Caroline made Lady Morgan the depository of all her secrets as to this connexion; the actors in the drama have passed away, and the story of their lives is public property. The details which may now be given, mainly under the hands of Lady Caroline and Lord Byron, will complete an interesting chapter in the poet's memoirs.

Lady Caroline may now appear on the stage.

Lady C. Lamb to Miss Owenson.

LONDON,
1811.

MY DEAR MISS OWENSON,

If it had not been near making me cry, what I am going to tell you might make you laugh; but I believe you are too good-natured not to sympathize

in some manner with my distress. It never occurred
to me that I should forget the direction you gave
me, so that having ordered the carriage, and having
passed a restless night, I was but just getting up when
it was ready. I ordered it to fetch you; where, was
the question—at York, was the only answer I could
possibly give; for York, alas, is all I remember. Now
they say there is a York lane, three York streets,
a York place, a York buildings, and York court.
I knew no number, but immediately thought of sending to Lady Augusta Leith; the *Court Guide* was
opened, it was for 1810; Lady A. Leith consequently
not where she now is, and where either of you are
I cannot think; but as I was obliged to go into the
country, I wrote this, and take my chance of its
ever getting to you. Should you receive it, pray
accept of my regrets and excuses, and do not treat
me as ill as I have you, but remember your kind
intentions some evening. I shall be back Saturday,
I believe; but General Leith goes Tuesday.

See me before you leave town, and send me your
number and street, I beg of you; the impression
you have made is, I assure you, a little stronger,
but I never can recollect one direction—do you think
the new man could teach me?

Yours very sincerely, C. LAMB.

My direction is always Melbourne House.

The two ladies soon met to become friends and
associates for ever. No contrast could be greater than

between these two women of genius; one highly born, adored by her husband, and every whim gratified without her own exertion; the other humble, if not obscure; adored by many, but with a dangerous kind of love; compelled to struggle for her daily bread and for her daily safety. Both played, most perilously, with the fire; yet both came from the burning bush unscathed. Lady Caroline was saved by her affections, Miss Owenson by her principles. She, too, was weaving most unconsciously her married destiny. On the death of his first wife, Dr. Morgan accepted the post of physician to Lord Abercorn. A man so handsome and accomplished, made a deep impression on the Marchioness, who set herself to provide him with a second wife. The affair of Miss Owenson with "*le bien aimé*" was now off; and Lady Abercorn's letters to Miss Owenson began to glow with praises of her young physician. Jane Butler (afterwards Lady Manners) mentions him in one of her letters in a rather droll fashion.

"We brought Dr. Morgan," she writes to Miss Owenson, "a physician, with us, who, I believe, is very clever in more ways than one, as he understands simony and all Mrs. Malaprop's accomplishments. I believe he is of your religious persuasion, and seems to think Moses mistaken in his calculations (this is *entre nous*)."

Lady Abercorn, from the beginning, had set her heart on a match between Dr. Morgan and Miss Owenson, and Miss Owenson entered readily into all the fun of such a suggestion. When Lady Aberdeen wrote to Miss Owenson a glowing account of Dr. Morgan's learning, and genius, and qualifications, and desired her to write a poetical diploma for him, Miss Owenson answered in pure *gaieté de cœur*, as follows:—

DIPLOMA NOS UNIVERSITATAS SANTÆ GLORVINA.

We learned Professors of the College,
The Alma Mater of true knowledge,
Where students learn, *in memoria*,
The philosophical amatoria,
Where senior fellows hold no power,
And junior sophists rule the hour,
Where every bachelor of arts
Studies no science—but of hearts.
Takes his degree from smiling eyes
And gets his FELLOWSHIP—by sighs;
Where scholars learn, by rules quite simple,
To expound the mystics of a dimple;
To run through all their moods and tenses,
The feelings, fancies, and the senses.
Where none (though still to grammar true)
Could e'er *decline—a billet doux*,
Though *all* soon learn to *conjugate*,
(*Eadum nos autoritate*)
We—learned Professors of this College,
The Alma Mater of true knowledge,
Do, on the Candidate *Morgani*,
(Doctissimo in Medicini)
Confer his right well earned degree,
And dub him, henceforth, sage *M.D.*,
He, having stood examination,
On points might puzzle half the nation,
Shown where with skill he could apply
A sedative, or *stimuli*,
How to the *chorda tympani*
He could, by dulcet symphony,
The soul divine itself convey.

How he (in verses) can impart
A vital motion to a heart,
Through hours which Time had sadly robb'd,
Though dull and morbid it had throbb'd.
Teach sympathetic nerves to thrill,
Pulses to quicken or lie still;
And without pause or hesitation,
Pursue that vagrant thing *sensation*,
From right to left,—from top to toe,
From head of sage to foot of beau,
While vain it shuns his searching hand,
E'en in its own *pineal gland*.

But did we all his feats rehearse,
How he excels in tuneful verse,
How well he writes—how well he sings,
How well he does ten thousand things,
Gave we due meed to this bright *homo*,
It would—*Turgeret Loc Diploma.*

                        GLORVINA OWENSONES.

On leaving England Miss Owenson again proceeded to Baron's Court. She used to relate that Dr. Morgan had heard so much in praise of Miss Owenson's wit, genius and general fascination, that he took an immense prejudice against her, and being a very shy man, he disliked the idea of meeting her.

He was one morning sitting with the Marchioness, when the groom of the chambers, throwing open the doors, announced "Miss Owenson!" who had just arrived. Dr. Morgan sprung from his seat, and there being no other way of escape, leaped through the open window into the garden below! This was too fair a challenge for Miss Owenson to refuse; she set to work to captivate him, and succeeded more effectually than she either desired or designed. The following letter gives no indication of the crisis so nearly at hand; it is to Mrs. Lefanu, and the tone is rather depressed.

Miss Owenson to Mrs. Lefanu.

[*No date.*]

CHERE, CHERE,

May the event your *sweet letter* communicated, and every event in your family that succeeds it, be productive of increasing happiness. Too much the creature of circumstances as they influence my manners or my conduct, my heart, ruled in its feelings by the objects of its affections only, knows no change, and the sympathy, the tender interest in all that concerns you, my *longest, kindest friend,* which chance recently discovered to you, has always existed under an increasing power since the first moment I pressed your cordial hand—I met the kind welcome of your full eyes. If I am too apt to visit abroad, I am sure to come home to you, and the increasing kindness with which you receive and forgive me, hourly quickens my return, and extends my contrition.

Tom and his bride are now as happy as is possible for human nature to be. I rejoice in their happiness. I pray that it may long, long continue, and above all, that it may add to the sum of your's and Mr. Lefanu's; for if ever parents deserved well of their children, you both have. I was received here with the kindest and most joyous welcome. I find the people and the place delightful—there never was such a perfect Paradise; the summer makes all the difference and the magnificent outlines I so much admired in winter, are now most luxuriantly filled up.

We have got a most desirable acquisition to our circle, in the family physician; he is a person of extraordinary talent and extensive acquirements; a linguist, musician, poet and philosopher, and withal a most amiable and benevolent person; he is in high popularity, and he and I most amazing friends, as you may suppose.

Miss Butler is here, merry and pleasant as ever. She is sitting beside me, and desires her compliments, congratulations and best recollections to your ladyship. Olivia writes of nobody but you. She seems in very low spirits about our father, poor dear soul! and *misses* me sadly. I need not say a word to you on the subject. I am sure you will see her often, and I know you cannot *help* being kind to her, and to any one who may stand in need of your kindness.

We expect the Duke of Richmond and suite the week after next. I expect Sir C. and Lady Asgill will also come at that time, so that we shall be a gay party. Olivia has been asked over and over again, but still declines the honour.

You see the king cannot make up his mind to leave us; he is *too kind!* I believe all things remain on the other side in *statu quo*. Write to me soon like a love, and tell me all that you think I most desire to know; above all, that you continue to love

Your own GLORVINA.

CHAPTER XXXVI.

ENGAGED TO BE MARRIED.

BETWEEN the last letter to Mrs. Lefanu and the next one to her father, not many weeks elapsed. This and the subsequent letters are all the indications that remain of her feelings and thoughts upon an event so important in her life, as her first real struggle against falling into love. She used to say, in after life, how little she was then aware of the blessing that had befallen her and how near she had been to missing it, through her own perverseness. There is no doubt that she had dreamed of making a more brilliant match.

Miss Owenson to Robert Owenson.

BARON'S COURT,
August 20, 1811.

MY DEAREST DAD,

I am the least taste in life at a loss how to begin to tell you what I am going to ask you—which

is, your leave to marry Doctor Morgan, whom I will
not marry if you do not wish it. I dare say you
will be amazingly astonished; but not half so much
as I am, for Lord and Lady Abercorn have hurried
on the business in such a manner, that I really don't
know what I am about. They called me in last
night, and more like parents than friends, begged me
to be guided by them—that it was their wish not
to lose sight of me, which, except I married a friend
of theirs, they might, as they never would acknowledge a *Dublin husband,* but that if I accepted Morgan, the man upon earth they most esteemed and
approved, they would be friends to both for life—
that we should reside one year with them, after our
marriage, or if they remained in Ireland, *two years,*
so that we might lay up our income during that
time to begin the world. He is also to continue
their physician.

He has now five hundred a-year, independent of
practice. I don't myself see the thing quite in the
light they do; but they think him a man of such
great abilities, such great worth and honour, that I
am the most fortunate person in the world.

He stands in the first-class of physicians in London, having taken his Doctor's degree at Cambridge;
his connexions are excellent, &c., &c., and in person
very distinguished-looking. Now tell me what you
wish, for I am still, as ever, all your own loving and
dutiful child,

SYDNEY OWENSON.

On the same subject, she wrote—after a few days—to most of her old friends. The letter to Mrs. Lefanu and Lady Stanley, may be given as specimens of the whole.

Miss Owenson to Mrs. Lefanu.

BARON'S COURT,
August 29, 1811.

MY DEAREST FRIEND,

Your inimitable letter was a source of great comfort to me. Your eloquent and exalted theories are still less powerful in their influence over me than your bright example. I have seen you the Providence of your family, and I admire and revere too much not to endeavour to imitate.

This event, the most unlooked-for and rapid of my life, has been accelerated by my friends here, and by the more than romantic passion of the most amiable and ardent of human beings, so as to leave me in a state of *agitation* and *flurry* that prevented me writing on the subject to any human being but my family—and even to them so incoherently as to leave them more to guess at from inference than fact.

The business was, indeed, *so hurried*, that it was all like a dream. The licence and ring have been in the house these ten days—all the settlements made; yet I have been battling off, from day to day, and hour to hour, and have only ten minutes back procured a little breathing time. The fact is, the struggle is almost too great for me—on one side engaged, be-

yond retrieval, to a man who has frequently declared
to my friends, here, that if I break off he will not survive it!! on the other, the dreadful certainty of being
parted for ever from a country and friends I love,
and a family I adore, to which I am linked by such
fatal ties, that my heart must break in breaking
them.

Lord and Lady Abercorn will not part with Dr. Morgan for a moment, as they suppose the whole family
would die if they did; so that, after my marriage, I
should have no chance of seeing you all before I went
to England, and I have, therefore, at last prevailed on
Morgan to permit me to go up for a *week* or *two*, while
I am yet a free agent. When I read that part of
your letter where you say Tom and his wife were to
live with you, I wept bitterly. Oh, if it were my lot
to live with those I love! but I am about to leave
them all. I write incoherently, for I am feeling
strongly; don't read this to Livy, but just what is
right and politic to mention to any one. To give you
any idea of the passion I have most unwittingly inspired, would be vain; but if I had spirits, I could
amuse you not a little. Tell Livy to repeat to you
some of his eloquent nonsense which I wrote to her.
Barring his wild, unfounded love for me, the creature
is perfection. The most *manly*, I had almost said
daring, tone of mind, united to more goodness of
heart and disposition, than I ever met with in a human being. Even with this circle, where all is acquirement and accomplishment, it is confessed that his
versatility of talent is unrivalled. There is scarcely

any art or science he has not cultivated with success; and the resources of his mind and memory are exhaustless. His manners are too English to be popular with the Irish; and though he is reckoned a handsome man, it is not that style of thing which, if I were to choose for beauty, I should select—it is too indicative of goodness; a little *diablerie* would make me wild in love with him. To the injury of his interests and circumstances, he has offered to settle with me in Dublin, since I appear so heart-broken at parting from my family; but *that* I would not hear of. He is just thirty; has a moderate property, independent of his profession; is a member and a fellow of twenty colleges and societies, and is a Cambridge man. This is a full-length picture drawn for your private inspection. He read your letter with bursts of admiration. He says you must have a divine mind, and that if all my country-women resemble you, his constancy will be sadly put to the test. We are to live one year with the Abercorns, which will save some income for furnishing a house in London, where we are to reside. *My man* is now playing Handel, and putting me in mind of dear Tom. He does not, however, play near so well; but has more *science* than any one, and sings the most difficult things at sight. He has so much improved me in Italian and singing, you cannot imagine. Ten thousand thanks for your benevolent attention to my poor old father—never did he stand more in need of it, sick, worn down and deprived of the attentions of a child he adores, and who has hitherto lived for him. You are all goodness, and to

part from you is not among the least of my afflictions.
God bless you ever,

S. OWENSON.

A thousand loves to all the fire-side circle; but
above all to Joe. I am quite shocked at the expense
of my last letter; but as I saw you got all your letters
at the *Castle*, I took it for granted they were free.

Miss Owenson to Lady Stanley.

BARON'S COURT,
1st September, 1811.

MY MOST DEAR FRIEND,

It is an age since we held any communion; in the
first instance (I was prevented by the fear of boring
you by a *platitude* of a letter, which could only repeat
what you know—that I love you. In the second, I
have been prevented writing since my arrival here
(now five weeks ago) by an event unexpected and
critical; in a word, in this little space of time, a man
has fallen in love with me, *tête baissée*, and almost
married me, before I know where I am or what it is
all about. I mentioned to you before, that Lord
Abercorn was to bring over with him a physician, and
as they wrote me word that he was a person of distinguished talent, a charming musician, and altogether an
interesting person, I sent him some comical professional
problems in my letters to Lady Abercorn. He answered
them by a poetical thesis—I sent him *a diploma*—and
thus prepared, we met under circumstances and in

scenes too favourable to the romantic feelings peculiar to his character, and which it was my lot to excite and feed. In short, almost without looking beyond the instant, his *empressement*, and the anxiety of Lord and Lady Abercorn to forward an event which would place me in England near them, took me unawares, and I gave a sort of consent to an event, which it is, and has ever since been, my incessant struggle to delay.

The fact is, there is much *pour et contre*, on the subject (Dr. Morgan having but a small patrimonial property, independent of his profession, in which he is still but young). The confidence his medical skill and success have inspired in this family, where there is a continual demand on his attention, have so raised him in their good opinion, that they have declared themselves his fast friends, and promoters of his interests for life. Indeed, it was at their instance, I was induced to listen to a proposal, which could have nothing in it very gratifying to my *ambition*. The man, however, is *perfection*. His mind has that strength of tone and extent of reflection, which you admire so much. He thinks upon every subject of importance with us, and is sometimes so daring in risking his bold and singular opinions, that while it raises him in my esteem, it makes me tremble for his worldly interests, so seldom promoted by this sovereign independence of principle and spirit, which throws rank and influence at such an incalculable distance. He is, with all this deep philosophy of character, a most accomplished gentleman. He speaks and writes well several languages, and is a scientific musician, a devoted naturalist, and has studied every branch of natural history with success. With these resources of *mind*, I never saw a wretch so thrown upon the *heart* for his happiness, or so governed by ardent and unruly passion, of which his most romantic *engouement* for me is a proof. I have refused and denied him over and over again, because if it is not in worldly circumstances a very good match for me, it is still WORSE for him. I am still putting it off from day to day, but fear I am too far committed to recede with honour. All this is *entre nous*, and should you mention the thing, *prônez* the business as much as you can, for upon all occasions, *il est bon de se faire valoir*. We are to live the first year with Lord and Lady Abercorn, and the next we hope to be in a baby-house of our own in London, and, oh! what happiness it will be to me to have one to receive you, dear Lady Stanley, when you come to town, instead of your going to an hotel; believe me, there is not a human being I should be happier to see, than your dear self, after my own sweet sister. The worst part of my story is, that I must then have to leave my country, and father, and sister, that I adore; when I think of this, I start from my promise, and have more than once *entreated* to be off, and in short, sometimes I am almost out of my mind between contending feelings; you would pity me if you knew and saw my struggles; pray write to me soon, and love me always,

Your own GLORVINA.

We expect the Duke and court here in a few days.

Lady Stanley's reply to the announcement of her friend's proposed, but not yet accomplished, marriage is both wise and kind.

Lady Stanley to Miss Owenson.

PENRHOS,
September 18*th*, 1811.

MY DEAR GLORVINA,

Shall I say the import of your letter surprised me? I know not. However, I think surprise was not the sensation predominant among the many it set afloat; that you should have met with a man who looked, listened, and entered the lists of love, *tête baissée*, was an event much of course; but that an equal to the admirable Crichton should be met at all, and moreover, that the destinies should just place him within the circle of Glorvina's influence, is truly a matter worthy of wonder, and particularly to me, who have hitherto adhered pertinaciously to a persuasion, that kindred spirits were subjected to the same laws as parallel lines, and never could meet on this ungracious planet. But, behold an exception! Receive, my dear Sydney, my sincere felicitations on your view of establishment. Yet rest assured, I do not fail of taking a part in your anxieties, but who can be married without such attendants? If every *contre* was nearly looked to, alack, poor Hymen! But in the main, establishment is good, in some lights almost expedient, since the delights of youth, of friends, of range, and frolic, are but passengers. On the subject of riches, it must be avowed, my worldly wishes are not completely gratified, but on that question, the interests of the heart must arbitrate, nor can I dispute with those sovereigns, and do they not appear with a powerful phalanx? and sweetly chime with the old song—" Et il en sera toujours de même, si j'en juge d'après mon cœur." Perhaps, ere this time, the conflict is over; I wish it may be so, and every sacrifice well compensated by the acquisition of a friend and associate, *à tout epreuve.* I have been sadly tardy in writing, but were details worth while, I could show I am more excusable than usual; I have been singularly engaged by company and hampered by business at the same time, and lassitude and chagrins spoilt every little interval. And now then, farewell, my dear Sydney. Imagine, and you may well imagine (do me but justice) how much I love to hear further of an event so interesting to me, and believe me, by every name,

    Most truly yours, &c., &c.,
       M. STANLEY

CHAPTER XXXVII.

BETWEEN CUP AND LIP.

WHEN she was fairly engaged, Miss Owenson's courage failed her. Dr. Morgan being very much in love, desired naturally that the marriage should take place with as little delay as possible. The Marchioness, to whom the drama and the *dénouement* were a pleasant excitement, had no idea that the ceremony in real life could be anything more than the last page in a novel, or the last words in a play, after the characters have grouped themselves. She sent for the marriage ring and licence, and would have proceeded to extremities, without consulting the wishes of one of the parties most interested.

Miss Owenson, however, contrived to obtain a short respite, and permission to pay a visit to her sister and father, in Dublin. Her father's precarious state of health was the plea she used. She was sent the first stage of her journey in all the state of a carriage and four horses, with Dr. Morgan riding beside the window for an escort. A fortnight was to be the term of her ab-

sence, and she promised very fairly, that if permitted
to go away, she would return without fail, at the time
appointed. She had no such intention. Her father
was ill; his health was quite broken up. As, however,
he was in no immediate danger, Miss Owenson had no
idea of stopping at home to keep him company. She
plunged at once into all the gaieties of Dublin society.
She was more the fashion than ever; and she enjoyed
the feeling of freedom and independence after the
stately restraints of her life at Baron's Court, of which
she had, by that time, become disenchanted.

Dr. Morgan was retained at Baron's Court by his
professional duty. Neither the Marquis nor the Marchioness
would grant him leave of absence. He was
extremely jealous, and knew his fair and slippery lady
love to be surrounded by admirers. He was especially
vexed by the attentions bestowed on her by Mr. Parkhurst,
one of the gayest men about town in Dublin
society; but he was unable to do more than write
eloquent letters of complaint and appeal, to which
the lady paid not the smallest attention. She always
owned, afterwards, that she had behaved exceedingly
ill, and that she deserved for ever to have lost the best
husband that ever a woman had; but at the time,
she only thought how she might prolong her absence,
if, indeed, she did not meditate breaking loose altogether.
The correspondence on both sides is characteristic,
and as the subject of love and love-making, of
woman's constancy and man's perfidy, is one of perennial
interest, some of this correspondence may be
given. The letters are printed as nearly according to

their date as can be ascertained. Both the Marquis
and Marchioness seem to have been kind throughout
the whole period, and to have shewn great patience
with their refractory *protegée*. In one of Morgan's
letters, under date Oct. 7, there is "a magic ———"
which requires a word of explanation. When Miss
Owenson had been particularly naughty, and wished
to make her peace, she would leave in her next note a
small blank space to represent a kiss. Morgan was at
liberty to believe that her lips had touched the paper,
and to act accordingly.

T. C. Morgan to Miss Owenson.

BARON'S COURT,
October 1, 1811.

MY DEAREST GIRL,

Here I am, again, safely returned from Strabane,
after going through a day's eating and drinking enough
to kill a horse. We had a most heavenly day, yesterday; but to-day, it has rained incessantly; we were
not, however, wet, being well provided with coats, so
that I am in no danger of dying this trip. Baron's
Court to-day is dulness personified. Lady Abercorn
received a shocking account of Lady Aberdeen from
Mrs. Kemble; and though I know how very little
such accounts are worth minding, yet her tears are
infectious, and I cannot help feeling alarmed and out
of spirits. Receiving, as I do, daily marks of their
kindness and good will, I cannot avoid sympathising
with them in their worst of all domestic calamities.

Yet, *true to human nature,* I am *selfish* enough to think much of the effect a fatal termination of this disease would have on us and our comforts. I trust that I am not laying up for *you* a winter's residence in the house of mourning—whatever the Apostles may say, *I* infinitely prefer the house of rejoicing. But to return to a more grateful theme, how is my best beloved after her journey? I hope to-morrow to hear a good account of you, and that you found your father and sister better than you expected.

Have you been gadding about much? Have you seen many people? Are you happy and comfortable? or are you, like me, looking forward anxiously to the happy time that will unite us for ever? Dearest Glorvina, love me as I adore you. How often I kiss the little gold bottle, and think of the sweeter roses on *somebody's* lips. Shorten time, by every means, that separates us, if you value the happiness of

Your ever devoted,
T. C. M.

T. C. Morgan to Miss Owenson.

Monday, October 7.

DEAREST, DEAR LOVE,

Will you, can you pardon my ravings? How angry I am with myself! I have at last got a sweet, charming, *affectionate* letter from you, and half my miseries are over. If my two last letters gave you pain, think what misery (well or ill-founded), what horrid depression must have been mine to inspire them. Your rea-

sonings are all very fine and very conclusive; but, alas, I parted with *reason* to a certain little coquette, and I can attend to and feel no language but that of the heart. Still, however, I must insist upon my distinction, that while I am ready to give up *everything* to your lovely, amiable *family feelings*, I can ill brook your associating any unpleasant idea with that of returning to *me*. If I know my heart, neither solitude, sickness, nor slavery would be unpalatable, if it gave me back to Glorvina. I would seek her amidst the plague, in an African ship, or, if such a place existed, in her *own father's* dominions. I have but one object in life, and *it is you;* and so little can I bear the idea of your preferring anything to me, that I have been angry with Olivia when she has had too much of your attention. Indeed, indeed it is *because I love*, that I cannot suppose it possible any feeling of disgust, or *ennui*, can associate itself with your return to me, and, I would fain hope, happiness. You cannot think so meanly of me as to suppose the dimity chamber could urge me to draw you from your *duties*. Trust me, love, you never win me more than when I see you, in imagination, discharging them; but when I picture to myself the *thoughtless, heartless* Glorvina, trifling with her friend, jesting at his sufferings, and flirting with every man she meets; when I imagine her more in love with the *vanities of this wicked world* than with me, I feel not *sure* of her. Do not think me cruel in reminding you that you have lost one husband by flirting, and that that makes *me* feel it is just possible you may drive another mad. I cannot, give you to the amusements of Dublin. God knows (if he takes the trouble to know) this "pile" is "dreary" enough without you; but it makes me curse the hour I threw away my love on one so incapable of returning it, when I see you looking forward to a *solitary* winter in it; trust me, dearest, a little *natural philosophy* will make time pass pleasantly enough, never fear.

I read part of your letter to Miss B——, relative to "Almighty Tact," and she laughed *tout son saoul*. She says, if there is one human being more thoroughly destitute of *tact* than another, it is Glorvina—and, indeed, I think so. In the instance of myself you have failed utterly. If you knew me, you would not combat my feelings by your affected stoicism; you would flatter my vanity with the idea of the separation being as painful to you as to me; you would soothe me with tenderness and not shock me with *badinage*. If you knew how much eloquence there was in the magic ——; if you knew the pleasure I felt in touching the paper that had touched your lips! Oh, Glor.! Glor.! have you been all this while studying me to so little purpose? In reply to *your orders*, know that I have not opened my lips to say more than—"a bit more," "very good," and "no more, thank you, MY LORD," since you have been gone. Lady Abercorn swears she heard me sing, "Il mio ben quando vena," and says I am Nina Pazza. In good truth, I believe she is right, for surely nothing but madness would distress itself, and what it loves more than itself, as *I* do. I assure you I have made myself quite ill, and others present; my calmness is acquired, unnatural, and deceitful. I am sorry, very sorry, for your poor dear dad; but hope he is not seriously worse; say everything that is kind to him from me, and tell him I hope we shall spend many a pleasant day together yet. Do you know you shock my tenderness by the *ease* with which you talk of Miss Butler. Surely we must adopt two terms to express our different loves, *one* word cannot imply such different affections. I WILL think and speak of nothing but you. As to my commissions, do not, best and dearest, put yourself to any inconvenience about them; when done you may send them by the mail, the pleasure of receiving anything from you is worth the carriage, though it even amounted to gold. There is, however, but *one* commission about which I am *anxious*, and that is *to love me* as I do you, EXCLUSIVELY; to prefer me to every other good; to think of me, speak of me, write to me, and to look forward to our union as the completion of every wish, for so do I by you. Do this, and though you grow as "*ugly*" as Sycorax, you will never lose in me the fondest, most doating, affectionate of husbands. Glorvina, I was born for tenderness; my business in life is *to love*. Cultivate, then, the latent feelings of the *heart*, learn to distrust the *imagination*, and to despise and quit the world, before the world leaves you. How, dearest, will you otherwise bear the hour when no longer young, lovely, and *agaçante*, you will see the *great ones* lay aside their plaything and forget their companion who can no longer give them plea-

sure; where, but in the arms of affection, will you
then find consolation? Fly, then, to me by times.
You have much wisdom to acquire yet, with respect
to happiness; and believe me, the *dimity chamber* is
a school worth all the Portico's in the world, Mrs.
Stoic. *There* nature reigns, and you will hear none
but the language of truth. Do you recollect folding
up a piece of blotting-paper with one of your letters?
I preserve it as the apple of my eye, and kiss it, as
I would you, all to pieces.

My sweetest life, I do not mean an atom of acrimony towards you in all this; but misery will be
querulous. I determine to pass over my sufferings in
silence; but find I cannot. Do not say I am selfish;
if I were, I should have pressed you to marriage when
I could have done it effectually. I should have opposed your leaving me; and now I should give up all
to you for comfort. I flatter myself, that *hitherto*
every sacrifice has been on my part. My only comfort is, that my wishes have given place to yours.

I do not wish you to *cut* any one; but I think
Parkhurst, too *particular* in his attentions; besides,
how can I bear that anybody can have the pleasure of
talking to you and gazing on you when I cannot. I
should be sorry you offended a *friend* on account of
any whim of mine; you can be civil to him without
encouraging *his daily* visits. Strangely as I show it,
I *am* obliged and grateful for your every attention,
and in this instance in particular; but indeed I do not
wish it. I have not so mean an opinion of myself to
be jealous of anybody's alienating your mind from me

by exciting a preference, *et pour tout le reste j'en sais assez.*

I have kissed your dear hair again and again, as I do the bottle, twenty times an hour; do not judge of my temper by this instance, for, believe me, I am not always, nor ever was in my married life, in the horrible state of mind I now am. You know I think ill of life in general, and kick against calamity as if I received an affront as well as an injury in it from fate. But trust me, no chance of life can reach me to wound as I am now wounded; when reposed on your dear bosom then my spirits will be calmed, my irritability soothed. If I thought there was the remotest chance of my giving you the uneasiness I know I now do, when once you are mine, I would release you from your engagement *au coup de pistolet*. No, no, my beloved, I hope, after all, we may be enabled to say, in our age, *c'est un monde passable*, at least it *shall* be so to you, if I can make it so. God bless you, my own dear, sweet, darling girl; don't, don't be angry with me, for I am very wretched without that. Mr. Eliot is come at last, and I must go dress and acquire steadiness for "*representation.*"

Adieu *ma belle, ma chère* Glor.

MORTIMER.

9 *o'clock.*

Pity and forgive a wretch whom nothing but your presence can console. God, God bless you, dear Glorvina.

T. C. Morgan to Miss Owenson.

DU CHEMIN DE CERBÈRE À LA PORTE D'ENFER.
Mardi, October 15*th*, 1811.

Faut-il que je m'egaye toujours? Combien cela est triste! Mais, soyons heureux c'est encore bien plus difficile. Egayons-nous pourtant. Pourquoi?—*La reine le veut!*

The Clitheroes are just gone with Bowen for the Giant's Causeway, the latter returns in the middle of next week; the former promise to repeat their visit soon. Oglander and the Major are gone shooting; and the little tail of nobility, Miss Butler and I, are going to ride if the weather permit. I really was *glad* you were not with us last night. We played magical music, "What's my Thought like?" and many other games *equally amusing*, for three or four hours; you would have been bored to death, as was almost your poor Mortimer. They made Lord Abercorn *go out* frequently, and though he was bored as bad as man could be, he did it with an ease and grace that was very pleasing; he certainly is thoroughly a gentleman on those points. Miss Butler seems thoroughly determined to go to Dublin, and then what will become of us? *Che farò senza mio ben,* we shall be given up to melancholy. What will become of me? *io morirò—ahi! ben mio*, how happy should I be could I behold thee and be near thee, and see thee with thy dear family, but what useless wishes, I love thee dearest! my wife, I love thee! and for thee I will do and endure anything, everything! adieu, my love, adieu!

   Farewell, dearest Glorvina,
     Your own, own
        MONTIMER.

Miss Owenson to T. C. Morgan.

        October, 1811.

"Do the P——s and Castlereaghs go to you at Christmas? when does the Butler come to town, and when do the Carberys leave you?"—answer all. I don't send you a kiss to-day, I am tired of the *diurnal act*, but I lay my head upon your bosom in a wife-like way, and suffer you to press me gently to your heart, which is more than you *deserve!* I am glad you changed your pen—I hate *poesy*—

> "When this you see,
> *Remember* me."
>
> "*His* mouth was Primmer,
> A lesson I took,
> I swore it was pretty,
> And then kiss'd the book."

that is the text, vide "Peeping Tom;" but I did not intend to make so free with you this three months, for you have behaved *very ill indeed* lately, and talked *like a fool* very often. Livy does not know what to make of you! but I forgive—lay by your nervousness, and get some common sense.

        S. OWENSON.

Miss Owenson to T. C. Morgan.

October 31st, 1811.

I am not half such a little rascal as you suppose; the best feelings only have detained me from you; and feelings better than the *best* will bring me back to you. I must be more or less than woman to resist tenderness, goodness, excellence, like yours, and I am simply woman, aye, dear, "every inch a woman." I feel a little kind of tingling about the heart, at once more feeling myself nestled in yours; do you remember —well, dear, if you don't, I will soon revive your recollection—I said I would not write to you to-day, but I could not resist it, and I am now going off to a man of business, and about Lady Abercorn's books, in the midst of the snow and pinched with cold. God bless you, love.

S. O.

Your song is charming; you are a clever wretch, and I love you more for your talents than your virtues, you *thing of the world*. What put it into your stupid head that I would not return at Christmas? did I ever say so, blockhead?

Well, I have only the old *story* to *tell*, no more than yourself—

> "And I loves you, and you loves me,
> And oh! how happy we shall be."

Take care of the *whiskers*—mind they are not to grow

thus—but thus.—[Here follows in the letter a couple
of droll portraits of Morgan, with the whiskers grown
and trimmed in the two fashions then in favour.]

T. C. Morgan to Miss Owenson.

Thursday, November, 1811.

You are a pretty pair of Paddies, you and your
sister. *Only see* how you enclosed your letter for me,
to Lord Abercorn, without seal and without direction.
Your second letter came at the *usual* time; but judge
my consternation, when Lord Abercorn gave me your
first at breakfast, *premising he had read three sides of
it,* under the supposition it was for him, till he came
quite at the end, to "my dear Morgan," which rather
surprised him. In good truth, the letter is so much
like the *Epistle General of St. Jude,* that it will do for
any church. Well, "the gods take care of Cato."
There was not a word of *his* frolics, of the stupidity of
B. C——, of Livy's not coming, or anything one would
much care about his reading; but I was in a special
fright till I could get an opportunity of reading it and
convincing myself; for Heaven's sake be more careful.
I think he must have laughed at your *jealous suspicions,* though I don't believe he has a very high
opinion of my *Josephism.* I wish I had something to
confess, just to *satisfy* you; but, ah, alas! you have
the best security in the world for my fidelity, the want
of opportunity for me to go astray. For unless I
made love to a young diablesse or an old witch, and
became the papa of an incubus, the devil a chance

have I of doing wrong. I should like to know the
"when and the who" of your thoughts; perhaps it
would give me *an idea*. Seriously, my best love, if
you doubt me, come and claim your own, for *I am*
yours and only yours.

Dearest girl, how much I wish I could say anything satisfactory to you about your father. I *cannot
judge* accurately, but all your accounts of him have
given me an unfavourable impression of his chance of
ultimate recovery. I should think the whiskey *bad*
for him; at least, if not rendered *necessary* by circumstances, it must be injurious. Your low spirits distress
me very, very much. Would to God I could be with
you to soothe and comfort you! I am, however, not less
so than yourself, as you must see by my awkward attempts at humour. I am very *irritable* at these times,
and do not know whether to laugh or cry.

My yesterday's letter (written in this mood) was
particularly dull and fade; I am very much pleased,
flattered, delighted by your second letter; it is so de-
cisive a mark of your tenderness and affection. Dearest
Glorvina, I *have no* love for any but you; you have
my *whole, whole heart*, and if my letters vary, it is because my spirits vary, and with them my *tone* of
thinking. When, when will the day come that shall
make me *yours* for ever. Glorvina, we have both
suffered much on each other's account; I feel, however, conscious we shall both be ultimately happy in
each other. God, God bless you! I am writing myself into dreadful spirits; I believe catching your tone.

You give a horrid picture of poor dad! He must

have been *very ill indeed* to require so much blistering.
I find you are quite in raptures with Dublin. Four
dinners beside evening parties in one week; that is
pretty well for a person who went there *merely* to
enjoy the society of her family for a few weeks. However, if you are amused, I am content. You must
want occasional *distraction*, and to be candid, I should
be all the better for it, if it were in my reach. Only
love me, and write good-humouredly. You do not
mention the Butler; she is, I suppose, as happy as the
day is long; give my love to her, and tell her I miss
her very much.

T. C. Morgan to Miss Owenson.

BARON'S COURT,
Wednesday, 2 *o'clock, Nov.* 14*th.*

DEAREST AND BEST,

Me voici de retour, and I have just read your dear
letter. Great God! how little able am I to bear any
crosses in which you are concerned. I cannot free
my mind from the idea of your having been *seriously*
ill. You say you are better, and I must believe you.
But once for all I implore and beseech you, in no instance conceal from me the *full extent* of any sickness
or calamity that may reach *you* or *yours*. It is only
the entire confidence that communications *are* made,
and that nothing would be hid that might happen ill,
by which absence is rendered supportable. An anxious,
fretful and *Rousseauish* disposition (like mine) will let
the imagination so much get the start of reason, that,

when once deceived, I should never feel happy by
any communication however pleasant its nature. I
should fancy ten millions of accidents, kept from
me *for my good.* I hope and trust you have acted
sincerely by me in this instance, and are as well in
health and about one-*eighth* part as happy as if you
really were "*on my knee.*" What an image! how
lovely! My bosom swelled in reading it, and the ob-
trusive drops, *for once* harbingers of pleasure, danced
trembling on my eyelids; *bless* you, BLESS you, dearest
love! I do kiss you with my whole heart, and pat
your dear *caen dhu* [black head]; and I, too, in my
turn, ask your pardon for worrying you in my last
but one, and for the two short hasty scrawls of Sunday
and yesterday. In each case, however, I really was
compelled to be so brief; I should not have written,
but, judging by myself, I thought a short letter infinitely preferable to no letter at all; I have just received your parcel, but have had no time to examine
anything. You have forgotten my lavender water, of
which I am in great want—*mais n'importe.* The ring
does *famously.* I kiss it every instant (*now*) and NOW
and NOW-W-W-W. Pray take care of the mourning
ring you took as a pattern, as I value it much. Lady
Abercorn played me an *arch trick* about it. By mistake, she opened the muslin and found the ring; she
and Miss Butler *abstracted it.* I missed the expected delight, and flew (*à la moi*) *all over scarlet,*
up to her to inquire if it was amongst her parcels,
and very soon discovered by her joking how the land
lay. Oh! I am a great fool, and it's all along of *you,*

you thing you! God bless dear *you*, though, for all that. Lady Abercorn will be obliged by the Irish extract from *Ossian;* her countenance quite brightened when I mentioned it. At this moment my imagination is wandering in delight. I kiss and press you in idea, and I am all fire, and passion and tenderness; the sensations are rather too nervous and will leave a horrible depression; but for one such "five minutes"— perish an eternity! This morning, in bed, at Sir John's, I read part of *The Way to Keep Him*, and I see now you take the widow for your model; but it won't do, for though I love you in *every* mood, it is only when you are *true to* NATURE, *passionate and tender*, that *I adore* you. You never are less interesting to me than when you *brillez* in a large party: "C'est dans un tête-à-tête, dans la Chambre de Basin que vous êtes vraiment déesse, mais *déesse*-FEMME." *A propos de la déesse*, your Paphian orders are *not* from Paphos, they are from the coldest chambers of your ice-house *imagination*. Venus disdains them, and Cupid trembles and averts his arrows, fearful of blunting their points: "Je n'ai qu'une seule occupation pour tous les jours, et presque pour toutes les nuits, et c'est de penser à Glorvina." I can neither read nor work, and the weather is horribly bad; how the time passes I can't say, for except writing to *you*, curse me if I can tell you any one thing I do from morning to night.

The *whiskers* thrive, and so, too, does the hair, but you really!

I cannot write another letter, and yet I cannot bear to part for two days in anger. Imagine all that is harsh and suspicious in this letter *unsaid*—*I know you love me*, however paradoxical your conduct, and I will try to be content; I cannot bear to give you pain; God bless my dearest love.

T. C. Morgan to Miss Owenson.

November, 1811.

I am very tired and it is late, so I shall write but a short letter to-day, and that is the better for you, dear, as I am thoroughly displeased with you and your cold, calculating, most truly unamiable epistle. As for favours, whatever this tremendous favour that you dread to ask, be, I suppose it will be granted—*if it can*. I have never yet been in the habit of refusing you the sacrifice of every one of my feelings and prejudices. In every instance you have done exactly what you pleased, and nothing else; and my wishes, right or wrong, have been held tolerably cheap by you; but this, I suppose, is to break me into an obedient husband by times. I could, however, better away with that, than the manner in which you have trifled with me in the business of delay. Why could you not at once have told me, when *you first conceived the idea in September*, as I remember by a conversation we had, that you did not mean to return till Christmas. You would have saved yourself some little trouble and me very much pain, besides freeing yourself from the necessity of stooping to something more than *evasion*. But I do not mean to reproach you. I know this is but a specimen of the roundabout policy of all your countrywomen. How strange is it that you, who are in the general *great* beyond every woman I know, philosophical, magnanimous— should, *in detail*, be so often ill-judging, wrong, and (shall I say) little. Ah, dearest Glorvina, you know not how I adore you; and what pain it gives me that you think so meanly of me as to imagine this little trickery *necessary*. Am I not worthy of your confidence? am I not always ready to live or die for your happiness? and though I may complain when I think your affections cold, and your views *merely* prudential, yet to your seriously-urged wishes I shall ever attend. Do not write harshly to me, nor go over again the worn-out theme of your last. It is mortification enough that you can be so dead to feelings that agitate *me*, almost to madness, that you can *wish* to stay from me! You do not mention how the letter missed, or whether you have gotten all mine regularly since. Dearest, I know I am cross; but it is because I *feel* strongly, and, perhaps, not always *correctly*. Believe, however, that none can be more truly devoted to you than your own, own

T. M.

Je vous donne mille mille baisers.

Miss Owenson to T. C. Morgan.

Wednesday, November, 1811.

"*Tout homme n'est pas maître de sa propre vie,*" if he has, by all the arts in his power, made that life indis-

pensably necessary to the happiness of another—this
you have done. Your life and love are necessary to
my happiness. I did not seek to associate myself with
either; it was you involved me, and you must abide
by it. You must live to love me, and to be loved by
me. Gracious God! how your letters harrow up my
soul! I would not willingly, purposely, give *you* one
pang for the best joy of my existence, and yet I,
too, am cruel, unavoidably so. The various feelings
by which I am eternally agitated and distracted, throw
me into various tempers, and I pass from one strong
emotion to another, almost insensible to their successive influence. I am the victim of the moment, and
moments, and days and weeks, are to me but various
seasons of suffering, each, in their way, too acute to be
long sustained.

The gaieties I mix in, are unparticipated by others.
You mistake me totally if you suppose I am the light,
volatile, inconsequent wretch you paint me. Much
as I am, and *ought to be*, flattered by the attention
and kindness of a very large circle of respectable and
distinguished friends; intimately associated as are all
my feelings, and habits, and social pursuits with my
sentiments for them, still, it is not they nor the festivals they give me, that could have a moment's influence with me. Oh, no, it is a far deeper feeling.

Yes, Morgan, I will be yours, I hope, I trust; God
give me strength to go through with it! I mean to
leave this house clandestinely; Clarke only in my secret. *My poor father!* I am very ill—obliged to
assist Livy, last night, with a heavy heart. The fa-

tigue, added to a bad cold and a settled cough, has produced a horrible state of exhaustion and nervous lowness. I scarce know what I write; your letters have overpowered me; my head is disordered and wild. You distrust me, and whether I marry or reject you, my misery is certain. Still I love you, oh! more than tenderly. I lean my aching head upon your heart, my sole asylum, my best and dearest friend. I must cease to write. The physique carries it. To-morrow I shall be in better health. Adieu.

Yours,
S. O.

T. C. Morgan to Miss Owenson.

November 26th, 1811.

DEAREST LIFE,

After three days of painful, miserable discussion, welcome, welcome to the *holy Sabbath*, and to pure, *unmixed* love. I know not why, but I enjoy to-day a *triste* sort of *calmness* in regard to you, to myself, and to all that life can give, which is ease and happiness when compared with the eternal flow and ebb of hope with which I am *usually* agitated. I will take advantage of it (while it *lasts*) in writing to you, contrary to my previous intention, and I do so, because I *can avoid* at all touching on your affairs.

I should much like to have been present at your *disputation* on the influence of *mental cultivation* on human happiness. You knew *my* opinion, as I had so lately mentioned it, though in a cursory way, in

one of my letters. I believe it is not very different
from your own. There can be no doubt, as far as
the sciences go, with which Davy is more particularly
acquainted, their happy influence on human life is
considerable, not only in the *aggregate* by "bettering
the condition" (that is the fashionable phrase) of
man, and multiplying his comforts, but *individually*,
in a way not at first sight very visible. The physical
sciences all consist in facts and reasoning on facts,
totally unconnected with morals, and, as Chamfort says,
"Le monde physique parait l'ouvrage d'un être par-
fait et bon, mais le monde moral parait être le produit
des caprices d'un diable devenu fou." The mind,
then, perpetually abstracted from the contemplation
of this influence, stimulated by brilliant discoveries,
and absorbed in the consideration of beautiful, well-
arranged and *constant* laws, is enlarged to *pleasurable
emotion*, at the same time that it rejoices in the consciousness of its increased powers over the natural
world. Those pursuits, on the contrary, which have
been supposed the most to influence happiness and to
tame the tiger in our nature,—the moral and metaphysical sciences, *belles-lettres*, and the fine arts, are, in
my opinion, of much more doubtful efficacy. Though
their influence, when opposed to the passions, is really
as nothing (indeed, they too often but co-operate with
them in corrupting the heart) yet they cast a sort of
splendour about vice by the refinement they create;
and render man, if not a better animal, yet certainly
a less horrible animal. As to the question whether
humanity is bettered by the multiplying wants, and

thereby drawing tighter the social bonds and making us more dependant on each other, on police and on Government, we cannot *decide*,—the advantages and disadvantages of each state are so little comparable; most probably what is lost on the side of liberty, is gained in security and the petty enjoyments which, by their *repetition* become important, so that, on the whole, one age is nearly on a par with another in this respect. As for the influence of these pursuits on the CULTIVATOR of them, there can, in my opinion, be hardly a dispute; he is to all intents and purposes a victim immolated for the public for which he labours. In morality, the mind always bent upon a gloomy and shaded system of things, is either tortured in making stubborn fact bend to graduate with *religious prejudices*, or if forced to abandon *these*, lost in seas of endless speculation; consciously *feeling* actually *existing evil*, and perfectly *sceptical to future good*. These sciences, too, generally are connected with a cultivated imagination, the *greatest curse in itself* to its unfortunate possessor. Imagination, always at variance with reason and truth, delights in exaggeration and dwells most constantly on what most affects the passions. Its food, its occupation is *pain*; then, again, how constant is that sickly squeamishness of taste which finds nothing to admire, nothing to approve; that sees the paucity of our conceptions and the endless repetition of them. In point of fact, I have rarely seen poets, painters, or musicians (I mean composers), *happy* men. Fretful, irritable, impatient; guided by enthusinsm (another word for *false conception*). [End missing.]

Miss Owenson to T. C. Morgan.

> "And if I answered you 'I know not what,'
> It shows the name of love."

Give me, my dear philosopher, ten thousand more such letters, that I may have ten thousand more excuses for loving you still better than I do. I glory in my own inferiority when you give that exalted mind of yours fair play. I triumph in my *conscious littleness*; I say, "*and this creature loves me.*" Yes, dearest of all the dears, this is a proud consciousness. I think precisely with you, and argued on the same grounds; but not with the same eloquence that you have done. Davy (Sir Humphry), *après tout*, is a *borné man*. I dined with him on Saturday last, and he lectured, tolerably, till every one yawned; I said twenty times in the course of the evening, to Miss Butler, "how much better *Morgan* would have spoken;" and so you would, dearest. Nothing takes a woman like *mind* in *man;* before that, everything *sinks*. When you talk *en philosophe* to me (even the Philosophy of Love) I adore you. When you make bad puns, and are "PUT IN MIND," I hate you. So, as you see, my love is a *relative*, not a *positive*, quality. You will know how to manage me, and I wish you every success, dear.

I shall not write much to you, to-day, because I am writing a long, long, letter to— to— the—Lord

Mayor!!! Aye, and going to send it to the *Freeman's Journal!!* Don't look frightened to death, you quiz! I always have something to talk to the chief magistrate about, at this season of the year, and now it is about *poor children;* but I will send you the paper, and that will best inform you. Just before I sat down to write to you, yesterday, Livy and I had four naked little wretches at the fire warming and feeding, and, to tell the truth, their sufferings added to my nervousness; and *you*, joking and dissipation, had an equal share in the wretched spirits in which I addressed the dearest and the best. "Oh! Father Abraham, what these Irish be!" but so it is,—it is next to impossible to follow the quick transitions of our feelings. Just as I had got thus far, enter Professor Higgins—our Professor of Chemistry. He came to arrange a collection of mineralogy for Livy, which Clarke bought her with a cabinet, and now, here we are, in the midst of spars, quartz, ores, madrepores, and petrifactions. I know the whole thing now, at my fingers' ends, and all in half-an-hour!!! The Professor says, I am a clever little soul! I have got a little collection, myself, which, with a harp, tripod, fifty volumes, and some music, constitutes all my household furniture—funny enough! Now, *coûte qui coûte*, no more dolorous letters; *à quoi bon?* if I were not to marry you, it would be because I loved you too well to involve you in difficulties and in distress. If I do marry you (and, like Solus, "I'm pretty sure I shall be married") I will make you the dearest, best, and funniest little wife in the world.

Meantime, I prefer you to your whole sex, and so, dearest of all philosophers,

Adio,
GLORVINA.

PS.—I shall not write to you to-morrow, love, because I am going out about business for poor papa, who is very poorly; but still, if not better, he is not worse. Here is a trait of poor human nature. When his head was blistered, he would only suffer the *size of the blister* to be shaved; but when the pain came to the front of his head, he was obliged to have it all shaven. Yesterday he said to me, "Tell Morgan, my dear, that I have made a great sacrifice to health; that I have lost the finest head of hair that ever man had, and that I prided myself on, because I should like to prepare him *for seeing me in a wig!*"

I wish you would accustom yourself to write a little every day in mere authorship. I mean we shall write a novel together. Your name shall go down to posterity with mine, you wretch. The snow very deep, and the cold insupportable.

SYDNEY O.

In the next note from Morgan to Miss Owenson, Mr. Parkhurst is again alluded to with bitterness. How far Miss Owenson went in her flirtations with this gentleman, it is hard to say; for when Lady Morgan, after her marriage, made a collection of the love letters of her old sweethearts, and presented it to Sir Charles, under the title of *Youth, Love and Folly*, she included none of Parkhurst's, if indeed she had any to include. Parkhurst had excited Ormsby's jealousy long before he disturbed Morgan's peace of mind. But there was nothing serious between them; at least, they never quarrelled and made each other miserable, as people in love usually do.

T. C. Morgan to Miss Owenson.

Thursday.

MY DARLING, INJURED LOVE,

I have behaved most ungenerously, most unjustly to you, and I am a beast. Do not despise, do not hate me, and I *will* endeavour to amend. I have sat building odious castles in the air about you till I fancied my speculations were realities. Do me, however, the justice to believe, that you have been a little the cause of my irritability. When you reflect that *you* told me * * * was coming to Baron's Court *only on your account*, and that I found you were not shocked at the indelicacy of his attentions—when you add to this that I found his name mentioned in *every one* of the first few letters you wrote, do you not think that a man *who really and truly loved*, might, nay must, feel anxious and uneasy. Never, for a moment, did I doubt your preference *for me*, nor dread his influence over your mind; but I was *angry* that you should indulge your vanity at the expense of my feelings and your reputation. I *was hurt* that you mentioned to Lady Abercorn his calling on you with so much apparent delight. But no more of this distressing subject. For God

Almighty's sake, for mine and your own, do not again, while you live, seek to hide a feeling or a thought from me; let us sacrifice together on the altar of truth, and communicate with unbounded confidence. Have you, indeed, been suffering and wretched, and have I added to that suffering by my conduct? You thought by hiding *your* grief to diminish mine, and you have overwhelmed me by your apparent indifference; the badinage and frivolity of tone in your letters (excuse me, dearest), have overcome me with a conviction of your indifference towards me, no kindness of *individual expression* could confute. Had you at first told me the extent of your wishes about absence, hard as they were, I *must* have yielded to you. But the little *preaching* of delay upon delay, has impressed me with the idea, that you wished THAT *delay* should terminate in *separation*. Tell me, tell me, dearest, even what you wish and *all* you wish, and I will, at any risk, gratify you if I can. Do not wrap yourself in stoicism, nor "disdain" to open your bosom to one whose *privilege* it is to share your griefs and to soothe your sorrows. When *you will* look to me for support, you *shall* find me a man capable of strong exertion, of *self-command* to act and to suffer for you. It is your indifference, your reserve, with which I cannot contend. I confess *I* cannot see any *adequate* reason for your dread of Baron's Court. They will not return to England till late in the next summer. Do you wish, do you really wish to delay my happiness so long? I do not think you can *avoid* coming here, without positively affronting the

Abercorns, nor can you long *delay it.* But, as far as *I* am concerned, do whatever will contribute to your own happiness, and leave *mine* to its chance. You know I had set my heart upon our being well and intimately known to each other by marriage, before the necessity of domestic arrangements should interfere with our enjoyments. When we go to England we shall have much to do and something to suffer. I was in hopes that by the cultivation of every tender feeling, we should have prepared each other to go through this with cheerfulness. But do as you will.

Sydney Owenson to T. C. Morgan.

November, 1811.

I told you I would not write to you to-day, dear, yet down I sat, determined on sending you a long letter when I had finished Lady L.'s; but, lo! a parcel of people (the Cahers) and their carriage seen at the door, others were obliged to be admitted, and one moment till this (five o'clock) I could not get, to tell you I love you the more I *think* of you, so take it for granted, my *life* is yours, and should be devoted to your happiness. God bless you! "Je t'embrasse tendrement *à la hâte*." Tell Lady L. that whatever Miss Butler may have written her—Lady Manners *seems*, at least, in too good spirits for anything very serious to be impending.

S. O.

T. C. Morgan to Miss Owenson.

Baron's Court,
Wednesday Morning, Nov. 27th, 1811.

And God bless *you*, my dear love, notwithstanding your shabby apologies for notes. Well, well, *you are amused—e basta cosi*—only, when you *are* at leisure, write me a dear, good letter, to make amends for your last week's *slender diet*. Your views of life are so different from mine, that at first they gave me great pain and uneasiness; use, however, reconciles to many things and I have already lost the *uneasiness;* perhaps the *pain* will soon follow, at least I feel a satisfaction in submitting my will to your's, which already diminishes it. *Nonobstant,* I wish you were more *independent* in your pleasures, and did not receive the bright lights in your picture of life so much *by reflection from the world.* For myself, I am not without a large portion of personal vanity, and am as pleased with *incense,* when offered, as others, but it is not a WANT *of habit* with me; and, on the whole, I had rather be *loved* than *admired,* and, I fear also, rather than *esteemed.* This, you will say, is weakness, " le bonheur n'est pour (*moi*) ni sur la même route, ni de la même espèce, que celui des autres hommes; *ils* ne cherchent que la *puissance* et les *regards d'autrui;* il ne (*me*) faut que *la tendresse et la paix,* ne suis je pas un vrai St. Preux ?" and so much the worse for me, if I am; a slight touch of ambition would *pepper* life; and truly, at little more than *thirty*, it is rather hard to find all "vanity and vexation of spirit." I am as convinced as of any mathematical fact, that the whole life can give is included in the four magical letters *home*. The *affections* are the only inlets to *real* satisfaction; and they, alas! are so often chilled, thwarted, or, by death and separation, *annihilated*, that I repent, most sincerely, "*of happiness I despair.*" Ah, Glorvina! you, you have roused me from that enviable state of apathy, in which the world passed as a panorama,—a dream; you have called forth the violent passions into action, which, I had hoped, slumbered for ever *with the dead*. I am again the sport of *hopes and fears*, and you are at once their cause, object and end. Dearest love, you have much in your power; oh! be merciful, be merciful! nor think it beneath your genius to strew some flowers in the path of him who lives but to adore you! But to *descend* to the common-place of life, Lady Abercorn *has* received another parcel of the books, and now finds she has got a copy of them already. She wishes, therefore, to know if the man will take them back, giving her something else in return? she will not *send* them till she gets your answer. The major is again returned from his *military duties*. How much more palpable his PECULIARITIES are after a little absence. *Have you burned the letters yet?* Why will you not put me at rest on that point? You complain of my temper sometimes, but you should afford the same pardon to sickness of *mind* as to *bodily* infirmity; your absence is the cause of it all.

T. C. Morgan to Miss Owenson.

November 29th, 1811.

How is this Glorvina? twice, already, you have failed writing. Is it so very painful to bestow five minutes recollection on me? though, in truth, I know not whether your silence is not less painful than your letters. How cold—how indifferent—what ill-timed levity, and ill-timed animadversion! I am, and have been, very, very ill; and you are the cause of it. I am sure neither health nor reason could long withstand the agonies I suffered on your account for these last twenty-four hours. I have not slept, and am now obliged to put myself under Bowen's care. The whole of yesterday was spent in answering your letter; but *I will not pain you by that exhibition* of my lacerated mind; I have already destroyed it. On the subject of *delay*, however, one word for all. As long as your presence is necessary to your family, so long (be it a month or a year) I freely consent to your absence from me; *but not one hour longer;* you have no *right* to demand it, and if you knew what *love* was, it is impossible you could *wish it*. But I fear you are a stranger to love, except as it affects the fancy. You may understand its picturesque effects; but of the anxious, agonizing alternations of doubt and confidence, joy and despair—of all that is tender, of all that is *heart* in it, I fear you are utterly ignorant. For what purpose can you wish a *protracted* stay?

Your plea about a "respected guest and a part of the establishment," is too childish for a moment's consideration. If you do not love me sufficiently to master such fancies—if my affection is so little esteemed, and my happiness so little valued, why have you led me into this fools' Paradise? You know you will not be able to *refuse* invitations to go out; for *them*, therefore, for your *Parkhursts* and *Ormsbys* (the devil take them) and not for your family, you will leave me in all the miseries of widowhood and solitude. I repeat it, this is *not* love. You say, before you knew me you were free as air; and I, too, was free; but you cannot give me back my former self, my "pleased alacrity and cheer of mind." Seek not, then, to torture me with your *coldness* and *carelessness*. Remember that, *attachment* means *bondage*, and that we are mutually bound to promote each other's happiness by every means in our power. Remember, that *savage freedom* is incompatible with the *social affections*, and that you have no right to render a being miserable, who lives and breathes only in your love. You cannot imagine the grief of heart, the tears, this early avowal of your wish to lengthen our separation has cost me. By heavens, there is no place so vile, so infectious, that I would not inhabit it with you; and you object to share *my* love in a *place* to which another and a more worthless passion—vanity, *has* chained you for nearly a year at once, with every circumstance that should have driven you away! How every unkind word, every doubtful expression with regard to your future conduct towards me, recurs to my recollection! *If you really do not mean to marry me*, your trifling with a passion like mine is worse than cruelty. For God's sake, be candid, and let me know the horrid truth at once.

Another thing—why do you keep secrets from me? Why suffer me to learn from others circumstances which so materially affect your interest?—as those of your father's health. For my sake, for your own, let there be no mystery between us, no separation of interests. Trust me, I was rejoiced to learn that he was better again, and that *you* were the cause of it— that is the true balm, the only balm you can pour upon the wounds made by your absence—it gratifies and consoles me.

Miss Owenson to T. C. Morgan.

December, 1811.

Great God! is there to be *no end* of this? is every *idle*, every mischievous person to change your sentiments towards me, and to destroy your confidence? what *have* I done, what *have* I said? to bring down this tirade of abuse and reproach? Your letter has distracted me. I thought myself so assured of your esteem, your confidence! I cannot write on the subject. If it is Miss Butler who has done this, I will never speak to her again.

Never mind what I said about *the bond*, no matter about that, or anything else. Your answer shall determine the moment of my departure. I will throw myself into the mail the night of the day I receive it, if you command it—*by all that is sacred*—at the expense of *health* and *life*, I will do as you desire. Livy goes *to a certainty*, except some misfortune happens, and means to leave this on the morning of the 2nd, so that she will, of course, be at Baron's Court on the night of the 3rd. If I have, indeed, been the cause of much pain to you, what remains of my life shall be devoted to your happiness. How different do we feel towards each other! I am all confidence, all esteem, all admiration, you *are in love* and nothing else. Any woman may inspire all that I have inspired—passion accompanied by distrust and suspicion—still I embrace you, my beloved, as tenderly as ever.

I am far from well. I have a most painful sore throat and oppression on my chest, with some remains of my cough; this is owing to my having gone into a bath at 105 degrees, when there was a hard frost; but the country will soon, I trust, put to flight every symptom of delicacy. God bless you! may your next bring me some comfort.

S. O.

Miss Owenson to T. C. Morgan.

December 3, 1811.

MY DEAREST DEAR,

The horrible struggle of feeling I sought to forget in every species of dissipation of mind, is over—friends, relatives, country, all are now resigned, and I am *yours* for ever—from this moment be it. The study of my life to deserve your love, and to expiate those errors of conduct which had their source in the long-cherished affections of the heart, by a life devoted exclusively to you. Oh, my dearest friend, passionately as you love me, you do not yet justly appreciate me, and know not all I am capable of when imperiously called on by feeling and by honour.

I have gained my point in putting off our marriage for three months, by which I have gratified the independent spirit of my character in avoiding any addition of obligation to those on whom we are already *too* dependant. I have satisfied the feelings of my heart by fulfilling the tender duties they dictate, to my father and my family. I have obtained a more thorough knowledge of your character from the development of your feelings in your letters; and I have satisfied my woman's delicacy, and the *bienséance* of the world, by avoiding the appearance of rashness in uniting myself for life to one whom I knew but a month, which, had I listened to you, would have been the case. I have now done with the little world, here, and shall go out no more; all that remains of my absence from you must be exclusively devoted to my family. I have informed them of my resolution with great firmness; it was received in silence and in tears; but no opposition was made, the effort is over, and I think we are all calmer, and even happier, than during the late interval of horrible suspense. I will return to you soon after Christmas-day, as we can decide upon a safe mode of travelling. Meantime, my heart and soul are with you, and as for the little body, that will come soon enough. Every moment I can spare from my poor suffering father, I am devoting to collecting everything on Irish story that can be had here. I have made out a most exquisite subject matter for an Irish novel which will help to furnish our London *baby-house*. Well, dear, we are now where we ought to be, and long, long may we remain so. Pray tell Lady Abercorn you are satisfied with me.

Here is one of my *wife-like* demands. Will you send to London for six yards of black velvet for me? Mrs. Morgan will get it, at *Grafton House*, for half-a-guinea a yard, and your friend of Pall Mall, will frank it over. This, dear, is no extravagance.

S. O.

Miss Owenson to T. C. Morgan.

Thursday, 11 *o'clock,* [1811].

I perceive it is easier to *command* your obedience than to *endure it.* You have taken me now, *au pied de la lettre.* Three weeks back you would have made another commentary on the text and tortured it into any sense but that in which you have now taken it. However, I submit uncomplaining, though not unrepining. Ah! my dear Morgan, *les absens ont toujours tort,* and that passion which, a month past, I feared might urge on its disappointment to exile, or even perhaps to worse, has now flown lightly over, like a summer gale, which leaves on the air scarce a trace of its fleeting fragrance. Well, " *Thou canst not say 'twas I did it.*" The inequalities, the inconsistency of my manner and my letters, the quick alternation from tenderness to reproach, from affection to indifference, the successive glow of hope and chill of despair, the brilliant playfulness of one moment, the gloomy affliction of the next—these were accessory, but not final, causes of your alienation, for your love, like your religion, is a tangible creed; faith alone will not nourish it, you must have the Real Presence; you must touch to believe, you must enjoy to adore, and in the absence of the goddess you will erect the *golden calf*, sooner than waste your homage upon an *invisible object*. Dearest, I have divined you well.

You will say, "My sweetest Glorvina, I would love you if I could; but how am I to find you? catch, if I can the Cynthia of the moment." And, dearest Morgan, you say true; but am I to blame if I am unhappy? "Who would be a wretch for ever?" and if you know the objects and the interests that alternately tear my heart, you would much less blame than pity me. In the morning, when I come down to breakfast, the dear faces I have so long looked on, turned on me with such smiles of tenderness, the family kiss, the little gossip that refers to the social pleasures of the former evening,—my whole heart is theirs,—I say, "no, I will not, cannot, part from you for ever." Then all disperse; your letter comes, your reproaches, your suspicion! divided between tenderness and resentment; wanting to give you *force*, but overcome by my own weakness—I know not what I write. My feelings struggle and combat, and I sink under it. Again—perhaps I go out—the brilliant assembly, where every member is my friend

or my acquaintance, every smile pointed to me, every
hand is stretched out to me, and where all is the
perfect intelligence of old acquaintanceship, mingled
with Irish wit and Irish cordiality. The reverse of
the picture — the dreary country, the stately, cold
magnificence, and the imposed silence; the expected
affliction, and where *I* too often find ridicule substituted for that *admiration* now too necessary to me.
Again you rush on me, and all is forgotten. Your
true, disinterested love! your passionate feelings! your
patience! you long endurance of all my faults! your
generous and noble feelings! your talents, your exclusive devotion to me! THEN, *my whole soul is yours!*
Father, sister, home, friends, country, all are forgotten, and I enter again upon life with you; I struggle
again for subsistence; I resign ease and comfort, and
share with you a doubtful existence. I give up my
career of pleasure and vanity to sink into privacy and
oblivion; and the ambition of the authoress and the
woman is lost in the feelings of the mistress and the
wife.

It was thus I felt *yesterday,* five minutes after my
cold letter to you. After dinner I threw myself on
the couch and heard the clock strike seven, and I was
transported into the little angular room! To surprise us all, the door opened, and, carried in between
two old servants, appeared the dear *father—papa!*
Hot cake ordered for tea, and a boiled chicken for
supper. We tuned the harp and piano, and Clarke
would play his flute in such *time* and *tune* as it pleased
God! There never was such a family picture. In the

midst of it all, papa said, "I am thinking, my dears, that if God ever restores me the use of my hands, I will write a treatise on Irish music for Morgan!!" Again, when he was going back to his room, he leaned on my shoulders to walk to the door,—" you are my support now, my little darling," and he burst into tears. Such, dearest, are the feelings alternately awakened in a heart so vitally alive to impressions of tenderness and affection, that in its struggles between contending emotions it is sometimes ready to burst. Oh, then, pity me, and forgive me; bear with me, examine the source and cause of my faults, and you will see them in that sensibility which makes a part of my physical structure, and which time and circumstances have fatally fed and nourished. You do not expect, do not deserve, perhaps do not wish to be *bored*, with this letter, yet I shall send it; keep it by you, and when you are angry with me, read, and forgive!

When the postman knocked, I said, "Ah! the rascal, after all his impertinent, icy Strabane letter, he has written." I flew to meet it—burst it open with a smile of triumph. It was from Lord Abercorn! the smile disappeared, and, with a sigh I sat down to write this; while you, perhaps, without one thought of the Glorvina, are writing verses on the charms of Lady Carberry.

Poor dear papa! The consequence of his little frolic last night are, that he is confined to his bed to-day, and symptoms of gout in his head. I am going to see him. God bless you.

S. O.

Lord Abercorn to Miss Owenson.

[Extract.]

You are not worth writing to, little fool, for though your words are fair, they are few and probably false.

Have you really the presumption to think I will condescend to write to her, who instead of writing two or three for one, thinks I am going to put up with a miserable cover of another letter?

As to "Livy," alas! I thought better of her. I thought better of her. I "give her courage by a tender line!" why was not one more tender than she deserved in my very last to you? But I see too well, that your calumnies (as I thought them) against her, are truths; and that she beguiled only to deceive me. The jackal, too, has been sneaking into the forest where the lion only should have stalked. Alas! alas! what has she to say to me for herself? and when will she say it?

T. C. Morgan to Miss Owenson.

DEAREST LOVE,

I *do* pity while I *blame* you. But your great instability, whatever be the cause of it, is equally cruel in *you* and equally unbearable to *me*. It is absolutely necessary for you to exert some firmness of nerve. Review your own conduct to me and think how very *unnecessarily* you have tortured with repeated promises, all evaded; while each letter has been a direct contradiction of the last. It is not the lapse of *time* I so much regret; and in whatever way our loves may terminate, *I beg you to carry that in your remembrance*. The same effort of self-denial, which gave you one month, would have given you *three*, had you asked it seriously and firmly. It is the eternal *fiddling* upon nerves untuned by love (perhaps too romantic) for you, that I cannot bear the repeated frustration of hope. The evident preference you give to *general society* over mine—your very dread of this place,—the instability of your affections *as depicted in your letters*, are all sources of agony greater than I can endure, and *it must have an end*. To finish this business, then, at once—*of your own mere motion* within this last week, you have fixed with me *and with your sister too*, to leave Dublin at Christmas, *and that much* I give to *nature* and to *amusement*. If you can *then* return to me freely and voluntarily (for I will be no restraint upon you) say so, and *stick to your promise*. If not, we had better (great Heaven! and is it come to this!) we had better *never meet again*. The love I require is no ordinary affection. The woman who marries me must be *identified* with me. I must have a large bank of tenderness to draw upon. I must have frequent profession, and frequent demonstration of it. Woman's love is all in all to me; it stands in place of honours and riches, and, what is yet more, in place of tranquillity of mind and ease; without it there is a void in existence that deprives me of all control of myself, and leads me to headlong dissipation, as a refuge from reflection. If, then, your love for me is not sufficiently ardent to bring you freely to me at the end of a three months' absence for your *own happiness' sake*, by Heaven! more dear to me than my own, do not let us risk a life of endless regret and disappointment. Deliberate; make up your mind; and, having done so, have the *honesty* to abide by your determination, and not again trifle with feelings so agonized as your unfortunate friend's.

As to your *two* chapters on story-telling, *I am* indignant enough at them, but my mind is too much occupied to dwell on that subject—only this; you assume *too high a tone* on these occasions. *I* set up no tyrannical pretensions to *man's* superiority, and have besides a *personal* respect for *your intellect* over other women's. I know too, that in the present instance, *you are right.* But I never will submit to an assumed control on the woman's side; we must be equals; and *ridicule* or *command* will meet with but little success and little quarter from me.

Oh, God! oh, God! my poor lacerated mind! but the horrid task is over, and now, dearest woman (for such you are and ever will be to me), take me to you, your own ardent lover; let me throw myself on your bosom, and give vent to my burdened heart; let me feel your gentle pressure, the warmth of your breath, and your still warmer tear on my cheek. Think, love, of those delicious moments! when all created things but our two selves were forgotten; of those instants wherein we lived eternities.

T. C. Morgan to Miss Owenson.

Wednesday, December.

My dearest Love,

I am indeed a wretch to inflict pain on so much excellence; but, alas! what can wretchedness do but complain! Recollect how often my hopes in you have been delayed a few days, the return of a post, a week, a month for you to go to town—three weeks delay in your departure added to this. And now, by every means in your power, you would delay them still further for an indefinite time. Recollect, too, the things you have said of yourself, your "exaggeration of your faults," the array of lovers you have dressed out; the times you have been on the point of matrimony and broken it off, and think what I must suffer with a mind making food for irritation even out of mere possibilities. Indeed, I was cut to the very heart of heart, when you first hinted at your dislike of this place being a sufficient motive for keeping *from me*. But when you renewed this plea, ere the first pang of parting had ceased to vibrate in my bosom, when you talked of happiness without me too great for comparison, can you wonder that I was horror-stricken and overwhelmed with misery. I doubt not, Glorvina, if I had duties to discharge incompatible with our meeting for some time, like you, I should discharge them, but I should *feel* the sacrifice, I should count the hours till we met, and should be, as I now am, a very wretch till that time arrived. I little thought when we parted at Omagh, that you meditated to leave me for a longer time than was originally fixed. I confess to you, I should have entreated you (on my knees I should) to have married me before you went. I should have then borne your absence with less uneasiness. Now, I have a sad presentiment we shall never meet again. I read and re-read your letter to feed upon your kind expressions, but all will not do. I sink into a despondence almost too great to bear; life is hateful to me, and the possibility of a *good* agent in creation scarcely admissible. For God's sake give me some idea when you think of returning. What hopes do the medical people give you of your father's recovering his limbs? Your last letter told me you feared he *never* would. If I had never been buoyed up with hopes of our speedy union, I could have better borne your absence. I am in so horrid a state, that I have already burned two sheets full written, least I should annoy you; and here I am writing worse than ever. Oh, God! oh, God! can I ever bear it? Can you forgive it? Lady Asgill too; how that woman frightens me! She is possessed of the only weapon *you* cannot resist—*ridicule.* You will never endure the object of her constant raillery. Really I do not see how she can affect you, now your father is ill. I did not part with every earthly happiness, with peace, with everything, that you might furnish out her dinner-tables. If you can dine out, you can come to me. I sent you home to *nurse,* and every hour taken from your duty to your father is a double fraud to me. Indeed, if I hear of your being gay, I shall go quite mad!— Glorvina, *I* cannot be gay.

Sydney Owenson to T. C. Morgan.

Saturday, 10 o'clock, December 11, 1811.

If you *are not, you ought to be*, very indignant at my last chapter upon *long stories*, for I certainly treated the subject rather *pertly;* but you know my way of preferring any one of the *deadly sins*, to the respectable dulness of worthy *bores;* and if there is any one thing on earth more insupportably *provoking* than another, it is to see a man like yourself full of that *stuff* which people call "*natural talent*," cultivated by a superior education, enlightened by science, and refined by philosophy, concealing his native treasures, and borne away by the bad *ton* of a bad style of society, substituting, in their stead, the "leather and prunella" of false taste. It is thus the *Irish peasant* plants potatoes on the surface of those mountains whose bosoms *teem with gold!* I have seen the best and the worst of English society; I have dined at the table of a *city trader*, taken tea with the family of a *London merchant*, and supped at Devonshire House, all in one day, and I must say, that if there is a people upon earth that understand the *science* of conversation LESS than another, it is the English. The quickness, the variety, the rapidity of perception and impression, which is indispensable to render conversation delightful, is *constitutionally denied* to them; like all people of slowly operating mental faculties, and of business pursuits, they depend upon *memory* more than upon *spontaneous thought.* When the power of, and *time* for, cultivating that retentive faculty is denied, they are then *hébête* and tiresome, and when it is granted (as among the higher circles) the omnipotence of *ton* is so great that every one fears to risk himself. In Ireland it is quite different; our *physique*, which renders us ardent, restless, and fond of change, bids defiance to the cultivation of memory; and, therefore, though we produce men of genius, we never have boasted of any man of learning—and so we excel in conversation, because, of necessity we are obliged to do the honours of the *amour-propre* of others; we are obliged to *give* and *take*, for thrown upon excitement, we only respond in proportion to the quantity of stimulus received. In England, conversation is a game of chess—the result of judgment, memory, and deliberation; with us, it is a game of battledore, and our ideas, like our shuttlecocks, are thrown lightly *one* to the *other*, bounding and rebounding, played more for amusement than conquest, and leaving the players equally animated by the game, and careless of its results.

There is a term in England applied to persons popular in society, which illustrates what I have said; it is "*he* (or she) *is very amusing*," that is, they tell stories of a *ghost*, or an *actor*. They recite *verses*, or they play *tricks*, all of which must exclude conversation, and it is, in my opinion, the very *bane* of good society. An Englishman will *declaim*, or he will *narrate*, or he will *be silent*; but it is very difficult to get him to converse, especially if he is *suprême bon ton*, or labours under the reputation of being a *rising man*; but even all this, dull as it is, is better than a man who, struck by some fatal analogy in what he is saying, immediately chimes in with the eternal "*that puts me in mind,,*" and then gives you, not an anecdote, but an absolute history of something his uncle did, or his grandfather said, and then, by some lucky association, goes on with stories which have his own obscure friends for his heroes and heroines, but have neither point, *bût*, humour, nor even *moral* (usually tagged to the end of old ballads). Oh, save me from this, good heaven, and I will sustain all else beside!

Dad's bedroom, 10 o'clock, letter arrived.

Ah, dearest love, what a querulous letter. While I, waiting impatiently for the post, was scribble, scribble, scribble, and would have gone on till night in the same idle way, had not your letter cut me short;—dearest, suspicious Morgan, you wrong me, indeed, you do, if you think me capable of evasion or deceit. When I left you, I had no plan, no object in view, but to gratify imperious feelings which still tyrannise and lead me on from day to day. It is not *I* who entreat permission to prolong my residence here, it is a father whom I *shall never see again*—it is a sister, whom I *may* never see again. It is friends I love, and who love me, who solicit you to leave me yet a little longer among them—you who are about to *possess me for ever!* My best friend, if after all I should be miserable, would you not blame yourself for having put a force upon my inclinations? If I come *voluntarily and self-devoted* to you, then the penalty lies upon my own head, and I must *abide the issue*. I will tell you honestly, and I have often told you so, you call it caprice or weakness if you will; but *I shudder at the place!* You will understand me, I *know* the susceptibility of my spirits, and I know the train of gloomy impressions which await them. I am *sure* of you! I am only delaying a good which may be mine whenever I please, and avoiding evils which *are certain*, and which once there, I cannot escape. Still, however, I am not the unworthy wretch you think. I am always more to be pitied than blamed.

God bless you dearest, ever.   S. O.

T. C. Morgan to Miss Owenson.

BARON'S COURT,
December [14], 1811.

My yesterday's letter will be a sufficient answer to yours of this morning. I can only repeat, that I will no more consent to delay and trifling, and that I consider your fulfilment of your sacred promise as the touchstone of your affection, and the only means of regaining my confidence, at present, I confess, somewhat in *abeyance*. I do not mean to *accuse* you of deceit, as you have so often said, but while your wishes extend in proportion to my facility in complying with them—while your love of pleasure (now no longer disguised) exceeds your love for me, and your regard for your own honour and pledged word—while your letters alternately breathe hot and cold as to *marrying at all*, you cannot wonder that I think you *tired of your bargain*, and I am anxious to reduce to certainty my hopes and fears on points so entirely involving my complete life. Professions of love are easily made; but if you really have that regard for me which I suppose, *place* cannot make so much difference. Your hatred of this place is an insult which any, less foolishly-fond than myself, would seriously resent. You complain of my irritable feelings; they are your own creation; from the very first hour of our intimacy, either from *want of tact*, or from disregard of it, you have kept them afloat, and when the cup is full you cannot wonder if a drop makes it run over.

[End wanting.]

T. C. Morgan to Miss Owenson.

Saturday, December 16th.

Ah, dearest, what have I done? positively nothing, but what I was always *prepared* to do, what I always felt *bound* to do—given up to yourself,—and considered you entirely your own mistress, to act as you pleased; *free as air, unpromise-bound*—to the very last moment of your approach to the altar; and yet, though our relative situation is not altered, I am fretful and uneasy, that you should *deliberate*. Perhaps I am mortified that deliberation should yet be necessary; whatever it be, I have not the courage to look the possibility of losing you in the face. Surely,

surely, it has not been a presentiment of *truth*, that has uniformly haunted me with the idea that you would not ultimately be mine. Do not say I am *meanly suspicious*, or that I have any *fixed notion* of your intending me unfairly; it is but the restless anxiety of a mind, naturally too susceptible of painful impressions, acted upon by circumstances *very peculiar*, and which (when once we are married) can never recur. "Je ne doute pas de votre sincerité; votre amour même n'est plus un mystère pour moi, mais j'appréhende quelques révolutions; quelles, et d'ou peuvent elles venir? Je n'en sais rien—je crois que je puis dire; je crains *parceque j'aime*." This is exactly my state; ah, my God! you deliberate!! and under what circumstances? surrounded by objects all acting forcibly on your senses and imagination, all opposed to my interests in you. Bored eternally by acquaintance who wish to retain you they know not why,—and no one by to take my part, to support my cause and plead with you for me. Alas! the paper can indeed carry my *complaints*, can show you the variety of my feelings, but it shows only the *désagrémens* of the passion, but the *inconvenience* to which (perhaps an ill regulated) love *appears* to threaten you. Little can it express the warmth, the tenderness of the feeling, still less can it convey the *kiss*, the sigh, the tear, the look which speak at once to the heart, and "outstrip the pauser reason;" ah! *les absents ont tort, en verité*, in this case. It is vain that the cold line is traced, without the expression that should accompany its delivery, the rhetoric of the eye is dumb and the heart cannot submit to mere *calculation and debate*. Dearest, dearest girl, I *have* a friend, an eloquent friend in your bosom; call him often to council; he will tell you far, far more than *words* can express; he will remind you of moments, blissful as they were transitory, moments when the world was but as nothing, compared to the passion, the tender self-abandonment of your friend; he will whisper of instants when father, sister, all were forgotten, or remembered only as less capable of conferring happiness than he who now addresses you. You have had, I admit, but a bad specimen of *my temper*. Irritable feelings but too idly indulged; but consider the unusual situation in which I am placed. You had always assumed a volatile, inconsequent air, and before I could be *assured of your love*, you left me. Honestly and fervently, I believed you *no trifling good*, and the *weight* of the loss has always pressed on me more than the *probability*, that I should lose you. I was uneasy because I was not *absolutely* and *entirely* certain of you.

Do you understand this? If I at all know myself, and can judge by my three years of married life, I am above suspicion and jealousy. I do not know that I ever felt one uneasy moment on that head. But while fate can snatch you from me, while you are anything short of my *married wife*, I cannot help taking alarm—I know not why—and from circumstances that won't bear analysis. Cannot you comprehend a sensation of uneasiness that crossed me (for instance) when I read your *friends'* satirical account of this place. It appears as if every body were *trying* to detain you and to picture your prospects in as dark colours as possible. Such have, however, been the *but* of every anecdote you have written me of *Dublin conversation*. Ah, my own sweet love, you cannot think how much *more than they ought*, such *trifles* prey upon a bosom agitated like mine. I should, indeed, be ashamed to confess this, if I did not feel it was *nature*, and a necessary part of a devoted affection. Our weather, contrary to your supposition, is fine, and Baron's Court in (my eyes) as lovely as ever. Were *you* out of the question, I could live here for ever. London and its gaieties would be forgotten.

Miss Owenson to T. C. Morgan.

December 18th, 1811.

My dear Friend,

Your letter to-day [of the 16th] came very opportunely. *Your dreadful epistle* yesterday [of the 14th] *totally overthrew me*,—it found me ill and low spirited, and left me in a high fever; in my life I never received such a *shock*—its severity, its *cruelty*, its *suspicion*. Oh, what a frightful futurity opened to my view! I went to bed almost immediately to hide my feelings from my family, but never closed my eyes all night; I am now languid and stupefied; my cold is very oppressive, it is an influenza going; my throat, however, is better.

From the style of your letter to-day, I suppose, I may stay to accompany my sister on the 2nd, that is, next Thursday, *the day week on which you will receive this*. Still I will go the moment your mandate arrives, *whether I am better or not*, and whether *my life is at stake* or no. It would be much better to die than to suffer what I did *yesterday*. I don't care a fig about being popular or unpopular. I am sick of that stuff and intend to be more savagely independent than ever. I am so very unwell, particularly in my head and throat, that I cannot write much to you. I have been obliged to give up *extracting*."

PS.—Write me word how my *large trunk* can be conveyed to Baron's Court, as I would send it off directly. My dearest, do not think of coming to *meet us*—we both particularly intreat you will *not*. We shall be quite full inside the carriage and cannot admit you (*maid inside*), and what use your riding beside the carriage? I entreat most earnestly you will let our first meeting be in your own little room. I will fly there the moment I arrive—but no human being must be present. My cold is better. If Livy does not *set off* at *daylight* on Thursday morning, no human power shall prevent me setting off in *the evening* without. She will decidedly *go, and on that day*, and so, *for once*, have confidence and believe. Who could invent such a lie, that I did not mean to go to Baron's Court till the middle of January? The idea never *suggested itself* to me; the 3rd was the most distant day I ever thought of. I suspect that wretched G., for reasons I have. God bless you, dearest and most beloved.

S. O.

1 will write to-morrow if the post leaves this, but I fear it does not.

Mr. Owenson to T. C. Morgan.

Dublin, December 23, 1811.

"Not know you? by the Lord *I do*, as well as he that made you, Hal;" why, I wouldn't be acquainted with any man that I didn't *find out* in speaking two sentences, or reading a couple of paragraphs of his letter. Well, then, although I know you these *fifty years*, I am at a loss whether to believe the *whole*, or the *half* of what I hear of you; to save you a blush (for I suppose you've *learned* to blush since you came to this *immaculate* country), I shall believe but *half*, and if you are but the tenth part of that half, by the Lord you are too good for a son-in-law of mine, who have been, however, half the while, little better than one of the wicked. Well, all's one for that; heaven's above all, and as we in the *south* say, "there's worse in the *north*." The cause of this saying arose from the hatred the southerns (especially the lower orders) had to the northerns, looking upon them as marauders and common robbers; and it was a common thing with nurses to frighten the children to sleep, by threatening them to call an *Ulsterman*. I remember this very well, myself. Now, if one man is speaking ill of another to a third person, that man will probably say, "Well, well, he is bad enough; but there's worse in the north."

"But hear, you *yadward*," here's a little bit of a thing here, that runs out in your praise as if you were "the god of her idolatry;" by-the-bye, you've had a good deal of patience with her lately; don't let her ride the *bald filly* too much; and if she won't go quietly in a *snaffle*, get a good *bit* and *curb* for her. But I have nothing to say to it; "among you be it, blind harpers."

For myself, here I am, "a poor old man, more sinned against than sinning." Instead of being the "fine, gay, bold-faced vil—" no, I'll change the word to *fellow*, I was wont to be—the very head and front of every jollification—I am dwindled into the "*slipper'd pantaloon*, with my hose a world too large for my shrunk shanks." I deny this, for my feet and legs swell so in the course of the day, that I can scarcely get hose large enough to fit me; but this swelling goes off in the night. "Can'st thou not minister to a *leg* diseased? if thou can'st not, throw physic to the dogs, I'll none on't;" time, however, is drawing near, when it will be "sans eyes, sans teeth, sans everything." With me, however, although "I owe heaven a debt, I would not wish to pay it before it's due;" therefore, if I could get these legs well, and the cursed teasing pain in my head somewhat banished, I should not fear lilting up one of *Carolan's planxtirs*, in such a style as to be heard from this to the *Monterlomy mountains* with the wind full in my teeth; for the old *trunk* is as sound as a roast, and never once in the course of a ten months' illness, was in the least affected, therefore, "who is afraid."

Sir Arthur and I will be left all alone and moody in a few days, as our ladies mean to set off immediately

to the hospitable mansion of Baron's Court, where, as
I am informed, the good things of this world are only
to be had; so, commending you to God's holy keeping, and wishing you neighbour's share of plumpud-
ding, this gormandizing season, I remain, then, in
truth and in spirit.

ROBERT OWENSON.

PS. You have worked a miracle—for eight months
back, I never could take a pen in my hand! I really
am astonished at myself now, bad as it is.

Sydney Owenson to T. C. Morgan.

December 24th.

I told you yesterday, dearest, that you should have
a long letter to-day, and here comes one as short as
myself. The reason is, that a good old Irishman has
sent me 20,000 volumes of old Irish books to make
extracts from, and I am to return them directly, and
here I am in poor Dad's room just after binding up his
poor blistered head, and I am just going to work pell
mell, looking like a little conjuror, with all my black-
lettered books about me. I am extracting from Ed-
mund Spenser, who loved Ireland *tant soit peu;*
dearest, your letters are delicious, 'tis such a sweet
feeling to create happiness for those we love; if we
have but *de quoi vivre* in a *nutshell house* in London,
I shall be satisfied, and you shall be made as happy
as Irish love, Irish talent, and Irish fun can make a

grave, *cold*, shy Englishman. Your song is divine. Here is Livy just come in and insists on saying so; but first I must tell you that poor, dear papa continues very ill and so low spirited, that it is heartbreaking to listen to him.

SYDNEY.

Postscript from Livy.

DEAR CHARLES,

I like and thank you for your pretty song,—it is quite in the *style* of Italian composition, and is the very thing for my weak natural voice, and I shall sing it with the Spanish guitar to great advantage. I suppose I may thank Madam Glo.'s loving epistles for your little *billet doux*.

I am yours, *en tout cas*,
OLIVIA.

December 24.

Irish books are pouring in on all sides—anonymously, too, which is very singular, and mostly "*Rebelly*" books as you English would call them. Has Lady Abercorn *Tuaf's Impartial History of Ireland*? I hear it is beautifully written, and full of eloquence. I think, to-morrow, Livy will have talked over her journey with Clarke, and something will decidedly be settled. Till then, and now, ever and ever yours in every way,

GLORVINA.

I write, as usual, in a hurry. There is a puff in

the Irish papers to-day, so like Stockdale, that I could
swear he sent it over for insertion. I'll try and get it
for you before I send this.

In the next letter it will be seen that Lady Abercorn speaks of her physician as Sir Charles. He was
not yet knighted, but Lady Abercorn had always proposed that when the Wild Irish Girl married she should
have a title, and His Grace of Richmond was ready to
lay the sword on Morgan's reluctant shoulders whenever her ladyship pleased.

Lady Abercorn to Miss Owenson.

December, 1811.
DEAR GLORVINA,

I own I think if you are not here by Christmas, you
use Sir Charles very ill indeed; let me give you a
piece of advice, which I know, from a long knowledge
of the world, that it is very unwise for a woman, when
she intends to marry a man, to let him for a moment
suppose he is not her first object; for after marriage,
people have more time to reflect, and *sometimes it
might so happen* that a man might recollect that
though he was accepted of for a husband, that past
conduct proved it was more *par convenance* than from
attachment; now I know you will say, that as Sir
Charles is not a very great match, he cannot ever
imagine you married him for aught but himself; but
that will not be so considered, and I recommend you
to play no longer with his feelings. I am sure Lady

Clarke will be of my opinion; I leave her to decide, trusting that she has a wiser head than you have. Tell Lady Clarke I do hope she will be here before Christmas; I am sure she will not be the person to put off coming.

I should be sorry to offend Mr. Mason; I am very sensible of his great goodness to me, and if there was a chance of his taking it ill my not wanting the MS., pray have it done. My objection to it is, that it has been so long about, that Lady Charlotte Campbell will have forgotten all about it; if, however, the Schoolmaster is come up to do it, let it be done, and, above all, express to Mr. Mason my *gratitude*. I only want the bookseller to change the books for others—they are damaged, and I have a set of them here. He might let me have No. 62, which is about the same price.

What is the cabinet? tell me. What is become of Miss Butler? bid her write to me.

Yours, dear Glorvina, sincerely,

A. J. A.

Miss Owenson to T. C. Morgan.

December, 26, 1811.

Lady Cahir has just sent me a magnificent edition of the *Pacata Hibernica*, to be returned this evening, by Miss Butler, who drinks tea with me, and I am extracting till I am black in the face, and I have scarce a moment to say how do you do? I had made up my mind before Lady Abercorn's letter, as you must have known by three letters you had previously received; but I thought it would please her to give her a little credit, &c., &c. I have written a very civil little billet to Mrs. Morgan, merely inclosing the address for Skinner, as it will save six days' delay. Are you angry? God bless you, which is all I have time to say.

Ever your own,
GLORVINA.

Miss Owenson to T. C. Morgan.

December, 27th, 1811.

"And the last *note* is shorter than the first." I totally despair of ever writing you a legitimate letter again, and you have met with a more formidable rival in O'Donnel, of Tirconnel, than all your jealous brain ever fancied in Generals, Aides-de-Camp, and Dublin LAWYERS. I have not yet got through the *Pacata*, and have obtained permission to keep it another day. I delight in my story, and my hero, and shall throw myself *tête baissée* this winter to the best of passions —LOVE and FAME. Heaven send the *latter* do not find its extinction in the *former*, and depend upon it, dear, had I asked your leave *to stay in Dublin three months*, you would have knocked me down. I will do all you desire on the subject of odious business, and I shall write to you (barring O'Donnel) to-morrow, fully on it, and if *I do not*, believe, as Suppho says, "the less my *words*, the more my love appears."

Dearest friend, protector, guardian, guide,—every day
draws me closer to you by ties (I trust) which Death
only can break. There was so much of FORCE in the
commencement of this business, that my heart was
frightened *back* from the course it would *naturally
have taken*. I have now had time *to reflect* myself into
love for you—how much deeper and fonder than that
mere *engouement* which first possessed me ; do not
fear me, my dear friend, once *decided* upon rational
grounds, I am *immoveable*, and I am as much *yours* as
if the Archbishop of Canterbury had given his blessing
to the contract ; by your wishing to get all business
out of the way, I suppose I am to be met at the door
by *Mr. Bowen** with his prayer-book in one hand and
you in the other, and "will you, Sydney, take this
man," &c., &c. Heavens, *what a horror!* but you
really *cannot mean* to take me, shattered and shaken
after a long, dislocating journey! Let me at least, like
other innocent victims, *be fed* before I am offered.

Miss Owenson to T. C. Morgan.

December 28th.

Why, I'm coming you wretch! Do you think I can
borrow Friar Bacon's flying chair or Fortunatus' wishing cap? Would I could; and at eight o'clock this
evening in the old arm-chair in the angular room—ah,
you rascal!—

> "Have you no bowels
> For my poor relations?"

* Lady Abercorn's chaplain.

No, you are merciless as a vulture, and I am worse off than

> "the maiden all forlorn,
> Who was tossed by the cow
> With the crumpity horn."

Well, no matter. I go on loving *ad libitum*—and without my "vanity and ambition," literary and personal, I cannot get on. As to our plans of travelling, they can be determined on in an hour. I do not think Livy could set off before the 5th of January.

Now, Stupid the First, read the following paragraph to the best of all possible marchionesses:—

"The injured Glorvina can read and put together as well as other people, and with respect to No. 9, acted with her accustomed wisdom—she bought *neither* edition until she described both to the Marchioness. The difference lies in this—the dear one *is dear* because it is a rare one, done upon much larger paper than the cheap; the engravings much finer by the execution,— and the binding splendid morocco and gold; the cheap one would be deemed a very fine book if not seen beside the other. The engravings are coarser, but the work, in Glorvina's opinion, equally good. The scarcity of the fine edition is its value. Mr. Mason is gone this day to look at both. I bought none till further orders." S. O.

T. C. Morgan to Miss Owenson.

Saturday, 4 o'clock, p.m.,
December 28, 1811.

A thousand thousand blessings upon my soul's best

hope for her dear letters. Oh! how welcome was the
stranger joy to my heart, yet *it was* a stranger, and its
first approach, almost pain. I grew sick as I read,
and trembled violently—tears flowed, welcome, heavenly drops; dear as the first showers in April, when
the cold east wind has long parched the fields. My
beloved Glorvina, you *will* come, then! you *will* be
here at Christmas? and no longer leave me to pine
at your absence, and doubt your love. Yet tell me
so again; tell me your arrangements; as yet I dare
not trust myself with this promise of better days. I
have had a long and dreary dream, and fear has not yet
quitted me. How weak, how inadequate are words to
express all that I would say to you on this event! the
ideas crowd upon my mind, and in vain seek for utterance. I would tell you of my love, my devotion,
my gratitude. I would do homage to your *virtues*,
to your *tenderness*, your *affection*, by heaven more
welcome to me than fortune's proudest gifts, her foremost places; but it must not be. Your imagination
must befriend me; think me at your feet, my long
frozen bozom thawed and melting into all that is tender, all that is affectionate. What an age of misery I
have suffered!—the pain, the grief of heart to think
hardly of you! Yet so it has been; you have suffered
in my estimation more than I dare tell; and though I
feel now that I *wronged* you, yet *was I not unjust*;
but thank God, thank God, all is again peace, and I
have nothing to regret, but the lingering flight of
slow-winged time. My sweet love, why do you not
take care of your health? Why do you suffer that
odious cough to remain? be more thoughtful of your-

self, for my sake; how much too happy should I be
was it possible to bear your sorrows and your sickness
for you—what a proud satisfaction in the endurance!
The bell has just rung, and I must bid
you a hasty farewell. Give my love to Livy, and tell
her, if I can manage a *billet doux* for her to-morrow
I will write.

MARINO.

T. C. Morgan to Miss Owenson

Saturday, December 29th.

I could almost fancy, my dearest life, that there
was something more than chance in your having inclosed
the *billet douceureux;* that *I*, too, might have
something pleasant to peruse to-day, and so sympathise
with you in the delight with which you are now
reading my letter of Thursday last. Ten thousand
thanks for it! How little do you know my temper;
that small note has a power over my mind beyond
comparison greater than your grave, sententious epistles;
you will never *scold* me into yielding a point;
but coax me, out of whatever you will, though it be
my heart's blood. I cannot think of your stupid Irish
post without vexation. Two whole days of torment
added to your sufferings, and to my repentance. But
I have *sinned*, and must bear your anger till the return
of post on Monday relieves me. When I look
back at my senseless irritability, I am more than
ashamed. It was the excess of love; but I am sure

un peu plus d'indifférence, would have been more excusable. However, at last you have gained a triumph, and I bow submissive at your feet. Enjoy your victory with moderation, and as you are stout, be merciful. You may partly guess what the sacrifice has cost *me*. You have not only vanquished love, and ardent, passionate, yet tender anxiety to possess you; but you have overcome my fixed *principles* of conduct and compelled me (according to my ideas) to risk our happiness, by protracting courtship; the *whims and caprices I* mean are those little peculiarities of habit, which can only be known to us by the close contact of matrimony. All the courtship in the world will never teach them. What the conquest has cost *you*, you do not know. If love had a triumph over reason, reason has, in its turn, gained the advantage of love. I love you certainly less than I did. It is more T. C. M. and Miss O., and less Mortimer and Glorvina. Yet I hope I have stock enough on hand, to carry us through the *vale of years*. "*Such as you are*," you are necessary to my happiness, so I must c'en marry you, *your* "*sensible men*" *and all*. I hope and trust all unpleasant discussion is over between us. Burn my "eloquence" that it may not rise in judgment against me, and *if you can*, forget the ungenerous *reveries* in which I have indulged. You must, I hope feel, *that in spite of my nonsense*, I am ready to sacrifice every feeling of self to your happiness. I do not wish *me faire valoir*, but you cannot conceive the convulsive throes of my mind, even now, at *trusting* my hopes into your possession. If you had asked Clarke, he would have told you in what funds my *little all* lies. My long *annuity* stands in my own name; my wife's settlement is vested in the Three per Cents., in the names (I think) of George Hammond, Anthony H. John Buckshaw and Francis Const, the trustees to the settlement. So ma'am you are accountable to no one on earth but *me*. Oh, that I could now *kiss* my thanks to you for the sweet avowal; prepare to find in me a *rigid accountant*, demanding the long arrear of love you owe me, and one who will not let you off "till you have paid the uttermost farthing." Thank your sister for her note, *she*, too, shall love me; *kiss* her for me.

Miss Owenson to T. C. Morgan.

GREAT GEORGE'S STREET, DUBLIN,
December, 29, 1811.

Packing to be off, you quiz! Don't grumble at this scrap, but down on your knees and thank God you get a line. I am all hurry and confusion, and my spirits sad, sad, and sometimes hysterically high; how much I must love you to act as I am acting! I shall write to-morrow; but not after. Oh, Morgan! give me all your love, tenderness, comfort and support—in five short days I am yours for ever. My poor father—do write to him—flatter him beyond everything on the score of his little

S. O.

CHAPTER XXXVIII.

LADY MORGAN.

LADY CLARKE's health was not strong enough to bear the journey to Baron's Court at such an inclement period of the year, and Miss Owenson had to go back and encounter her fate alone. In narrating this part of her history, she admitted that she felt rather doubtful of her reception. The carriage was in waiting for her; but quite empty. On her arrival, the Marquis was stately, and the Marchioness stiff, in their welcome; but Sir Charles, who had been knighted by the Lord Lieutenant, was too enchanted by her return to be able to recollect that he had ever been displeased, and in the course of a quarter of an hour, she quite convinced him that he had been in the wrong, altogether, and that her own conduct had been, not only right, but admirable. She was soon reinstated in all her former favour. The following letter from Miss Butler to Lady Clarke shows how matters stood ten days afterwards. It was an act of courtesy on the part of his Grace the Duke of Richmond to Lord Abercorn to

confer knighthood on his family physician, who had
done nothing to deserve it on public grounds. Morgan, himself, cared nothing about it; but to please
Miss Owenson he would have been content to pass
under any denomination.

Miss Butler to Lady Clarke.

BARON'S COURT,
January, 1812.

MY DEAR LADY CLARKE,

The vice-regal party are here, and are all running
after the grouse, at this moment. The Duke is to make
Dr. Morgan (of the Linnean Society, and Fellow of
the Royal College of Physicians in London) a *Knight*.
The ceremony is to take place in a few hours. The
coquette has behaved very well, for these ten days
past; she really seems now attached to him. She is
afraid Lady Asgill has quizzed *Sir Charles* Morgan to
you; for a reason Miss Owenson has, she thinks every
body would rather *have the mate*. He is in as great
a frenzy as ever about her. He left me, last night
most suddenly, in the midst of an Italian duett,
before the whole *Court*, to go and listen to what *his
love* said to *Mr. Parkhurst*. I was rather offended at
being so publicly disgraced and deserted, considering
that he thinks me *the first of women*, and that I have
great capabilities. However, I must tell you, Glorvina is minding her P. P. P.'s and Q. Q. Q's.

Yours, sincerely,
J. BUTLER.

Lady Morgan used to tell, very comically, of her dismay at finding herself fairly caught in the toils. Any romance she had felt about Sir Charles, was frightened out of her for the time being, and she said she would have given anything to be able to run away again. Neither was much delay accorded to her. On a cold morning in January, she was sitting in the library, by the fire, in her morning wrapper, when Lady Abercorn opened the door, and said, "Glorvina, come up stairs directly, and be married; there must be no more trifling!"

Her ladyship took Miss Owenson's arm, and led her up stairs into her dressing-room, where a table was arranged for the ceremony—the family chaplain, standing in full canonicals, with his book open, and Sir Charles ready to receive her. There was no escape left. The ceremony proceeded, and the Wild Irish Girl was married past redemption.

The event had at last come upon her by surprise. No one of the many visitors in the house knew of it coming on thus suddenly; nor was the fact itself announced till some days afterwards, when Lord Abercorn, after dinner, filled his glass and drank to the health of "Sir Charles and Lady Morgan."

END OF VOL. I.

INDEX.

A.

Abercorn, Marquis and Marchioness of, 383, 384, 389, 390, 392, 408, 410, 411, 415, 418, 489, 517.
Aberdeen, 500.
Abingdon, Mrs., 81.
Actors, 113.
Address Prefatory, 1.
Anecdote of an Irish audience, 21.
Anecdote of the O'Connor Don, 64.
Anecdote of liberal professions, 115, 137.
Anderson, Mrs., 110.
Arbitration about theatre, 85.
Archdeacon, King, 382.
Atkinson, Joseph, 13, 288, 332.

B.

Ballad singer frozen to death, 9; Dysart's humanity to, 10; lines on, 10.
Baron's Court, 389, 394, 395; Miss Owenson's return to, 416.
Baron Smith and Miss Owenson, 354, 362.
Barrington, Sir Jonah, 367, 383.
Barrington, highwayman, 104.
Battle of the Boyne, lines in commemoration of, 102.
Bollingham Castle, 30.
Beef Steak Club, 180.
Benson, Captain White, 193, 195, 199; suicide of, 199.
Billington, Mrs., 82, 83.
Birthday, 6.
Blake, Mr., 45—48.
Book of the Boudoir, 323.
Brocklin, 154, 165, 167, 171.
Brennan, Pat, 17, 19, 20, 32.
Butler, Miss, 481.

C.

Castlereagh, Lord, 424.
Catholic Emancipation, 62.
Clarkville, Lady, 312, 330, 365, 383.

Cats with stings in their tail, 32.
Childhood, Lady Morgan's early impressions of, 16, 22.
Children's prayers, 33.
Chimney sweeps, 80.
Christening dinner, 11.
Christmas day, 7.
Clarke, Sir A., 341.
Clasagh na Valla, 44.
Clontarf House, 109.
Coach, hackney, anecdote of, 437.
Cochrane, Lord, 418.
Condemned felon, the, 359, 362.
Crawfords, family of the, 214.
Criticism on *Ida*, 351, 352.
Crofton, Lady, 301.
Croker, John Wilson, 327, 333.
Crossley, Francis, 242.

D.

Daly, Richard, 12, 24, 25.
Dermody, 79, 83, 92, 97, 128, 131, 176, 201, 205, 216, 217; death of, 227.
Death of Mrs. Owenson, 62.
Devonshire, Duke of, 420, 421.
Diary (1811), 329.
Diploma, poetical, by Miss Owenson, 415.
Dominic Street, 172.
Dr. Morgan and Dr. Jenner, 372.
Drumcondra, 90, 93, 96.
Dublin, life in, 321, 460.

E.

Edgeworth, Mr., letter from, 281.
England, Miss Owenson's departure from, 446.
Everard (original of story of Wild Irish Girl), 270, 278.

F.

Faror, Father, 70.

VOL. I.   M M

530 INDEX.

Farren, Miss, 112.
Featherstone, Mrs., 153, 167.
Featherstone, Miss, letters to, 207.
Felon, the condemned, 353.
Ffrenches of Bordeaux, 25, 26.
First Publisher, 185—190.
Fisher, Dr., 70, 50.
Fontaine, 137.
Freedom of the 6 and 10 per cents, 26.

G.

Garrick, 50.
Ginger, favourite cat so called, 32, 33.
Giordiani, 12, 57, 79, 81, 113.
Glorvina, sobriquet for Lady Morgan, 277; bodkin for the hair, 408.
Goldsmith, Oliver, 52, 55, 56.
Goldsmith, Miss, 82.
Governess, second engagement, 214.
Government patent to Theatre Royal, 25.
Granville, Lord George, 437.

H.

Hamilton, Lady, 410.
Hartington, Marquis of, 420, 421.
Hastings, Marchioness of, letter from, 176.
Highwayman, 104.
Hill, Miss, 57.
Hills of Shrewsbury, 280, 327.
Hitchcock, Robert, 81.
Home picture, 211.
House, Longford, 43, 295.
Huguenots, 106.

I.

Ida of Athens, 334, 348, 351; criticism of by Lady Charleville, 361.
Inchbald, Mrs., 253.
Inniskillen, 241.

J.

Jenner, Dr., 372, 374, 376, 378, 379.
Jephson, Captain, 12.
Jesuit, Father Farr, 76.

K.

Kane, O'Hara, 12.
Kilkenny, 114—122.
Kilkenny theatricals, 114.
Kinigad Mail, 169.
Kirwan, Richard, 370.
Knight, Payne, 395.

L.

Lady Morgan painted by herself and Sir Thomas Lawrence, 425.
Lamb, Lady Caroline, 441, 442.

Langley, Rev. Mr., 78.
Lawrence, Sir Thomas, 395, 426, 427, 434.
Lawsuit about Music Hall, 114.
Lefanu, Mr., 146—149, 151.
Lefanu, Mrs., 233, 217, 322, 335, 417.
Leigh Hunt, 111 (lines on Lady Morgan).
LETTERS :—
 Sydney Owenson to her father, 123—161, 177, 449.
 Miss Owenson to Mrs. Lefanu, 238, 258, 303, 359, 393, 447, 451.
 Mr. Wallace to Miss Owenson, 397.
 Miss Owenson to Mr. Wallace, 400.
 Miss Owenson to Lady Stanley, 327, 332, 349, 419, 425, 435, 454.
 Lady Stanley to Miss Owenson, 341, 457.
 Sydney Owenson to Mrs. Featherstone, 200, 222.
 Sydney Owenson to Miss M. Featherstone, 235.
 Sydney Owenson to her sister, 280.
 Miss Owenson to Miss Featherstone, 207.
 Duke of Devonshire to Miss Owenson, 421.
 Miss Owenson to the Duke of Devonshire, 422.
 Miss Owenson to Sir C. Ormsby, 325, 335, 359, 384, 423.
 Mrs. Lefanu to Miss Owenson, 23, 247.
 Francis Crossley to Miss Owenson, 243.
 Everard to Miss Owenson, 278.
 J. Atkinson to Miss Owenson, 282.
 Mrs. Tighe to Sydney Owenson, 322.
 J. W. Croker to Miss Owenson, 337.
 Lady Charleville to Miss Owenson, 339, 365, 383.
 Miss Owenson to Messrs. Longman's, 345.
 Baron Smith to Miss Owenson, 360—362.
 Miss Stanley to Miss Owenson, 363.
 Sir J. Barrington to Miss Owenson, 367, 385.
 Dr. Jenner to Dr. Morgan, 374—382.
 Archdeacon King to Miss Owenson, 387.
 Marchioness of Abercorn to Miss Owenson, 408, 411, 415, 416, 517.

LETTERS continued:—
   Lord Abercorn to Miss Owenson, 410, 439, 492.
   Sir Thomas Lawrence to Sydney Owenson, 427, 434.
   Lady Caroline Lamb to Miss Owenson, 442.
   T. C. Morgan to Miss Owenson, 461, 462, 464, 471, 473, 476, 479, 485, 488, 490, 499, 502, 507, 509, 521, 522.
   Miss Owenson to T. C. Morgan, 469, 470, 477, 482, 487, 492, 493, 495, 501, 506, 511, 515, 516 (P.S. from Olivia Owenson, 516).
   Mr. Owenson to T. C. Morgan, 513.
   Miss Butler to Lady Clarke, 527.
   Mr. Edgeworth to Sydney Owenson, 203.
   Mrs. Inchbald to Sydney Owenson, 253.
   Robert Owenson to Miss Owenson, 317.
London, Lady Morgan's first journey to, 251; second visit to, 323; third visit to, 412.
Longman's, the Messrs., 343, 345.
Lynagh, Counsellor, 9—13.

M.
Macklin, Rev. C., 12, 73, 74, 78.
Mamally, 12.
Mahon, Hon. Mrs., 24.
Marriage of Miss Owenson, 523.
Marriage of Olivia Owenson, 341.
Match, Hurling, 42.
Miller, publisher, 417.
Missionary, the, 407, 414, 424.
Moira, Countess of, 35, 175. See Hastings.
Molly, 63, 67, 95, 124, 127, 133, 193.
Moore, Thomas, 181—183; evenings with, 182—184.
Morgan, Dr., 378, 444, 445, 461, 525, 527.
Music Hall, first arrival at, 16; curious night in, 21; opened as National Theatre, 24; turned into wine vaults, 27; made comfortable for dwelling-house, 27; let out for public meetings, 27; lawsuit about, 114.

N.
National Theatre, arbitration about, 21.
Novice of St. Dominic, 251, 253.

O.
O'Haggerty, Countess, 132.
O'Leary, Father Arthur, 11, 12.
Opera, Whim of the Moment, 299, 316.
Ormsby, Sir C., 324, 325, 355, 383, 421.
Ormond, Lord, 114.
Ossory, bishop of, 334.
Owenson, Olivia, 29, 193, 317, 318, 320, 341; marriage of, 341.
Owenson, Mac Owen, 42.
Owenson, Robert, 45, 59, 81, 111, 208, 317, 342; his bankruptcy, 121; ill health of, 460.
Owenson, Miss, early prayers, 33; drawing master, 37; early verses, 85; writing master, 39; visit to Kilkenny, 116; her residence in Dublin with Molly, 120; her admirers, 183; engaged to be married, 442.

P.
Patterson, Captain and Mrs., 425, 436.
Pellegrini, Dr., 136.
Phillips, Sir Richard, 240, 252, 254; letters from, 268, 270, 271, 274, 275, 291; quarrel with, 343, 414.
Portarlington, great Huguenot school at, 68, 99, 103—105.
Poems—by Miss Owenson, offer of £100 for, 201.
Priory, Stanmore, Lord Abercorn's seat, 424.

Q.
Quentin Dick, 252.
Quarterly's Review of Ida, 352.

S.
Satin shoes, 421.
Schools, 100, 110.
Self, 1811, 420.
Servants, Irish, 67.
Shea, Mrs., 133; anecdote of, 187.
Shrewsbury, Miss Owenson's visit to her relations at, 279.
Sketches, Patriotic, 280.
Smith, Baron, 352.
Society in Dublin in Miss Owenson's childhood, 70.
Stage, Mr. Owenson's opinion of for his daughter, 81, 208.
Stanley, Lady, of Pewrhos, 321, 327, 332, 333, 335, 414, 419, 423, 435, 454.

Stanley, Miss, 363.
St. Clair, 184, 206, 209.
St. Dominic, Novice of, 251, 255.
Steele, Lady, 154.
Stephenson, Sir John, 179—181.
Sydney, Crofton, 42.
Sweeps, chimney, 30—31.

T.

Taafe, Miss Mac, 290.
Torson, Madame, 92, 98, 100—105.
The O'Connor Don, 61.
Theatre, National, opening of the, 24; arbitration about, 25.
Theatre, Kilkenny, 115.

Tighe, Edward, 10.
Tighe, Mrs., 19, 222.
Tully, Mark, 17.

V.

Vauxhall, 64.

W.

Walker, Mr., Irish Music, 259, 261, 319.
Walace, 895—897, 400.
Weichsel, Madame, 52.
Wild Irish Girl, 276.
William Fort, 214; leaving, 251.
Worgan, Dr., 62.

www.ingramcontent.com/pod-product-compliance
Lightning Source LLC
Chambersburg PA
CBHW031945290426
44108CB00011B/685